BUILDING WEB COMMERCE SITES

BUILDING WEB COMMERCE SITES

*by Ed Tittel, Charlie Scott,
Paul Wolfe, and Mike Erwin*

IDG BOOKS WORLDWIDE, INC.
AN INTERNATIONAL DATA GROUP COMPANY

Foster City, CA ■ Chicago, IL ■ Indianapolis, IN ■ Southlake, TX

Building Web Commerce Sites

Published by
IDG Books Worldwide, Inc.
An International Data Group Company
919 E. Hillsdale Blvd., Suite 400
Foster City, CA 94404

Library of Congress Catalog Card No.: 96-079058
ISBN: 0-7645-3032-1
Printed in the United States of America
10 9 8 7 6 5 4 3 2 1
1B/QS/RS/ZW/FC

Distributed in the United States by IDG Books Worldwide, Inc.
Distributed by Macmillan Canada for Canada; by Contemporanea de Ediciones for Venezuela; by Distribuidora Cuspide for Argentina; by CITEC for Brazil; by Ediciones ZETA S.C.R. Ltda. for Peru; by Editorial Limusa SA for Mexico; by Transworld Publishers Limited in the United Kingdom and Europe; by Academic Bookshop for Egypt; by Levant Distributors S.A.R.L. for Lebanon; by Al Jassim for Saudi Arabia; by Simron Pty. Ltd. for South Africa; by Pustak Mahal for India; by The Computer Bookshop for India; by Toppan Company Ltd. for Japan; by Addison Wesley Publishing Company for Korea; by Longman Singapore Publishers Ltd. for Singapore, Malaysia, Thailand, and Indonesia; by Unalis Corporation for Taiwan; by WS Computer Publishing Company, Inc. for the Philippines; by WoodsLane Pty. Ltd. for Australia; by WoodsLane Enterprises Ltd. for New Zealand. Authorized Sales Agent: Anthony Rudkin Associates for the Middle East and North Africa.

For general information on IDG Books Worldwide's books in the U.S., please call our Consumer Customer Service department at 800-762-2974. For reseller information, including discounts and premium sales, please call our Reseller Customer Service department at 800-434-3422.

For information on where to purchase IDG Books Worldwide's books outside the U.S., please contact our International Sales department at 415-655-3172 or fax 415-655-3295.

For information on foreign language translations, please contact our Foreign & Subsidiary Rights department at 415-655-3021 or fax 415-655-3281.

For sales inquiries and special prices for bulk quantities, please contact our Sales department at 415-655-3200 or write to the address above.

For information on using IDG Books Worldwide's books in the classroom or for ordering examination copies, please contact our Educational Sales department at 800-434-2086 or fax 817-251-8174.

For authorization to photocopy items for corporate, personal, or educational use, please contact Copyright Clearance Center, 222 Rosewood Drive, Danvers, MA 01923, or fax 508-750-4470.

 ™ is a trademark under exclusive license to IDG Books Worldwide, Inc., from International Data Group, Inc.

ABOUT IDG BOOKS WORLDWIDE

Welcome to the world of IDG Books Worldwide.

IDG Books Worldwide, Inc., is a subsidiary of International Data Group, the world's largest publisher of computer-related information and the leading global provider of information services on information technology. IDG was founded more than 25 years ago and now employs more than 8,500 people worldwide. IDG publishes more than 275 computer publications in over 75 countries (see listing below). More than 60 million people read one or more IDG publications each month.

Launched in 1990, IDG Books Worldwide is today the #1 publisher of best-selling computer books in the United States. We are proud to have received eight awards from the Computer Press Association in recognition of editorial excellence and three from *Computer Currents'* First Annual Readers' Choice Awards. Our best-selling *...For Dummies®* series has more than 30 million copies in print with translations in 30 languages. IDG Books Worldwide, through a joint venture with IDG's Hi-Tech Beijing, became the first U.S. publisher to publish a computer book in the People's Republic of China. In record time, IDG Books Worldwide has become the first choice for millions of readers around the world who want to learn how to better manage their businesses.

Our mission is simple: Every one of our books is designed to bring extra value and skill-building instructions to the reader. Our books are written by experts who understand and care about our readers. The knowledge base of our editorial staff comes from years of experience in publishing, education, and journalism — experience we use to produce books for the '90s. In short, we care about books, so we attract the best people. We devote special attention to details such as audience, interior design, use of icons, and illustrations. And because we use an efficient process of authoring, editing, and desktop publishing our books electronically, we can spend more time ensuring superior content and spend less time on the technicalities of making books.

You can count on our commitment to deliver high-quality books at competitive prices on topics you want to read about. At IDG Books Worldwide, we continue in the IDG tradition of delivering quality for more than 25 years. You'll find no better book on a subject than one from IDG Books Worldwide.

John Kilcullen
President and CEO
IDG Books Worldwide, Inc.

*Eighth Annual
Computer Press
Awards ≥1992*

*Ninth Annual
Computer Press
Awards ≥1993*

*Tenth Annual
Computer Press
Awards ≥1994*

*Eleventh Annual
Computer Press
Awards ≥1995*

FOREWORD

Today, one of the greatest challenges facing would-be merchants online is mastering the technology necessary to make it easy for customers to make purchases when they visit a Web site. Fortunately for everyone, this task is getting easier all the time.

As you'll learn in the pages of this book, there are lots of options available for turning your Web site into a commercial venue, or for building a commercial Web site from scratch. From digital forms of currency, to third-party payment systems, to online credit card processing, these options are numerous, interesting, and increasingly competitive with traditional marketplaces. There are even emerging systems to handle very small transactions—called micropayment systems for that reason—to make it easier for information vendors and content providers to sell small bits of information for equally small sums of money.

In this book, you'll find each of these topics covered, along with important areas like processing financial transactions online, providing confidential transport of sensitive financial information, verifying the identities of the parties to an online transaction, and more.

The authors don't merely cover the theory and operations behind electronic commerce, they also explore the business side of online commerce. Topics like establishing a merchant banking relationship, handling the application process, and calculating the many costs involved in online commerce are all addressed here. Likewise, they cover the details involved in installing and using a variety of payment systems, including ICVERIFY, the credit card electronic transaction processing software solution offered by my own company.

Throughout this book, the emphasis is on practical, hands-on information and real-life problems and solutions. The sample applications provided will take you through design, implementation, testing, installation, and use of several possible electronic commerce alternatives, across an interesting variety of platforms.

At ICVERIFY, we think that electronic commerce represents a technology frontier with as much potential for the twenty-first century as the American West posed in the nineteenth. Armed with the information in this book, and an appreciation of the hard work that underlies the many exploits on any frontier, we believe you'll be able to partake of its bounties.

Whatever electronic commerce solution you choose, you'll benefit by implementing one. Of course, we're biased where our own products are concerned—we can't help but think they're the best of the bunch. Please check them out at http://www.icverify.com (and in the pages of this book).

Good luck on this brave new frontier. We'll see you soon in cyberspace!

Steve Elefant
Chairman and Co-Founder
ICVERIFY Corporation
Oakland, California

PREFACE

Welcome to *Building Web Commerce Sites*! This book attempts to deliver a usable snapshot of one of the most exciting and literally remunerative aspects of the World Wide Web. With all kinds of businesses and organizations attempting to capitalize on the Web, electronic commerce is a huge and burgeoning opportunity for software developers, consultants, and Internet service providers all over the world. Electronic commerce also happens to be a particularly mutable beast these days, where numerous options abound, where current implementations often compete, and where standards—especially programming standards—are emerging and amorphous, rather than well-defined and clearly established.

Because of the rapidly shifting intellectual landscape, *Building Web Commerce Sites* will not only discuss many of the leading electronic commerce technologies and interfaces, and delve into programming details, it will also arm you with pointers to online resources galore. Whether code, tools, or techniques, our primary aim in this work is to educate you sufficiently about how commercial transactions may be conducted online, so that you can add these kinds of capabilities to your own (or your customer's) Web pages without losing too much sleep in the process.

Beyond the technology and the code, *Building Web Commerce Sites* also explores and explains the business aspects of conducting commerce online. It's essential to understand that collecting money from customers in cyberspace is not something you can do alone and unaided—you must establish a relationship with a credit handling company of some kind, whether a merchant bank, a credit card processing company, or a dispenser of electronic cash (or its equivalent). Such relationships, alas, are only available at some cost to you (or your customers). They must be negotiated with great care, and with a profound understanding of what those costs are, how they are incurred, and how moneys flow from your credit handler's coffers into your own (or your customers').

Finally, *Building Web Commerce Sites* includes a CD-ROM that contains not only all of the code examples you'll find in this book, but also a set of HTML pages that provides pointers and links to all of the material on the CD. In addition to our own work, you'll need to use these pointers to lead you to a broad set of third-party software on the CD, including various application programming interfaces and server software. Also, we've included pointers to the many vendors we mention in the text, all of whom can be reached online (as you'd expect for anyone whose business is providing electronic services tools or technology). All of the many URLs mentioned in the book can be accessed through the HTML documents on the CD, as can the vendors mentioned in the book's various appendixes. In short, you'll find the CD is laid out to make the contents of the book as accessible online as we hope it is in print!

Who Should Read This Book?

Beyond the merely facile answer "everyone," this book is aimed at a fairly specific audience. Its primary focus is on those individuals who will be involved in using the Web to specify, design, build, test, or otherwise rely upon the results of commercial transactions undertaken through that medium. However, our book is not strictly aimed at those individuals who'll write the code that brings transaction ability to a Web site, or to a specific Web page or set of pages.

Individuals who must understand and manage the development process will benefit from this book as well, because it deals with business issues and relationships that underlie these technologies. Internet service providers who wish to establish electronic relationships with their customer base should also find these materials particularly illuminating, since they already have a customer base from whom they need to collect monthly services fees and other charges. Organizations seeking to use the Web as another outlet for their goods or services will also find this book interesting—be it those executives, managers, or members of an IT department who are tasked with "going commercial" on the Web on behalf of their employers.

In short, if you want to know more about how electronic commerce actually works on a Web page, you should find this book both useful and illuminating. Likewise, if you want to understand the business implications of doing business online. But if you're in search of the gory details of cryptography, key escrow and management, digital signatures, and other important underlying technologies, you'll find that this book points to lots of resources in each of those areas, but doesn't delve deeply into technical details at that level.

As you'll learn in the introductory chapters, electronic commerce has fundamental requirements for security, reliability, authentication, non-repudiatability, and credit handling. We believe, however, that the techniques by which these requirements are met are not as important to those individuals who use these technologies are they are to those who develop them. Since our book is aimed at those people who will be using electronic commerce within the larger context of mounting and managing a Web presence, we eschew deep technical discussions of underlying terminology and technology. Instead, we concentrate on the nitty-gritty details required to design HTML documents and related Web server programs to help our readers conduct transactions with their customers via the World Wide Web.

One final caveat about this book's intended audience: We're aiming our efforts at small- to medium-sized businesses that don't necessarily need to deal with large-scale, high-volume payment systems. Although readers in Fortune 1,000 companies will probably find our book's contents interesting and informative, we don't address the needs of companies that must conduct many thousands of transactions per day, probably on multiple servers at many locations around the country, or the globe. The focus here is on single-server based Web sites, with more modest needs for customer interaction and transaction processing.

If you expect your Web site(s) to handle more than a thousand payments per day, or need to collect and synchronize payment information from more than a handful of servers, you'll need to consider solutions well beyond the scope of what's covered in this book. In that case, you'll probably want to follow some of the many pointers we provide throughout the text, and probably won't benefit as much from the source code included herein as will readers from smaller operations.

What Did We Assume?

We assume you, our gentle reader, are already familiar with the Web, that you know how to use a Web browser, and aren't afraid to use search engines like Yahoo!, Excite, or AltaVista to research whatever topics you like. We also assume a passing familiarity with Web server technology and related configuration and installation, and that you are familiar with the Common Gateway Interface (CGI) used to construct Web page extensions and enhancements of all kinds. We also assume you're familiar enough with HTML to construct a Web page by hand—or as the output of a program—and that you understand the basics of using the HTML <FORM>-related markup sufficiently to construct interactive forms on your Web pages. If this is not the case, let us make a few preliminary recommendations:

- For more information about HTML, check out our two companion books, *HTML For Dummies, Second Edition,* and *MORE HTML For Dummies,* by Ed Tittel and Stephen N. James (IDG Books Worldwide, 1996).
- For more information about Web servers and Web technology, check out our book entitled *Building Windows NT Web Servers,* by Ed Tittel, Mary Madden, and David B. Smith (IDG Books Worldwide, 1996). If a more general perspective is desired, check out *Building Successful Internet Businesses: The Essential Sourcebook for Creating Businesses on the Net,* by David Elderbrock and Nitin Borwankar (IDG Books Worldwide, 1996).
- For more information about CGI programming and Web extensions, check out our companion books, *CGI Bible* and *Web Programming SECRETS with HTML, CGI, and Perl,* both by Ed Tittel, Mark Gaither, Sebastian Hassinger, and Mike Erwin (IDG Books Worldwide, 1996).

Because UNIX remains the most popular platform for Web servers of all stripes, we assume a rudimentary familiarity with UNIX among our readers. We do, however, cover Windows NT, Windows 95, and Macintosh, in our discussion of Web server platforms in Part II.

Because Perl remains the most widely used programming language for CGI programs on the Web, we built our example programs in Part III in Perl (we used Perl 5, but didn't take advantage of too many of its special features in our programs, so either Perl 4 or 5 should be able to interpret this code).

Pieces and Parts

Building Web Commerce Sites is divided into three parts. Part I provides an introduction to the concepts and underlying principles of electronic commerce, especially as it relates to commerce via the Web. Part II covers those Web servers, tools, and application programming interfaces that our survey of the market's offerings showed us to be best-suited for use in small- to medium-sized businesses. Part III takes these servers and tools and provides instructions on how to configure and install the necessary Web server software, and then provides examples of Web sites that handle payment via electronic cash or credit cards.

Part I: The Essentials of Web Commerce

Part I introduces the basic concepts, terminology, standards, and technologies related to electronic commerce in general, but concentrates its coverage on those elements that touch most directly on the Web. Chapter 1 includes a brief history of commerce as it has been practiced online, and provides a tour of some of the most common kinds of commercial venues already online, along with a quick look at some interesting examples. Chapter 2 tackles the issues involved in ensuring the confidentiality of secured Web transmissions, and in creating techniques to positively identify the parties to commercial transactions online. Along the way, it also tackles some of the encryption schemes in wide use, and examines some of the secure transport mechanisms used to keep the contents of Web transmissions safe from prying eyes.

In Chapter 3, the focus changes from exchanges of credit information to various implementations of payment systems that involve so-called "digital cash," and other alternative methods of payment that don't involve sending sensitive information over the Internet. You'll also learn about so-called micropayment systems, which support low-cost charges (sometimes even fractions of a cent, which helps to explain the general name for such technologies). In Chapter 4, we tackle the other side of the credit equation—namely, credit cards and how transactions that do involve delivery of sensitive information over the Internet are handled safely and securely.

Throughout Part I, the emphasis is on establishing a foundation you can use throughout the rest of the book. If you're already familiar with the concepts and minutiae of electronic commerce, feel free to skip this part. If you're not, you should find it a useful first pass over this domain.

Part II: Electronic Capitalist Tools

Part II tackles a number of platforms for which secure Web servers are available—including UNIX (Chapter 5), Windows NT and 95 (Chapter 6), and Macintosh (Chapter 7). For each platform, the leading secure server solutions are also covered, including a discussion of the benefits that each one can deliver, as well as the potential problems it can pose. Along the way, products from Open Market, Stronghold, O'Reilly & Associates, Netscape Communications, and Quarterdeck/StarNine are covered in some detail. As always, we also provide pointers to other potential candidates in the secure Web server sweepstakes.

After Chapter 7, the focus turns from the secure Web server platform to the details of the electronic payments systems that can be used to manage the nuts and bolts of an online financial transaction. Chapter 8 examines the major electronic cash alternatives, including DigiCash's Ecash and other cash systems; it also examines the system available from First Virtual Holdings, a company that processes credit card payments without transmitting any sensitive information across the Internet. Chapter 9 examines a variety of turn-key and integrated solutions for electronic commerce, including Netscape's Live Payment, Open Market's OpenTransact, CyberCash, and WebMaster's CommerceRoom systems. Finally, in Chapter 10, you'll learn the salient details about ICVERIFY, a popular credit-card verification system that represents the largest segment of all those Web sites that support electronic commerce today.

Throughout this part of the book, the emphasis is on understanding what options make sense, how existing systems behave, and how much effort is involved in incorporating them into real-live electronic commerce solutions. The idea here is to acquaint you with the tools in an electronic capitalist's toolbox, to help you select those that best fit your particular needs.

Part III: Building a Web Commerce Site

Part III seeks to employ everything you learned about the theory and practice of electronic commerce in Part I, and about the tools of that trade in Part II, as you explore the requirements and integrate the components necessary to mount a commercial presence on the Web. Chapter 11 kicks off this process with a self-evaluation questionnaire designed to help you assess and determine your own needs. Chapter 12 moves on to server installation, and steps through the various stages involved in setting up a document hierarchy, placing the necessary CGI programs, dealing with a certificate authority, and anticipating—and plugging—potential security hazards on your system.

Chapter 13 sets up a Web site to handle First Virtual transactions, including establishing a vendor relationship, building the appropriate CGIs to process customer input, installing and testing those programs, and managing the payment cycle with First Virtual.

Chapter 14 covers the same ground for credit card based transactions, beginning with obtaining a merchant banking relationship, working with a financial clearinghouse, and installing the ICVERIFY software. It then presents the necessary CGI programs to incorporate ICVERIFY functions into your Web pages, talks about installing and testing them, and explains how to handle credit card authentication and billing practices.

Chapter 15 concludes the book with a lengthy rumination on further developments to a Web site to enhance its commercial potential and viability. We begin with a discussion of marketing practices, discuss the value of handling multiple types of payment, and cover the practices of good Web maintenance, as they relate to a commercial site. Finally, we conclude with a report on some new directions in electronic commerce standards and software, to help prepare you for the inevitable changes that the coming years will bring.

How to Use This Book

If you're a relative newcomer to electronic commerce, we'd strongly recommend that you read Parts I and II in their entirety before tackling the implementation details covered in Part III. You can then pick and choose among those topics in Part III that interest you most, and dip in again from time to time as other topics catch your eye.

If you're a seasoned Web hand, already familiar with the basics of electronic commerce, you'll probably want to skim the first part, and read only those sections in Part II that you don't already know. But even if you're already somewhat familiar with encryption, public and private keys, authentication techniques, and certificate authorities, you may still be able to glean some useful information about new and emerging commerce standards and technologies from Part I. Parts I and II both include useful coverage of a variety of online resources and search techniques that you might find interesting. We also strongly recommend a look at Chapter 9, entitled "Integrated Solutions," because of the many powerful and flexible integrated payment handling systems now available as development platforms.

But experienced Web professionals will probably find Part III includes the most useful content in this book, because it tackles the special set up and configuration issues that electronic commerce adds to a Web site, and because it provides working examples of the code that's necessary to use either First Virtual Holding's or ICVERIFY's payment systems within your own Web pages. Here, we'd recommend reading the chapters that match your specific requirements, after completing the needs assessment questionnaire in Chapter 11.

Conventions Used in This Book

We've tried to be clear and consistent about what's in this book. This can get tricky sometimes, so we used the following typographical conventions to distinguish among a variety of elements that you're likely to encounter while programming.

- When we include fragments of code or whole programs in the text, we'll set them off like this:

```
# Because these lines start with a '#' they're valid
# comments in a variety of programming languages.
```

- When we name UNIX or other programs, system commands, or special terms, they'll show up in italics, as in "the *grep* command provides a way to manipulate data based on pattern-matching and regular expressions."

If you can follow—and master—these simple rules, you'll be well-equipped to keep up with the content of this book. It's not too much harder than mastering the details of any programming language we know of, so we're pretty sure you can handle the job.

But Wait, There's More!

In addition to the materials you'll find in the book itself, don't neglect to check out the contents of its accompanying CD-ROM. As mentioned earlier, you'll find pointers on the CD-ROM to all of the resources mentioned throughout the book, plus links to the vendors and products that are covered herein as well. We strongly recommend that you check out what's available on the Web from these vendors before digging into the contents of the CD too deeply, simply because the accelerating pace of change in electronic commerce requires that you be sure this version is not already obsolete.

Please feel free to share your feedback with us about this book. You'll find all of the authors' e-mail addresses on the "About the Authors" pages; we'd encourage you to use them. Tell us about what you like or don't like about the book, about what's missing or any inaccuracies or outright mistakes you might catch. If you run across some especially useful resources related to electronic commerce that we fail to mention in the book, please feel free to share them with us—we'll even give you credit in our second edition if we use your pointers (should we be lucky enough to warrant a revision).

Bon Voyage!

We hope you find the materials, code, pointers, and information in this book useful. We hope you'll jump right in, and that these materials will advance your fortune, if they don't change your life. We'd like to close by saying thanks for buying our book, and enjoy your reading!

ACKNOWLEDGMENTS

We have too many parties to thank for their contributions to this book to mention all of them by name. Please accept our heartfelt thanks anyway—we couldn't have done it without you!

Ed Tittel

I'm truly grateful to announce that my team and I have formed a real, honest-to-gosh corporation, LANWrights, Inc. Therefore, I'd like to start my acknowledgments with special thanks to Michael Stewart, Dawn Rader, and Natanya Pitts, my colleagues and co-workers. Next, of course, are my thanks to the writers of this book, including Charlie, whose idea led to this work and who acted as our technical guru throughout the project; Paul, who struggled with impending fatherhood while writing this book (and then had a baby before it was all over); and Mike, who despite being the busiest guy I know, found time to help out with this project. I'd also like to thank two unnamed authors and friends: Claire Sanders, who wrote Chapter 9, and Sebastian Hassinger, who was going to be a major contributor, but had to drop out for family reasons. Finally, thanks to my family, near and far, for putting up with the occasional inattention that writing books will sometimes cause.

Charlie Scott

I would like to dedicate my portion of this book to my father. I would also like to thank my wife, Mary, for being understanding whilst I've been working on this and other books (the last one for a while, I promise!). Special thanks to Sebastian Hassinger of OuterNet for doing all of the original research and software procurement for Internet credit card transactions. Thanks to Ed for having me work on *Web Programming SECRETS* (which gave me the bug to do this book) and for managing this project from proposal to final chapter. Gracious thanks to my other co-authors—Paul, Mike, and Claire—for their expertise and hard work. And to the LANWrights staff, Dawn Rader and Michael Stewart, for putting our patchwork of submissions together into a complete book.

Paul Wolfe

This book is dedicated to my daughter, Taylor Rayna Wolfe, born September 16, 1996. I bow before my wife Brenda and my sons Nikolaus and Lukas for their love and patience in many nights away from home. Thanks to Ed Tittel for cracking the whip, and Dawn Rader for her gentle reminders. To my OuterNet brothers, Mike Erwin, Sebastian Hassinger, and Charlie Scott, who have all labored hard to build a bullet-proof network, without which my contribution to this book would not be possible. Finally, all my love to my Mom, Dad, and Sis, for their continued support of my dreams.

Mike Erwin

I would like to personally acknowledge Sebastian Hassinger, who did a fantastic job in laying down the groundwork for all of the commerce code that I created for this book. His excellent work in researching and preliminary development was much appreciated during the creation of this work. I also want to extend a full "thank you" and "well done" to Charlie Scott, whose vision it was in the first place to create all of this, and who saw it out to the end. Charlie drew together a variety of people to supply input and was a great project manager for all aspects of this book. Lastly, I want to personally thank Paul Wolfe and the rest of the OuterNet team for allowing us to use the facilities for our testing and debugging of the various pieces of code that we produced herein.

From all of us

All of the authors would like to thank Sameer Parekh, President of Community ConneXion, Inc. (makers of Stronghold: Apache-SSL), for his assistance. Likewise for Bill Tyner, president of Tyner Associates, who helped us begin to understand the nuances of doing business on the Web. Ed also wants to thank Marshall Rose, late of the NetWorld + Interop Program Committee, now at First Virtual Holdings, for alerting us to the fascinating quirks that are the hallmark of all genuine electronic commerce technologists.

Another round of thanks is due to our production team at IDG Books, starting with Mike Roney, our acquisition editor. Thanks also to our development editor Susannah Davidson, our copyeditors Katharine Dvorak and Lothlórien Baerenwald, and our technical editor, David Elderbrock.

The publisher would like to give special thanks to Patrick McGovern, without whom this book would not have been possible.

Contents at a Glance

Contents

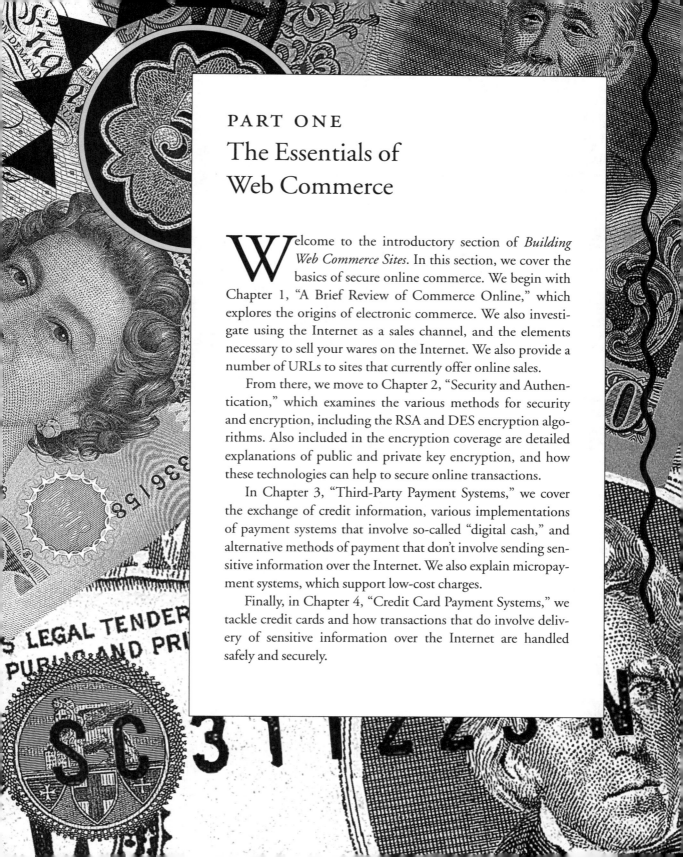

PART ONE
The Essentials of Web Commerce

Welcome to the introductory section of *Building Web Commerce Sites*. In this section, we cover the basics of secure online commerce. We begin with Chapter 1, "A Brief Review of Commerce Online," which explores the origins of electronic commerce. We also investigate using the Internet as a sales channel, and the elements necessary to sell your wares on the Internet. We also provide a number of URLs to sites that currently offer online sales.

From there, we move to Chapter 2, "Security and Authentication," which examines the various methods for security and encryption, including the RSA and DES encryption algorithms. Also included in the encryption coverage are detailed explanations of public and private key encryption, and how these technologies can help to secure online transactions.

In Chapter 3, "Third-Party Payment Systems," we cover the exchange of credit information, various implementations of payment systems that involve so-called "digital cash," and alternative methods of payment that don't involve sending sensitive information over the Internet. We also explain micropayment systems, which support low-cost charges.

Finally, in Chapter 4, "Credit Card Payment Systems," we tackle credit cards and how transactions that do involve delivery of sensitive information over the Internet are handled safely and securely.

CHAPTER ONE

A BRIEF REVIEW OF COMMERCE ONLINE

W e can define commerce in its broadest sense as the exchange of something of value for goods, services, or whatever else a buyer seeks from a seller. The key ingredients include: buyers, sellers, and the exchange of valuables—usually money or some equivalent—for whatever a seller offers and a buyer seeks to purchase. The basis for the exchange may be negotiated, along with delivery terms, quantities, quality, and a whole slew of other factors. But the basics remain the same: buyer and seller agree to an exchange, and figure out a way to consummate the transaction.

In the beginning, all exchange was done through a system of bartering: A buyer would have to offer something of value to a seller in exchange for something he or she wished to obtain. The introduction of cash, however, makes such transactions infinitely easier. Cash creates a relatively constant way to measure value, provides a compact way to accumulate or transfer value, and even acts as a sort of place-holder for value to occupy as it moves through an economy. Simply, cash makes commerce possible, even if cash is only a polite fiction and nothing more, as anyone who's ever experienced rampant or hyperinflation can attest.

Even before the ascendancy of the Internet, people conducted electronic business transactions, starting with the introduction of the telegraph system in the nine-

3

teenth century. To begin with, "wire transfers" of funds between branches of a bank and among separate banks have been practiced for some time. Then, too, the infamous "ticker tape" that records the ups and downs of the stock market has been with us since the turn of the century.

Thus, there's ample precedent for conducting commerce electronically, well before the Internet appeared on the scene. But the introduction of the Internet certainly broadened the audience from a couple of hundred thousand companies (and other organizations savvy enough to exploit electronic banking services or electronic data interchange [EDI]), to as many as fifty million potential shoppers, many ready to part with some of their cash while they're doing their online things, whatever those might be.

Why All the Excitement?

Beyond the sheer size and scope of the audience—which by itself includes potential vendors, service providers, banks, and others—anything that can be represented digitally can move across the global internetwork that is the Internet. Thus, the Internet is more than just a way to communicate, it's also a channel across which all kinds of information can move, including data, documents, numbers, audio, video, and computer programs. Many businesses correctly perceive that there's much potential business to be done in this medium.

From a commercial standpoint, the Internet is a 24-hour-a-day operation, whose worldwide scope means that there's always somebody, somewhere ready to do business. It's a great vehicle for delivering time-sensitive information because it can transfer data from sender to receiver within minutes or hours, rather than days. As the Internet is accessible from just about anywhere (nearly every country represented in the United Nations has some kind of Internet access), data transfer seldom costs more than the charge for making a local call (and in many places, that cost is simply part of basic telephone service, or basically free), plus the charges to access the Internet that a service provider levies (and again, this is often so cheap, it too is "almost free").

Because data on the Internet is completely computerized, it's easy to search for things. The explosion in the popularity of the World Wide Web is due as much to the presence of powerful search engines such as AltaVista, Yahoo!, Excite, and others, as it is to the availability of all that data in the first place. These search engines help users find particular items in the unimaginably large storehouse of information the Web represents. Not only do we get the haystack and the needle, as it were, we also get the tools that help us to separate one from the other.

Finally, one of the biggest benefits of the Internet is its unique ability to connect almost any two parties in the world, if only via transitory e-mail (but also increasingly through audio or video channels as well). Because of this potential for person-to-person, or business-to-business communication, the Internet offers the same kind of reach as the global telephone system (and in many cases, of course, these two systems overlap when modems are used to access the Internet).

In addition to the many benefits the Internet confers, there are some inevitable drawbacks. Scarcity of bandwidth and the expense of high-bandwidth connections and related equipment still conspire to keep some of the richer uses of the Internet, such as voice, video, or multimedia data, restricted to a small subset of the user community. Even though the Internet can sustain voice, video, and multimedia data, it still isn't ready to switch completely over to such high-bandwidth applications. The infrastructure's not there yet, therefore limiting the amount of electronic commerce that can take place over the Net. Likewise, electronic forms of communication, especially for document delivery, don't yet compete on an equal footing with print. Print communication still works better for portability and readability as documents get longer (try taking a terminal into some of the places you like to read—you'll get the idea). But taken together, print and online documentation can work well, especially since rich text representations such as Adobe's Portable Document Format (PDF) can be delivered electronically and then printed for local use. This can aide in the online sale of software applications that require extensive documentation.

The Internet: Just Another Sales Channel?

To be successful on the Internet, commercial enterprises must exploit its special capabilities. They must also cater to its unique clientele, which can differ considerably from the customers that come in through the front door or via the mailbox. Some pundits have likened doing business on the Internet to setting up shop in the third world, where a knowledge of the local culture is an essential ingredient to creating a successful business. Likewise, catering to the Internet crowd means understanding its likes and dislikes, and the most effective means of communication and solicitation. This is becoming less true as the Internet population comes increasingly to resemble the population at large, but an understanding of one's target audience is as important on the Internet as it is in any other business venture.

Since the first step in establishing any kind of relationship, business or otherwise, involves an exchange of information, the Internet supplies an especially usable way to communicate, whether with customers, suppliers, or partners of any kind. Because the Internet is available around-the-clock, and provides an easy way for users to download all kinds of information, it's a great way to get a business relationship going. If you add the Web's ability to provide interesting and easy access to all kinds of current and up-to-date information, it makes great sense to use the Internet as an icebreaker to establish communication with just about anyone after your public offerings. That's why so many companies and organizations have already established a presence on the Web, and why so many more are at least thinking about it, if not already in the process of doing so.

The notion of an online information center is one that's hard to beat, and one that aptly describes what kinds of offerings you'll find at so many corporate or organizational Web sites today. Such sites usually include the following elements:

- Contact information, including branch or local office locators to help visitors contact the organization

- Products and services available, with pricing, ordering, and delivery information where appropriate, to permit visitors to obtain initial information about the organization's offerings

- News, press releases, and coverage of current events and "What's New" items, to report on recent activities and newsworthy events

- A search engine, especially for large or complex Web sites, to help visitors find specific items

In addition, such sites often include at least some of the following elements as well:

- A list of current employment opportunities, to permit the organization to recruit from among its visitor population

- An organizational backgrounder, history, officer biographies, and other self-descriptive documents, to permit visitors to learn more about the organization and its key personnel

- Financial information, especially for publicly-held organizations that must report such data to shareholders, to allow visitors to examine public records online

- Information about beta releases, planned products, or technologies under development, to permit visitors to gauge the organization's direction and future plans

- Pointers to related information, standards, professional societies, or other affiliations important to the organization, to position it within a broader industry and societal context

- Reader feedback solicitation, to permit visitors to provide comments, criticisms, or ask questions about a site's content and information

Many corporate sites offer all of these features; most include at least some of them. High-tech companies—in particular, those with technology investments in the Internet—sport some of the most comprehensive offerings. For some excellent examples, visit any or all of the following company Web sites:

Microsoft: http://www.microsoft.com
Novell: http://www.novell.com
Sun Microsystems: http://www.sun.com

Increasingly, commerce is on the minds of these organizations. Many of them are investigating the Internet as a potential sales channel, and most already use the Internet to deliver updates, patches, and fixes for their existing products.

Once a presence on the Internet is established, it's only a small additional step to begin conducting business online. We anticipate that the Web's increasing presence and popularity will cause many organizations to migrate their business activities to the online world. It's already possible to make travel arrangements, buy tickets to sporting events or shows, check bank or credit card balances, and track overnight shipments on the Web; it's just a matter of time before paying routine bills, ordering office supplies, and taking care of business in general heads the same way.

Bullish on the Internet . . .

The financial markets in general, and the stock market in particular, operate entirely in real-time—or as close to real-time as the regulating bodies will let stock tickers get (usually, a 15-minute delay is required). Most of the major financial news services, stock brokerages, commodities and currency trading firms, investment banks, and other financial players have already staked out a presence on the Internet. Much trading of all kinds is already taking place in cyberspace, courtesy of these and other interested firms.

In general, such operations usually offer an online stock ticker, along with a variety of financial news feeds, and other information offerings. Those brokerages or financial analysis firms that produce special reports routinely make these reports available online, along with historical trading information, market analysis, and other kinds of financial data. Likewise, subscriptions to additional information services—such as financial newsletters or special reports—are often available for an additional fee.

In addition to trading stocks, bonds, money markets, commodities, and other financial instruments, these operators can provide access to financial planning, expert advice, tax planning, and other sophisticated and customized offerings. If "follow the money" is a prime principle of investing, most of these firms have also heeded this dictum in providing ways to interact with investors at all levels.

These days, it is easy to gather information regarding electronic commerce on the Internet. There are literally thousands of sources of financial information and trading opportunities available online, from major financial publications like *Money Magazine* and the *Kiplinger Report*, to information reporting services like Value Line, to discount brokerage firms like Charles Schwab, to the major Wall Street firms like Prudential Investments.

Even the Securities and Exchange Commission (SEC) filings are available online, at `http://edgar.stern.nyu.edu`. For an excellent entry point into the online financial world that covers resources from classes to financial databases online, please visit the KiwiClub server at the University of Texas (the alma mater of several of the authors of this book) at `http://kiwiclub.bus.utexas.edu/`.

To Err Is Human, To Shop (Online) Divine!

Perhaps one of the business models that's weathered the translation from a prior incarnation (from a mail- and telephone-based approach) to the Internet is catalog shopping. Other than dealing with the inconvenience of sticking close to a terminal to shop, there's really not much difference between calling into a telesales operation to place a catalog order, versus filling out an order form yourself online. In most cases, shoppers fill out paper forms in advance anyway, to have the information they need ready for the person who takes their order, so there's no fundamental change involved in performing these functions online.

Catalog companies like electronic catalogs because they're easier to maintain and keep current. Whereas a printed catalog might have to last two or three months, an electronic analog can be updated daily without inconveniencing the customer, or confusing the order-takers. Then, too, the rising costs of paper—up over 300 percent in the last four years—makes electronic catalogs more economical than paper versions, especially for companies that offer large collections of merchandise.

Here, too, companies discovered that paper and electronic versions need not be incompatible. L.L. Bean, for instance, still prints seasonal catalogs of selected merchandise for its mail-order customer base. But a quick jump to their Web site, at `http://www.llbean.com/`, shows that customers are able search the complete collection of L.L. Bean products online, whereas paper and mailing costs prevents the company from printing the same information in any single paper catalog. The Web site also gives L.L. Bean the opportunity to provide camping and fishing information, as well as publicize their shooting, biking, fly-fishing, and other training programs.

Other catalog businesses that have flourished on the Web include bookstores, specialty foods stores, wine shops, music stores, and florists. Because catalog shopping represents a large business sector—over $50 billion in 1996, according to a study published in the *San Diego Business Journal* (available at `http://www.businessite.com/Entry/BusinessNet/bj/bjinwells.html`)—many companies are eager to investigate the online side of this business. In fact, several companies offer automatic conversion tools to take the kinds of databases normally used to generate paper catalogs, and use the same data to create online versions "automagically." Given the presence of such sophisticated tools, it's obvious that this represents a major market niche.

The following is a sampling of some outstanding online catalog shopping sites, all of which offer online commerce and are worth visiting (or avoiding, depending on the state of your budget):

Bookstores
Amazon.com: `http://www.amazon.com/`
Computer Literacy Bookstores: `http://www.clbooks.com/`

Music
CDnow: `http://www.cdnow.com`
CD Universe: `http://www.cduniverse.com/`

Specialty foods
Alligator Bob's Gourmet Alligator: `http://www.gatorbob.com/`
Godiva Chocolatier: `http://www.godiva.com`
Pepper Plant Hot Sauce: `http://www.pepperplant.com/`

Florists
Amazing Arrangements: `http://www.durhamnews.net/~amazing/`
The Ultimate Thought, Inc: `http://www.walrus.com/~tut/`

Home Shopping Network online
Internet Shopping Network: `http://internet.com`

Online Catalog Resources
Buy IT Online: `http://www.buyitonline.com/`
The Catalog Site: `http://www.catalogsite.com/`

The final elements in this list are both clearinghouses of online shopping and catalog information; either one makes a great spot to start an online shopping expedition. What's amazing is the huge number of vendors that not only have online sites, but that will accept orders online as well.

Moving Products Across the Net

For digital wares of all kinds, the Internet—which some pundits have equated with the "Information Superhighway" as promoted by the Clinton administration—provides a natural delivery channel. It should therefore come as no surprise that both software and content vendors (that is, those companies that make digital wares) and resellers (those companies that sell such wares to other dealers, or to the public) are adopting this approach with varying degrees of intensity, investment, and success.

Although some of the earliest Internet software stores are nothing more than online catalogs, software giants like Microsoft and Novell are investigating transferring licenses for their products to distributors electronically to expedite delivery and drastically reduce the cost of goods. Especially for the international marketplace, where help screens, menus, and other user-interface elements must be translated into other languages, this method of distribution promises to speed delivery, and to reduce the current 3- to 6-month gap that commonly separates an English-language release of a major product from any of its counterparts in other languages.

Companies such as Egghead, Inc., and CompUSA, Inc., have made significant investments in online catalog operations, which are starting to pay off handsomely for both companies. Each of the Web sites of these companies features "virtual stores" online where, in addition to searching for products by name or category, users can walk electronic aisles and browse images of shelves, laid out just like those in the stores operated by these chains. For an interesting illustration of how the "virtual store" concept can be realized, visit either of their sites at:

Egghead: `http://www.egghead.com/`
CompUSA: `http://www.compusa.com/`

In addition to phone and mail order-taking, both companies also support ordering online. We expect this to be the wave of the future, coupled with electronic delivery of software (and possibly, snail mail delivery of manuals and media for customers who want to pay extra for these more tangible products). Publishing giant CMP offers a similar Web site called software.net where demo programs and entire packages can be downloaded with ease. Its sister Web site, shareware.com, provides a search engine and pointers to thousands of freeware and shareware software packages all over the world. Visit these sites at:

```
http://www.software.net/
http://www.shareware.com/ .
```

Other online software delivery operations are more like electronic malls, in that they create "virtual storefronts" where users can browse offerings from a large number of vendors within the confines of a single Web site. Infohaus, from First Virtual Holdings, Inc., falls into this category, and functions as a marketplace for digital materials of all kinds, including text, image, audio, video, and software products. The Infohaus has made a home for affiliated vendors too small or uninterested in hosting their own Web sites, and created a venue to generate revenue for their own credit transfer operations. Visit the Infohaus at:

```
http://www.infohaus.com/ .
```

Beyond the Obvious

Using the Internet to deliver digital data is its most blatant and obvious application. But beyond the merely obvious, the Internet has spawned a number of interesting and useful commercial applications that exploit its broad reach, easy access, and tremendous consumer appeal. The following sections detail some of the less predictable niches where the digital and real worlds have converged in unusual but fruitful ways.

The online auto advantage

Buy IT Online lists nearly one hundred online services and information resources under the category "Auto." Although it's still impossible to actually purchase an automobile online, it's by no means difficult to research such a purchase. In fact, next to buying a home, buying an automobile is one of the few other "big ticket" purchases most people must make from time to time. Even though autos themselves may never be available online, for those inclined to research their next vehicle purchase, the Internet offers a real surfeit of information, from the "Big 3" (Chrysler, General Motors, and Ford) themselves, new and used dealerships, and aftermarket companies, to car purchasing agents, fleet sales operations, and other vehicle sources of all kinds. The following are a few noteworthy sites to inspect along the way:

Chrysler Corporation
```
http://www.chryslercars.com
```

Clickable Systems International, Ltd.
```
http://www.clickable.com/cars.html
```

CyberCar
`http://www.cybercar.com`

Dealernet
`http://www.dealernet.com`

Delco Electronics
`http://www.delco.com/`

Ford Motor Company
`http://www.ford.com`

Looking for just the right . . . ?

The searchability of electronic information adds tremendously to the value of using such data when looking for a particular item or piece of merchandise. If you've ever spent the morning circling listings in the classified section of a newspaper, whether you were looking for a job, an apartment, a vehicle, or even a garage sale in your neighborhood, you'd surely jump at the chance to easily zero in on what you're after electronically, instead of reading each and every entry just enough to see whether it matches your interests.

Newspapers such as the *San Jose Mercury News*, *USA Today*, and countless local papers, have launched online versions of their printed product. In almost every case, the most popular service they offer is a search engine for their classified ads. This lets readers search the content by keyword, and sometimes by concept, which can be a tremendous aid when searching for something in particular. A quick jump to Digital's AltaVista search engine using the term "matching service" turns up 1,000 hits—all of which offer some kind of online matching capability for everything from personal relationships to business investments, and quite a few interesting points in-between. A few examples of this genre include the following:

Financial Aid Matching Service (students with financial aid)
`http://plan.educ.indiana.edu/~www/famatching.html`

Silverplate Matching Service (silver and silverplate patterns)
`http://www.compumedia.com/~eugene/`

Career Matching Service (people with cosmetology jobs)
`http://www.imagenetworker.com/public_html/career/career.html`

Electronic wagering, sports lines, and more

Although gambling is usually under the jurisdiction of local authorities—and is in fact illegal in many locales—the Internet's global reach makes it possible to bring people who want to wager together with those who'd like to take wagers. Given the right medium of electronic exchange, there's no limit to the wagering that can occur. The same thing is true of the various lines of information used to set wagers. Even though such information may not be freely disseminated in many jurisdictions, it still serves as the basis for informal wagering of all kinds, like football, soccer, or baseball pools. Finally, local restrictions on contraband material can be overstepped on the Internet. For example, a great deal of controversy has surrounded online access to material, such as erotica and pornography, that is found objectionable by some locales but not everywhere (particularly outside of the U.S.).

We can't endorse the use of the Internet for such purposes, but we're no more able to control these forms of human behavior than anyone else. Suffice it to say that there's plenty of commerce underway on the Internet that might fail to meet the rules and regulations in many places. For that reason, we left the pointers out of this section and let those with sufficient interest find their own forms of such diversion.

The Mechanics of Electronic Commerce

Hopefully, we've demonstrated the appeal of electronic commerce and some of the many areas in which it's practiced online. Now, we'll turn our attention away from the "what" and concentrate a bit on the "how." In other words, we'll examine what's involved in handling a commercial transaction online, and expose some of the issues and concerns that have somewhat slowed the rush to switch our economy completely over to this new medium of exchange.

Plain vanilla commerce

First, it's important to understand the basic elements of a commercial transaction of any kind. Next, we'll explore those areas of particular concern when buyer and seller may be at opposite ends of the world, without the ability to present physical documentation, or proof of identity and the ability to pay for—or deliver—the goods or services that are involved in the commercial transaction.

Consider a credit card transaction at your local department store. If the clerk follows the rules for such transactions to the letter, here's what's supposed to happen:

1. You present the merchandise you wish to purchase, and the clerk asks, "Will that be cash, check, or charge?" You answer, "charge."

2. The clerk rings up the merchandise; asks for your credit card. Typically, he or she will swipe the card at the cash register, or in a special credit check device. Either way, the financial clearinghouse (FC) that handles the card gets a phone call. Assuming everything's okay, the dialog for this communication goes something like the following:

    (Store) Card number 1234 5678 9101 1121 requests a purchase of $112.20.
    (FC) Card number 1234 5678 9101 1121 has sufficient remaining credit to cover the purchase. Approval code F578X25.

3. The approval code is entered onto the credit card purchase form (either by hand, or by the cash register software).

4. The clerk asks you to sign the credit card receipt.

5. You sign the receipt, and the clerk compares the signature on the receipt to the one on the back (or front) of your credit card to make sure it's really your card. Sometimes, depending on local laws, he or she may ask to see a photo ID.

6. Since everything worked out, you get your merchandise and your credit card back.

But here's what's really going on, in terms of the financial transaction that's taking place:

1. The merchant makes sure the credit card is valid by checking with the financial clearinghouse.

2. Having ascertained the card's validity, the merchant makes sure it contains sufficient remaining available credit to cover the cost of the current transaction.

3. Having ascertained validity and ability to pay, the merchant makes sure that the purchaser is indeed the person who's using the card (but since the merchant will usually be paid even if this latter element is untrue, this check is less religiously applied than items 1 or 2).

An electronic equivalent

In reality, electronic commerce doesn't differ too much from the department store credit card purchase we just described, but it does introduce additional concerns, especially when the Internet is involved. Here are some of the issues we address throughout the rest of this book:

■ Proof of identity becomes quite a bit trickier. Because all that can be presented online is a pattern of bits, there has to be some way to make sure that the pattern of bits that's presented identifies a particular individual (or more usually, an account belonging to a particular business entity, whether an individual, corporation, or whatever).

■ The security of the communications involved between buyer and seller becomes an issue. Because traffic on the Internet can be intercepted and inspected at any point between buyer and seller, or vice-versa, it's worrisome that sensitive financial information may be available to parties other than those immediately involved in the transaction itself. Although it's a truism that sending credit card information by e-mail is no more risky than giving your credit card number to someone over the phone, it's still a risk nonetheless. For some reason, the electronic version worries people a lot more than the telephone scenario.

■ The ability to pay is also trickier in a purely digital world. Most credit card check systems use built-in security mechanisms, and only connect to the clearinghouse that serves the credit check network to which a merchant belongs. On the wild and wooly global Internet, merchants want to be doubly sure that they're communicating with a genuine authority on a purchaser's ability to pay, rather than a "very good imitation." The difference between the two might be both subtle and expensive!

■ Although it's often overlooked, the ability to deliver can also raise issues. Whereas the purchaser may enter a transaction in perfectly good faith and tender the necessary cash to make a purchase, what's to guarantee that when the seller collects the cash that they'll actually deliver the goods or services that were just paid for. In other words, it's important that all parties to a transaction be properly identified, if only to properly assign liability later.

The only entirely new element here is the need to maintain confidentiality for the communications between buyer and seller (and other parties that may get involved along the way, like the financial clearinghouse in the credit card example mentioned earlier).

Many experts liken communications across the Internet to a giant party line where everyone can "hear" what everyone else is saying. To preserve the confidentiality of sensitive communications, like those used to conduct commercial transactions, some kind of special data scrambling is required. The scrambling keeps others who may attempt to read these communications from obtaining the confidential information. What makes such scrambling special is that what gets scrambled on one end of a communication must then be successfully unscrambled on the other end, restoring the original content. If the original information gets lost, no communication can occur.

Summary

In this chapter, we examined some of the applications for electronic commerce, and some of the many venues in which it's currently practiced on the Internet. Along the way, we've pointed out some interesting examples, and some Web sites that practice what we preach. We concluded with an introductory high-level examination of what's different about electronic commerce, after examining what's involved in a credit transaction. In the chapters that follow, we'll increase the level of detail and information about this subject, as we explain what's involved in electronic commerce in detail, and then examine some of the many options for implementing software to conduct electronic commerce. By now, you understand the basic elements. By the time you've finished this book, you will understand many of the details, and know how to use them for your own protection, if not to your best advantage.

CHAPTER TWO

SECURITY AND
AUTHENTICATION

In Chapter 1, we examined the mechanics of a credit card transaction involving human interaction as a way to set the stage for exploring its electronic equivalent online. At the end of that discussion, we raised the issues of confidentiality (on the Internet any party in between the buyer and seller can inspect the messages sent from sender to receiver) and authentication (the mechanisms used to confirm the identities of buyer and seller and possibly other interested third parties, like the merchant banks or clearing houses that actually process financial transactions). In this chapter, we'll examine those issues in greater detail, as we explore and explain the prevailing methods used to handle confidentiality and authentication, and talk about some of the technologies used to implement these methods.

Securely Transferring Information

Because the messages that move via e-mail on the Internet (and indeed the contents of protocol packets of all kinds) can become an open book on any server through which they pass, maintaining the confidentiality of commercial transactions is a worthy focus for concern. In fact, we agree with the experts who declaim that giving one's credit card information over the phone to an order-taker is every bit as risky as sending that information in clear text across the Internet.

But there's a substantial difference between the Internet and the telephone. Although there's plenty of opportunity for a telephone order-taker to play a role in potential credit card fraud, you'd have to place your order on a party line of vast dimensions to match the replication of e-mail information on every server involved in forwarding a message from sender to receiver across the Internet. In fact, we think it's the number of potential access points that gives people the willies where electronic commerce is concerned, rather than the degree of exposure of sensitive information.

Is security really that important? In a word, "Yes." It's a great deal more important for business-to-business transactions, perhaps, than for individual purchases, but all parties involved in a commercial transaction expect that the information they exchange is limited strictly to the parties involved.

By definition, access to account information of all kinds is sensitive. Access to this information provides one link to a chain of information elements that can let one party impersonate another, thereby giving impersonators the ability to access funds that aren't rightfully theirs. Much of the security that's built into the various electronic commerce technologies and systems we'll be investigating in this book has been deliberately designed to deny access to any information about commercial transactions to those who have no right to that information.

For most electronic commerce systems, the key to security is based on encryption, where a complex mathematical transformation is applied to data that is sent over an insecure line. The process of encrypting data includes applying a special value to plain text, called an encryption key, which scrambles the data by rearranging it and replacing the original values with a set of substituted values. These values are based on the value of the key plus a rigorously defined set of mathematical operations based on the key and the original plain text. The result is a collection of seemingly random bits that look and behave exactly like garbage in its encrypted form.

Obtaining access to the original data on the other end of the connection depends on whether the user has possession of a "magic number," or decryption key, which can be used to reverse the encryption process. Essentially, using the decryption key, along with an understanding of the original transformation process that encrypted the data in the first place, permits that process to be undone, and the data to be restored to its original form.

Today, existing electronic commerce systems—and other secure forms of communication, like those used by governments to transmit classified documents via satellite—rely on one of two of the following standard encryption methods:

- Private-key encryption, also known as symmetric cryptography
- Public-key encryption, also known as asymmetric cryptography

These methods are called cryptography, which literally means "to write secrets," because they involve rewriting a data stream to make its contents as unreadable to parties that do not possess a key as is practical and (moderately) efficient. Please read on to learn more about each of these methods, and to appreciate their differences.

Private-key encryption

Private-key encryption uses the identical key to decrypt a message that was used to encrypt the message in the first place. This requires that the sender and receiver both have copies of the key, which usually means they've exchanged or agreed upon its value beforehand. One of the best-known private-key encryption schemes is the Data Encryption Standard (DES) used by numerous financial institutions—and the U.S. Government—to transmit data to automatic teller machines over public telephone lines (which, by definition, are unsecured).

In the field of cryptography, much of the discussion, and a great deal of intellectual horse-power, is devoted to the definition and creation of public and private keys. Since the value of a key must be hard to guess, most keys rely on performing mathematical operations on one or more large prime numbers that are literally calculated to be unique and hard to reproduce. Because it's necessary to know the prime numbers that go into creating a key, and calculating large prime numbers is itself a time-consuming computing job, it's the compounding of difficult calculations within a very large search space that makes larger keys safer than smaller ones, and the cracking task increasingly onerous as keys increase in size.

In fact, you'll sometimes see estimates about how long it would take a computer to crack a particular key that will strain credulity (as described in the sidebar on RSA Data Security later in this chapter). Such calculations presuppose that there are no special tricks that would allow a key to be cracked by knowing the trick, rather than figuring out the key by brute force. Such calculations also ignore the fact that many computers working in parallel can greatly compress the time required to employ the necessary brute force, rather than a single machine working by itself in patient obscurity.

It's quite interesting that the U.S. Government has done quite a bit to restrict cryptography technology suitable for export to 48-bit keys or less. (For more information on this topic, please see the next sidebar, entitled "The DES Conspiracy.") "Export-safe" versions of Netscape Navigator and the various commerce servers also available from Netscape Communications use 40-bit keys. Since the length of the key is directly related to its crackability, this strikes most knowledgeable observers as way too short. By way of comparison, the current commercial version of RSA encryption uses 768-bit keys, and 1024-bit key lengths will be accommodated within the next year or so.

WHAT'S IN A KEY?

The Digital Encryption Standard (DES) is the official encryption standard for the U.S. Government. Originally developed by IBM in the 1970s, DES was adopted by the Federal Government in 1977. This adoption led numerous manufacturers to implement the encryption algorithm, defined by the National Bureau of Standards (now known as the National Institute of Standards and Technology, or NIST) later that year. The availability of fast, cheap hardware has stimulated its use in many market sectors, including finance (it's what's behind Electronic Data Interchange, or EDI) and numerous types of "scrambler phones" and other, relatively secure communications equipment.

DES operates on 8-byte (64-bit) blocks of data, and uses a 56-bit key to perform its encryption tasks. DES is designed to be implemented in hardware, to make it relatively fast and efficient to apply. According to numerous sources, the claim is that this encryption scheme has never been "broken"—which is to say, there are no known instances of someone decoding a message encrypted with a DES algorithm through a brute force attack. However, IBM's original design called for a 128-bit key, which would have mathematically guaranteed too large a search space to make brute force techniques effective. The key length specified in the NIST standard, however, was reduced to 56-bits at the request of the U.S. National Security agency.

Also, at that same agency's request, IBM refused to publish its approach to designing the DES algorithm in its current form. This has led academic cryptographers to speculate that there may be "tricks" that permit the encryption scheme to be broken at will. The overall effect of a short key, a secret design scheme, and other attempts at government interference has been to promote the widely-held belief that the government did not want to promote an unbreakable encryption technology, because that could prevent them from tapping phones and obtaining access to encrypted data when they deem it necessary.

Certainly, more recent controversies around the export of public-key technologies and the so-called "Clipper" chip (which includes a special "back door" for wiretapping use) have not caused this speculation to abate. Nevertheless, DES is widely used and provides a reasonable—if not impenetrable—degree of security.

To use DES most effectively, its implementors recommend that you change keys often. (Government traffic uses a one-time keypad approach, so that each message uses a unique key, based on tearing off a sheet from a set of shared pads of predefined keys.) The requirements of sharing secret keys means that it's absolutely essential to manage their security, which is why they are usually kept under lock and key with strictly enforced access protocols to their repositories. The implementors recommend further that all keys themselves be encrypted with a "master key," so that compromise of one key will not provide system-wide entry. For the greatest security, they also recommend multiple encryption passes, up to three times, to scramble the data as much as possible.

For further information on DES, including references to published versions of its source code, visit the following Web site:

THE DES CONSPIRACY

```
http://www.quadralay.com/Crypto/source-books.html .
```

Once the keys have been delivered to their intended users, private-key encryption is an excellent method to ensure the security of data that's to be transmitted over unsecured links of any kind. The problem, of course, is that exchanging keys usually requires some other method of transfer than the link over which encrypted messages travel. Otherwise, a problem of infinite regress will occur, because the keys themselves will need to be encrypted. Most systems that rely on private keys, therefore, rely on other methods to exchange keys, whether via a diplomatic pouch for delivery of one-time-use only key pads, or in the form of a file that's manually installed on an automated transaction machine (ATM) device by a technician performing a service call, or access to an encrypted file of keys for which the "master key" is manually installed.

For mass market digital use, private-key systems often depend on shared access to a trusted provider of keys, so that sender and receiver can declare their intent to exchange encrypted information, and then obtain a key for one-time use. Given some method of identifying themselves unambiguously—which we'll discuss later in this chapter—this provides a reasonable way to use private keys safely and securely, but also relatively spontaneously as well.

Public-key encryption

Public-key encryption schemes rely on the use of two keys: one that's used to encode a message for transmission, and another that's used to decode that transmission at the receiving end. The encrypting key is based on a mathematical translation of the private key that is designed to be extremely difficult to decode; therefore, it can be freely shared with anyone via e-mail, file transfer, or other methods. Its free dissemination and availability explains why it's called the public key. Anyone with access to the public key can use it to encrypt a message that's virtually guaranteed to be readable only by someone who possesses the other key in the pair. This decrypting key should be the exclusive property of the receiver only, and is therefore called the private key.

The best-known public-key encryption scheme in broad commercial use today is called RSA. Named after its inventors: Rivest, Shamir, and Adelman—all originally professors and colleagues at MIT—RSA encryption is used for a broad range of applications, from encrypting passwords on networks by companies like Microsoft and Novell, to protecting account information in financial packages like Quicken, to outright personal encryption packages like Phil Zimmerman's Pretty Good Privacy (PGP) software. Much of the command set for the DOS version of PGP is displayed in Figure 2-1, and is available through http://www.pgp.com/.

Public-key systems also enable the use of special digital tokens, called digital signatures. Anyone who creates an e-mail message, or some other kind of electronic document, can include a code that is generated with his or her private key. Any recipient can then use the public key to decode enough of that code to verify that the message was encoded with that individual's private key. Figure 2-2 shows what VeriSign delivers for free to Netscape e-mail users who wish to obtain a digital signature to authenticate their e-mail.

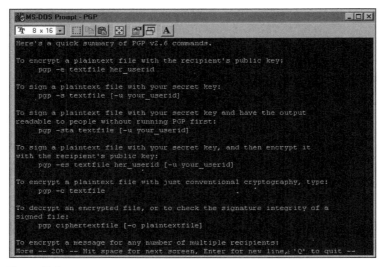

Figure 2-1
Phil Zimmerman's PGP program provides lots of useful encryption options, and is free to download.

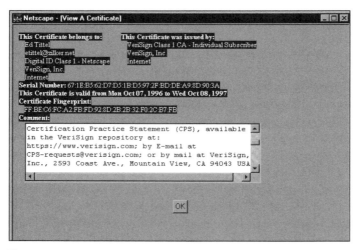

Figure 2-2
At http://www.verisign.com/ you can sign up for your own digital signature, which results in a certificate that looks like this.

Most electronic commerce systems use either private- or public-key encryption techniques to ensure secure communications. Some newer encryption schemes even use both private- and public-key encryption schemes in tandem—most notably, the emerging standard for Internet-based credit card transactions known as Secure Electronic Transactions (SET), engineered by MasterCard and Visa in the third quarter of 1996 (covered in more detail at the end of this chapter).

RSA Data Security, Inc., is a Redwood City, California-based company that virtually owns the public-key encryption technology business (and they do, in fact, own a patent on their encryption algorithm, which they've vigorously—and successfully—enforced in U.S. courts on several occasions). Founded in 1982 by its eponymous founders, Rivest, Shamir, and Adelman, RSA's encryption technology is embedded in Microsoft Windows, Novell NetWare, Intuit Quicken, Lotus Notes, and hundreds of other products. RSA is also the parent company of VeriSign, one of the digital certificate authorities currently operating on the Internet at:

`http://www.verisign.com/`.

RSA technologies appear in existing and proposed standards for the Internet and World Wide Web, ISO, ANSI, IEEE, and in business, financial, and electronic commerce networks, both public and private, around the world. RSA develops and markets platform-independent developer's kits and end-user products, and is available for consultation on cryptography techniques. For more information about the company, its software and APIs, and access to its many informative publications, API descriptions, and standards documents, visit the RSA Data Security Web site at:

`http://www.rsa.com/`.

RSA has taken steps to ensure the unbreakability of its security schemes and key-generation methods. In 1977, Ran Rivest (who developed the public-key encryption system at the heart of the RSA algorithm) publicly challenged anyone to break their original 129-bit key. Rivest had originally calculated that it would take 40 quadrillion years (4×10^{13}) years to crack a test message that he encoded with a prime number 129 digits long. But by devising an attack strategy that executed in parallel on over 1,600 machines around the world, an MIT graduate student named Derek Atkins, broke the code in a mere eight months!

That's probably exactly why today's commercial RSA implementations use much longer keys that are much harder to break. In fact, the current RSA keys are 768 bits long, which are considered formidable, even for parallel cracking techniques. By the end of 1997, 1,024-bit keys will also be available, making an extremely difficult cracking task even more challenging.

But taking a parallel and distributed approach to code-breaking makes predictions about code unbreakability questionable. Academics, students, and security analysts have also repeatedly demonstrated the relative weakness of codes crippled by the U.S. Government's export limitations. In fact, several different groups broke the 40-bit version of Netscape encryption, most recently in France in the summer of 1996, when a graduate student was able to "bust" Netscape's 40-bit version over a holiday weekend when he gained access to half-a-dozen supercomputers that were otherwise idle.

But given that a financial transaction takes a fairly short period of time, regular replacement of keys will foil would-be crackers. Even those with the resources to bring thousands or ordinary computers (or even a handful of supercomputers) together still can't crack codes fast enough to break through before a key is replaced. Perhaps that's why RSA's technology has proved "secure enough" to appear in a wide range of software products and systems. According to RSA's estimates in late 1996, over 75 million software packages in daily use employ their security technology.

RSA'S MARKET HEGEMONY

Certification and certificate authorities

In addition to providing a secure method for encryption, the mere possession of a private or secret key can also demonstrate identity. The concept of a digital signature rests on creating a message that only the holder of a particular private key can read—the ability to read that message provides proof that the reader is the holder of the key, and hence, creates a reasonable expectation that the reader is the desired recipient. For instance, if the designated user receives an encrypted message that reads "send an e-mail message to xy14$z529@test.com" and then follows those instructions, it's a clear indication that the user not only received the message, but was able to read and act on its contents. This ability demonstrates the user's identity in an unequivocal way—so long as the key is only in the hands of its rightful owner.

This assumption—namely, that only the designated holder of a key can use it—is what enables digital signature technology to work. By creating a message that only the keyholder could create, or acting on encrypted instructions that only someone with a private or secret key could follow, either approach "proves" the identity of one party to a communication.

Since electronic commerce really requires that both parties of a transaction be able to provide proof of identity, some security schemes rely on the presence of a third party to perform authentication services, which in turn often issue their own digital tokens, or certificates, to indicate acceptance of a bearer's identity. This third-party authentication effort is called certification, and the certificates issued are subject to various conditions of expiration, qualification, and use. The nature of this activity also explains why such third parties are called "certificate authorities."

Some commerce schemes require the parties of a transaction to tender a certificate, in addition to the details of that transaction, as a way of demonstrating authenticity of the parties involved. This approach also confers another benefit—since obtaining a certificate is a voluntary act, tendering a certificate provides a way to keep transactions from being repudiated, by either buyer or seller.

The logic behind this notion of non-repudiatability goes something like this:

1. A certificate is required to consummate a transaction.

2. A certificate can only by obtained by solicitation.

3. Obtaining a certificate requires that the obtainer provide proof of identity.

4. Tender of a certificate not only provides proof of the participant's identity, but of the participant's volition in pursuing a particular transaction.

Of course, the whole thing rests on the confidentiality of each party's private or secret key, which is used to obtain a certificate in the first place. That's why following all reasonable precautions in protecting your keys is very, very important.

Protecting your keys

According to the security experts both inside and outside the government, the only really safe way to protect a key or password is to store it in a safe, whose combination is known only to authorized personnel. Of course, this creates the problem of what to do with the combination—as you'll quickly learn, one key very often leads to another!

Beyond this dictum, we'd like to suggest some worthwhile ways of hiding keys, and then some incredibly dumb things that you should never, ever, do with keys. For one thing, a 768-bit key translates into 96 characters, which is quite a lot to write down in the first place, and real challenge to key in correctly should you ever need to edit it! The longer the key, the more secure it may be, but the more likely it also becomes that that key is recorded somewhere on a computer (because cutting and pasting beats re-keying every time).

Most reasonable key-based software won't require you to enter your key every time you use it. Instead, it will ask you to enter the key twice, and only permit you to proceed when (a) the two keys are identical, and (b) the key is verified as correct. After that, you may never need to re-enter the key again—unless the software that needs it must be re-installed on a machine that crashed (normally, keys will transfer, even across upgrades). Of course, keys do occasionally expire, so you may have to perform this intricate process on a regular basis.

THREE TIPS FOR SAFE, SECRET KEY STORAGE

All the following tips assume that you have at least one hard-copy of the key value in your possession, and that storage in a safe is not an option.

1. Store it in a locked drawer or filing cabinet.

2. Place it in a known location (such as between pages 100 and 101 of a book nobody ever reads) that's out of sight. Or append it as an unlabeled comment in a text file on your computer that includes the string "key" nowhere in its name.

3. Rent a safety deposit box, and store the key there.

NEVER DO THIS WITH YOUR KEYS!

1. Keep them on a sticky note on your computer screen.

2. Create a neatly labeled folder named "keys" and keep all your keys in there.

3. Carry the key on a slip of paper in your wallet.

4. Write the key down in your organizer in the address book under "key" or any other descriptive, easy-to-find name.

If you're a little bit crafty, you can usually avoid unwanted sharing of keys, yet still retrieve them when you need them. Think about it: these keys can be the ticket to a lot of your money (or your organization's money), so treat them like the valuable assets they are.

Paradigms for Secure Web Information Transfer

In practice, most developers don't build encryption systems, either based on public- or private-keys. Instead they use them through incorporation of specific external software libraries made accessible by one or another of a series of application programming interfaces (APIs). Some understanding of this technology is useful because it helps to instill a proper degree of caution, especially where managing keys is concerned. But the details of the mathematics and algorithms used are largely irrelevant to building electronic commerce solutions. It's enough that these technologies are available, and that they work more or less as advertised.

As the individuals who construct electronic commerce systems, developers tend to be far more interested in the APIs that deliver secure access and the best techniques for their use. In the sections that follow, we'll cover some of the major contenders in the secure API market, and explain what's behind these various sets of programming interfaces. In later chapters, you'll get plenty of opportunity to wrestle with the details.

Here, our goal is to introduce the cast of players in the secure Web access game, so you'll not only have a better idea of your options, but also be somewhat familiar with the APIs we cover in more detail in chapters 5 through 10, where you'll also learn about secure Web servers and related services. We again cover APIs in chapters 12 through 14, where you'll be exposed to some of the details involved in building, installing, and using a secure Web-based electronic commerce application.

At this point, we introduce some of the options used to create secure Web traffic, primarily through the use of a secure transport protocol. These methods share a common approach to providing security—namely, the insertion of an encryption layer in the protocols normally used to ship requests for Web data (or transaction information, for electronic commerce applications on the Web) to Web servers, and to send replies to such requests back to clients. As you'll soon see, some of these techniques apply to more than just the Web's HyperText Transfer Protocol (HTTP).

Netscape's Secure Sockets Layer (SSL) protocol

Netscape Communications designed and specified a data security protocol called the Secure Sockets Layer (SSL), that has been widely adopted in many applications. SSL interposes itself between application-layer protocols like HTTP, Telnet, the Network News Transfer Protocol (NNTP), and the connection-oriented transport protocol, TCP. SSL provides a variety of security services including data encryption, server authentication, message integrity check, and optional client authentication for TCP/IP connection.

SSL relies heavily on public-key technology, based on a royalty-free license from RSA. SSL-enabled servers and clients are available from commercial vendors such as Netscape, Microsoft, IBM, Spyglass, and public-domain implementations such as Apache-SSL, which is included on the CD-ROM in the back of this book. Netscape's products all incorporate SSL to provide security services.

SSL delivers the following three basic security services, all of which rely on public-key encryption:

1. **Message privacy.** SSL provides message privacy through a combination of private- and public-key encryption techniques. All traffic between an SSL server and SSL client is encrypted using a key and an encryption algorithm that's negotiated during an SSL handshake phase. By encrypting the contents of network traffic, this approach thwarts would-be network eavesdroppers who may be able to see, but not decrypt, such messages.

2. **Message integrity.** SSL includes integrity checks to guarantee that message contents do not change between sender and receiver. SSL uses a combination of a shared private key and special hashing functions to detect and reject altered (or erroneous) packets.

3. **Mutual authentication.** SSL uses public-key certificates to authenticate both parties to any communication, where both certificates are exchanged during the handshake phase. Each party must successfully use its private key to decrypt encrypted data from the other party during that phase to demonstrate that it not only holds a particular certificate, but can also prove its identity through a "test decryption."

SSL is an open, royalty-free protocol that was submitted to the World Wide Web Consortium's (W3C) working group on security for consideration as a standard security mechanism for Web browsers and servers. Netscape representatives are participating in the development and standardization of robust security technologies and protocols for use on the Internet. They also announced their intentions to support whatever security standards emerge from the efforts of this working group, in concert with the Internet Engineering Task Force, or IETF.

A reference implementation of SSL, called SSLRef 2.0, is available for noncommercial use, or may be commercially licensed from Netscape. Anyone is free to implement his or her own version of SSL from its specifications without the obligation to license that technology from Netscape. For more information on SSL, please visit Netscape's Web site at:

`http://home.netscape.com/`.

The site search utility will provide ample materials on SSL if you use that acronym as a search term. You will also find the mailing list at `ssl-talk@netscape.com` to be a valuable source of SSL news and information.

EIT's Secure Hypertext Transfer Protocol (S-HTTP)

Enterprise Integration Technologies is a company that has pioneered important technologies for the Internet and the Web, including Secure HTTP (S-HTTP) and the CommerceNet Consortium (an assemblage of commerce-minded companies with online interests available at `http://www.commerce.net.`). It's now a wholly owned subsidiary of VeriFone, Inc., a leading company in the ATM industry, and a supplier of ATM technology to banks around the world. It's safe to say that at EIT, the focus is on electronic commerce, pure and simple (or as complex as it needs to be).

S-HTTP is a security-enhanced version of the original HTTP application-layer Web protocol. It was released by EIT to members of CommerceNet in late 1994, and provides general transaction security services necessary to conduct electronic commerce, including transaction confidentiality, authentication, message integrity checks, and proof of origin. Today, CommerceNet members use EIT's reference implementations in field tests of electronic commercial applications on the Internet. A commercial implementation of S-HTTP is available from Terisa Systems (a joint venture between EIT and RSA Data Security). For more information, please send e-mail to `info@terisa.com` or `shttp-info@eit.com`.

Much like SSL, S-HTTP supports end-to-end secure communications by handling encryption of messages at the application level. This means that all S-HTTP traffic is already encrypted before it reaches the network, and can only be decrypted upon receipt by a party in possession of the proper keys. Yet S-HTTP is completely interoperable with HTTP, and sites can mix S-HTTP materials with HTTP at will. Of course, only S-HTTP-enabled browsers will be able to read the S-HTTP materials (which are recognizable by URLs that end with .shtml instead of the more customary .html).Today, Internet Explorer 3.0, Netscape Navigator 3.0, and Mosaic 3.0, among others, all support S-HTTP.

S-HTTP also supports private-key operation; therefore, it requires neither client-side public-key certificates, nor public keys, to operate. This permits spontaneous transactions to occur even between parties not in possession of each other's public keys. Even though S-HTTP can use widely available certification techniques and certificate authorities (such as VeriSign), it does not require certification to work. Clients may be automatically set up to initiate a secure transaction, typically by following an HTML hyperlink to a secure document, and then filling out an order or payment form whose contents will automatically be encrypted before transmission.

S-HTTP provides flexible selection of cryptographic techniques, including private and public keys, and supports multiple transaction modes and related parameters. When clients and servers establish communication, option negotiation is used to establish an agreement on how a transaction should proceed. The options that are negotiable include the following:

- Should the transaction include a digital signature or not? If signed, what algorithm should be used?

- Should the transaction be encrypted or not? If encrypted, what algorithm should be used, DES or RSA?

- If a certificate is required, what kind should be used, SET, VeriSign, and so on?

S-HTTP uses a model called "late binding" to establish the way a transaction will be conducted—that is, rather than building a particular kind of logic into an application, S-HTTP permits all of the necessary choices to be made while the transaction is being set up, during the negotiation process. While this leads to more complex coding, S-HTTP also supports the most flexible possible transaction processing model.

In S-HTTP, messages may be protected in any of three ways—digital signature, authentication, and encryption—where any combination of these three methods can be used in a single transaction. The details of operation are quite similar to those explained for SSL in the preceding section, and will therefore not be covered again here.

S-HTTP also supports multiple key management mechanisms, including shared private keys, public-key exchange, and Kerberos ticket distribution. (Kerberos is a well-known security and access control service used on many TCP/IP-based networks. Kerberos can issue security tokens, called tickets, as proof of identity or for use as session-level keys.) Other session key mechanisms are also supported, to permit keys delivered in previous secure exchanges to be used in subsequent sessions.

Where digital signatures are used, messages may either contain the required certificate, or include instructions for the receiving party to contact an independent certificate authority to obtain the required information. S-HTTP even includes a bulk encryption mechanism, so that keys can be securely transferred and applied to large-scale data transfers or other lengthy online information exchanges.

For more details about S-HTTP, we recommend perusing the draft specification, which is available at:

```
http://www.eit.com/creations/s-http/
    draft-ietf-wts-shttp-00.txt
ftp://ds.internic.net/internet-drafts/ .
```

Today, because neither SSL nor S-HTTP has emerged as a clear choice, and a security standard for Web transactions has yet to be set, most of the major Web browsers—including Netscape Navigator, Internet Explorer, and Mosaic—support both methods.

TradeWave's Virtual Private Internet (TradeVPI)

Using security technologies and authentication methods that are already available today, companies can use the Internet as if it were a virtual private network, reserved for their exclusive use. TradeWave Technologies labels this scenario a "VPI" for virtual private Internet, and defines it as a network circumscribed by ". . . security mechanisms and procedures that allow only appointed users access to the VPI and the information that flows through it," in *Electronic Commerce over the Internet and the Increasing Need for Security: A White Paper*, by Dr. Alexander Cavalli, VP, Strategic Development, TradeWave Corporation, December 8, 1995, and available at:

```
http://galaxy.tradewave.com/tradewave/products/vpiwp.html .
```

According to TradeWave's view of the world, VPIs enable organizations to use the Internet as a secure medium to share proprietary data, conduct commercial transactions, yet still retain access to its huge storehouse of publicly available information.

TradeWave depicts a virtual private Internet as consisting of the following two components:

1. A network security platform

2. A set of applications that use the security platform to provide VPI services

These components must separate both users and services from the public Internet by a firewall, as shown in Figure 2-3. Note also that the firewall protects the Trade Authority that dispenses certificates for users and servers alike.

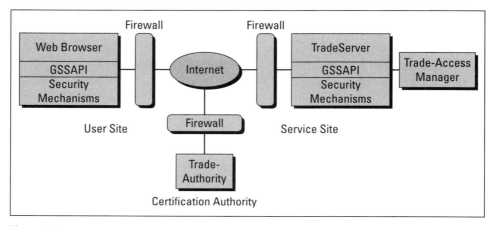

Figure 2-3
The GSSAPI, or generic security service API, and a set of predefined security mechanisms, are the keys to imposing a VPI atop the public Internet.

Entry into the VPI is rigorously guarded by the Certification Authority that operates at the Trade Authority server. Once on the VPI, users are still subject to further levels of security and access control.

In practice, TradeWave's VPI technology can be used for business-to-business electronic commerce as an analog to EDI, except that it runs on the Internet, instead of using secured communications lines on private or public networks. TradeWave has done a good job of making its technologies open and readily available to both businesses and merchants that wish to exploit its technologies. But since it's not aimed at traditional retail, this technology will probably not be as widely deployed as some of the other alternatives we cover in this chapter, and elsewhere in this book. Nevertheless, we find it to be an interesting model, and the company to be a useful source of information about electronic commerce in general.

For more information on VPIs or TradeWave, visit their Web site at:

```
http://www.tradewave.com/ .
```

MasterCard and Visa's
Secure Electronic Transactions (SET) architecture

For most of 1995, it looked like MasterCard and Visa, the two giants of the credit card industry, were dead-set on pursuing independent paths to handling Internet commerce. But by February, 1996, these two organizations agreed jointly to embrace a common standard for electronic commerce. This agreement united major players in the secure transaction arena, including companies like GTE, IBM, Microsoft, Netscape, SAIC, Terisa Systems, and VeriSign, behind a single approach. Unfortunately, this technology is still so early in the development cycle that we can't provide samples of code, nor too many of its internal details.

The roles of these individual companies illustrate of the scope of the effort that's currently underway:

■ IBM and GTE want to make sure their hardware and banking networks can handle the protocols that will emerge from SET.

■ Microsoft and Netscape want to be sure their browsers and other transaction handling software will support this future standard. With the two major players in Web clients and servers engaged, the rest of the industry is sure to follow.

■ SAIC will provide the RSA-based encryption technology used in S-HTTP and in Visa's earlier collaborations with Microsoft, called Secure Transaction Technology (STT), for SET.

■ Terisa Systems will leverage its experience in commercializing APIs for S-HTTP to do the same for SET, once the technology's fully integrated.

■ VeriSign, working with GTE, will provide the certificate authentication mechanisms that SET will demand that sellers, customers, and credit companies use.

In keeping with the capabilities of all of the security approaches and protocols we've reviewed so far, SET's primary business requirements should come as no surprise.

■ **Ensure confidentiality for payment and ordering information**. This is where encryption comes in. SET will use state-of-the-art public and private-key encryption technologies.

■ **Guarantee integrity of all transmitted data**. Digital signatures and a hash function will be used to create a unique hash value that will be included with the message by the sender. When recalculated by the recipient, a match with the sent value is required to accept the transmission. SET uses this technique to prevent tampering.

■ **Establish the identity of a cardholder**. Digital signatures and cardholder certificates will be used to mathematically demonstrate a cardholder's identity. SET users this technique to prevent fraud.

■ **Establish a merchant's ability to accept bankcard payments.** As we'll discuss in detail in Chapter 4, a merchant must have a financial relationship with a merchant bank, or some other financial institution, that can process credit card payments. SET merchants will be required to furnish digital signatures and merchant certificates to mathematically demonstrate their identities.

■ **Ensure maximum interoperability among network and software providers.** To facilitate the broadest possible adoption, SET aims to be as platform-independent as possible. Users must be able to use commonly available client-side software, and merchants must be able to use any software that meets SET standards. To this end, SET will use specific, documented protocols and message formats that will be made available to all software vendors who choose to support this standard.

As more information becomes available about SET, and standards begin to emerge from its implementors' efforts, it will no doubt be covered heavily in the trade press. Online, you'll find useful sources of information about SET at any of the aforementioned vendors' sites, but also at the following Web site:

    http://www.mastercard.com/set/set.htm.

which is the repository for the current SET documents. Likewise, a search at any of the good search engines (we had particularly good results from AltaVista and Yahoo!) should turn up much information on this subject.

The Joint Electronic Payment Initiative (JEPI)

In an effort to avoid a the proliferation of incompatible standards for electronic commerce, the W3C and CommerceNet have also proposed an Internet payment protocol known as the Joint Electronic Payments Initiative (JEPI). Although SET already appears to have attained industry-wide support, credit card transactions represent only one of the many ways to pay for purchases over the Internet. Other payment schemes include digital cash, electronic wallets, and debit cards (several of which you'll learn more about in Chapter 3). Furthermore, vendors sometimes wish to entice shoppers with electronic coupons or "frequent flier miles" for purchases. These kinds of options are not currently supported in other transaction models, and adding support for such capabilities would undoubtedly complicate them further.

The JEPI standard seeks to provide a single unified protocol for all users, including Web servers and browsers, as well as payment vendors. The reasoning behind this standard is that JEPI's universal adoption within client/server products would ensure interoperability between different electronic commerce systems and applications.

Many of the pre-eminent Internet electronic commerce vendors—including Microsoft, Netscape, IBM, Open Market, CyberCash, the Financial Services Technology Consortium (FSTC), GC Tech, and VeriFone, among others, have committed to support JEPI. Together, the W3C and CommerceNet hope to have a working prototype in place by the end of 1996, or early 1997.

At present, JEPI aims to meet four primary goals by this deadline. These goals include the following:

1. Building a standard mechanism for Web clients and servers to negotiate payment

2. Piloting the new negotiation process in a live market environment

3. Publishing the result as an open standard

4. Submitting the results to a recognized standards body (probably the Internet Engineering Task Force or IETF, the technical and standards management arm of the Internet Architecture Board that "runs" the Internet), under the aegis of the W3C for change control

Here's how the JEPI effort is divided among the organizations that are supporting this initiative: CommerceNet is providing overall project management and marketing support for JEPI. The W3C is providing technical leadership and implementation support. Participants are divided into three project teams, each with its own specific deliverable.

1. **Browser and Server Vendors**. Refine mechanisms for connecting to payment middleware.

2. **Payment Vendors**. Test payment middleware in a real-world environment.

3. **Merchants**. Test alternative user interface designs to study customer acceptance.

While these teams are busy building prototypes, we're looking forward to seeing the fruits of some of these efforts.

In the meantime, the best resources for JEPI information that we found included the W3C mailing list archives and in the press releases and new items published by the companies mentioned earlier in this section. You'll find the W3C's various list archives at the following URL:

```
http://lists.w3.org/Archives/Public/.
```

Summary

In this chapter, we explored the basic mechanisms that make secure networked communications possible, including encryption, public and private keys, authentication, and certification. Along the way, we also covered the prevailing current standards and APIs for electronic commerce, and mentioned a few up-and-coming contenders in this somewhat crowded implementation area. Undoubtedly, you'll find it worthwhile to keep as current as you can on these technologies and programming interfaces, because this appears to be a market that's ready to explode, both in terms of new options and capabilities, and in terms of anticipated use.

CHAPTER THREE

THIRD-PARTY PAYMENT SYSTEMS

Electronic commerce strikes fear in the heart of every credit card holder on the Internet. Everyone dreads the day when, after buying flowers for Aunt Brenda from that flower shop Web site, the credit card bill comes in with the balance maxed out and the list of transactions filling several pages. Merchants, on the other hand, want consumers to overcome these fears, for with electronic commerce they see the potential for an overnight global market.

Of course, nothing as complex and sensitive as Internet commerce moves as fast as lightning—many consumers, financial institutions, and other corporations still view the Internet as nothing more than a "hacker breeding ground." But at the same time, the public's conception of the Internet has continued to evolve. From its beginnings as a technological enigma, we've begun to witness the dawning of a sense of "virtual community." Many people now turn to the Internet for such things as news and information more readily than they do traditional media such as television and libraries.

Only now are both consumers and merchants beginning to see the potential of the Internet to transact business. It's this enormous potential that has given rise to the perceived need for secure transaction of financial data.

The Electronic Commerce Evolution

Before 1994, electronic commerce was nothing more than a virtual garage sale. On many of the `.forsale` newsgroups, consumers and merchants took chances and unfortunately got taken on a regular basis. A seller would post a product on the newsgroup and a buyer would respond. In most cases, the buyer was expected to send payment for the item, sight unseen, to the seller, who then, in most cases, would send the product. This approach is obviously rife with security issues. What if a buyer's check bounces? What if the product is defective—how does a buyer know a refund would be issued? And as far as credit cards went, only the naïve felt comfortable sending their account numbers in a clear-text e-mail message. The only recourse for buyer and seller alike was vague mail fraud legislation, which didn't even apply to overseas or "small ticket" transactions.

The advent of online payment systems

In 1994, the first third-party payment systems began to appear online. DigiCash was one of the first to implement a virtual money system, with which clients and merchants could transact business in relative safety. Of course, security holes exist in any mail-order business, and for this very reason, credit card companies steered clear of Internet commerce until only recently.

Third-party systems developed payment and merchant systems based on the RSA security system for transmitting encrypted data over the Internet. As this technology became more widely accepted, and with the development of actual secure Internet protocols for use on the World Wide Web, banks and credit card companies began to look at the Internet with renewed interest.

Many third-party organizations, such as CyberCash, were actually founded by people in the banking and network security industries who quickly implemented secure credit card transaction systems for use over the Internet. Today, the need for third-party systems has been diluted, with options like ICVERIFY and other systems that allow merchants to set up their own secure credit card verification systems, independent of a third party.

Numerous solutions exist today for conducting business transactions on the Internet. Of those remains the trusted third-party payment organizations, which act as intermediaries between buyer and seller, and function as clearing houses for Internet transactions. Only the organizations have access to a buyer's credit card information and a merchant's bank account information.

Two's a crowd; three's a . . . party!

Most third parties issue some sort of intermediary program or process for ensuring that the buyer's sensitive information never goes across the Internet. For example, First Virtual issues a VirtualPIN, which is an alias for the buyer's credit card number, while CyberCash and Ecash use an application that runs on a buyer's computer and keeps track of the amount of "virtual cash" available. All three use secure methods to insure data security in transit, mostly through RSA public- and private-key systems (discussed in Chapter 2) which are independent of either the Web browser or the corresponding Web server.

These electronic payment options open up a new vista for both consumers and merchants. The idea of a secure, nearly-same-as-cash payment system on the Internet gives a "Mom and Pop" flower shop in Bogota worldwide business options, and allows a user in Singapore to order products without leaving his desktop. The client software used by most third-party systems gives consumers a management and security tool that tracks all of their Internet purchases, both for personal or business use, and provides them with a well-deserved sense of financial security. Third-party verification systems were one of the first to support secure Internet commerce, and their features and benefits remain valid in today's fast paced electronic marketplace.

Benefits of Trusted Third Parties

Third-party payment systems offer not only the option to use virtual money over the Internet, but also provide these services quickly, securely, and—in comparison to pure credit card systems—cheaply. The overhead necessary to run a credit card clearing system is more than a small merchant can bear in many cases. The merchant must obtain merchant identification information (through a lengthy application process), third-party verification licenses (such as ICVERIFY), and then purchase, set up, and maintain a complex, often platform-specific, server. With most third-party payment systems, the application process takes a few minutes, the server is intuitive and usually runs on most platforms and, most important, is often extremely cheap, if not free.

Client software is likewise easy to use and, in most cases, contains a host of management features to track and log Internet transactions. "Client software" for credit card systems consists of a form to fill out on a Web page developed by the merchant. Such systems are not only arbitrary and random, they can also be far from intuitive. Because intermediary credit card verifiers often charge hefty set-up and maintenance fees in addition to recurring charges and transaction percentages, merchants using such systems must charge accordingly. With trusted third-party systems this is usually not the case. Although many of them do charge for their server software and, like First Virtual, take a percentage of a merchant's transactions, the overall costs are much lower than what the credit card service companies charge. And, as we said before, often both the server and client software is free.

So why doesn't everyone use this method? It boils down to the enigmatic nature of the Internet. Trusted third-party payment organizations, and Internet businesses as a whole, are far from being universally trusted or accepted. The technology and concept of virtual payment is still too new, even though the transactions are as secure and simple as using an automatic teller machine.

Another major factor blocking universal deployment of trusted third-party payment systems is receipt of payment by participating merchants. With a credit card system such as ICVERIFY, once a transaction is approved by the credit card company, the funds could be deposited in the merchant's bank within 48 hours. With some third-party solutions, the funds may be held for up to 90 days pending a customer's refusal of a transaction. This can cripple many businesses who might otherwise look to the Internet as a money machine.

If a user can download an order form, mail it to a merchant, and receive its product in less than 90 days, why go to the Internet for electronic commerce at all? There are many reasons, as we'll attempt to explain in this chapter. In fact, numerous trusted third-party payment providers already offer solid Internet commerce solutions with good value for both consumers and merchants.

Almost-same-as-cash

"Almost-same-as-cash" usually applies to a consumer rather than a merchant. For the consumer, virtual payment software systems and processes are as easy to use as opening a wallet and pitching change on a countertop, or handing a store clerk a credit card. Applications such as Ecash and CyberCash run as background applications that prompt users when it is time to pay. Users then click on appropriate amounts and payment methods, confirm their purchases, and the transactions are made. Minutes later, these users will receive an e-mail or HTML message that asks for confirmation, and eventually, an approval code and a receipt. All account information and balances are automatically updated and tracked in the commerce-handling application.

Other payment systems, such as First Virtual, require only that a user enter a VirtualPIN number in the appropriate field on a merchant's order form. First Virtual's verification and clearing system handles the rest. Because the payment system actually charges a customer's credit card, First Virtual withholds payment to its subscribing merchants for a "reasonable amount of time" as defined in their terms and conditions agreements. This could be up to 91 days, which makes this not-very-much-like-cash to those merchants who don't want to submit to the kinds of detailed and searching credit checks merchant banks routinely require.

Overall, third-party systems appear to favor ease of use and speed of the sale on the consumer side, but not on the merchant side of the transaction. Depending on the third party and the system used, a merchant could wait for payment as long as three months. In fact, a consumer could conceivably mail a check to a merchant, and the merchant could send the product to the customer in that amount of time—or less.

In fact, some third-party systems, like CyberCash, work from the same kind of standard credit card clearing systems found in most retail stores, which speeds the funds resulting from a transaction from a consumer's pocket to the merchant's bank account. The drawback to this kind of system is the overhead inherent in such standard credit card accounts, that merchants must open with a bank or financial institution. These accounts are not granted to just any sideline business, and most are fairly expensive to set up, both in recurring costs and in the percentage of any transaction charged to the merchant. This in turn affects consumers, because merchants must recover these costs by raising the price of the products they offer on the Internet.

Anonymity

One consumer benefit to electronic commerce is that most trusted third-party systems maintain user privacy, either by issuing a username and credit card number alias, or by totally masking the customer's information from the merchant. This not only gives users peace of mind with regard to the feeling that some "Big Brother" organization is tracking their spending habits, but it also eliminates the possibility of the consumers getting on yet another mailing list, either electronic or otherwise.

In today's electronic world, consumers are increasingly paranoid about the possibility of a criminal accessing their private information somewhere on the Internet. The beauty of most trusted third parties is that they usually maintain only one gateway to the Internet. Rather than conducting the business of transaction verification and such over the public network, they use the gateway only to receive and send encrypted packets, either requesting verification or responding to the request. All data transactions with banks and other financial institutions are conducted on private, secure ATM lines, the same way credit cards are verified in a retail store, or cash machines communicate with banks. Records of transactions, personal information, and other sensitive data are never transmitted in the open on the Internet, further protecting the privacy of the consumer.

Third-party involvement

In most transactions, the involvement of a third party is usually a good thing. When a merchant sets up a credit verification system directly with a bank or financial institution, there is a fairly complex and revealing application process in which the financial institution requires a certain amount of detailed information to ensure that the business and the people running it are legitimate. However, once the application process is over, and the merchant is approved, the possibility of fraud, misuse, and faulty merchant systems can become real considerations. Of course, the consumer has final say as to whether any transaction is valid; but often, contention over a charge comes only after the customer gets the bill from a credit card company and happens to catch erroneous charges.

With a third-party payment system, the merchant in most cases still has to apply through a financial institution that requires the same intensive survey of the business and its participants. However, with many of the Internet payment systems, the merchant never processes the transaction or even receives the customer's credit card information. With First Virtual's VirtualPIN, the credit card number and relevant information are never transmitted over the Internet. With CyberCash, the customer's encrypted credit card information is never decrypted until it reaches CyberCash's private network, after passing through a firewall. The encrypted packet still passes through the merchant site, but the merchant's system merely strips off any order information and adds an encrypted merchant and terminal identification number before sending the entire package along to CyberCash. In this system, only the trusted third party has access to both credit card information and merchant banking information, and this data is processed away from the public Internet.

A Sampler of Trusted Third Parties

The main trusted third-party payment organizations are as old as the concept of secure Internet commerce itself. Many of the founders and developers of these systems were innovators in the fields of Internet security, networking systems, and the Internet as a whole. The organizations described in the following sections each take a different yet valid approach to electronic commerce.

CyberCash

CyberCash provided the first real-time, secure, digital signature-based credit card authentication service over the Internet. CyberCash approaches the problems of electronic commerce similarly to ICVERIFY by acting as an intermediary among consumer, merchant, and credit card clearinghouses. Both CyberCash and ICVERIFY require a merchant to obtain a merchant identification and terminal identification number from a bank or financial service agent. And CyberCash maintains a close relationship with about 20 such institutions. The advantage of CyberCash over ICVERIFY is that both the server and client software are free and work in tandem to process transactions, provide reporting and accounting to both merchant and consumer, and ensure that the merchant receives payment while protecting the rights and privacy of the customer.

HISTORY

CyberCash, Inc., was founded in 1994, and has offered secure credit card transaction services over the Internet since April, 1995. Started by Bill Melton and Dan Lynch, CyberCash does not lack expertise in either financial or Internet technologies. Melton is also the founder of VeriFone, Inc., the transaction automation company that has made credit card authorization terminals omnipresent on retail outlet counters. Dan Lynch is the founder of Interop, the premier trade show for the computer networking industry, and a well known expert in the field of computer networks, particularly the Internet. From 1980 to 1983 he led the ARPAnet team that made the transition from the original NCP protocols to today's TCP/IP-based Internet protocols.

Since its inception, CyberCash has developed solid relationships with financial institutions, its client merchants, and end-users by offering a solid, secure, and affordable solutions for electronic commerce. By building relations with well-known banks and financial service agents, such as Wells Fargo and First USA, CyberCash simultaneously established a feeling of trust and confidence in both the company's solution and the concept of Internet commerce in general. This kind of reputation has been much sought after by companies that have more recently begun to offer similar Internet services.

CONCEPT

CyberCash is fairly simple technically—it uses familiar Internet secure and open protocols to send and receive data. The consumer uses a local application, called the Wallet, to store credit card information, relevant account numbers, and so on. The server side has two parts: the merchant's Web server, which is independent of the actual financial transaction; and the CashRegister server, which also resides on the merchant side. At a remote location, CyberCash's third-party server actually decrypts and processes credit card information.

The merchant's Web server receives only order information, and an indication that the order was paid by credit card. The CashRegister strips off the order and forwards the encrypted payment information to the CyberCash server over the Internet, digitally signed and encrypted with the merchant's private key. The CyberCash server then takes the packet from the Internet behind its firewall to complete the transaction process through secure ATM lines. Fifteen to twenty seconds later, the merchant's server receives an authorization code, which is then processed according to how the merchant's Web server has been set up. All encryption of the transaction is at the message level, and thus independent of browser or secure protocol.

Ecash

Ecash, from DigiCash, approaches the idea of Internet commerce from a totally different perspective that CyberCash. Ecash is digital money that is downloaded by an Ecash client from a participating bank and stored on a customer's local computer. Ecash can be spent at merchant systems that accept that form of exchange; accepting merchants, in turn, must deposit Ecash receipts at a participating bank.

HISTORY
In October of 1994, DigiCash began a trial distribution of the Ecash client software and the Ecash payment system. A virtual bank called the First Digital Bank was set up that was run by DigiCash. Trial users would deposit real money in the bank and draw Ecash against this balance. The trial ran for a year and a half, ending in April, 1996. At that time, DigiCash no longer allowed new users to come online and suspended the program other than to support users already using the application. The Ecash concept has since been licensed by several banks, the first of which was the Mark Twain Bank in St. Louis, Missouri. There are currently three banks using the Ecash system. These Ecash participating banks can be reached at:

```
http://www.digicash.com/Ecash/Ecash-issuers.html .
```

CONCEPT
The basic concept of Ecash is secure, same-as-cash, Internet banking. The user transacts business on the Internet as if browsing through a store with a pocket full of money. In this case, the money is withdrawn from the Ecash account at a participating bank that issues Ecash in electronic "coins" distinguished by serial numbers. The number of coins is calculated by the user's Ecash client software before any withdrawals are made. Requests for coins are then encoded with a private key that is generated when the client software is installed. Refer to Chapter 8 for a more detailed discussion of Ecash.

The beauty of Ecash is that it behaves exactly like cash—spenders are completely anonymous because Ecash "coins" maintain their own identities using unique serial numbers. When a merchant receives Ecash, such payment is instantly valid as long as the issuing bank can match the serial numbers to valid issued Ecash coins that have not already been spent. Ecash coins are encrypted during transit using standard digital signature technology available on the Internet from such places as VeriSign at:

```
http://www.verisign.com .
```

The convenience of Ecash, both for consumers and merchants cannot be ignored. Merchants receive virtually instant compensation for the sale of an item without having to go through the trouble of applying for merchant IDs or interacting with a credit processor. The second, and by far the greatest, feature of Ecash is that there is no separate server software to buy, install, or run.

First Virtual

The First Virtual Internet Payment System (FVIPS) provides a safe, secure method for electronic commerce over the Internet. Neither client software for users, nor servers or special hardware for merchants are required. All transactions are handled via normal Internet e-mail based on a user's VirtualPIN, which is chosen by the user as an alias for a credit card when an account is established. This VirtualPIN may be used to complete a form on a merchant's Web site, or transmitted to a merchant via e-mail. The consumer's VirtualPIN remains integral to the information that is forwarded by the merchant to First Virtual along with the amount of the sale and the merchant's VirtualPIN.

If a transaction is confirmed, an e-mail message is sent to the buyer for explicit confirmation. A buyer replies "yes" to accept the transaction, "no" to decline, or "fraud" to indicate that its was initiated without the buyer's consent (any fraud reply automatically cancels the VirtualPIN). Once a "yes" reply is made, confirmation is sent to the seller, and the customer's credit card is charged. After a reasonable amount of time, the merchant's bank account is credited via Direct Deposit, less First Virtual's fees.

HISTORY

In October of 1994, First Virtual Holdings, Inc., announced to the world that it had developed a secure and easy method for conducting electronic commerce over the Internet. At that time, there were only a few companies emerging into the Internet commerce world, and many more who were frantically trying to develop a secure means of transacting business. First Virtual's approach was decidedly different from developers of that time. First Virtual scoffed at accepted data encryption methods used by most third-party systems, and the basis for secure Web protocols such as S-HTTP. However, First Virtual's idea apparently worked, because First Virtual currently serves over 100,000 customers and over 1,000 merchants in 144 countries. Financial Services Online reported earlier this year that First Virtual moves over $60,000 in daily payment transactions. Recent news from the First Virtual Web site indicates that it has upgraded and expanded its computer systems, and restructured and simplified its fee schedules.

Information about subscribing to First Virtual's payment system, either as a buyer or a seller, can be obtained from its Web site at:

```
http://www.fv.com .
```

CONCEPT
The First Virtual Internet Payment System employs an easy concept, built on a familiar Internet service: e-mail. All transactions and confirmations are conducted simply and efficiently using existing technology with which every Internet user, whether buyer or merchant, is familiar. The merchant needs only to write a CGI script that will build an e-mail message from the Web site's order form, including the following information: the buyer's VirtualPIN, the merchant's Seller's VirtualPIN, the amount of the sale, the currency used, and a description of the transaction, such as the product name (we provide a sample CGI script that fulfills all these functions in Chapter 13). Then it must be mailed to First Virtual for validation and for the creation of a customer confirmation message. Once a customer confirms the transaction by e-mail, First Virtual notifies the vendor, and payment can be processed. That's it! You'll find a more detailed description of this process from the point of view of both customer and merchant in Chapter 8.

First Virtual's payment has garnered attention, accolades, and a fair amount of market share not only because its cleverly managed to handle transactions without having to transfer sensitive information across the Internet, but also because the company makes it much easier and cheaper for small-scale merchants to participate in electronic commerce than any of the credit card-based options. In fact, for those merchants who don't mind waiting for their funds to be disbursed, First Virtual makes it nearly painless to establish a presence online. They even offer a "virtual mall" called the InfoHaus where First Virtual vendors can hawk their wares on a site that's been created and is managed by First Virtual itself.

Micropayment Systems

Today, there are many sources of valuable information online, ranging from specialty databases to periodic publications of all kinds (daily, weekly, monthly, and occasional). Then, too, vendors can distribute all kinds of digital wares over existing networks and intranets with ease, given the ubiquitous presence of Web browsers, FTP clients, and other software suitable for handling file transfers from vendors to their customers.

What's missing from this tantalizing situation is a way to provide small bits of information in exchange for small amounts of money. For all of the other types of payment systems we examine in this book, the minimal cost of a transaction is seldom less than fifty cents to a dollar. But many pundits believe that users would be willing to pay anywhere from fractions of a cent to fifty cents to obtain online access to documents and other information. What's missing is a way to manage the payment process: that is, to collect small sums from buyers and deliver those sums to sellers, yet still leave room for a fraction of the transaction to make the handling process worthwhile.

Such small-time exchanges are known in electronic commerce jargon as "micropay-ments" because they're too small to register on ordinary payment systems, or are too minuscule to be worth the cost processing in many, if not most, of the payment sys-tems already available. The challenge for all payment systems is to keep the costs of doing business to only a small fraction of the total cost. But here, the problem is that as the size of a transaction decreases, keeping the processing cost correspondingly small becomes increasingly difficult.

On the seller's side of this equation, the challenge is to provide a mechanism to sup-port those merchants who might be interested in offering materials at extremely low costs. Obviously, such a system is only workable for digital information, where the same system that handles a customer's order for merchandise can be used to fulfill that order. Even the cost of a postage stamp or a long-distance phone call could easily swamp the costs of a micropayment transaction, so other forms of delivery or response to an order are not economically viable. Nevertheless, there are numerous vendors for whom these circumstances are quite appealing, including the following:

- Information providers of all kinds, such as companies like Mead Data Central, Dow Jones Information Services, Value Line, and others of that ilk

- News and information publishers, such as the news wire services, newspaper publishers, vertical market newsletters, syndicated publications (like comic strips, columns, personalities), magazines, and other periodicals

- Stock and commodities reporting services, for quotes or price information, or market news and information

- Online classified advertisements, job listings, or other forms of promoting potential exchanges between buyers and sellers, where the information has value to both sides of the transaction

In fact, as long as the information offered at micropayment rates is volatile, and its information content has sufficient value to warrant a small payment for access, this model appears to be a viable way to bring consumers and producers together. Today, of course, such information exchanges are largely underwritten by those ubiquitous advertising banners from vendors who hope to benefit from their association with these venues. In the future, micropayment technology may make such forms of subsidy or third-party support unnecessary.

In the sections that follow, we examine a few of the micropayment schemes cur-rently available on the Internet. Many of them are still in prototype stages, or are not yet fully deployed for commercial use, but others are in daily use and provide a way for some prestigious vendors (for example, *The Christian Science Monitor*) to deliver cus-tomized and tailored information "packages" to subscribers on a daily basis.

Clickshare

Today, Clickshare is one of the few micropayment systems in daily use on the Internet, but it's still very much in start-up mode. In short, Clickshare offers a micropayment system that permits merchants to participate in a transaction-handling system that consolidates charges over a billing period, for once-a-month billing on a credit card. This lets Clickshare handle the details of tracking and charging for microtransactions itself, but incur only a single, more expensive monthly credit card transaction cost for each user account. This system has been designed to be extremely easy for users to sign up for and use, and to be relatively easy for vendors to incorporate into their Web sites (but it can also work with other forms of online access, including FTP, e-mail, and other, proprietary techniques).

HISTORY

Clickshare Corporation is a spin-off of Newshare Corporation, a privately held Massachusetts-based supplier of interactive media products to newspapers, broadcasters, and the public through Newshare Syndicate and the Newshare Common Resource Center. Newshare Corp. is developing a nationwide electronic brokerage for the delivery of time-sensitive, general-interest news and advertising materials to publishers, both on- and off-line. These materials will be organized both geographically and by interest area for direct consumer use. Newshare's goal is to become a worldwide licenser of local- and topic-specific information franchises that share users and information through the Clickshare micropayment service.

Since 1994, Newshare Corp. has devoted increasing resources and attention to developing and bringing to market the Clickshare Access and Payment Service, to track movements and settle charges for digital transactions on the World Wide Web. In Fall 1995, Clickshare Corporation was incorporated as an independent company, but remains primarily owned by Newshare Corp. At present, Clickshare is in the process of bringing in additional strategic and technical partners, investors and other allies—with the goal to establish Clickshare as a widely used solution on the Internet for digital microtransactions.

CONCEPT

From the user perspective, Clickshare employs a simple, one-time sign-up and only a single password for access to any related merchant offerings. Users supply a password only once, at the beginning of a Web session, and it's provided automatically for all Clickshare-based microtransactions thereafter during a session. Clickshare also consolidates all charges for microtransactions. They provide a daily summary of activity via e-mail, and users are charged on a single billing on an account they've already established elsewhere—today, that means a credit card account, but efforts are underway to let users charge microtransactions to their phone, cable, newspaper, or ISP bills as well. Clickshare also helps to ensure user privacy, yet gives advertisers enough demographic information about purchasers to help them bankroll those Web sites that give information for free, while also managing all the details required from for-a-fee information providers.

For vendors, Clickshare server software is based on standard Web server technology (primarily UNIX-based NCSA software at present, but ports to Apache and Windows NT platforms are already underway). The vendor package includes auxiliary software for registration database management, an e-mail redirector (for reporting activity and transactions), and a set of testing and verification tools to make sure the service has been properly installed, and is working correctly. Clickshare also claims that adding its services to an existing Web server will not add significantly to the server's processing overhead, nor consume excessive amounts of system resources.

Once a user has registered with Clickshare (at `http://www.clickshare.com`) accessing for-a-fee information is easy. During the sign-up process, a phone number is provided for supplying credit card information to set up an account, or users can elect to send that information in an encrypted online session. At this point, a password of the user's choosing is also assigned. Next, users must log in at the Clickshare site, and provide their password to enable microtransaction purchases. Thereafter, at any Click-share vendor site, they can purchase whatever they wish (most transactions cost 10, 25, 50, or 75 cents right now). The next day, the user receives an activity report by e-mail that tallies up all charges for the preceding day's Clickshare transactions. To use Clickshare follow these steps:

1. Start a Web session
2. Click bookmark to login to ClickShare at

   `http://www.newshare.com/cs/welcome.html?TVS3Dlogin`

3. Select "Clickshare Publishing Members"
4. Select "Publisher"
5. Select item(s); charges will be posted to ClickShare account.

Continue steps 4 and 5 as needed. Charges will be posted to an activity report and e-mailed to the user the next day

See Figure 3-1 for a diagram of how Clickshare works.

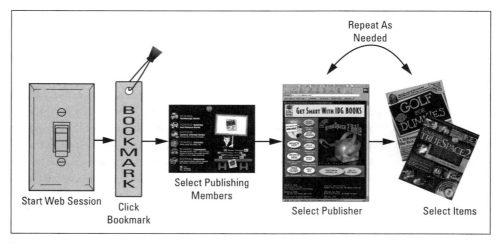

Figure 3-1
How to use Clickshare.

To become Clickshare vendors, merchants must sign up for an account with the company and deploy their CGI programs (or Web server) to create microtransaction Web pages. The initial fee structure requires a one-time enrollment and licensing fee of $1,995, plus an annual fee for each user that the vendor enrolls in the Clickshare system (volume discounts kick in after the 10,000 user mark is passed), plus a maximum transaction fee of 20 percent for each purchase executed by the Clickshare system. To its credit, Clickshare offers a great deal of support to its licensed vendors, including software, HTML files, and information sharing and promotion among its customer base.

Here's how the environment works: The Clickshare-enabled Web server at each Clickshare vendor site maintains a persistent connection to the Clickshare Authentication Service. Billing entities—the Clickshare service providers that maintain the billing relationship with an end user—request authentication tokens for valid users, vendors—the Clickshare service providers that vend information or other for-a-fee digital content—ask that these tokens be validated. The Authentication Service has been set up to be able to handle in excess of 1 million requests per day, and its protocols and services have been built to be as efficient and lightweight as possible. Typical response times for validation are 20 seconds or less, making this a viable system for working with customers online.

For more information about Clickshare, visit its Web site at:

```
http://www.clickshare.com/.
```

You should find a great deal of information at this site; we found the online documentation to be both helpful and informative.

CyberCash's CyberCoins

Since we've already introduced and discussed CyberCash, the company, earlier in this chapter, we can cut right to the chase on their new micropayment system, known as CyberCoin. You'll find this new system prominently displayed on their home page at:

```
http://www.cybercash.com.
```

CONCEPT

CyberCoin is an extension of the existing CyberCash system, and can be used for microtransactions (which they define as falling in a range of $0.25 to $10.00) on the Internet. CyberCoin uses the same electronic Wallet and payment-handling scheme as CyberCash, but it's aimed at a different kind of market, and will typically be used for pure information purchases, rather than as a completely general medium of exchange.

The CyberCoin service was also created to allow consumers to use an existing bank account to transfer money to their Wallet; in other words, banks that support CyberCoin provide the accounts that "hold" the money that's transferred into the Wallet. Thus, all money transfers remain within existing banking networks. Unlike digital cash systems, CyberCash only represents money electronically; actually, it "points" to funds that are held in a bank! Because of the requirement for bank involvement, CyberCoin is not necessarily anonymous, but the software's been written not to supply consumer data unless it's volunteered by the buyer.

Furthermore, the Wallet makes a transaction log entry for every transaction made, thereby creating an electronic "receipt" for each purchase. These receipts act just like their paper equivalents with real money, to provide proof of purchase and a payment record. To prevent consumers from being charged without receiving their goods, CyberCash uses the same confirmation scheme for CyberCoin as for its other payment system—that is, the company confirms delivery of payment and goods through the use of public and private key encryption. Only when it has been confirmed that the data requested has been delivered to the consumer's machine will the money be transferred into the merchant's Cash Register. Here's a step-by step description of how it works:

1. The Web user sees something worth buying at a site that accepts CyberCoins. If the user has already downloaded the CyberCash wallet, the Web browser knows to open the wallet when the "PAY" button is activated (see Figure 3-2).

Figure 3-2
PAY button for CyberCoins.

2. The customer decides how to pay. This choice is restricted to different credit cards today, although CyberCoins will eventually be able to extend to debit cards, electronic checks, and electronic cash (see Figure 3-3).

3. When the customer sends the payment information for the transaction and confirms the purchase amount, he or she sets the transaction in motion, launching the request for approval for the charge.

4. The merchant is then sent an encrypted charge payment message. This message is accompanied by the customer's order information, although the merchant can't see the customer's credit card information (see Figure 3-4).

5. The confirmed payment message and order information is received by the merchant's SMPS software, which then adds its own merchant identification information before passing the payment request to the CyberCash Gateway Server. Figure 3-5 shows how this payment information is digitally signed and encrypted with the merchant's private key.

Figure 3-3
Use a credit card.

"Encrypted credit card info":
":>K#@!&^())%$!###&?:^"

Figure 3-4
Customer order information is sent to the merchant.

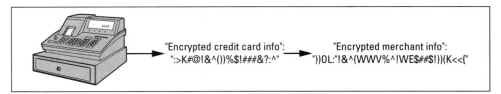

"Encrypted credit card info":
":>K#@!&^())%$!###&?:^"

"Encrypted merchant info":
"))OL:"!&^(WWV%^!WE$##$!))(K<<{"

Figure 3-5
Encrypted merchant information.

6. The CyberCash Gateway Server's firewall system then decides whether to accept the charge authorization request. If it accepts, it takes the transaction off the Internet, decrypts the message with a hardware-based crypto box (see Figure 3-6).

7. The Cybercash gateway sends the request, as Figure 3-7 shows.

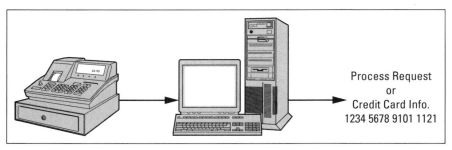

Figure 3-6
Processing the charge authorization request.

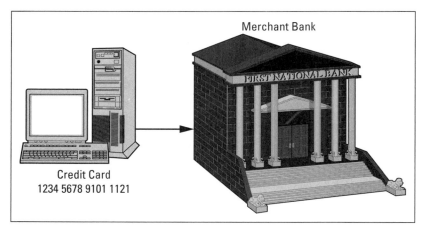

Figure 3-7
Sending the request via the Cybercash gateway.

8. The authorization request is then forwarded by the merchant's bank to the bank that has issued the credit card, or to American Express or Discover. The approval (or denial) is sent to CyberCash (see Figure 3-8).

9. CyberCash returns the resulting approval or denial code to the merchant. The merchant then sends it to the consumer (see Figure 3-9).

Currently, user Wallet software is available at no charge, but only for Windows 3.x and Windows 95, with a Macintosh implementation planned for early 1997. Merchant software is available at no charge for the Solaris and BSDI UNIX platforms; a Windows NT merchant implementation is scheduled for delivery before the end of 1996.

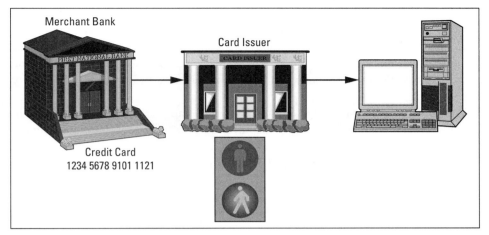

Figure 3-8
Merchant forwards request to issuing bank. Issuing bank sends approval/denial code.

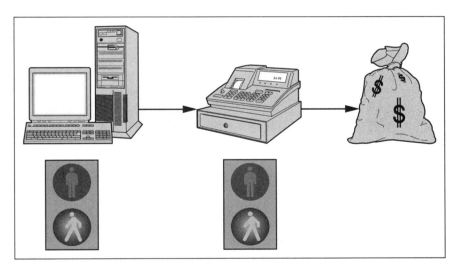

Figure 3-9
Merchant forwards approval/denial code.

Given CyberCash's success in its more conventional payment system, we're excited about the possibilities inherent in the CyberCoin model. CyberCash's use of the banking system to handle the funds is particularly appealing to many, because it prevents digital counterfeiting of funds. But a relatively low adoption rate as this chapter's being written also indicates that micropayment schemes have not yet been passionately embraced, or fully accepted, in the context of the online marketplace. But this could easily change, as witnessed by Netscape's recent announcement of its intention to bundle CyberCoin in its LivePayment product.

CMU's NetBill

NetBill is designed as a dependable, secure, and economical payment system for purchasing digital goods and services via the Internet. It is an offshoot of a research project undertaken at Carnegie-Mellon University in Pittsburgh, PA, where a team of faculty and graduate students implemented the environment as a prototype of a micropayment system.

At present, NetBill is only deployed on the CMU campus, where it can be used for small purchases. Because it has yet to be deployed commercially, we'll treat it as a kind of design scheme for a possible micropayment system, and skip the usual company background and history section. Hence, we'll jump right into its concept and operation.

CONCEPT

NetBill has been specifically designed to support the exchange of small amounts of money for purely digital information. That's why the system seeks to facilitate exchanges as small as a couple of cents, rather than the 25 or 35 cent minimum we've seen in the previous implementations. On the buyer's side, this makes it possible to acquire all kinds of information for truly little costs, while on the seller's, it makes it possible for small operators to enter the marketplace for little more cost than the price of a PC and the labor necessary to create and deploy what digital information or capability they have to sell.

In the NetBill environment, when a user wishes to buy from a merchant's server, a NetBill server that maintains account information for both parties must be accessed. These accounts are linked to NetBill holdings at conventional financial institutions, so a NetBill transaction transfers information from the merchant to the buyer, debits the buyer's account, and credits the merchant's account. Whenever necessary, the balance of funds in a NetBill account can be increased from another bank account or credit card; likewise, merchants can access their earnings by withdrawing moneys from their NetBill accounts. The concept of NetBill works as follows:

1. User starts a Web session.

2. User goes to NetBill vendor site, and requests a for-a-fee item.

   a. The NetBill server accesses user and vendor balances.
   b. User balance compared to transaction cost is calculated.
   c. If the balance is sufficient, then the user account is debited, and the vendor account is credited.

3. The transaction clears, and the item is downloaded to the user.

4. All charges are posted to the user billing record, and an activity report is sent monthly (although the frequency of the transmission is adjustable). Figure 3-10 shows a diagram of how this process works.

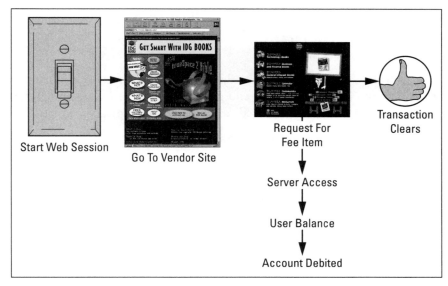

Figure 3-10
NetBill in action.

One appealing aspect of NetBill is its flexibility. The system has been designed to accommodate a variety of pricing models, so that users may be charged per item, by some kind of subscription fee unrelated to access, or may be subject to a variety of discount or special pricing plans. This kind of capability is important to meet the widely differing requirements of the kinds of vendors who will participate in micropayment schemes.

NetBill uses its own special protocol to handle charges across a wide range of services. NetBill delivers transaction support through code libraries that may easily be integrated with existing client-server software. These libraries use an application-based, transaction-oriented protocol to communicate between clients, servers, and NetBill, but the normal communications between client and server remain unchanged. This approach allows NetBill to work with delivery mechanisms based on HTTP, FTP, and even MPEG-2 streams.

The client library is called the checkbook, and the server library the till. Each has a well-defined API that permits integration with a wide range of applications. The current prototype has been integrated with Mosaic on the client side and several *httpd* servers. Because these libraries handle all security and payment processes, the underlying applications do not have to address encryption, authentication, or non-repudiation issues. In fact, all networked communications between the checkbook and the till are encrypted to provide confidentiality and tamper proofing.

While this system is not yet deployed commercially, it offers great functionality and capability. It is also one of a very few systems that have been designed to keep their transactions costs below a penny per transaction. We think these things make it quite attractive, and possibly worth investigating should it ever appear outside the halls of academe. For more information, visit the NetBill site at:

`http://www.netbill.com/` .

You'll also find the design document for this system quite informative, for many reasons that range from good background and market analysis, to a clear, straightforward presentation of the technology involved. You can obtain a copy at:

`http://www.ini.cmu.edu/netbill/pubs/CompCon.html` .

DEC's Millicent

Like NetBill, Millicent is more of a design for a micropayment system than an actual commercial environment; also like NetBill, it's been deliberately designed to support purchases costing less than one cent. Because fractions of a penny are often called "millicents," we think this is how the system designed at Digital Equipment Corporation got its name. Here again, we'll jump right into the concept information.

CONCEPT

DEC's goal in designing Millicent is to support transactions that are inexpensive yet secure and reliable. By building a system around accounts based on scrip, and relying on brokers to sell scrip, they claim to have created a design that meets these goals.

Here's how it works: A piece of scrip represents a customer account with a particular vendor; at any moment, a vendor may have scrip outstanding (that is, open accounts) with customers who've been active recently. The spendable balance of the account is the value of the scrip still outstanding. When a customer makes a purchase, the cost of the purchase is deducted from the value of the scrip and what's left over is issued as new scrip, representing the change. When customers conclude their transactions with a vendor, they can redeem any remaining scrip, thereby closing their open account with that vendor.

In this scheme, scrip brokers act as intermediaries between customers and vendors. Customers would establish a long-term relationship with a broker, like the kind of relationship they might also have with a bank, a credit card company, or an ISP. Brokers buy and sell vendor scrip as a service to both of the other parties, so broker scrip provides a form of currency that customers can use to buy vendor scrip, and vendors to issue for unredeemed vendor scrip at the end of series of transactions. Here's a step-by-step description of how Millicent works:

1. User starts a Web session.

2. User visits a broker site, and obtains generic broker scrip by drawing on his/her bank account.

3. Then, the user visits a vendor site, and exchanges generic scrip for vendor scrip.

4. When the user requests a for-a-fee item, the user's scrip balance with vendor is debited, and charges are credited to vendor's account. (Repeat this process as needed, and repeat steps 2 and 3 if more scrip is needed.)

5. User terminates the vendor account, converting remaining vendor scrip to generic broker scrip (if any).

6. User deposits remaining broker scrip (if any) with the broker. The user can leave the scrip with the broker, or return it to a bank account. Note: Brokers can convert scrip to cash for vendors or users. Figure 3-11 shows a diagram of how this all works.

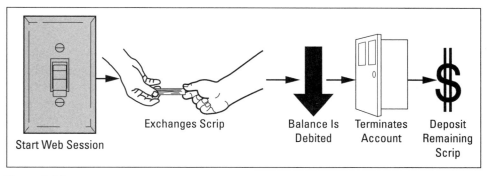

Start Web Session   Exchanges Scrip   Balance Is Debited   Terminates Account   Deposit Remaining Scrip

Figure 3-11
How Millicent works.

Millicent has been designed for minimal account overhead as follows:

■ Local verification. Scrip is verified at the vendor site, so no additional communication is required other than that between customer and vendor. This also eliminates the potential bottleneck imposed by a centralized certification or authentication service.

■ Cryptographic costs may be reduced to match the scale of payments involved. Scrip isn't worth much, so it doesn't need expensive protection. Ideally, it should only cost slightly more to "break" the scrip than it's worth to keep it safe.

■ Brokers help reduce accounting costs. By establishing accounts with customers and vendors, most costs can be shifted by moving funds from one pocket to another, rather than requiring actual fund transfers from one broker to another.

Because Millicent is built to handle small, cheap transactions, it also requires other protocols for account setup between brokers and customers or vendors. This is also true for those occasional transfers of real funds between brokers, customers, and vendors that will sometimes be necessary. Encryption and digital signatures are reserved for those occasions where they're necessary, and don't provide a constant source of overhead for the whole payment system.

According to DEC, the range of potential uses for Millicent is extremely wide. Today, Millicent is suitable for transactions from as little as a tenth of a cent to several dollars. The lower bound is set by the computational cost of performing a genuine transaction for a broker, where autonomy must be guaranteed and exchanges reliable. The upper bound is set by the value of a transaction at which the cost of "breaking" low-overhead security is exceeded. But this price range covers a great deal of valuable exchanges, including print and information services like magazines, news sources, databases, directories, and some forms of entertainment (comics, serials, or personality pieces, for instance).

Like DEC, we too believe that Millicent offers a good model to support these kinds of transactions. That's why we recommend that you keep an eye on this technology, and watch for news of its deployment. In the meantime, you can find a detailed architecture document on Millicent at:

```
http://www.research.digital.com/SRC/millicent/papers/
    millicent-w3c4/millicent.html.
```

Summary

There are many trusted third-party Internet payment systems out there, but not all are compatible with a merchant's idea of business. We hope that this chapter has elucidated the possibilities of approaching electronic commerce with regard to third-party systems, and will help any merchants out there that hope to start on the road to Internet commerce by giving them a good idea of the steps involved. You should also have attained an appreciation for, if not a working knowledge of, micropayment systems like Millicent, CyberCoin, NetBill, and ClickNet.

The important thing to remember is that most trusted third-party and digital cash systems favor the buyer. Thus, like credit card payments anywhere, the buyer has the final say as to a transaction's validity. Fraud on either side of a transaction is a reality in this age of electronic payment, though it's not common. Merchants are well advised to understand their rights in this regard before venturing into any form of commerce online.

CHAPTER FOUR

CREDIT CARD

PAYMENT SYSTEMS

B rowse the Web site of any company that makes a secure Web server and you'll
probably see that server being marketed as an "electronic commerce solution"
that allows you to "securely take credit card information over the Net." Actually, with a secure server, you're only getting part of the solution. Although it's true
that the secure server allows you to securely receive credit card information from a
customer, the server doesn't do anything with the information once it has it. What
you're missing is the *payment* system.

The payment system is what actually authorizes a credit card for use. This means
that the card has been verified to have enough available credit to make the purchase,
and that it's not stolen. It's also what makes the charge on the card. The payment system can be driven by a human or by a completely automated Web site.

In this chapter, we discuss why it has taken so long to bring credit card payment
to the Internet, and describe the concepts and entities involved in credit card payment. We also look at existing credit card payment techniques from the standpoint
of integrating them into a Web site. The ultimate goal of this chapter is to make you
familiar with the background and concepts of this financial system. Later in this
book we discuss how to interact with the players involved and how to set up your
own credit card-accepting site.

What's the Delay?

The big question on everyone's minds is: "Why has it taken so long for credit card sales to be made over the Internet?" The World Wide Web itself has been around since 1992, so why has it taken four years for Web commerce to take its first steps? This is one of those questions that would cause a cacophonous debate in a room full of Web developers, salespeople, and credit card merchants, so we'll save you from that headache and try to explain it here.

The security quandary

Many observers say that transaction security has held Web commerce back; that consumers are unwilling to risk having their credit card information float freely over the Net. This argument is somewhat bogus. People risk their credit card information all the time without thinking twice about it: They make credit card orders over their cellular phones, which anyone with a scanner can pick up. They leave charge slips on restaurant tables while the waiter is away (a prime time to be snatched), which contain not only their card information, but also their signature.

The Internet, however, is something new to most people, so it's tinged with a little mystery and perhaps a little evil. It also has the reputation of being lawless. In reality, it's not that easy for a random hacker to "sniff" credit card numbers from upstream on the Internet. We're not saying that it hasn't been done, but it's very much a matter of being in the right place (network-wise) at the right time. It also takes the right software, the right access, the right skills, and someone who knows what to look for. On the other hand, anyone can sift through the garbage can outside of a gas station for sales slips. In addition, the same credit fraud laws that protect consumers who had their card number stolen from that garbage can would protect someone whose card number was snatched from the Internet as well.

Thanks to public-key encryption technology and the resulting protocols it has spawned, secure information transmission has been possible over the Internet for years, and secure Web servers have been around since 1994. The transaction security argument doesn't really apply anymore. In fact, it's almost safe to say that the Internet is one of the most secure places to use your credit card, since the information may never even be seen by human eyes.

Looking for the right solution

Practically every company involved in Internet credit card transaction processing is touting their product as "the solution." What's truly amazing is how long it took these companies to come up with their "solution." In the meantime, they're making it sound as if accepting credit cards over the Net without their solution is an impossibility. This isn't actually the case. In the next section, we overview what it takes to accept credit cards over the Net, and outline ways to do it with solutions that have existed for a while.

Accepting Credit Cards

It's not as if accepting credit cards is anything new. Credit itself is an ancient concept and credit cards linked to financial institutions have been around for about 30 years. It's also not as if credit cards aren't an accepted part of our lifestyles. In 1994, Visa, the world's most prolific and accepted card, was in the hands of 391 million consumers in 247 countries.

You also don't absolutely need a network of fancy and expensive equipment to accept credit cards. The hardware and software you use (if any) will depend greatly on the design of your storefront and, most importantly, volume of transactions.

The players

It's rare that you'll ever deal directly with the major credit card companies. For instance, you won't call Visa to process a Visa card, or American Express for an American Express card. Instead, you'll contact a third-party known as a processing network. The "go-betweens" between the credit card companies, the banks, and you, the merchant, greatly simplify things. They dilute the merchant application process and transactions into communication between two or three parties, rather than across multiple banks and card issuers. The players involved in this process include the merchant, the transaction processing network, and possibly a merchant bank. We take a look at what each of these does in the following sections.

THE MERCHANT

The merchant is the company that intends to accept credit cards as a form of payment. It's up to the merchant to set up a bank account and initiate the relationship with the other parties involved—the merchant bank and the transaction processing network. The merchant is easy to spot as the one who sweats the details through the entire merchant application process: Will I be accepted by the merchant bank? How can I work down these percentages? How much is the chargeback fee? In short, this is you.

THE MERCHANT BANK

The merchant bank is the organization from which you (the merchant) obtain a merchant ID number (discussed later in this section). To complete this request, you must submit a number of financial and trade references as well as other information regarding the origin of your company. We outline the application process step-by-step in Chapter 14.

You'll come out of this process with a merchant ID number. The merchant bank can also set up a relationship with a transaction processing network for you. Often, the transaction processing networks act as merchant banks themselves, or have a subsidiary that's a merchant bank. FirstUSA, for example, is a large merchant bank that's also a processing network.

THE TRANSACTION PROCESSING NETWORK

The transaction processing network is where the money actually changes hands. There are dozens upon dozens of processing networks in the United States, each of which has its own focus and coverage. In addition to processing the major credit cards, some can process debit (ATM) cards, overseas credit cards (such as Japan's JCB), and authorize checks. The transaction processing networks are often referred to as just "the networks" or "the processors."

The processing network is who you actually call—either data or voice—to verify the credit card information, and who process the transaction in real-time or batch. They deposit the transacted money into your commercial bank account. They're also the people to whom you pay the credit card discount rate, lease any point-of-sale (POS) equipment from, and pay any general and processing fees. We look at these fees in detail in Chapter 14. National Data Corporation (NDC) is an example of a large processing network.

DON'T DISCOUNT THE DISCOUNT RATE	A note on confusing terminology: The *credit card discount rate* is the percentage per transaction that a processing network pays itself. This is usually a fixed rate between 1 and 4 percent, and is based upon your gross sales. The word "discount" typically has many good connotations for a consumer—which you are when using a processing network's services. An example is an item on sale having a "discounted" price. In this case, however, discount means that the processing network takes a few pennies from every dollar you make through credit card sales, on top of whatever monthly fees they may have.

The essential items

Now that you have an idea of the players involved in a credit card transaction and what they do, we can move on to what's needed to process credit cards. This section covers not the hardware or software needed, but the accounts and relationships you'll need for credit card transactions. This boils down to three items: a commercial bank account, a merchant ID number, and a relationship with a processing network.

COMMERCIAL BANK ACCOUNT

Your company must have a commercial bank account in which the processing network will place the incoming funds, and deduct any charges or fees. This account can be opened with any bank, including the one you already have. It's a good idea make this a separate account from your other accounts, such as payroll or general account, and just transfer the money into those accounts when needed. Thousands of transactions per month could potentially take place in this account. This high volume means that there's a higher chance for error, so it's better not to have other accounts "tainted" by problems arising from mistakes.

MERCHANT ID NUMBER

The merchant ID number is a unique number that designates your company to the merchant banks and the processing networks, and is used in any transaction between these entities. This number is given to you by your bank or merchant bank (depending on which one you use).

A RELATIONSHIP WITH A PROCESSING NETWORK

The relationship with a processing network is either set up by your merchant bank, or else your merchant bank *is* your processing network. Whichever way, the processing network you choose should be willing to process the types of transactions you wish to perform—Internet-based sales in which there's no direct customer contact and no signature recorded.

An overview of credit card transactions

Now that you know who and what's involved in a credit card transaction, we'll go over the procedure step-by-step.

1. **Sale.** A sale is made between a merchant and a customer. The customer gives the merchant his or her credit card number and expiration date.

2. **Authorization.** The merchant attempts to authorize the credit card for the purchase by contacting the processing network. The merchant sends the credit card number, expiration date, the amount of purchase, and comments to the network. The network, in turn, compares this information against a database maintained by the card's issuer (Visa, MasterCard, American Express, Novus, and so on) to determine if the customer has enough available credit to make the purchase, or if the card has been reported stolen. The network responds back to the merchant with an approval code or a denial.

3. **Settlement.** Approved transactions are then "settled" with the processor. The settlement is where funds are exchanged between the parties involved. Settlement can either take place immediately after the authorization, or in a batch that occurs at merchant-selected times. After settlement, the money is transferred into the merchant's bank account at a time agreed upon with the processing network.

The jargon in the financial world of credit card processing can be fairly mind boggling, and many banks and processing networks have their own terminology. If you're ever unsure about any of the steps, contracts, or definitions, by all means ask your merchant bank or network. When it comes to the quick change of funds inherent in credit card processing, there's no room for confusion.

Point-of-sale options

This section covers the basic tools needed for point-of-sale transactions. We don't cover Web payment options specifically here, but instead focus on the common POS hardware and software you might find in a retail environment and discuss how easy or difficult it might be to fold them into a Web commerce solution. These tools boil down to the telephone authorization/sales slips, electronic payment systems, and software payment systems.

THE BASICS: TELEPHONE AUTHORIZATION AND SALES SLIPS

The most simple point-of-sale credit card payment system requires only two things: a telephone and a sales slip. The telephone is used to make a voice call to your processing network to authorize the card. The sales amount for which you need authorization depends upon the agreement you have with the processing network. For smaller amounts, you may not need authorization.

The sales slip is a form supplied by your processing network on which you, as the merchant, fill out the credit card and vendor information (or take an imprint of this information from the credit card and a plate that contains vendor information). You also write in the authorization code, the price and a description of the products, the tax, and the total, and have the customer sign the slip. The sales slip is a two- or three-part carbon form: The customer gets one copy, the processing network is sent another, and you may have one as well. It's up to you to mail the sales slips to the processing network. When the network has received and tallied these slips, it deposits the funds into your bank account.

Before the days of magnetic strips and credit card swipers, this is how all credit card transactions were done. Low-volume retail and service centers still use voice authorizations and sales slips. Even department stores keep sales slips handy so that they can process cards in a pinch, such as when their POS systems go down.

ONE SOLUTION FOR LOW-VOLUME SALES If your Web site is a low-volume system as well—say, around ten or so transactions per day—then the old voice authorization/sales slip method may work for you. In this scenario, you would dump all of the information entered by the customer in a Web form into a secure flat file or database file. You would then call your processor with the credit card information and write the sales slips by hand.

You'll find a few advantages to this method:

1. You won't have to purchase or lease an electronic payment system, such as a Personal Identification Number (PIN) pad or electronic cash register.

2. The Common Gateway Interface (CGI) programming would be simple, compared with making a payment gateway of some sort.

There are, however, multiple disadvantages to using sales slips:

1. Cards aren't processed and funds aren't deposited into your account as quickly as they would be through an electronic payment system.

2. Per-transaction voice authorization is typically twice as expensive as doing it electronically.

3. Because you're doing the authorizations in batch, you don't know if the card has been approved or disapproved immediately. This precludes you from safely offering some services, such as providing instant access to an FTP site, since you won't know if the card is valid until later.

4. Somebody has to make all of those authorization calls and fill out the sales slips. (We're sure that you can think of better ways to spend your time!)

The disadvantages far outweigh the advantages, which strongly suggest that you avoid doing voice authorization and sales slips if possible. There are definitely better—and faster—ways to do it.

ELECTRONIC PAYMENT SYSTEMS

In the early 1980s, electronic payment systems started to take hold in the retail market. This equipment could immediately call a processing network through a modem data connection, authorize a credit purchase, then upload a batch of all sales and credits in the evening. This instant access meant that more customers could be processed through a retail line faster, and that merchants could receive payments sooner. The common electronic payment systems include: payment terminals (external hardware devices) and POS equipment (the modern equivalent of a cash register).

PAYMENT TERMINALS Payment terminals are a familiar sight at retail establishments and they're probably the most popular electronic payment means. Gas station customers are even able to pay for their own gas using a payment terminal built into the gas pump. These devices consist of a numeric keypad with special function keys, a magnetic stripe reader, a modem line, a port for connecting to a sales slip printer, and a port for connecting to a POS system. Authorization and payment is typically made by either swiping the card through the stripe reader, or entering the number by hand. If it's a debit card transaction, then the customer's PIN can also be entered into a connected PIN pad. The terminal then makes a call into the processor's network, verifies the card information, retrieves the authorization code, then stores the information in the batch. Figure 4-1 shows two popular payment terminals.

Figure 4-1
Two common payment terminals: A VeriFone OMNI 460 (left) and OMNI 380 (right) with printer and PIN pad.

Quick Payment Scheme for Low-Volume Web Sites As with voice authorization and sales slips, payment terminals are suitable for credit card payment for low-volume Web sites. You would capture the credit card information the same way you would with that payment system, except that instead of performing the authorization by voice and mailing in the sales slips, you enter the information manually into the keypad.

The advantage of the payment terminal over sales slips is that transactions are processed much faster by the network and, consequently, the merchant receives its money sooner. This system still has many of the same disadvantages, however. You still won't be able to grant access to certain parts of your Web site instantaneously based on authorization, because authorization won't occur until the card information is entered by hand. Also, you or someone in your company will still have to enter the card information by hand. Last, the payment terminal itself, which can be obtained from your processing network, sells for around $600 and leases for around $30 per month. Some networks claim to give you the terminal for free, but still charge you $15 per month as a maintenance fee.

Again, we suggest that, if at all possible, you don't use the payment terminal method for processing Web-based sales. It may be handy, however, to keep one around in case there are ever problems with the system you do decide to use.

More information about payment terminals can be found at the companies that make them, including VeriFone, at:

```
http://www.verifone.com.
```

POINT-OF-SALE EQUIPMENT POS equipment is a fancy term for a retail system that integrates a variety of features into one workstation or a group of networked workstations. These workstations combine an electronic cash register, electronic payment systems, network connectivity, and interoperability with back-office software, such as an inventory database.

POS workstations are typically based on PC hardware (such as Pentium processors and ISA or PCI bus cards) and run PC operating systems (such as Windows, UNIX, DOS, and OS/2). There are a number of options you can get for them, such as touchscreens, PIN pads, and scanners. An example of a POS system is shown in Figure 4-2.

Figure 4-2
NCR's 7450-FS32 POS workstation has a PC architecture and includes a touch-screen.

POS Equipment as a Web Solution Unless you already have POS equipment, using this equipment as a solution to Web transactions isn't recommended. For Web transactions, POP equipment doesn't give you any benefit over payment terminals. Not only do you have all of the problems associated with those devices, but you're paying a larger amount of money to have them. The price of POS equipment starts at around $2,000.

More information about POS equipment can be found from the manufacturers, including NCR at:

```
http://www.ncr.com.
```

SOFTWARE PAYMENT SYSTEMS

Software payment systems are designed to either supplant or enhance POS equipment. These solutions run on a regular computer platform, such as DOS, Windows, OS/2, UNIX, or Mac OS. There are even some that run on mainframe systems.

The benefit of software payment systems is that, since they run on a typical computer operating system, they can be integrated with existing software, such as POS software, transaction databases, and Web servers. Another benefit is that a computer-based POS system is extremely scaleable—you only buy peripherals such as a cash drawer, magnetic strip reader, or printer when you need them. This greatly cuts down on costs. Finally, software payment systems are typically more open and developer-friendly than other means of payment—they provide the speed of electronic payment systems without proprietary boundaries.

There are a growing number of turnkey Web payment solutions available, such as CommerceRoom, LivePayment, and the Microsoft Merchant System. Rather than cover these solutions here, we're going to focus instead on solutions that though not made for the Web, with the right CGI program "glue," can be turned into a Web payment solution. More information about the turnkey solutions can be found in Chapter 9.

THE TURNKEY WEB PAYMENT SOLUTIONS

MACAUTHORIZE AND PCAUTHORIZE MacAuthorize and PCAuthorize are two credit card transaction software solutions from Tellan Software, Inc. These two products can be easily integrated with POS software that runs on regular Macs and PCs, and their setup is handled through an easy-to-use Graphical User Interface (GUI), as shown in Figure 4-3. MacAuthorize requires a Macintosh Plus or better running MacOS System 7 or later. PCAuthorize is for Windows 3.1, 95, and NT systems, and can be downloaded from `http://www.tellan.com/products.html`. Both solutions require a Hayes-compatible modem to call the processing network.

Figure 4-3
MacAuthorize's transactions screen makes sales intuitive with its resemblance to a sales slip.

MacAuthorize includes the following features:

■ Supports AppleEvents and AppleScript, providing easy access for other applications such as databases and Web servers

■ Support for all major credit cards

■ Support for approximately 20 processing networks, though the list continues to grow

■ Instant authorization via modem call-in to your processing network

■ Customer billing address verification

There is also a multiuser gateway version of MacAuthorize called Mac Authorize*Hub. The Hub is designed to allow multiple networked Macintosh computers to process credit card transactions with the same gateway. In addition, the Hub is especially attuned to Internet commerce.

Any application that can initiate AppleEvents or run AppleScripts can act as a client, including the MacAuthorize*Client software, AppleScript, FileMaker Pro, and WebStar. For more information about MacAuthorize and PCAuthorize products, visit the Tellan Web site at:

```
http://www.tellan.com.
```

MacAuthorize Makes a Good Web Payment System The easy integration of MacAuthorize and MacAuthorize*Hub with AppleEvents and AppleScript make this product an excellent choice for a Web payment system. In fact, Pacific Coast Software, Inc., has a suite of CGI programs for doing commerce on the Internet with MacAuthorize and WebSTAR (the popular Macintosh Web server, the SSL version of which we will review in Chapter 7) called Web Commerce Solution. These applications include a shopping cart, a catalog database middleware program, a purchase tracking system, and a payment system. A free sample HTML payment form and AppleScript authorization CGI is available from Pacific Coast Software. It can be found in the MacAuthorize Demo, which is located at:

```
http://www.tellan.com/Demo.html .
```

For more information about Pacific Coast Software and Web Commerce Solution, visit the following Web site:

```
http://www.pacific-coast.com .
```

Another benefit of MacAuthorize is that almost all of its features can be accessed via the Web using the AppleEvents and AppleScript CGIs—it doesn't contain an abundance of features that you'll never use. Finally, MacAuthorize is reasonably priced: The single-user MacAuthorize sells for approximately $350, and the single-user MacAuthorize*Hub sells for approximately $450. This is even cheaper than most electronic payment terminals.

The only drawback with MacAuthorize is that you can't have a multimerchant setup if you're an Internet Service Provider (ISP) wanting to provide credit card services for a number of your customers—there's only one field for vendor information. For single-merchant Web sites, however, it's an excellent solution.

ICVERIFY   The company, ICVERIFY, Inc., was founded in 1988, and its ICVERIFY product is one of the most accepted pieces of electronic payment software around. It's available for DOS, Windows, and UNIX systems, in both single-user and network versions. Like MacAuthorize, credit card authorization is performed with ICVERIFY by calling up your processing network via a modem.

ICVERIFY's interface is less intuitive than MacAuthorize, but it's much more powerful (see Figure 4-4 for an example). In addition, ICVERIFY is extremely open for development—most of its features are accessible through a text or command-line interface, and authorization requests and answers are all in text files.

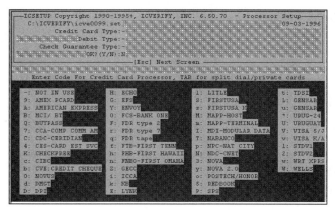

Figure 4-4
One of the DOS versions of ICVERIFY's merchant configuration screens.

Some of the other features of ICVERIFY include the following:

- Support for over 80 processing networks—it's accepted by 99 percent of the banks in the U.S.

- Multimerchant capabilities—more than one vendor can use a single copy of ICVERIFY, each with his or her own merchant ID number and processing network, so each has funds deposited into his or her own accounts

- Automatic billing of recurring transactions (such as monthly payments)

- Accepts all major credit cards as well as private cards (a card that's verified by the private network of the company issuing credit, such as a gas company)

- Authorizations and transactions can be processed either in real-time or in batch

- Reports can be viewed online and saved in a comma/quote delimited file for further processing by an in-house or third-party application, such as a spreadsheet

There are many other ICVERIFY functions, but these are the ones that will affect a Web developer the most. For more information visit the ICVERIFY corporate site at:

```
http://www.icverify.com.
```

The Best for Integration   ICVERIFY's open structure makes it an excellent option for a Web payment system. Because it uses text files for authorization, processing, and reporting, it is quite easy to write a CGI program in almost any language for online payment. Consequently, it has become our choice for creating a sample Web commerce solution. We outline the steps in setting up ICVERIFY in Chapter 10, and make a simple CGI "glue" for ICVERIFY in Chapter 14.

Like MacAuthorize, ICVERIFY is also quite reasonably priced. It can be purchased for less than $280 for the single-user version, and for less than $400 for the multiuser version.

Requirements for Credit Card Payment on the Net

For any payment system to be worthy of usage on the World Wide Web, it must pass certain criterion. These demands aren't ordained by some cabalistic standards society, but are what has been created through the synergy of the trade press, Internet consumers, and Internet marketing companies. The collective Web marketing presence has spoken, and it has said that credit card payment on the Net must have the following features: It must be fast, open, and secure.

Fast

Internet Web servers have the potential to accept hundreds of different client connections simultaneously. There could be dozens of people visiting your Web site at any given time. Any number of these visitors may decide to make an online purchase and, optimally, you should be able to authorize more than one credit card at a time. If this isn't possible, then authorizing them as fast as possible is the next best thing. If customers have to re-submit a form several times while waiting for a turn at authorization, they may end up going away.

MODEM DIAL-UP AUTHORIZATION

Currently, most processing networks require you to dial-in to them via modem. Many are still using the same technology they originally installed in the 1980s, meaning that you may be calling into a low-speed (300 or 1200 Bps) modem. The rather specialized and insular back-end of credit card authorization means that most of the networks haven't had to keep up with the times. The connection time to call in and authorize a card is around 20 seconds or so, which is actually not too bad—the line can be held up for several minutes to allow multiple consecutive transactions to be processed. Of course, the more modems and phone lines you have, the more transactions you can process.

LEASED-LINES AND OTHER OPTIONS

If you can afford it, you may also get a leased-line or satellite uplink to your processing network. This connection would be faster than a typical modem connection because you wouldn't have to dial-in each time you needed to authorize cards. Typically, only large retail chains or high-traffic, 24-hour gas stations have these types of connections to their networks.

AUTHORIZATION VIA THE INTERNET

The fastest authorization solution is one that actually uses the Internet itself to talk to a transaction processing network. By using high-speed connections to the Internet, several connections could be opened simultaneously.

So far, progress on this has been slow because of security concerns. There are many parties involved in the transaction process that must agree on how the communication will take place. Among them: the credit card issuers (Visa, MasterCard, and so on), the merchant banks, the processing networks, and the authorization software developers. The credit card issuers take precedence when it comes to this issue—they can refuse to let any processor who doesn't follow their standard to take their card over the Net.

Indeed, MasterCard and Visa collaborated with Netscape, Microsoft, IBM, GTE, VeriSign, and others, to create the Secure Electronic Transactions (SET) open standard for conducting bank card transactions over the Internet. American Express also agreed to adopt this standard, which uses specially developed RSA public-key cryptography for security. As this standard becomes finalized and adopted into products (which the group expects to happen toward the end of 1996), we should see it proliferate even in the processing networks, and expect a jump in Web commerce. More on the SET draft can be found at:

    http://www.mastercard.com/set/.

Open

The word "Open" is quite popular when used to describe Internet technologies. Primarily, it describes a technology that's not proprietary, and doesn't require the payment of royalties to use it. It doesn't mean that the software license is necessarily free. "Open" just means that the algorithm or specification is free for anyone to adopt, but programs developed using the algorithm or specification don't have to be. For instance, Netscape's SSL specification is free to use, but you must pay Netscape to use one of the SSL servers.

This meaning can be extended to software applications that are developer-friendly. In other words, the software makes things easy on programmers by allowing them to import and export file formats, or control the program through a number of ways. This allows a developer to simply integrate the software application (or their application's data) with their own programs.

The best of the electronic commerce solutions will be open. It's much nicer to be able to bring payment software into your current environment, rather than having to use a specific Web server or database.

Secure

We've already addressed the concerns about security at the beginning of this chapter, as this is probably the area in which the greatest advancements have been made in electronic commerce. And we've already discussed most of the solutions available today: SSL, S-HTTP, VPI, and PCT. Any of these can be used for customer to merchant communication.

For merchant-to-processor communication, it's worth mentioning that modem dial-up to the processor is quite secure. The information travels across the modem connection directly to the processor, so it never moves through different networks in-between as it would if it traveled through the Internet. As we've also said, SET is beginning to address the security concerns about transferring bank card-specific information over the Internet, including to processing networks.

Summary

In this chapter we examined the reasons for why such an old technology like credit card authorization hasn't been speedily adopted on Web sites. The ultimate reason, we believe, is that people don't realize how easy it actually is to integrate. To take credit cards, you must have a merchant ID, a bank account, and a relationship with a credit card processing network. A number of ways to take credit card transactions already exist, but the software solutions, such as MacAuthorize and ICVERIFY, are the easiest to develop CGI "glue" programs for. In the coming chapters, you'll learn how to obtain a merchant ID and add the processing power of ICVERIFY to your Web site.

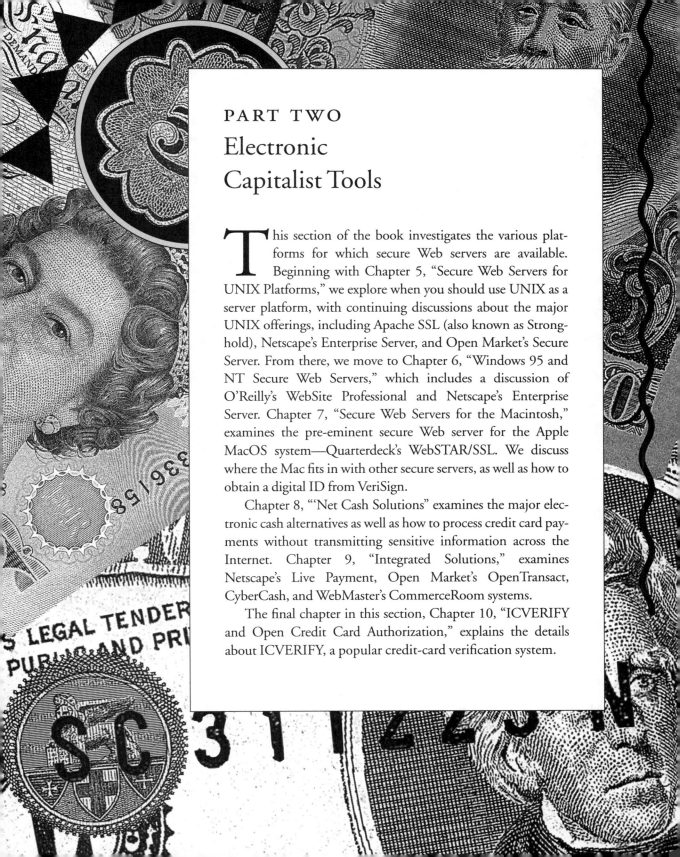

PART TWO
Electronic Capitalist Tools

This section of the book investigates the various platforms for which secure Web servers are available. Beginning with Chapter 5, "Secure Web Servers for UNIX Platforms," we explore when you should use UNIX as a server platform, with continuing discussions about the major UNIX offerings, including Apache SSL (also known as Stronghold), Netscape's Enterprise Server, and Open Market's Secure Server. From there, we move to Chapter 6, "Windows 95 and NT Secure Web Servers," which includes a discussion of O'Reilly's WebSite Professional and Netscape's Enterprise Server. Chapter 7, "Secure Web Servers for the Macintosh," examines the pre-eminent secure Web server for the Apple MacOS system—Quarterdeck's WebSTAR/SSL. We discuss where the Mac fits in with other secure servers, as well as how to obtain a digital ID from VeriSign.

Chapter 8, "'Net Cash Solutions" examines the major electronic cash alternatives as well as how to process credit card payments without transmitting sensitive information across the Internet. Chapter 9, "Integrated Solutions," examines Netscape's Live Payment, Open Market's OpenTransact, CyberCash, and WebMaster's CommerceRoom systems.

The final chapter in this section, Chapter 10, "ICVERIFY and Open Credit Card Authorization," explains the details about ICVERIFY, a popular credit-card verification system.

CHAPTER FIVE

SECURE WEB SERVERS FOR
UNIX PLATFORMS

I n this chapter, we look at a few secure Web servers available for the various flavors of the UNIX operating system. We discuss why UNIX secure servers seem to be going the way of the dinosaurs, when you should use a UNIX secure server, and what servers are available. Then we focus on two specific servers: one that represents solutions for the budget-minded, experienced server user, and one for the less-experienced user willing to spend a little more for a turnkey solution.

Why UNIX Secure Servers Are Becoming Scarce

Since UNIX was the first OS to have a World Wide Web server designed for it, there should be no surprise that UNIX would also boast the largest number of secure servers available (although Windows NT comes in at a close second). Nearly every major Web server vendor has a UNIX version of their product. The only notable exception is WebSite, which at first seems contrary to O'Reilly & Associates' reputation for being UNIX gurus. O'Reilly is not the only company to shun the UNIX secure Web server market. CompuServe/Spry used to sell its Internet Office secure server for a number of UNIX platforms, but no longer does; a decision driven more by the market than technology, however. As more and more companies and individuals run their own Web servers, they tend to lean toward the platforms they already own and are familiar with, usually Windows 95 and NT. That way, they can maintain homogenous platforms and don't have to bear the cost of hiring or training a UNIX administrator.

When to use UNIX

Windows 95 and NT are not always the best solution for every situation. There are times when one needs the raw horsepower of a UNIX server, such as

- when you're allowing other people to have Web sites on your server, as in the case of an ISP. Only UNIX has the robust, multiuser capabilities and quota systems needed to administer access rights and calculate billing for disk use.

- when you're running more than 16 virtual Web hosts. That is, you have sixteen different IP addresses pointing to sixteen separate document roots on a single server, giving the illusion that it's actually sixteen different Web servers housing the pages. NT has resource limits which prevent you from adding too many before performance is severely impeded. With UNIX, you can add practically as many sites as your configuration allows (which usually means the more RAM you have, the more virtual Web hosts you can have).

- when your site is getting a large number of hits. How many? Unfortunately, there's no plug-in formula for figuring this out, and you may not know you should have set up that UNIX server until it's too late. Based on our own personal observations, anything over 5,000 hits a day is moving from the "small" to "medium" range, and anything over 50,000 hits a day is moving from "medium" to "large." As a point of reference, some of the most heavily visited sites on the Net—such as Yahoo!, AltaVista, or c|net—experience at least 500,000 hits per day.

To summarize, we recommend a UNIX secure server for ISPs or companies that plan on handling a large number of transactions over the Web. Of course, make sure you have an experienced UNIX administrator on staff, or available on contract, to handle the OS management issues.

A wide selection of servers

Despite the shrinking market share, there are a large number of secure servers available for UNIX platforms. Table 5-1 shows a list of some of them, including the platforms on which they are available and their price as of the third quarter of 1996.

As you can see from Table 5-1, if you're using one of the major commercial versions of UNIX, you're in luck: There's a secure server available for you. SunOS, Solaris, OSF/1, HP-UX, and IRIX are the most prevalent. If you're running one of the free versions of UNIX, such as Linux or FreeBSD (available on the Internet or from CD-ROM distributors), there are a few servers available for you as well. Someone running an "orphaned" or less-popular flavor of UNIX, such as Apple's A/UX, Novell's UNIXWare, or SCO's UNIX may run into problems finding a secure server for their platform.

TABLE 5.1: THE PLATFORMS AND PRICES OF A FEW UNIX SECURE WEB SERVERS

SERVER NAME	UNIX PLATFORMS	PRICE
Stronghold: Apache SSL	IRIX, Solaris, OSF, HP-UX, Linux, FreeBSD, SunOS, AIX	$495
Netscape Enterprise Server	OSF/1, HP-UX, AIX, IRIX, SunOS, Solaris, BSDI	$995
Open Market Secure Server	HP-UX, Solaris, SunOS, OSF/1, AIX, IRIX, BSDI	$1,120

SERVERS FOR A VARIETY OF BUDGETS

When most secure servers first came out, in 1994, they were priced between $2,000 and $5,000 per "instance" of the server binary that you executed on your system. This means that even if you want to run one instance of your secure server at port 443 for your outside electronic commerce, and another instance at port 1776 for an intranet database, you would have to pay for two licenses.

The instance rule still applies to most secure servers, but server prices have dropped substantially. For instance, less than a year ago, Open Market's Secure Server sold for $4,995. Today, it's priced at just above $1,100, and during certain promotions you can get it for less than $1,000!

The reason for the dramatic decrease in price is competition. It used to be that Netscape and Open Market were the only solutions, but now there are many more, and the increased competition has caused both companies to position themselves as "high-end" solutions.

At the inexpensive end of the UNIX secure server market is Stronghold: Apache SSL. Coming in at $495 (or free for non-commercial use), it's within the budgets of most small companies.

PRICE ISN'T THE ONLY DIFFERENCE BETWEEN SERVERS You shouldn't necessarily jump to use the least expensive server on the market. Each server has its own special features and tools, and its own level of future expandability. For instance, Netscape and Open Market have made it easy to plug their numerous other commerce applications into their servers. Also, you're paying for support: Open Market and Netscape are both known for their support staff, while the Community ConneXion (the distributors of Stronghold) have more limited technical support services. As a Web developer, you have to decide how turnkey you want your solution to be, and whether or not you have the time and expertise to puzzle through potential problems.

OBTAINING A UNIX SECURE SERVER

Many UNIX secure server manufacturers let you purchase and download their secure server products directly from their Web pages, while others prefer to ship their products to you. You usually have to fill out a form stating that you are a U.S. or Canadian citizen, that you plan on using the server in the U.S. or Canada, and that you won't ship the server to someone outside of the U.S. or Canada. Table 5-2 shows you where you can obtain selected servers, and what their evaluation period is, if there is one.

TABLE 5-2: UNIX SECURE WEB SERVERS, THEIR URLS, AND THEIR EVALUATION PERIODS

SECURE WEB SERVER	URL	EVALUATION PERIOD
Stronghold: Apache-SSL	`http://apachessl.c2.org`	30 days for the commercial version (the non-commercial version is free)
Netscape Enterprise Server	`http://www.netscape.com/comprod/server_central` `/product/enterprise/index.html`	60 days
Open Market Secure Server	`http://www.openmarket.com/servers/`	30 days

As you've probably gathered, obtaining a UNIX secure server to evaluate and learn is really quite easy. In the following section, we examine two Web servers in particular: Open Market's Secure Server and Stronghold: ApacheSSL. They're good examples, respectively, of the high-end, turnkey variety, and the more hands-on, basic variety. Let's explore the benefits and limitations of each in detail.

Stronghold: Apache-SSL

Stronghold is the marriage of two popular free Internet products: The Apache *httpd* Web server for UNIX systems, and the SSLeay Secure Sockets Layer implementation. Apache has long been known to the UNIX Web server community as a stable and progressive alternative to NCSA's *httpd*, and Apache was also one of the first UNIX Web servers to implement virtual hosts. SSLeay is the first free SSL implementation ever created. The Apache was built from scratch using the SSL specification written by Netscape. Because Netscape wants SSL to be an open Internet standard, the specification doesn't have to be licensed. Outside of the U.S., SSLeay is free; but within the U.S., commercial users of SSLeay are required to pay a licensing fee to RSA for use of the RSARef. More information on the original Apache can be found at:

`http://www.apache.org .`

And more information on SSLeay can be found at:

`http://www.psy.uq.oz.au/~ftp/Crypto/ .`

Ben Laurie first combined Apache and SSLeay to create a secure server distribution that's available outside of the U.S. The Community ConneXion now maintains the U.S. version, which uses the licensed RSARef. More information on the trials and tribulations of creating a public version of SSL can be found at:

```
http://petrified.cic.net/~altitude/ssl/ssl.saga.html .
```

Maintained by privacy experts

Stronghold is maintained by the Community ConneXion, a nonprofit Internet service and presence provider that concerns itself with electronic privacy issues. In addition to developing Stronghold, they operate a number of other privacy-related services, such as an anonymous re-mailer. You can visit their Web site, shown in Figure 5-1, at:

```
http://www.c2.org .
```

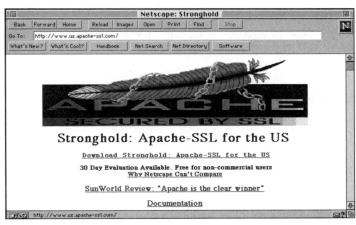

Figure 5-1
The Community ConneXion Web site, home of Stronghold: Apache-SSL.
©1992 C2Net.

As privacy advocates, the Community ConneXion has made Stronghold available at no cost to individuals and organizations who do not intend to use the application for commercial purposes. This means that nonprofit organizations can use Stronghold for their Intranet applications without having to put up nearly $1,000 for a commercial secure Web server such as Netscape's Enterprise Server.

A classic cheap-and-easy solution

Stronghold has all the elements of a classic UNIX *httpd* server. UNIX users familiar with installing and configuring NCSA or CERN's *httpd* will have no problem with Stronghold. In keeping with the tradition of these inexpensive servers, Stronghold also comes with an agreeable price tag.

BASED ON THE POPULAR APACHE *httpd* SERVER

As we've said, Stronghold is built around the popular Apache WWW server. This makes it easy for companies currently using Apache to integrate Stronghold into their Web server environment.

Although Apache doesn't have commercial-level technical support, as of July 1996, it owns 35 percent of the Web server market—UNIX, Windows NT, or otherwise! This statistic comes from a survey taken in July, 1996 by Netcraft, a company that polls a large number of Web servers each month with an HTTP request to find out what variety they are running. You can get current and historical survey data from Netcraft's Web site at:

```
http://www.netcraft.co.uk/Survey/Reports/ .
```

The aforementioned survey found that 104,086 servers are running Apache, taking into consideration only those servers that are Internet accessible—that figure doesn't include intranet servers! In other words, this large user base may be all the technical support you'll ever need. There are Apache listservs, FAQs, and USENET newsgroups to assist you with whatever problem or question you might have.

The FAQ is maintained by the Apache developers at:

```
http://www.apache.org/docs/FAQ.html .
```

You can report any bugs you may find in the Apache server to:

```
apache-bugs@mail.apache.org .
```

Finally, you can find support in a USENET group, where a number of Apache developers can be found, at:

```
comp.infosystems.www.servers.unix .
```

If you've already been using Apache, you'll be able to migrate the Apache configuration files to Stronghold rather easily. Stronghold also boasts the best features of Apache, including

- support for an unlimited number of Virtual Hosts, allowing you to have multiple IP addresses assigned to different document roots.

- database support for user authentication.

- mSQL public domain database support.

- UNIX "db" authentication.

- "keep-alive" persistent HTTP connections to allow multiple requests to be sent over the same TCP connection. Defined in the HTTP 1.1 draft, it speeds up access time for browsers that support it.

- caching a proxy server to allow HTTP access for clients behind a firewall.

- status and information modules that let you pull up real time configuration and resource data. An example of status output is visible in Figure 5-2.

- support for the Apache API.

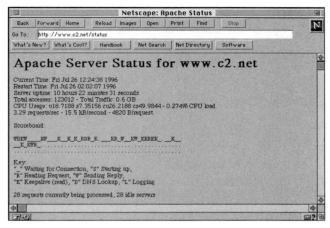

Figure 5-2
A sample status data output from the Community ConneXion Web server.
©1992 C2Net.

Thanks to these features, Stronghold holds its own in the secure Web server market against its more commercial and expensive competitors.

IT'S VERY SIMILAR TO NCSA'S *httpd*

Apache and Apache-SSL are both based on the NCSA *httpd* server, which (along with CERN *httpd*) is one of the granddaddies of the Web server family. In fact, Apache uses some of the code originally developed for NCSA; and likewise, NCSA has adopted some of the next-generation enhancements and code created for Apache over the years.

Because many other Web servers have used NCSA's *httpd* as their model, someone new to Apache will still find themselves in a largely familiar environment. Webmasters who've been using NCSA's *httpd* will notice that the configuration files for Apache and NCSA are both very similar, which makes for an easy migration.

Sioux is an Apache-based SSL server developed by Thawte Consulting of South Africa. Because it was created outside the U.S., it's not bound by the export restrictions that force Netscape and Community ConneXion to have "exportable" versions of their products with weaker encryption keys. It's also possible to get your Sioux certificate signed by VeriSign. (See Chapter 12 for more information about certificate authorities.)

Sioux currently costs $550 in the U.S. and includes many of the same features as Stronghold; plus, it also includes the Python programming language for CGI development. If you're outside North America and want to find a cheap secure server solution that's similar to Stronghold, visit Thawte at:

```
http://www.thawte.com/products/sioux/ .
```

**SIOUX:
APACHE-SSL
FOR THE
REST OF THE
WORLD**

IT'S CHEAP

Any way you cut it, Stronghold is one of the best values on the UNIX secure Web server market. The Community ConneXion has a very simple pricing structure for Stronghold: Free for non-commercial use, or $495 for the commercial version. The reason it's so inexpensive is that the Community ConneXion is a nonprofit organization. The $495 fee merely covers the licensing fee for the RSARef when you use it for commercial purposes.

For you to get Stronghold for free, you need to ensure the Community ConneXion that you are not going to use it for revenue-generating purposes. This doesn't necessarily mean your organization has to be nonprofit, or that if it is nonprofit, the fee is automatically waived. Even a nonprofit organization can use the server to hold an online "bake sale" to generate income. Acceptable uses here include using it for teaching purposes in an educational institution, to provide basic services at a charity or other nonprofit organization, or to host a community freenet (a free network available to all users in a community, to provide Internet access to those who otherwise couldn't afford it). This isn't the Community ConneXion's rule, but that of RSA for licensing the patented RSA public-key cryptosystem technology.

Best for those experienced with UNIX Web servers

To use Stronghold, you're going to need a UNIX administrator at your disposal. Either you should be one yourself, have one on staff, or have one on contract who can remotely administer the server, perform upgrades, and so on. The reason for this is twofold: 1) It's available only for UNIX, and 2) there's no turnkey technical support.

COMMERCIAL-LEVEL SUPPORT, BUT NO HAND-HOLDING

Although Stronghold has commercial-level support for its commercial licensees, it may not be the level of support you need. Although phone support is available from the Community ConneXion, they prefer that you report bugs and pose questions via e-mail. In addition, the Community ConneXion Web site contains a FAQ and documentation for the server at:

```
http://stronghold.c2.net/about/purchase_faq.php .
```

You can also subscribe to a user-support mailing list. Just send e-mail to `majordomo@c2.org` with the following in the body of the message:

```
subscribe apachessl-users .
```

There is also a mailing list for commercial users of the product. You are automatically added to this list when you download the software.

To report bugs in Stronghold, send e-mail to:

```
apachessl-bugs@c2.org .
```

For technical support, send e-mail to:

```
apachessl-support@c2.org .
```

Our suggestion for those of you wishing to use Stronghold is to first attempt to install the Apache *httpd* server on your system. If you can accomplish this, then Stronghold should be simple to install.

ONLY AVAILABLE FOR UNIX PLATFORMS

The downside of Stronghold is that, like Apache, it's only available for UNIX platforms (and, unfortunately, not as many as Apache itself). A die-hard UNIX lover would say, "So what? What else do you need?" But the fact is, most Web server environments are becoming amalgamations of a variety of different platforms. A company may have a UNIX server to house its main pages because of the number of connections it allows, but also have a Windows NT Web server for a WWW front end to their MS Access database. When working in an environment like this, it's nice to have some homogeneity in how you interact with your Web server, such as Netscape's browser-based administrative pages.

Also, although Stronghold has a very nice script that helps guide you through the installation process, you may still run into the foibles that occur when installing *anything* on a UNIX system: Are permissions correct? Do you have port 443 open? Who should you run the Web server as? In other words, you should know your way around a UNIX system before you attempt to install Stronghold.

Perhaps some enterprising developer out there will take charge and port the Apache and SSLeay code to Windows NT and other platforms, so we can have a choice of Stronghold servers.

Open Market's Secure Server

Open Market, Inc. has been a leader in electronic commerce products since early 1994. The following sections takes a look at the Open Market server, its highlights, and its shortcomings.

It's a server with room to grow

Open Market's Secure Server is one of the most comprehensive servers on the market. Rather than trying to infuse the Internet industry with their own standards, as Microsoft and Netscape are doing, Open Market takes a more holistic approach and attempts to encompass as many competing technologies as possible. This is one instance where the "everything but the kitchen sink" approach seems to work. Their angle is that it's difficult to tell if the next new hot technology will become an industry standard or disappear without a trace. Why would an information manager want to invest in a product that gambles its livelihood on one server API, security protocol, or browser? Open Market attempts to take the risk out of buying its product by supporting everything. Combining this philosophy with server features and tools that complement (rather than clobber) existing Web server paradigms, makes for a powerful Web server.

SUPPORTS A NUMBER OF ENCRYPTION TECHNIQUES

As previously mentioned, Open Market's Secure Server doesn't depend on one model to provide its security. It fully supports SSL, S-HTTP, and Microsoft's new, exportable Private Communications Technology (PCT). The only one it doesn't seem to support is TradeWave's VPI. By supporting all of these encryption systems, Open Market can operate securely with practically any Web browser that supports security.

But Open Market's approach goes beyond just trying to be compatible with a large number of browsers—Open Market itself doesn't even make a browser, a rarity for a Web server product company. They see security as a matter of degree, with different situations and data calling for different protocols and different levels of encryption strength. Open Market describes their feeling about this on their Web site:

> *You don't protect the loose change in your pocket the same way you protect your life savings; you don't protect the information about your CFO's surprise birthday party the same way you protect the formula for your Secret Sauce.*

We couldn't have said it any better. But Netscape assures us that SSL doesn't really stand for Secret Sauce Layer protocol!

EXTENSIBLE WITH OPEN MARKET'S OTHER PRODUCTS

Open Market's other Web commerce products can be used in conjunction with the Secure Server. Combining them, you can create a turnkey Web commerce solution for your company. Here's a brief description of some of the products:

OM-Transact. Provides the back end of the Web commerce system, including customer support, order management, and transaction processing.

OM-Axcess. Actually uses and extends Secure Server to provide a way to limit access content to only certain users. It includes a variety of tools to make it easy to set up an online financial center, electronic publishing house, or Intranet information server.

OM-WebReporter. Comes with Secure Server now. It allows you to configure and control detailed Web reports through a browser-based GUI.

Adding such features may raise the cost of your Web commerce site, but you have to pay the price for ease-of-use.

INCLUDES WEB REPORTING SOFTWARE

Secure Server also includes Open Market's WebReporter package, which can provide statistical data on your Web site. This includes summarizing which pages are hit the most and by what hosts, and tracking the amount of time someone visited your site and what pages referred them to your page. This is configured to be either viewed on the Web or e-mailed to you. The software itself is highly configurable, so you can generate reports that best reflect the statistics you want. Figure 5-3 shows an example of a summary report generated from an example on Open Market's Web site.

FastCGI EMPOWERS YOUR CGI PROGRAMS

Open Market's FastCGI interface for their secure Web server allows you to get the performance of a vendor-specific API Web server application from your standard common gateway interface (CGI) programs. This is achieved by running the CGI program all the time. This increases CGI speed because the user doesn't have to wait for the CGI to start up before it handles the request. In addition, FastCGI maintains a cache of the user authentication information,

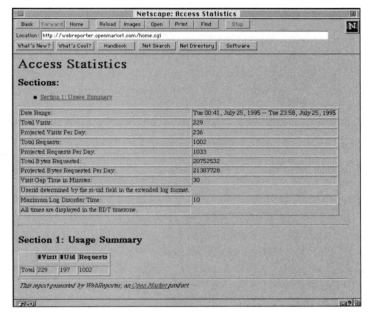

Figure 5-3
A summary report generated by WebReporter of a sample Web log, on Open Market's Web site for July 25th, 1995. Despite the date, this represents the latest and greatest version of the company's software.

which can save time when accessing a database that requires a user to be granted permission via user name and password.

Like CGI, FastCGI is language-independent, meaning that programs can be written in any language that has a FastCGI application library. So far, these languages include C/C++, Java, Perl, and TCL.

FastCGI is already receiving praise from the Web server community. Besides being available for Open Market's Secure Server, there's also a FastCGI module for Apache. NCSA is planning on including the standard FastCGI module in future releases of the *httpd* server. More information on FastCGI can be found at:

```
http://www.fastcgi.com/ .
```

It's a powerful server, but accessibility is limited

Because of Open Market's ease of use and all-in-one approach, it's a good choice for someone who doesn't have much experience with UNIX Web servers. It's also a good option for companies that don't have a large IS staff, or don't have much time to put into learning a new product. Unfortunately, two things impede small companies from making Open Market their secure server of choice: price and platform.

A LITTLE PRICEY FOR A SMALL BUSINESS

At $1,120, Open Market's Secure Server comes in a little high for many small businesses. If you only need to run a single instance of the server once on your Web server, the cost is cut down somewhat. Nonetheless, many companies only need one or two pages to be secure (such as a credit card information form), and won't want to spend so much on a server on which they'll be serving few pages. Therefore, we suggest that only small companies who need a plug-and-play solution, whose Web business depends on them having their own private secure Web server, purchase this product. We also suggest this product for those who require the ability to run securely and insecurely on a single execution of the server.

CURRENTLY LIMITED TO HIGH-END UNIX PLATFORMS

Many of the same reasons it would be nice to have an Apache-SSL for Windows NT applies here as well. Oddly enough, though many of Open Market's other products (such as OM-Transact) are available for Windows NT, Secure Server itself isn't. In addition, Secure Server is only produced for the high-end (and expensive) UNIX server market, such as AIX and IRIX. There are no OM secure servers available for the free UNIX operating systems of Linux or FreeBSD.

Summary

As with most products in the computer industry (and especially the Internet product industry), the more turnkey you need your solution to be, the more you're going to pay. After describing secure servers for UNIX in general, we suggested Stronghold as an inexpensive solution that requires some in-house experience to set up and run. On the other hand, Open Market's Secure Server, although more expensive, makes installation and configuration a little easier, and has better support for the new user. Hopefully, you now have a better idea of what type of UNIX secure Web server best suits your needs.

CHAPTER SIX

WINDOWS 95 AND NT SECURE WEB SERVERS

As the idea of Web publishing has taken hold of the business world, both on the Internet and private intranets, it's natural that most Web server developers would focus on the Windows 95 and Windows NT platforms. With the proliferation of these platforms, as well as overall Windows system administrators' knowledge of the Windows environment, developers have specifically targeted Windows for secure Web engines.

The Windows Platform Web Server Push

This chapter focuses on why Windows NT network administrators should consider making Web commerce engines standard components. Here, we focus on two widely used secure Web servers: O'Reilly's WebSite Professional and the Netscape Commerce Server. Though these are not the only such solutions available, both are easily implemented and integrated into existing Web structures, and are well supported by their manufacturers. In addition, other less common secure solutions are briefly covered. As always, system administrators must consider their own unique networking requirements to determine which is the most beneficial solution.

The versatility of the Windows NT/95 client server model

The beauty of Windows NT is its versatility and widespread use. Most system administrators are already familiar with NT implementation and its various quirks. NT serves
not only as a Web commerce platform, but also as a gateway server to a broad range of
other platforms. Using NFS or Samba, a network of Windows NT, Windows 95, Macintosh, and UNIX-based machines can service a variety of Internet commerce needs. This
flexibility enables the Windows platform to fit easily into any plans for internetworking
and Net commerce.

In addition, most credit card validation systems software is developed for NT or
DOS. Though an equal amount of software is developed for specific flavors of UNIX,
these versions not only require knowledge and possession of that particular OS, but
also limit the Web server to UNIX-based utilities. With a Windows NT Web server,
one can take advantage of a broader range of CGIs, including Perl, C++, and Visual
Basic; not to mention ActiveX controls (which currently don't work on UNIX). Logs,
transactions, and more can be pushed through to specific Windows NT applications,
without the need for in-house development of specific administrative tools, as is so
often the case with UNIX.

Likewise, security is a big issue when it comes to Internet commerce. Windows NT
offers permissions and firewalling equal to that found in UNIX. In addition, any NT-
based Web server software, such as O'Reilly's WebSite Professional, typically provides its
own onboard security and permissions functions. With the use of SSL and HTTP-S,
transactions and pages may be secured individually, providing an extra layer of security.

The proliferation of the platform and commerce software

As with every application, the demand for certain platforms and operating systems
drives the development process. With Web commerce servers, this is equally true. The
Windows OS and the Intel platform are the most widely used throughout the world,
and will likely continue to be so for the foreseeable future. What this means to system
and Web administrators is that they will have a wide variety of choices when selecting a
secure Web server.

We chose O'Reilly's WebSite Professional and the Netscape Commerce Server.
O'Reilly's WebSite Professional, which is one of the newer entries in the commerce
server field, has impressed Web gurus worldwide with its easy setup and comprehensive
documentation (as you might expect from such a preeminent publisher of computer
books). The Netscape Enterprise Server is probably the oldest in the industry (a vener-
able two years old at this point), and gives administrators an easy-to-use interface for
configuration. The real drawback is its price, which tends to run about double that of
WebSite Professional.

O'Reilly's WebSite Professional

O'Reilly Software has long been a leader in World Wide Web publishing, serving, and
development. Their WebSite is an industry-wide recognized, solid solution for an

organization's Web server needs. With the recent addition of WebSite Professional, O'Reilly takes the strengths of WebSite and expands them into secure document transmission. There are several benefits to using WebSite Professional, not the least of which is its versatility with regard to secure document transmission protocols. While most commerce servers support either S-HTTP or SSL, WebSite Professional supports both. This enables a system administrator to easily integrate an existing secure server, or to transfer the job directly over to WebSite Professional. Also, WebSite Professional is the least expensive of Windows NT secure Web servers, at $499 list price.

Features

There are many advantages to implementing WebSite Professional as a secure Web server. Easy installation and configuration, outstanding documentation, and a familiar WebSite management interface are just a few of the cosmetic benefits. These and other features, such as its versatile use across platforms and secure protocols, its support for a variety of CGI programs, and its onboard Web publishing tools, are discussed in the following sections.

PLATFORMS AND PROTOCOLS

One of the main benefits of WebSite Professional is its versatile deployment on a variety of Windows platforms. Unlike some Windows-based Web servers, WebSite Professional can be installed on and run from a Windows NT Server, Workstation, or a system running Windows 95. This enables the Web administrator to divide his or her resources more efficiently, by not being limited to say, the main NT server as a file system and a Web server. The server load can be distributed across the network, without a loss of security, or wasted processor load.

Likewise, WebSite Professional supports the two main secure Web protocols, S-HTTP and SSL. This not only provides for a combination of secure protocols, but also gives the system administrator the opportunity to easily integrate this secure Web server into an existing Web server model. Thus, if the organization was currently using Netscape Commerce Server, which is limited to SSL, the move to WebSite Professional would not be painful, because the current secure infrastructure would be compatible with the new Web server.

DEVELOPMENT TOOLKITS AND CGIs

As with its predecessor, WebSite, WebSite Professional offers a broad range of software development toolkits (SDK), and a variety of CGI options. In addition, it supports all major Web architectures and standards, enabling the system administrator and the network development staff to use the programming, Web authoring, and secure transaction tools with which they are familiar. For example, Professional implements WebSite Application Programming Interface, which extends the Web server's capabilities with regard to program-to-Web-to-program integration.

THE ODBC DATABASE TOOL Open Database Connectivity (ODBC) is a database access API controlled by Microsoft. ODBC provides a standard interface for various database programs and systems, thereby enabling a single application or interface to communicate with a database engine. As seen in Figure 6-1, most Windows-based development tools and applications that commonly interact with database programs now support ODBC, though O'Reilly's WebSite Professional is one of the first secure Web servers to package such a toolkit with its product.

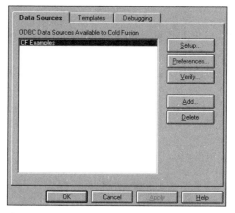

Figure 6-1
The Cold Fusion database interface supports access to ODBC databases on Windows NT.

CGI 1.3 / VISUAL BASIC 4 TOOLKIT WebSite Professional fully supports both Windows CGI, Visual Basic 4, and Visual Basic 3. Using any of these toolkits, developers can create interface programs to shuttle and process data received from a Web site, and produce the desired results.

SERVER-SIDE JAVA AND TOOLKIT Java is the most recent innovation to the Internet programming world, and Professional fully supports the Java Developer's Kit 1.01 (JDK) for Win32. WebSite Professional uses Java to create server-side applications, instead of using Java applets, as would normally be the case. Use of this toolkit requires the JDK 1.01, which is available at Sun Microsystems's Web site:

        http://java.sun.com .

API AND TOOLKIT The WebSite Application Programming Interface (WSAPI) and Microsoft's Internet Server Application Programming Interface (ISAPI) are both supported and provided with a toolkit. WSAPI provides a faster and more robust way to accommodate server-side applications needs, and to handle Web page-to-program interfaces. WSAPI also provides for integration with Microsoft's ISAPI, making it easy to integrate with existing Web interface programs.

PERL 5 AND API PERL 5 SDK The most recent version of Perl for Win32 is installed with WebSite Professional. This enables easy implementation and integration of existing Perl components and libraries into the existing Web structure. Essential Perl libraries are available at the WebSite Central Web page:

```
http://Website.ora.com .
```

In addition to these SDKs, WebSite Professional supports integration with Borland's Delphi, Visual C++, and Visual Basic, or any other Windows-based development environment. Likewise, integration of popular Windows-based applications, such as spreadsheets, databases, and scheduling programs, can be integrated efficiently into the Web environment, making the information and functionality contained in these applications available to the user across the Internet. This opens up vistas as yet untapped with regard to linking remote offices to the most recent data through a wide area intranet. Through the use of secure functions inherent to a commerce server, this information can be delivered securely, quickly, and to a wide variety of platforms and clients.

CONTENT DEVELOPMENT AND PUBLISHING

WebSite Professional comes with the HotDog Standard HTML authoring tool by Sausage Software (see Figure 6-2), which supports a variety of content development tools, including Netscape Navigator Gold and Microsoft's ActiveX and FrontPage. The purpose of having use of all these applications is to create "one button publishing," enabling the developer to craft a Web site, and then upload the entire site while maintaining crucial links to other documents. If you've ever developed Web pages with a standard text editor, you'll realize what a big time saver this functionality is.

With the HotDog Standard HTML editor, the Web development team has a ready tool for creating and publishing Web sites quickly and efficiently. Some of HotDog's features are innovative and integrate many of the features supported by a broad range of browsers, such as extensions inherent to Netscape Navigator, or Microsoft Explorer. The following is a list of its main features:

- graphical user interface for formatting documents in HTML
- support of both Netscape's and Microsoft's extensions to HTML, and proposed HTML 3.0 elements
- Windows 95-style interface in Windows 3.1 and Windows NT
- useful dialog boxes enabling easy creation of forms and tables
- management functions that minimize errors by finding duplicate links and converting DOS files to UNIX format
- a plethora (fifty) of interface customization options
- internal file manager enabling designers to drag and drop files to a document; files are instantly converted into links to the appropriate file
- support for editing of CGIs

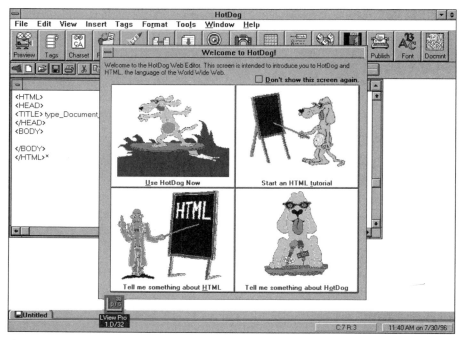

Figure 6-2
HotDog Standard provides an excellent shareware tool for creating Web documents.

In addition, WebSite Professional comes standard with a powerful indexing tool, search engine, WebView maintenance tool, and image map editor (MapThis!). Professional also supplies a broad range of Server Side Includes utilities that keep track of page access, or display the current date and time. Several standard page generation "wizards" are also included, enabling developers to easily create and update "What's New" pages, "Under Construction" pages, and more.

WebSite's built-in indexing tool, WebIndex, creates an index for every document, or any portion of a document or site. As shown in Figure 6-3, its interface is highly customizable, and enables administrators to index every word in every document, or only certain areas of documents, such as the head, body, or title. WebIndex even supports multiple indexes for use by different users or groups. Through the included WebFind form, users can employ standard Boolean logic to search the index for desired information. WebView is WebSite's built-in maintenance tool. As seen in Figure 6-4, WebView displays a graphical tree of unique icons that depict, track, and report on the status of links and files, both internal and external to the Web site. This enables administrators to easily identify and correct any broken or mismapped links.

Image maps may be quickly created or altered using MapThis!, an image map editor. As indicated in Figure 6-5, its interface is graphical, enabling designers to map images and embed links easily without any complex image analysis or background programming. MapThis! can likewise display or edit any NCSA-formatted image map, even though it may have been imported from a different Web server.

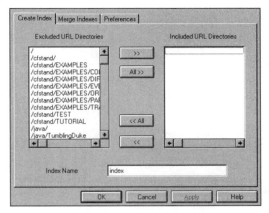

Figure 6-3
WebIndex can create indexes on a per-document or per-site basis.

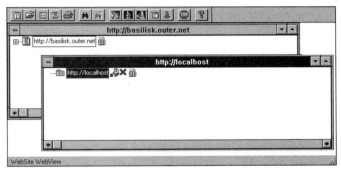

Figure 6-4
WebView shows status on individual Web sites.

WebSite's Server Side Includes feature supports a broad range of display and tracking features, which enables a page access to counters that return daily and total accesses to any given page, or other display options such as current date and time. There are 30 variables that can process and display standard HTML markup verbs for various purposes.

The WebSite Wizard function enables easy creation and publishing of standard pages, such as What's New, a WebFind Search page, and basic home pages. Using easy to understand templates, the Wizard takes the work out of creating and maintaining such essential pages on any Web site. In addition, files and images are easily uploaded to a Web space, where they maintain their link integrity. All these management and publishing tools provide true "one-button publishing."

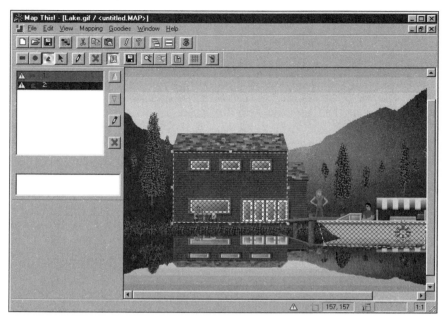

Figure 6-5
MapThis! offers a great variety of image map manipulation capabilities.

Cryptographic security

WebSite Professional is a fully functional secure commerce Web server that supports both the Secure Sockets Layer (SSL) and Secure HTTP (S-HTTP). Because WebSite Professional supports both of these secure protocols, and a variety of file system permissions systems, a multilevel security scheme can be implemented for an organization's Web site.

Regardless of the security protocol, the system administrator must obtain a public and private key certificate for use with the specific secure site. These certificates are requested, obtained, and authorized by a Certification Authority (CA), such as VeriSign. On the server side, certificates and keys are maintained through WebSite Professional's Certificate Manager function.

PUBLIC/PRIVATE KEYS AND THE CERTIFICATE MANAGER

WebSite Professional provides an easy-to-use application for requesting, storing, and maintaining public and private keys, and handles security certificates through its Certificate Manager. The system administrator uses the Certificate Wizard to request a certificate from a CA. This Wizard provides an intuitive form, wherein relevant information is entered and transmitted via e-mail to the CA (see Figure 6-6). Note that Certificates must be obtained for all virtual servers separately, because each one is unique and assigned only to a specific site.

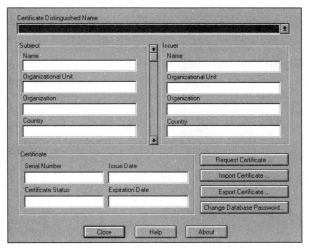

Figure 6-6
The basic wizard commands make it simple to handle certificates.

Once obtained, keys are stored in a certificate database. This enables Web administrators to use and maintain each one individually, to assign keys to specific virtual sites, and more. The Certificate Manager application is extremely secure, as is the database of certificates obtained for the entire site. The Certificate database is password-protected, so losing the password to the Certificate database could be fatal to a site. Therefore, system administrators should save the private keys and the database password onto a floppy disk, and store the disk offsite, in a secure place. Losing or compromising either the keys or the password is a severe security breach, necessitating the application for a new certificate and the installation of a new Certificate Manager.

SSL AND WEBSITE PROFESSIONAL IMPLEMENTATION

The SSL is a secure transmission protocol developed by Netscape Communications Corporation that provides data security between application protocols, such as HTTP, and standard networking protocols, such as TCP/IP, the underlying Internet protocol suite. SSL resides between the application functions used to handle network I/O and the data to be secured—in this case, Web pages and the data they contain when returned from client to server (with credit card numbers or other sensitive information).

When using an SSL-capable browser, the SSL protocol encrypts and decrypts transmitted data from the point of request (the Web server), to the point of retrieval (the client's browser). SSL uses a different port for secure Web page transmission, port 223, instead of the standard Web port, 80. This way, secure and insecure Web pages can reside on the same Web server, or even in the same directory, without compromising data security. WebSite Professional enables administrators to change these port number assignments, if necessary, for an additional level of security.

Implementing SSL into a WebSite Professional site is fairly easy. The administrator can either add SSL links to any page on the Web site, or require SSL protection for a specific URL. This is handled from the WebSite Server Properties administration window. There the Web administrator can select the directories or individual URLs that will require an SSL connection. Links that map to secure documents must be annotated by the https:// reference, rather than the standard http:// tag. Likewise, the client that requests a secure page must use a Web browser that supports the SSL protocol.

Once implemented, the function of the secure server basically stays the same as before, except that the server can handle both secured and unsecured pages. Ordinary unsecured page requests operate as they always have. But when a client requests a secure page, using the https:// markup tag, the server and the client perform a "security handshake," where they exchange and verify security certificates, and session keys are exchanged. If these prove to be valid (that is, authentication completes successfully), the keys are used so that the secure document, or documents, are encrypted and transmitted, then decrypted on the other end of the secure exchange.

CGIs, regardless of their implementation language, function the same way in this environment. That is, if a CGI is invoked on a secured page, the data it collects will be secure when transferred back from a client to the server. This enables secure posting of data on forms (such as credit card numbers) to a program (such as a credit card verification) that can then return a secure authorization code to the client. All of this is set up and maintained through WebSite Professional's Server Properties administration screen.

WebView, the WebSite Professional site management tool, uses an "unbroken key" icon to indicate that a document is secure—the same technique used in Netscape Navigator's browser display that indicates a secure link has been established. Therefore, administrators can easily recognize secure pages, as well as those that should be but are not.

WEBSITE PRO'S S-HTTP IMPLEMENTATION

While SSL provides security at the connection level, S-HTTP actually secures an entire document. The standard protocol identifier for Secure HTTP is shttp:// and must be used in document links to ensure proper delivery of an S-HTTP request. As with SSL, the end user must access secure documents with an S-HTTP enabled browser.

Figure 6-7 shows how S-HTTP is applied on a per-document basis within WebSite Professional, using its property page. S-HTTP is applied using specific styles—either predefined styles that are included with the package, or those created by the local administrator or some developer. S-HTTP styles can include three security options that govern requests for and responses to secured documents. These options, Encryption, Authentication, and Signature, may be used in any combination, depending on the security needs of the document. They're set using WebView's document properties function, and are fully customizable by the administrator.

To be more specific,

■ **Encryption** means that data to be transmitted is encrypted before transmission, and decrypted upon reception.

■ **Authentication** means that user and server certificate data is examined, to establish and confirm both sender's and receiver's identities.

■ **Signature** means that the user furnishes a digital signature used to positively identify him or her, for the purpose of making a financial transaction of some kind.

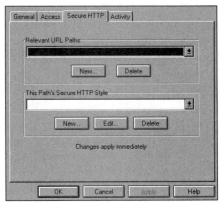

Figure 6-7
WebSite's easy S-HTTP administrator enables you to set a path to secure documents and directories quickly and easily.

Secure pages are set up by specifying an URL in the WebView properties window. Once a style is selected for that page, related request and response options may be enabled or disabled from the S-HTTP style dialog. Standard styles included with Web-Site Professional are: memo, receipt, article, communiqué, and price list. Each has its own properties, as far as how the server is to handle the secure transaction involved, as dictated by the options discussed earlier. Thus, it's possible to indicate if a response must be signed, if it is to be encrypted upon transmission, and if authentication is to be applied. These properties may be altered or removed by the system administrator, and new S-HTTP styles can be created using the S-HTTP style edit box.

When using S-HTTP in combination with a CGI program, security information must be passed through the proper CGI variables; otherwise, the document either fails to perform its intended function, or it may even be returned in an unsecured state.

Drawbacks

Though it may not seem that WebSite Professional has any problems, there are a few. The main drawback seems to be its youth. Being less than a year old, there are few such servers in operation on the Internet, compared to some of the other, more established secure servers, such as Netscape Commerce Server for Windows NT, or Apache SSL for UNIX. As WebSite Professional is implemented on a larger scale, it is possible that problems may develop that will require attention from its developers.

Netscape Enterprise Server

From the industry leader in World Wide Web browsers, servers, applications, and strategies, comes Netscape Enterprise Server, seen in Figure 6-8. Netscape began its Internet commerce vision two years ago with the release of Netscape Commerce Server. Though it lacks many of the features commonly found in Web servers today, such as content creation and site management tools, the Netscape Commerce Server remains a highly successful commercial Web server package.

Netscape Enterprise Server, on the other hand, includes a standard set of development, content creation, and site management tools (and more), making it an integrated commerce-oriented Web server package. These features, combined with a speed upgrade and advanced connection-level capabilities, have made it possible for Netscape to tout Enterprise Server as the fastest Web server on the market. Enterprise Server runs on multiple platforms, with versions available for SunOS, HP-UX, and AIX, to name a few; on Windows NT, it requires the Server Version 3.51 Service Pack 4 or Windows NT Server 4.0. So, if your network administrator has been looking for a reason to upgrade the NT Server, this should be reason enough.

Features
Netscape Enterprise Server has inherited and enhanced the common features of its predecessor, Commerce Server. These include

- easy configuration (10-minute installation, even for inexperienced Web administrators),

- a familiar Netscape Navigator administration interface,

- and other standard Web server features, including CGI support, management functions for processor management, log reporting, server activity, page activity, and more.

And though Netscape Enterprise Server only supports the Secure Sockets Layer (S-HTTP) protocol (developed by Netscape), the server utilizes its own permissions and authorization functions, enabling the server to allow or deny access by user name and password, DNS or IP, and named groups. On Windows NT, this extends and enhances the built-in security and permissions management.

In addition to these capabilities, Enterprise adds many administrative functions, programming tools, and content development features. From a graphic display of an entire Web site using the LiveWire add-on, to an onboard Java compiler, Netscape Enterprise has become the leader in third-generation Web servers. Here's a more detailed list of these features, each with a brief explanation:

- **Site management.** Enterprise Server's management features appear through a familiar Netscape Navigator interface, as seen in Figure 6-9, providing for seamless integration, configuration, and ongoing administration.

- **Remote administration.** By setting an administrative port ID, a Web administrator may access the management engine from anywhere on the Internet, using Netscape Navigator. An administrative user name and password are all that is required. This is a distinct advantage over WebSite Professional and other NT-based Web servers, and gives Netscape Enterprise Server the same versatility as most UNIX-based Web servers.

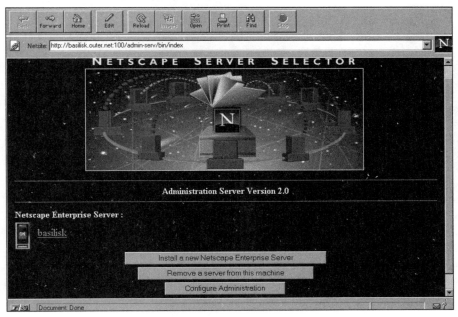

Figure 6-8
The familiar Netscape interface to the administrative functions of Enterprise Server make Web site management intuitive and easy. ©1996 Netscape Communications Corp. All rights reserved. This page may not be reprinted or copied without the express written permission of Netscape.

- **Simple Network Management Protocol (SNMP).** Support for SNMP provides standards-based remote monitoring and management capabilities from any SNMP management application (such as SunNet Manager, NetView, or OpenView).

- **Logging and reporting.** Enterprise Server supports Common Log Format, Flexible Log Format, and Proxy Log Format, enabling administrators to generate reports based on hit rates, transfer site identifiers, pages and documents accessed, and request origination data. These logs can pinpoint the heaviest traffic times, and any errors which a server encounters during operation, including unauthorized access attempts and security problems.

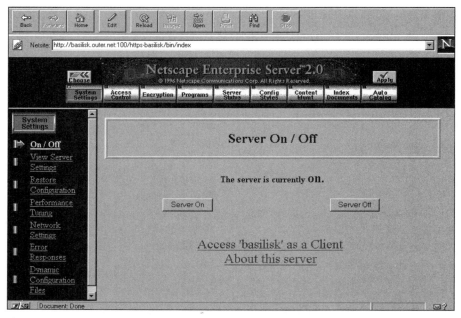

Figure 6-9
The core administrative screen enables the webmaster to access all management functions from a handy, top-level tool bar. ©1996 Netscape Communications Corp. All rights reserved. This page may not be reprinted or copied without the express written permission of Netscape.

- **Automatic indexing.** This enables administrators to index the site or sites in question quickly and easily, and to build powerful search facilities. (This is now a standard for most Web servers.)

- **Historical configuration.** This function enables administrators to reinstate past configurations, should the current one become corrupted, or otherwise unusable.

- **Common server management.** This general administrative tool enables system administrators to configure multiple servers from the same interface.

- **LiveWire visual site management tool.** LiveWire provides a graphically browsable snapshot of the organization for an entire site. This enables the administrator to drag and drop files and directories to new locations and even restructure an entire site, quickly and efficiently. LiveWire automatically updates links on pages to correctly map to images and other files within a site, and checks the status of external links on a periodic basis. LiveWire also supports document and image conversion, and includes an onboard JavaScript compiler.

DEVELOPMENT AND CGI SUPPORT

Though not as rich in development tools as WebSite, Enterprise supports a wide range of development options. Here's a list of its capabilities in this area:

- **CGI scripting.** Enterprise supports a wide range of CGI and WinCGI scripts to interface Web pages to applications and other programs. ActiveX support is expected in the next release of Enterprise.

- **Application management.** As with the general site administration, management of applications is possible remotely from any node on the network.

- **Java and JavaScript support.** Enables deployment of server- or client-side Java programs for development of cross-platform Internet applications.

- **Support of development tools.** Including Java and C, and traditional HTML and VRML editors. (These tools must be acquired separately.)

- **NSAPI server extension.** Enables developers to modify or enhance the performance and behavior of the Netscape Enterprise Server itself. As with other Application Programming Interfaces, NSAPI provides for an interface for a variety of programming languages, such as C and C++.

CONTENT DEVELOPMENT TOOLS

Compared to WebSite Professional, Enterprise Server is noticeably lacking in content development tools. Though it lacks an onboard HTML editor, Netscape's Navigator Gold, should be easy to integrate with Enterprise Server. What Enterprise *does* implement, with considerable success, is a multiple version document control function (the content management screen is shown in Figure 6-10). Here's a list of relevant features:

- **MKS integrity engine.** Enables users to check out documents, edit them, then upload changed versions to the server. While this happens, the document is locked, prohibiting other users from editing that document. The engine also enables documents to roll back to previous versions, in case changes need to be undone. Version control enables groups of Web designers to work on the same set of documents, while maintaining document and data integrity.

- **Dynamic server-parsed HTML tags.** These tags enable designers to dynamically insert content into a Web page and update information automatically. Such volatile data as office supply requests, manufacturing test data, and other changing content is easy to include and display.

SECURITY, COMMERCE, AND SSL

Enterprise Server offers multiple levels of security, and can be configured to use SSL for transmission of secure documents, as well as a standard set of permission and authentication engines, to grant or deny access to files or directories. Netscape Enterprise Server supports a wide variety of security options, which can be used either on their own or in combination with Windows NT's built-in security and permission systems. Here are some of the specifics:

■ **Advanced access control.** As seen in Figure 6-11, Enterprise comes equipped with flexible read/write access control across files or directories, allowing or denying users by use of X.509v3 certificates, user names and passwords, domains, IPs, or via grouping of memberships.

■ **Secure Sockets Layer 3.0 support.** For intranet or Internet secure document transmissions, Enterprise implements SSL. As noted in the WebSite section, SSL provides security at the connection level, allowing authorized users with valid certificates access to secured documents and files.

■ **Client-side certificate authentication.** Enterprise's certificate authentication function enables the server to authenticate clients using public key certificates (X.509v3). CA configuration can be dynamic or static, depending on the needs of the organization.

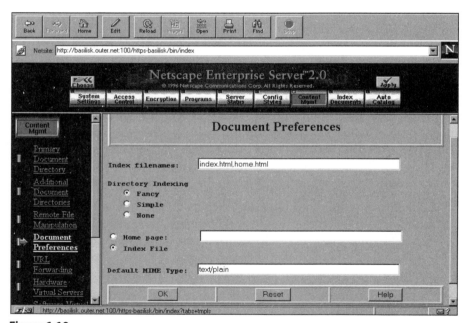

Figure 6-10
Enterprise Server's content management screen enables the webmaster to set specific variables for each document or directory within the Web server. ©1996 Netscape Communications Corp. All rights reserved. This page may not be reprinted or copied without the express written permission of Netscape.

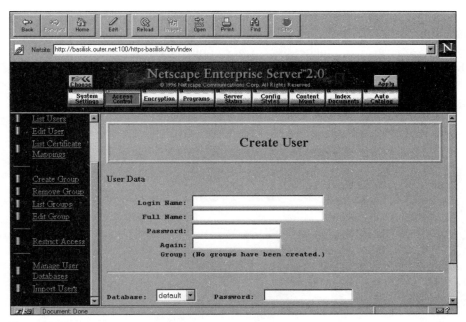

Figure 6-11
A very flexible user and group access management function enables the Web administrator to regulate access to sensitive files and directories using a "log in and password" procedure. ©1996 Netscape Communications Corp. All rights reserved. This page may not be reprinted or copied without the express written permission of Netscape.

IMPLEMENTING SSL AND OTHER SECURITY OPTIONS From the Netscape Configuration Manager, implementing SSL is easy and intuitive. Dialogs walk the administrator through the necessary procedures. From generating a key pair, to applying for and installing a certificate from a CA, there's built-in guidance and support along the way. As pictured in Figure 6-12, Enterprise stores its certificate information in a file that is password protected, accessible only to the Web administrator.

Netscape Enterprise Server, like Commerce Server, enables administrators to implement a user database, much like a password file on a UNIX system. This database allows or denies access to individual pages or sites based on user names, domain names, and/or IP addresses. This database is independent of the user access privileges inherent in Windows NT; by using this database, the Web server can be further secured from unauthorized access.

Drawbacks
Some of Netscape Enterprise Server's more obvious drawbacks are that you have to pay extra for the management and development features that are included with WebSite

Professional, such as programming kits and a built-in certificate manager. The reason for the product's lack of features appears to be an effect of Netscape's deliberate Internet solutions strategy. For a higher price, you can buy Netscape's Suite Spot package, which includes many of these features with added capabilities.

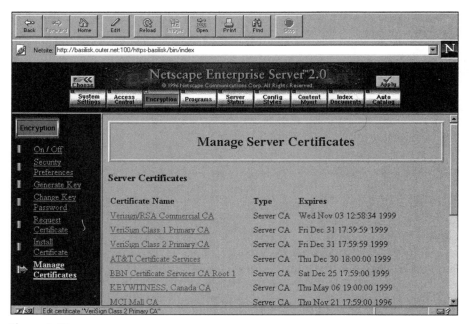

Figure 6-12
The Certificate Manager allows the Enterprise Server administrator easy access to all security certificates installed on the server.

There are several drawbacks to using Enterprise Server as a Web commerce engine. The main objection is price—Enterprise Server ($995 list) costs about twice as much as WebSite and other popular commerce servers (and infinitely more than Microsoft's IIS, which is bundled with Windows NT 4.0). Nevertheless, Enterprise Server is touted as the fastest commerce server on the market, despite the fact that its predecessor (Commerce Server) had functionality issues that caused some concern. Though Commerce Server seemed to perform on the high end with regard to throughput and latency, under a very heavy load it tended to shut down quietly, with no error messages. Enterprise doesn't appear to have this problem and delivers the same high performance (albeit at a premium price).

Furthermore, Enterprise Server's distinct lack of software development kits and well-rounded content development tools, as well as the fact that SSL is its only secure protocol, makes Enterprise a far from complete Web site solution. The recent introduction of Netscape Navigator Gold means that an easily integrated Web page design tool is now available, but Enterprise itself lacks an onboard editor. For that reason, we suspect that Navigator Gold may be bundled with Enterprise Server in the future. Even so, Navigator Gold is still considered a bit buggy and limiting (based on current beta versions), whereas HotDog's interface and options are viewed as much more useful. Likewise, Enterprise lacks an image map editor, requiring the purchase of a third party product.

Choosing a Secure Commerce Server

As with any wide-scale network services implementation, system administrators must weigh the needs of the network against the packages available. This is not an easy job, by any means, because there are assuredly many more Web servers in general, and commerce servers in particular, than most administrators have time to consider. To help in this decision-making process, we suggest that the main points any administrator should consider are features, security, compatibility, and price.

Some simple tables that compare WebSite Professional to Netscape Enterprise Server follow. While perusing their contents, be sure to remember that these are not the only solutions available for Windows NT-based secure Web servers, but they are the most broadly used packages for that platform today.

We're of the opinion that the O'Reilly product is a better value than Netscape Enterprise Server, especially for smaller organizations that may not need the extra performance that Enterprise Server can provide. As you examine their comparison in these tables, however, feel free to draw your own conclusions.

TABLE 6-1: MANAGEMENT FEATURES

POINT	WEBSITE PRO	ENTERPRISE SERVER
remote administration	No	Yes
intuitive interface	Yes	Yes
site snapshot management	Yes	Yes
automatic indexing	Yes	Yes
standard logging	Yes	Yes
historical configuration	No	Yes

TABLE 6-2: CONTENT DEVELOPMENT

POINT	WEBSITE PRO	ENTERPRISE SERVER
HTML editor included	Yes	No
image map editor	Yes	No
CGI editor	Yes	No
document integrity	No	Yes
dynamic link insertion	No	Yes
Server Side Includes	Yes	No

TABLE 6-3: DEVELOPMENT FEATURES

POINT	WEBSITE PRO	ENTERPRISE SERVER
support for Java	Yes	Yes
Java development kit	Yes	No
support for CGI & WinCGI	Yes	Yes
support for Perl	Yes	Yes
API support	Yes	Yes
Visual Basic support	Yes	No

TABLE 6-4: SECURITY

POINT	WEBSITE PRO	ENTERPRISE SERVER
SSL	Yes	Yes
S-HTTP	Yes	No
permissions and authentication	Yes	Yes
security logging	Yes	Yes

TABLE 6-5: COMPATIBILITY

POINT	WEBSITE PRO	ENTERPRISE SERVER
Windows NT server	Yes	Yes*
Windows NT workstation	Yes	No
Windows 95	Yes	No

(* *Windows NT 3.51 Service Pack 4 or Windows NT 4.0*)

Summary

Given that a recent survey of offerings shows us that over a dozen Web servers are available for Windows NT, with at least half providing secure transaction support, you may be tempted to do some investigation on your own in this area. To that end, we'd like to provide you with an excellent search and comparison tool. If you visit David Strom's WebCompare site, prepared for *InfoWorld*, you'll find a current listing of Web server offerings available, along with current comparisons and benchmarking information. We can hardly recommend a better place to start your own search. Visit this URL

```
http://webcompare.iworld.com/
```

and you should come away well-equipped with the latest data to help you select a secure server for NT (or other platforms) that meets your needs—and your budget!

CHAPTER SEVEN

SECURE WEB SERVERS FOR THE MACINTOSH

I n this chapter we discuss the operating advantages derived from using a Macintosh at the core of your Web commerce. We also look at the preeminent secure Web server that's available for the MacOS (WebSTAR/SSL), and cover a generic setup and walkthrough of a server that's fully configured for secure transactions.

Where Does the Mac Fit in with Other Secure Servers?

The Macintosh, typically regarded as a desktop workstation, graphics machine, or even, in some circles, as simply a toy, is frequently overlooked when an IS department goes shopping for a small- to medium-sized network server solution. The Macintosh *should* be considered, because of its ease of set up, simplicity of maintenance and use, and relatively low cost.

UNIX may be overkill

The Mac has a considerable advantage when compared to other, larger servers, particularly of the UNIX variety. UNIX servers, by their very nature, house complex and daunting operating systems, full of Internet services. This makes a UNIX Web server only *one* of *many* services that a normal system could run, which in turn often makes the security of the total system suspect.

Monitoring everything that a UNIX machine does at any one instant is more than most casual network administrators have time for. If your intention is to run a small- to medium-sized server, or if you have limited technical resources, the Mac may be a great answer to your Web security needs. Plus, if you outgrow the machine, upgrading to a larger, more robust system is always a possibility.

The Mac advantage

Mac systems, by virtue of their systems architecture, are much less susceptible to security compromises than most UNIX systems; therefore, they're a better option for a secure Web server. If that isn't a good enough reason to use a Mac, consider this: Secure servers are usually used for low-traffic, highly confidential data transport, which is well within the operating parameters of what a typical Mac can handle. In addition, you or your company may already have an extra Macintosh available that is adequate for use as a secure server. There may be an AppleShare server on your network that has almost no current load, which is a great place to plant a fledgling Mac Web commerce server.

When a Mac makes sense as a secure server

Here are four situations for which we recommend using a Macintosh as a secure Web server, with an explanation for each scenario:

YOU'RE NOT CONNECTED

If your operation is a predominantly Macintosh shop, even if you aren't using any sort of Internet server software—even if you aren't connected to the Internet—using a Mac is *ideal* because of the low technology and learning investment it will take to get things running. Just as it's better not to jump into deep water without a floatation device, it's better not to jump into equipment and software that you will need hours of training to handle, or that might force you to hire a full-time system administrator to manage.

YOU'RE ALREADY USING A WEBSTAR SERVER

If you already use a WebSTAR server, you should consider obtaining their secure server. After all, you've already survived the hard part by obtaining the experience and expertise required to manage and maintain a Web server and its associated Internet or network connection. Even if your office is dominated by PCs, installing a Mac secure server is a sound idea, if that's what you already know how to manage.

YOU NEED A QUICK COMMERCE FIX (OR TEST)

Large Web sites with hundreds of CGIs and thousands of documents can use Macs to establish an immediate toehold for secure transactions, or simply to test new secure pages before they're placed into production. As you'll learn later in this chapter, setting up a Mac for secure transactions only requires around two hours of effort, provided a digital ID has already been obtained. If you compare this to the effort required to set up a PC- or workstation-based secure Web server, the Mac option makes a lot of sense.

YOUR SITE USES MAC CGIS

For any Web site that already uses Macs running WebSTAR with custom-built CGI programs, installing a secure Macintosh Web server makes perfect sense. Whether they're using those CGIs to deliver form or query reply data, such as from a database, or from some other custom ACGI, it's almost perfunctory to add a secure Web server to the mix. Even large sites and/or those with multiple points of Web access that funnel the bulk of their traffic to Web servers running on UNIX, can still rely on smaller Macintosh-based servers to handle lesser volumes of secure traffic.

To summarize, we recommend a Macintosh secure server for small Mac-based companies; organizations that already use Mac servers or are Mac-literate; organizations that need simple internal solutions or that only want to test the ins and outs of Web-based commerce; and companies looking for a quick setup and simple operation of a secure Web server.

Are Mac servers secure?

Some may ask, "Is the security on a Mac as good as a *real* server?" Our answer is an emphatic "Yes!" All SSL Servers conform to a protocol guideline originally proposed by Netscape to enforce uniformity in all secure connections. Although the details involved are beyond the scope of this book, SSL is more that just a "secure Web transfer" protocol. SSL provides a secure low-level connection, which can be used for e-mail, news feeds, or even Telnet streams. Anything that uses TCP/IP can ride atop an SSL stream.

The encryption technology used to scramble the bits at the sending server's end, and then used again by the receiving browser to unscramble them, relies upon one of two fancy mathematical algorithms. Macintosh-based secure Web servers, like their UNIX or NT brethren, can use any of the techniques currently available to encrypt data. These techniques fall primarily into three main categories (refer to Chapter 2 for more details):

- RC4-40 (an international standard for use worldwide)
- RC4-128 (a U.S.-only technique; imposes higher security and longer wait times for encryption and decryption)
- DES (typically used by the U.S. Government and in UNIX password files)

Netscape users are given a choice for their preferred level of encryption. In researching this book, we learned that the international version of Netscape supports only the least secure of these three encryption methods, RC4-40. Due to the U.S. restriction on the export of cryptosystems, the international version of Netscape is less secure than the U.S.-only one. One quick way to tell is to connect to a site that supports RC4-128 and examine the picture of the key in the left hand corner of a Netscape window. If the key has 2 teeth, it uses 128 bit encryption (RC4-128); but if it has only 1 tooth, it uses 40 bit encryption (RC4-40). To make our browsers provide a more secure form of transport, we were required to upgrade to the domestic version of Netscape, which may be found at

www.netscape.com .

The domestic version supports all three varieties of secure connections. If your browser does not appear to include all of these choices under the Securities Option menu, the odds are that you will need to download the domestic version from the URL we just mentioned. Of course, if you are primarily involved with International Web commerce, this may not be required. We recommend it anyway, because each and every secure connection is negotiated afresh by the server and the browser every time a secure link is requested. If you use the domestic version of Netscape, it will use the higher level of security where it's supported, and will only temporarily lower your security level for international exchanges.

WebSTAR/SSL: The Only Choice

In our quest for secure Macintosh-based secure Web servers we found only one real choice, WebSTAR/SSL. That's why it serves as the focus for the remainder of this chapter. One big plus is that it comes with its own security toolkit. Another big plus is that if you already have a regular WebSTAR server, you can simply upgrade it to SSL level. Quarterdeck offers the security toolkit and a commerce toolkit as add-ons, which, respectively, enables the WebSTAR server to provide SSL capabilities, and adds support for commercial transactions using the First Virtual Internet Payment System.

Although it differs considerably from a real-time online transaction-processing system, the First Virtual Internet Payment System is highly secure, quite affordable, and requires no additional hardware or software. Though it can be somewhat clumsy when compared to a credit card swipe system, it offers an excellent compromise between cost and capability. First Virtual is also especially well-suited to products that require small, incremental payments.

When shopping for a Mac . . .

As with all things, money is usually a strong contributing factor when shopping for a new product. According to Quarterdeck, it's a major factor that contributes heavily to the following statistic:

> *Recent studies have shown that over 20% of the Web servers in use on the Internet today are using WebSTAR servers on the Macintosh.*

WebSTAR requires a computer with a processor capable of handling a large workload. Since encryption techniques are CPU-intensive, you need a high-performance computer for your commerce server. The makers of WebSTAR/SSL recommend the following minimum configuration for their software:

- A Power Macintosh computer (RISC Chip based 601/603/604)

- 12MB of RAM (The server will operate with less, but 12-16MB is optimal.)

- System Software 7.0.1 or later (a requirement of the server software)

- A dedicated TCP/IP connection, such as a T1, fractional T1, or ISDN line

A brief history of WebSTAR

WebSTAR and WebSTAR/SSL both started out as MacHTTP, written by Chuck Shotton in the late 1980s. It's still possible to obtain a copy of MacHTTP at various places on the Internet. But as you will learn in the next few paragraphs, a wealth of features have been added to this application, making the commercial versions much more capable and robust. Not the least of these features is the SSL toolkit, which is the focus for this chapter.

WebSTAR/SSL boasts the following features:

■ Supports HTTP/1.0

■ Handles URLs that reference HTML, JPEG, GIF, and other binary formats

■ Handles CGI applications with AppleScript and AppleEvents

■ Provides access control based on IP addresses or domain names

■ Performs user name/password authentication on a per-file or per-folder basis

■ A native PowerPC implementation of WebSTAR/SSL is available

■ Supports Apple's Open Transport; handles more than 64 TCP/IP streams simultaneously

Starting with version 1.3, WebSTAR sports a list of enhanced features, which are detailed briefly in the sections that follow. These enhancements put WebSTAR on par with better-known, robust UNIX- and NT-based solutions, making it more acceptable for production use than its predecessors may have been.

CONNECTION SPEED UPGRADE

To increase its throughput and connection processing, WebSTAR now makes use of the Thread Manager built into the MacOS. (The Thread Manager is built directly into System 7.5 but requires an extension to System 7.1.) The Thread Manager provides a cleaner multitasking environment for WebSTAR, enabling it to handle more simultaneous connections without having to spend time waiting for each thread to complete. Quarterdeck claims that controlled laboratory tests prove WebSTAR can handle over 1,000,000 discrete connections in a single day (24 hours), through the good agencies of the Thread Manager.

REMOTE ADMINISTRATION

One of the features that makes WebSTAR great when compared to other Web servers, no matter which environment they support, is its remote administration capabilities. WebSTAR includes a Macintosh application called WebSTAR Admin that enables system administrators to control their Web servers from any location on an AppleTalk network, using a secure connection. WebSTAR Admin can also control multiple WebSTAR servers, which makes it a great tool for any webmasters who must manage servers distributed across multiple sites.

Furthermore, starting with WebSTAR 1.2, administrators can also use the Internet and a browser to configure their servers. WebSTAR now includes an administration component in the form of a CGI program, which permits administrators access to nearly all of WebSTAR's functions through a simple and comfortable browser interface. For example, administrators can examine the maximum number of simultaneous users allowed, inspect default home page assignments, control server logging, and restart the server, all from within a set of Web-based control pages. Figure 7-1 shows what WebSTAR Admin looks like.

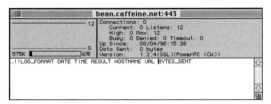

Figure 7-1
The WebSTAR Admin Status screen is an example of the easy-to-use interface.

BACKGROUND-ONLY VERSION

WebSTAR/SSL, like its counterpart WebSTAR, comes with a background-only application. This is good for internal security, and even performs a little better than the one that runs within a display window on-screen. The product's backgrounding feature prevents administrators from accidentally making the Web server unavailable when they unintentionally exit WebSTAR.

As most Mac users can attest, accidentally hitting ⌘Q, instead of ⌘W, can easily shut down applications, sometimes without the user's knowledge; not to mention the common mishap of using a keyboard that is connected to a different computer than you think. This is especially true in situations where the Mac Web server is housed with a variety of other servers in one room. There is also the potential for confusion when several machines use a common switch box for access.

URL PROCESSING IMPROVEMENTS

One nice feature of WebSTAR is its capability for handling the preprocessing and postprocessing of URL requests. Preprocessing a request enables local programs to take action on an URL before it ever hits the Web server. Consequently, it's possible to balance the load across multiple servers, or redirect URL requests to other servers based on their contents. Postprocessing supports operations that would be applied after a Web server has already responded to an incoming request.

Like UNIX servers, WebSTAR supports HTML file aliasing, pointing to files, folders, or even external volumes through a name translation that's completely invisible to outsiders. For security reasons, WebSTAR will not allow users to access aliases that point outside the document root on the volume where the WebSTAR document folder resides, but it does permit users to refer to remote volumes as if they were located within the root folder. Hence, Macintosh network mount points, CD-ROMs, and AppleShare volumes that reside on other network servers can be made available to service user requests (albeit indirectly).

CGI IMPROVEMENTS

With the rise of a complete scripting language for the Macintosh, developed by Apple itself, called the AppleScript Development Environment, WebSTAR supports almost everything in AppleScript worth supporting. WebSTAR is recordable, attachable, and scriptable, and there's a vast selection of pre-existing scripts ready to download, purchase, or modify based on your site's requirements.

Typical scripts deliver support for clickable maps, text search, CGI form handling, database access, and audio or video capture and playback. WebSTAR also supports extended Apple Events, enabling better interaction and integration with applications such as ListSTAR, not to mention customized applications that you might create or purchase for your Web site.

CGIs can be created with almost any programming or scripting language, such as Apple's MacApp Development Environment, Metrowerk's Code Warrior compiler Suites, MacPERL, or the Frontier enhancements and additions to AppleScript. Basically, all of these are just general application development tools, which can be distilled down into the process of taking input from a FORM, conducting a series of operations based on the variables retrieved from it, and outputting the results as an HTML page.

Earlier WebSTAR implementations limited the amount of return data from a CGI to 32KB, but the current version of WebSTAR can deliver unlimited amounts of such data, making constant "server push" technologies available through WebSTAR.

LOCALIZATION VIA STRING RESOURCES

The current version of WebSTAR can be modified with ResEdit, or a similar resource editor, to localize the Web server to your part of the world. Most built-in messages are available as String Resources (STR#) in the application's resource fork for you to modify or localize to some language other than English.

Obtaining the WebSTAR/SSL secure server

Just as most manufacturers of UNIX secure servers allow you to download and test their servers from the Internet, so Quarterdeck allows you to do the same with WebSTAR/SSL. And as with UNIX server vendors, you'll need to provide Quarterdeck with some information about yourself and your location first. The demo version of WebSTAR/SSL is available at `http://www.starnine.com/webstarssl/webstarssl.html`, and the evaluation period is thirty days.

Obtaining a digital ID from VeriSign

As with all Secure Servers, WebSTAR cannot be used—or even started—without assigning it a digital ID from one of the certificate sources certified by RSA and VeriSign. Although they claim a three to five day turn around, our ID took about two weeks to obtain when all was said and done. Digital IDs cost around $250 for the first year. After that, it will run about $100 to maintain the worldwide active key.

Before firing up WebSTAR/SSL, you need to run the following ID applications, send a letter to VeriSign, and wait for a signed certificate to follow. Once your certificate is in hand, you can extract the key and put your server to work.

Next we explore the different applications contained in the folder shown in Figure 7-2, what they do, and why they're needed.

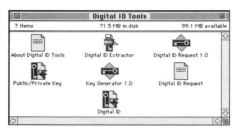

Figure 7-2
The digital ID applications needed for full server operations.

KEY GENERATOR
This application creates a public/private pair of keys for use with your WebSTAR/SSL server. The keys are stored in a file called Public/Private Key, which must be placed in the same folder as the WebSTAR/SSL application; otherwise, it will not operate correctly. The file will look like garbage if you open it with a text editor. Remember the password that you used to create this file, because you'll need it later in the configuration process. Try not to write it down where others might accidentally see it. You don't want anyone running their own secure Web server using your digital ID!

REQUESTING A DIGITAL ID
Digital IDs are used whenever two parties negotiate a secure communication channel by using a third party as a point of reference. In this case (and in most cases with secure servers) that third party is VeriSign, a subsidiary of RSA, the encryption company.

What VeriSign does is to authenticate your identity. This is why you should keep the Public/Private Key file secure. It's also essential that your password be uncrackable. A good password or passphrase is one that is hard for you to remember, impossible for anyone else to guess. Most security experts recommend a password that consists of two randomly generated words, separated by punctuation marks or numbers, including a mixture of upper and lowercase letters. Do not use your birth date, spouse's name, or anything even potentially obvious.

By running the Digital ID Request application, and by entering all its fields correctly, you should end up with a text document called a Digital ID Request. You'll need to mail this document to VeriSign for processing, which may take up to a week to complete. Be sure to use the same password you used to create your public/private keys in the previous section in this form, because it's your only method of authentication for this postal transaction.

RECEIVING A DIGITAL ID

If all goes as planned, you should receive an e-mail response from VeriSign that includes a text document as an attachment. This document should be extracted using the Digital ID Extractor tool, which creates your Digital ID file. Take this file and place it with your Public/Private Key file in the WebSTAR/SSL main folder. This will fully enable your server to conduct secure transactions from here on out. Also, store a copy of the original VeriSign certificate file elsewhere, for good measure.

WebSTAR/SSL setup and configuration

As you can see from Figure 7-3, once a digital ID has been entered and the server launched, it looks pretty much like its sibling, the generic version of WebSTAR. In the discussion that follows, we review some of the most important elements in this display.

Figure 7-3
The WebSTAR/SSL Main Status Screen.

The main fields contained on this window have the following attributes:

- **Total.** The total number of clients served.

- **Max.** The maximum number of concurrent incoming connections.

- **Listening.** The number of TCP/IP sessions listening for a new connection from a browser. Ones that are currently handling clients are taken off the listening list and added to the current list while these sessions are active. Server memory should be set to allow for about 100KB per listener.

- **Current.** The total number of connections currently serviced by the Web server.

■ **High.** Reflects the peak number of simultaneous users since the application was launched. Use this as a gauge to determine if you have the maximum number of users set correctly. This field is also known as the "high-water mark."

■ **Busy.** The number of clients that have been refused service because the server was too busy. If this value is non-zero, you may need to increase the Max Users setting. If you are on a super-busy network, or demand on the server is such that the machine will always be busy, consider installing another server to help balance this load.

■ **Denied.** The number of clients denied access based on a failure to authenticate with the allow/deny security scheme. Realm security violations are not logged here.

■ **Timeout.** The number of connections terminated because the server timeout interval had elapsed, usually caused by a CGI application consuming too much time before it returns its results. This could also happen if a client were to disappear from the network, usually caused by a crashed machine, terminating browser software, network failure, or modem lockup.

Mistakes and MIS-steps with WebSTAR/SSL

If you've already been using WebSTAR for the Macintosh, using the SSL version will be a breeze. As a matter of fact, many sites do an installation of WebSTAR/SSL in the same folder where the currently server resides. This puts all Web related documents together in one easy-to-find place. You don't have to worry about the servers fighting over control files, because WebSTAR and WebSTAR/SSL use different setting and log files, which can be configured to root at a different point in the server's folder hierarchy. This is recommended because it keeps secured documents out of the main tree and vice versa.

It is important to remember that you only need to keep a small subset of your HTML files (or CGIs) in the document root of the SSL server. This is because the encryption and decryption phases of the Web server's communication from client to server is laborious, and can significantly slow down access to your server.

Many files on a normal Web server don't need to be encrypted, so our advice to you is to sift through your site to figure out what needs to be secure and what doesn't. Place all of the secure pages in a different tree and root the SSL server there. From pages in the normal document root, you can refer to secure pages using the https protocol tag and a full path in the new secure root. From pages in the secure tree, refer links back to the normal server the same way (as full paths with the standard http tag). All other paths, in either of the two trees, can be relative within each of the respective trees.

If you are rooting both of your HTML document trees together, refer to secure documents using full path names, rather than relative ones. By using a relative path, such as /main/stuff.html, requests to a secure server may force all such documents through encryption. That's because unless it's explicitly defined, a partial URL referenced in a document retrieved via WebSTAR/SSL will attempt to use the https:// protocol rather than the regular http:// protocol. As you can guess, this could lead to a ton of unwanted encryption, making your server appear slow and unwieldy to clients. Using a full path, such as `http://www.website.com/main/stuff.html` or `https://www.website.com/main/secure.stuff.html` is how to guarantee that links take the client where you want them to go.

Other common problems with WebSTAR/SSL and the regular WebSTAR application derive from the allocation of main memory to the servers. Here's the relevant material, taken directly from the WebSTAR technical manual:

> *The following formula is a basic guideline for allocating WebSTAR application memory:*
>
> *100K X Max_Users + 750K = WebSTAR application memory*
>
> *However, if you are running CGI applications, you may want to allocate more application memory to the WebSTAR server. Most sites allocate a minimum of 2.5MB for the default 12 connections. Up to 4MB of memory is recommended for 25 connections. To access your WebSTAR server once it is running, you'll need client software, such as Netscape Navigator or Mosaic. If you run a browser on the same Macintosh as the server, you will need at least 2MB of free memory, and server performance will decrease while the browser is running.*

Consider two servers

If you are able to, we suggest running two different Web servers on two different machines. Run one machine using the regular version of WebSTAR, the other with the SSL version. By using two machines, you move the processing power needed for secure transactions to one machine, leaving the other to deal with the bulk of the traffic. This creates a nice segregation of secure and insecure material as well, especially if you are seriously concerned about the physical security of the hardware hosting the SSL server.

For example, a company we recently consulted with required a secure server for low volume traffic, in order to assist employees with benefits options and payroll deductions. Initially, this server was married with the other servers that made up this client's intranet. The customers of this system were the company's own employees, and the privacy of all employee records needed to be guaranteed; hence the need for a solid Web security program. Because the company had already been using Macs to handle a variety of their intranet needs, adding a Mac-based secure Web server the perfect solution. For them it was easy to set up and use, and it provided the necessary security.

Troubleshooting and some tips

While running a WebSTAR/SSL server, we ran into a few things you might need to consider regarding its operation. The following are detailed tips for quick reference.

"SSL HANDSHAKE FAILED"

If WebSTAR/SSL launches normally, but while trying to connect to the server your browser comes back with a "No Data" page, or does not complete, and the server reports that "SSL handshake failed," you may have a corrupt digital ID. To cure this, simply get out your extra copy of the original VeriSign certificate file that you stashed away for good measure (see "About Digital ID Extractor"), and regenerate your ID.

If you try to set up two servers using the same digital ID, it will also give you the "SSL Handshake failed" message. Remember, the certificate is customized all the way down to the name of the machine that the ID is intended for, so it can't work on another machine. There is no way around this problem; to run two servers you need two unique digital IDs.

"-23009"

Another common message is "-23009," which you might notice in your log file. As with the regular WebSTAR application, this message indicates that there are too many TCP/IP connections allocated to the server. Using the older TCP/IP software for the Macintosh (MacTCP) the limit stands at sixty-four *total* connections. The most likely cause for this error occurs when you run both your regular server and an SSL server on the same machine, and both are set to sixty-four connections, or the sum of their connections is greater than sixty-four. If your servers are busy enough to merit this configuration, you need to either split the servers across two different machines, or rework the data on the servers to lower the aggregate number of simultaneous users.

Another, probably better option, is to install Apple's new TCP/IP protocol stack on your server, Open Transport (OT). This software is typically shipped with Apple's new operating systems (System 7.5) but you can also download it from a variety of Apple public FTP servers. Some Macs have the software installed, but it may be disabled. To switch your system from MacTCP to OT, check in your Apple Extras folder for an application called Network Software Selector. This enables you to change the selection.

PROXY SERVERS

Even though we ran into these problems specifically on our Mac SSL server, variations can occur on any SSL server. For instance, your SSL server is connected to the Internet and users connecting from AOL, CompuServe, or GEnie complain that they are unable to access your pages. You check the server and all is well. The reason for this behavior is that SSL transactions cannot occur through a proxy server. Proxy servers are used to firewall private networks from the Internet by enabling them to connect to third-party sources through a known intermediary machine. In fact, that's how AOL, CompuServe, and GEnie support Internet access. The solution is for your customers to use another connection that does not go through a proxy server. Another possibility is that you have set up your server inside your network, which only allows access via a gateway proxy server. The solution here is to allow port 443 access across your network gateways, if that's acceptable to your network operations team.

RELATIVE REFERENCES

The most common problem is the misuse of relative references in your HTML. This is relevant only if you run a regular, unsecured server alongside an SSLserver in parallel, where both use the same directory structure. It's common practice to use relative links rather than fully qualified path names in most HTML documents. Some HTML generation tools even create tags with relative links. The problem is that once a page is handled by the SSL server, all subsequent pages are routed through that server as well, because everything is encrypted from that point forward. This makes the server sluggish. One solution is to use full path names in all documents, and to explicitly use the https:// protocol tag when a page needs to be pulled from a secure server.

Another solution is to make all references from the SSL server that point back at the unsecured server, and vice versa, fully qualified. This way, you can corral a user to use whichever server they need to be using, without the unwarranted encryption along the way.

Summary

The Macintosh is a good secure server choice for a variety of reasons. Mac systems are intrinsically more secure, and easier to work with than the sometimes daunting task of running and maintaining a UNIX server. If you're already using a Mac Web server, or have a Macintosh-based operation, a Macintosh secure Web server may indeed be the best choice for you. The in-depth examination of the WebSTAR/SSL secure server software (the only real choice for the Macintosh) divulged some useful secrets about that server's operation, and should help you decide if using a Macintosh-based commerce site is right for you. You now have all the information you'll need to get started using a Macintosh secure server. The next chapter will further expand the electronic commerce equation by describing some secure Internet payment solutions.

CHAPTER EIGHT

NET CASH SOLUTIONS

In Chapter 3, we introduced some third-party payment systems. This chapter provides more detail about how to install and use these various options. We explore several of the companies' solutions that provide electronic equivalents for cash exchanges or alternatives to shipping sensitive information across the Internet. We start with two of the major digital cash vendors—CyberCash and Ecash. Next, we examine the mechanics of the payment system offered by First Virtual Holdings, which handles credit card transactions through a masterful bit of indirection that keeps its Internet communications wholly devoid of sensitive information of any kind.

The main trusted third-party payment organizations are as old as the concept of secure Internet commerce itself. Many of the founders and developers of these systems were innovators in the fields of Internet security, networking systems, and the Internet as a whole. You should be able to recognize the thought and expertise that was poured into these systems from their level of complexity and capability, not to mention that all of them provide viable solutions for transacting business on the Internet.

CyberCash

CyberCash provides real-time, secure, digital signature-based credit card authentication service over the Internet. CyberCash approaches the problems of electronic commerce similarly to ICVERIFY—it acts as an intermediary among consumers, merchants, and credit card clearinghouses. CyberCash requires its merchants to obtain merchant identification and terminal identification numbers from merchant banks or financial service agents. To make things easier for would-be customers, CyberCash maintains close relationships with about 20 such institutions. One advantage of CyberCash over ICVERIFY is that both the server and client software are free. Both components work in tandem to process transactions, provide reporting and accounting to both merchant and consumer, and ensure that the merchant receives payment while protecting the rights and privacy of the customer.

Since its inception, CyberCash has developed solid relationships with financial institutions, client merchants, and end-users by offering secure and affordable access to electronic commerce services. By building relations with well-known banks and financial service agents, CyberCash helped to promote its own solution and the concept of Internet commerce. This kind of reputation has been much sought after by subsequent newcomers to this marketplace.

Technically speaking, CyberCash is fairly simple. It uses familiar Internet secure and open protocols to send and receive data. The consumer side uses a local application, called the Wallet, to store credit card information, relevant account numbers, and so on. Seen in Figure 8-1, the server side includes two components: the merchant's Web server, which is independent of the actual financial transaction, and the CashRegister server.

At a remote location, CyberCash's own server actually performs the decrypting and processing of credit card information. The merchant's Web server receives only the order information, and an indication that the order was paid by credit card. The CashRegister strips off the order and forwards the encrypted payment information to the CyberCash server over the Internet, digitally signed and encrypted with the merchant's private key. The CyberCash server then takes the packet off the Internet behind its firewall to complete the transaction process through separate, secure ATM lines. Fifteen to twenty seconds later, the merchant's server receives an authorization code, which is then processed according to how the merchant's Web server has been set up. All encryption of the transaction is at the message level, and thus independent of browser or secure protocol.

CyberCash's commerce model mirrors the concept of normal electronic credit card clearing systems that you find in any retail store. The customer accesses a merchant's Web page, selects items for purchase, and at some point reaches a page that summarizes those items and their prices, assigns a transaction number, and so on.

At this point, a *Pay* button on the Web page launches CyberCash's local Wallet application. The consumer clicks on the credit card to be used for the transaction, confirms payment, and sends order and payment information to the merchant using a secure Internet protocol. The merchant sends the encrypted information on to CyberCash's gateway server, which decrypts and processes the transaction. Please note that the merchant receives no address or billing information from the CyberCash process, and must develop appropriate scripts, such as a simple information form, within their Web page to capture this information.

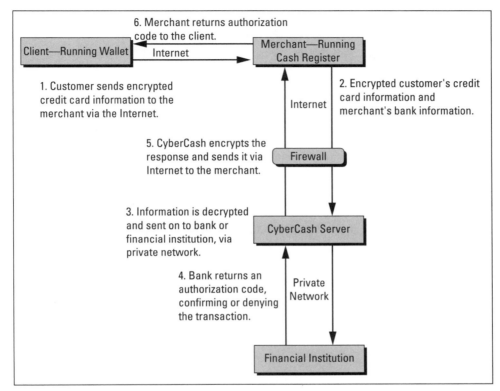

Figure 8-1
The CyberCash payment process model keeps merchants from accessing a customer's credit card information, and is thus safer than telephone orders.

CyberCash application—the user

Using the CyberCash Wallet is as easy as using any other desktop application. The client software actually stores, encrypts, and tracks transactions on all credit cards that it handles. As part of the installation process, the application automatically links its file extension (.CYB) to itself in a preferred Web browser's helper application function. Thus, once the user reaches a point in a Web shopping session where payment is required, the browser automatically launches the Wallet software, which handles the transaction from there. The important thing to note is that the Wallet itself does all encryption processes, thereby eliminating any need for a browser to run secure protocols like SSL or S-HTTP.

The Wallet application is able to use several Wallets, and can support multiple users or track business and personal transactions separately. Each individual Wallet is password-protected, and associated with a particular user through a CyberCash-issued user name and a customer-supplied password. The best thing about the client software is that it is free to users.

OBTAINING THE CYBERCASH WALLET

The easiest thing about CyberCash Wallet is obtaining it! The client software is available on our CD-ROM, or it can be downloaded from the CyberCash Web site, which contains information about the application, supporting merchants, and even an online user's guide, from this URL:

```
http://www.cybercash.com.
```

SYSTEM REQUIREMENTS AND INSTALLATION

CyberCash Wallet runs on the following systems:

- Windows Versions 3.1, 3.11, or Windows 95 (80386 or higher)
- Windows NT 3.51 or greater
- Macintosh system 7.1 or greater

To run on Windows, the application requires 3MB of disk space and at least 4MB of RAM. The Macintosh version needs the same amount of disk space, but at least 8MB of memory. Both versions require a TCP/IP stack—either WinSock for Windows, or MacTCP, or Open Transport for the Macintosh. Obviously, you also need a connection to the Internet. The Wallet client acts like any other Internet client program, such as Fetch or WinFTP, by communicating directly with the host from the user's desktop over a SLIP or PPP connection.

Both the Windows and Macintosh versions of the Wallet application are packaged in an installation program that guides the user through various options, such as the directory that houses the program and the preferred browser that modifies it with a helper application call. The installation program searches the user's hard drive for all Web browsers installed and allows the user to choose one, some, or all of the currently installed browsers for operation with the application. Once installed, a CyberCash program group (for Windows platforms) or folder (for Macintosh) is created, and the application icon appears, along with an Uninstall icon and a basic Read Me file.

All that's left at that point is launching the application and setting it up.

SETTING UP

Once the installation process is complete, the user must launch the CyberCash Wallet application and go through several steps to initially set up the application. The information and conditions below are required before setting up the application:

- A user name and valid e-mail address
- A TCP/IP connection to the Internet

- A valid credit card number and associated information
- Billing information, such as address and phone number

The set-up process is fairly straightforward and is outlined in the figures below:

1. Enter a Wallet ID (normally the actual user's name with no spaces, i.e., JohnSmith) and a valid Internet e-mail address, as seen in Figure 8-2. The language variable isn't a variable at the moment, as only US English is supported.

Figure 8-2
Enter a Wallet ID and e-mail address to set up your CyberCash Wallet.

2. Now enter and verify your password, as shown in Figure 8-3. This will protect multiple individual Wallets run on the same system or a single Wallet from unauthorized access.

Figure 8-3
Enter and verify your CyberCash password.

3. The system now takes over, generates security keys, and logs into the CyberCash server to set up the user name and security information (see Figure 8-4). If the proposed user name is already in use, the system will respond with a suggested user name, appending a number to the proposed name, as in *bubba90-87* shown in Figure 8-5.

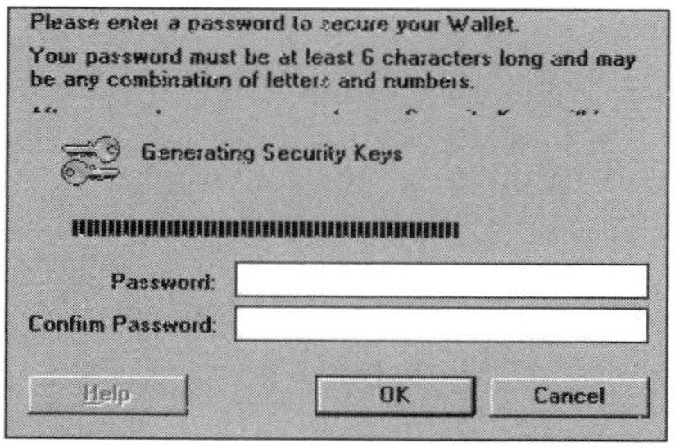

Figure 8-4
The system automatically generates all required security keys.

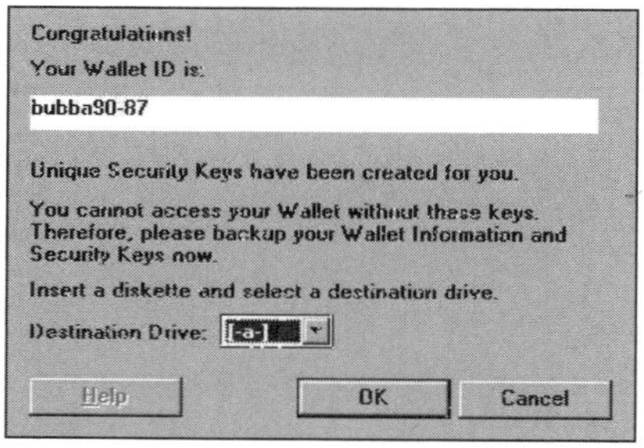

Figure 8-5
It's a good idea to back up your keys and other Wallet information!

4. Now the application prompts the user to back up security keys and other Wallet information to an offline storage media, such as a floppy. This process is optional, but strongly recommended; once lost, the information must be regenerated to continue using the application.

5. Finally, a credit card must be linked to the application. This operation is not optional, and valid credit card information must be entered to finish setting up a Wallet (see Figure 8-6). This requires a valid credit card, including number, card type, expiration date, name on the card, and card name (such as GoldMastercard), as well as billing and contact information.

6. The application makes a second TCP/IP connection to the CyberCash server, confirming the validity of the credit card (see Figure 8-7). This process takes a few seconds.

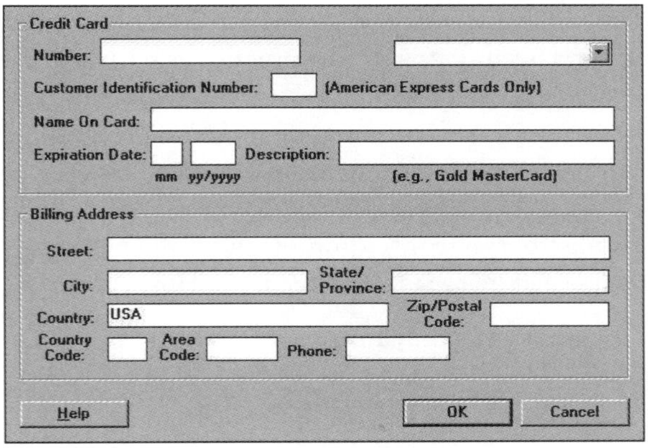

Figure 8-6
Link a credit card to this application, and you're done.

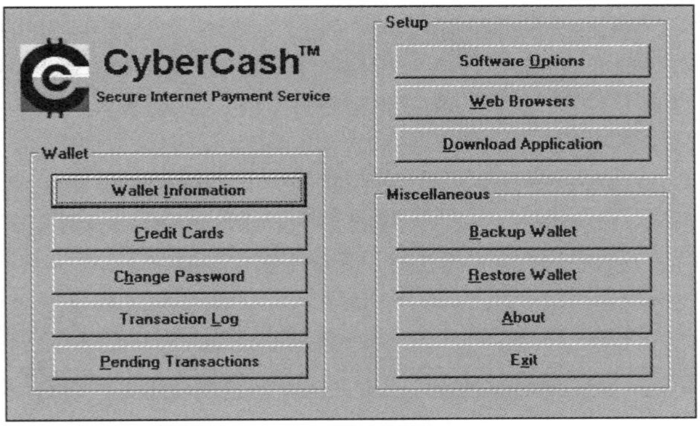

Figure 8-7
The system checks the status of the credit card.

7. Now the user is ready to use the CyberCash Wallet. From this main screen, the user can add more credit cards to the Wallet, view or print the transaction log, view pending transactions (those still uncleared by CyberCash), and perform other administrative functions, such as backing up or restoring the Wallet, linking other browsers, setting a proxy server, or downloading a new release of the Wallet software.

Once set-up is complete, the user is ready to shop the World Wide Web, securely and easily.

SPEND! SPEND! SPEND!
Simply by linking to a CyberCash-capable merchant with a Web browser and selecting items for purchase, consumers can initiate transactions by clicking the Pay button. The Wallet client then launches, asks for confirmation of the transaction, and sends the

user's encrypted information to the merchant and, eventually, to CyberCash. The transaction is recorded in the transaction log, and, until a confirmation is returned, the pending transaction log. Fifteen to twenty seconds later, the user receives a confirmation of the transaction, denoting whether it was authorized or denied, and the amount. This is the customer's receipt, in addition to any output from the merchant's Web server.

CyberCash naturally maintains links to merchants running the CyberCash payment system from their Web site. A minimall merchant list page is available at:

```
http://www.cybercash.com/cybercash/shopping/ .
```

The merchants listed are divided by category, and all support the CyberCash payment system.

CyberCash application—the merchant

CyberCash merchants need to have many things to run a CyberCash payment service. System requirements are listed later, but more important, the merchant will need a credit card account from a bank or financial institution, which is harder to obtain than you might think. We cover the details of the application and qualification process in Chapter 14, where you'll develop a keen appreciation for its potential twists and turns.

The CyberCash merchant side uses a server called CashRegister, that receives a customer's order and encrypted payment information, strips off the order, adds the merchant's encrypted bank information, and forwards this packet to a CyberCash server for further processing. It then waits for a return authorization code from the customer's bank, and returns this information to the merchant for further processing, as well as notifying the customer of the state of the transaction. CashRegister runs on a variety of platforms (see the system requirements that follow), and interfaces with CGIs for Web server order processing , payment information, and payment authorization codes.

OBTAINING THE CYBERCASH CASHREGISTER

Once the decision has been made to go with the CyberCash payment system, the merchant must go to the CyberCash Web site and fill out a Merchant Inquiry Form. This form defines some variables for CyberCash, such as what products the merchant wishes to sell on the Internet, Web server and platform specifics, and the name of the financial institution used to accept credit card payments via CyberCash.

Once the form is submitted, CyberCash issues a user name and password, giving the merchant access to a private FTP site from which to download the CashRegister software.

SYSTEM REQUIREMENTS AND INSTALLATION

CyberCash has versions for the following platforms:

- Solaris V2.4
- BSDI V2.0.1

- Sun OS V4.1.3/V4.1.4
- Windows NT V 3.51
- SGI Irix V5.3
- HP/UX V 9.0.7
- Linux Slackware V3.0

CyberCash is also compatible with these Web servers:

- Netscape
- Apache
- CERN
- Microsoft IIS
- Spry
- Spyglass
- Oracle
- Novell
- Quarterdeck

CONCLUSION

CyberCash is a viable Internet payment solution for both consumer and merchant. For the merchant there are a few more steps other than implementing a payment solution by hand, as with ICVERIFY, but the consumer confidence in a secure credit card transaction solution makes the extra work worth it. Also, since the CyberCash payment system handles encryption and decryption internally, the need for a secure Web server is eliminated. The CyberCash CashRegister server is free to qualified merchants, reducing the potential overhead in getting their products out there on the Internet.

For the consumer, CyberCash provides a ready-made solution to Internet shopping, with the easy to install and use Wallet software and the security of knowing a qualified third party is processing the transactions. The future of Internet commerce probably looks a lot like CyberCash.

Ecash

Ecash, by DigiCash, approaches the idea of Internet commerce from a totally different perspective. Ecash is actual digital money, downloaded by the Ecash client from a participating bank and stored on the customer's local computer. The Ecash can then be spent at merchant systems that accept Ecash, and the merchant, in turn, deposits the money in a participating bank. The beauty of Ecash is that it is exactly like cash: The spender is kept completely anonymous, as Ecash *coins* maintain their own identity using a serial number. When the merchant receives Ecash in payment, the payment is instantly valid, as long as the issuing bank can match the serial numbers to validly issued Ecash coins that have not already been used. The Ecash coins are encrypted using standard digital signature technology available on the Internet and obtainable from such places as VeriSign.

The convenience to both consumer and merchant cannot be ignored, as the consumer benefits from an easy-to-use local client that can send Ecash payments via e-mail or over the Web. The merchant gets virtually instant compensation for the sale of an item without having to go through the trouble of applying for merchant IDs and such from a financial institution. The second, and by far the greatest, feature of Ecash is that there is no separate server software to buy, install, or run. The program that enables the consumer to pay for things with Ecash is the same program that enables the merchant to accept payment of Ecash.

The basic concept of Ecash is secure, same-as-cash, Internet banking. The user transacts business on the Internet as if browsing through a store with a pocketful of money. In this case, the money is withdrawn from the Ecash account at a participating bank that issues Ecash in electronic coins, which are distinguished by serial numbers. The number of coins is calculated by the Ecash client before a withdrawal is made, depending on the amount of money requested. Such requests for coins are then encoded with a private key that is generated when the client software is installed.

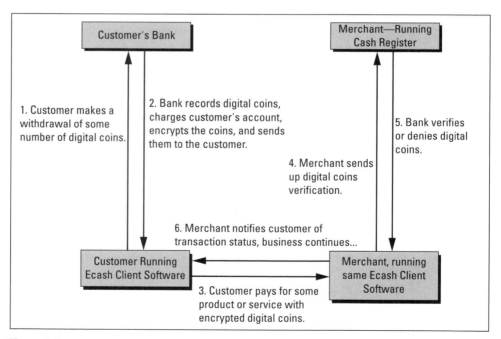

Figure 8-8
This diagram shows the flow of digital coins from the issuing bank to the customer's local machine, from there to the merchant's Ecash client, and up to the issuing bank for verification.

The Ecash client connects to its digital bank and makes a request for the coins. The bank issues the coins, records their serial numbers, debits the customer's account, and sends the packet of coins back to the Ecash client. These coins are stored on the user's local machine and managed by the Ecash client software that runs in the background as the user browses the Internet. Once a user decides to make an Ecash transaction, the client software takes over and transfers the Ecash from the client machine to the merchant's machine that is running the same client software. The merchant's side receives the Ecash and sends it up to the merchant's digital bank for verification. Once verified, the merchant's account is updated, and the merchant ships the product out to the customer. Simple, right? Not too slow, either—the whole process seldom takes more than a minute!

Because the coins are transmitted across the Internet, security and privacy are naturally major concerns. First, the coins are protected by individual serial numbers kept on record at the issuing bank. Once a transaction has taken place, and the receiving merchant deposits the electronic coins, the bank's system checks the validity of the coins against its record of serial numbers issued. If everything matches, the merchant's account is credited with the correct amount. However, if the coins are fraudulent in any way—for example, if the user counterfeited the coins by copying them, the bank also maintains a record of serial numbers that are no longer valid (that is, that have already been spent). At this point, the merchant is automatically notified, and the client can be denied the product.

A second level of security is handled at the level of actual data transmission, using RSA's system for secure Internet communications. During setup, the Ecash client generates a pair of keys, public and private. The private key encodes all digital coins before sending them over the Internet. At the merchant end, the user's public key is used to decode the digital coins, thereby allowing the merchant's Ecash client to read them properly. This ensures secure transmission of Ecash, both from the client to the issuing bank and to the merchant, and from the merchant to its issuing bank.

Privacy, though not necessarily considered a security feature, is also built into the Ecash system. Because the issuing bank records only the requests for digital coins and their respective serial numbers, the privacy of the requester is maintained. The merchant end is not so lucky, nor is the client who wishes to deposit unused or newly received Ecash. The bank will have to know whose account to credit, and needs all the necessary information to do so. Thus, the spending habits of innocent individuals cannot be traced or otherwise extrapolated from a single source, although all deposits of Ecash are definitely on record.

The reason for this is that Ecash is automatically forwarded and recorded by the bank, so digital coins cannot be hidden or laundered. Second, for those criminals who make their livings from bribes, extortion, or the black market, customers can always prove that payment originated from the customer's Ecash client. Although this obviously leaves some loose ends, the customer's privacy is controlled, and at no time can the merchant or the issuing or receiving bank know from whom digital coins come, unless the customer volunteers that information.

Ecash client software

Unfortunately, DigiCash no longer offers the Ecash client software, because their Ecash trial period has ended. However, there are presently three banks worldwide that have licensed the Ecash payment system, and use the Ecash client for their customers. Only one of these banks is in the U.S., the Mark Twain bank. Ecash information pages and client software download information is available at:

```
http://www.marktwain.com/ecash.html.
```

Once an account is opened with an issuing bank, they'll provide the client software free of charge.

Figure 8-9
The Ecash client software allows the user to withdraw digital coins from an Ecash-capable bank account and use the coins to pay for items at Ecash-capable merchant Web sites. (ECash™)

SYSTEM REQUIREMENTS

The Ecash client is available for the Windows, OS/2, Macintosh, and UNIX platforms. With all platforms, a TCP/IP connection to the Internet is required.

WINDOWS AND OS/2 PLATFORMS:

- Operating System
  - Windows 3.1, 3.11, NT 3.1, or 95.
  - IBM OS/2 3.0 (Warp) (if Windows emulation installed)
- TCP/IP Stack
  - WinSock 1.1-compliant network software is needed (built into NT, Windows 95 and OS/2)
- Processor and Hardware
  - A 80386 CPU or higher
  - 4 MB of RAM

- 3 MB of Hard disk space
- Modem or other connection hardware (for Internet connection)

MACINTOSH PLATFORMS:

- Operating System
  - System 7 or higher is needed
- TCP/IP Stack
  - MacTCP, version 1.1.1 or higher or OpenTransport
- Processor and Hardware
  - 68020 CPU or higher
  - 8 MB of RAM
  - 3 MB of hard disk space
  - Modem or other connection hardware (for Internet connection)
- Supported UNIX Flavors
  - Linux
  - FreeBSD
  - SunOS
  - Solaris or NetBSD 1.0 on a Sun4 (Sparc)
  - A/UX
  - HP-UX
  - SGI
  - NeXTstep
  - BSDI
  - OSF/1 (DEC Alpha)
  - SCO UNIX (and compatibles)
  - Solaris 2.4 for Intel

CONCLUSION

Ecash is certainly an innovative and secure solution for doing same-as-cash transactions over the Internet. The client software is multifunctional, eliminating the need for costly servers on the merchant side, and the payment process is straightforward and equally convenient for all parties. Even following the emergence of real-time credit card transactions as a primary vehicle for Internet commerce, there remains a need for electronic cash systems. Ecash is a solid solution and has grabbed a visible share of the trusted third-party market that's doing business on the Internet.

First Virtual

The First Virtual Internet Payment System provides a secure and safe method for electronic commerce over the Internet. There's no client software for customers to figure out, nor servers or special hardware for merchants to set up. All transactions are handled over normal Internet e-mail, based on the user's VirtualPIN, chosen by the user as an alias for a credit card. The VirtualPIN can be entered in a form on a merchant's Web site, or transmitted to a merchant via e-mail.

This information is then forwarded to First Virtual along with the amount of the sale and the merchant's VirtualPIN. If this information is confirmed valid, an e-mail message is sent to the buyer for confirmation. The buyer replies *yes* to accept, *no* to decline, or *fraud* to indicate that the transaction was initiated without the buyer's consent. A fraud reply automatically cancels that VirtualPIN. Once a *yes* reply is received, confirmation is sent to the seller, and the customer's credit card is charged. After a reasonable amount of time (up to ninety-one days, depending on the merchant's creditworthiness), the merchant's bank account is credited via Direct Deposit, less First Virtual's fees.

This process can be cumbersome, especially for merchants who might wait several days for initial confirmation, and up to three months for payment. However, First Virtual's system not only ensures security and guards against fraud on both sides of a transaction, it also allows merchants to get involved in Internet commerce without incurring the additional overhead of running a credit card verification system, such as ICVERIFY. Likewise, there is no need for data encryption or a secure Web server because there is no sensitive data transmitted over the Internet.

First Virtual's innovative system is backed up by Electronic Data Systems (EDS) which maintains credit card information and handles electronic settlement of transactions over their private network. First USA Merchant Services acts as a clearinghouse for merchant information.

Although First Virtual still operates as it has from its inception, recent news from its Web site indicates that the company has upgraded and expanded its computer systems, offering ten times its original capacity. The company has also restructured and simplified its fee schedule for both merchants and buyers. These are clear indications that First Virtual is an accepted and trusted third-party system for transacting business on the Internet.

Information on becoming a buyer or a seller with the First Virtual can be obtained from the following URL:

```
http://www.fv.com .
```

The First Virtual Internet Payment System is built on e-mail, the prototypical Internet service. All transactions and confirmations are conducted simply and efficiently using existing technology with which every Internet user, buyer, or merchant is familiar. The merchant needs only to write a script that will compose an e-mail message from the contents of an HTML-based order form that includes the following information: the buyer's VirtualPIN, the merchant's Seller's VirtualPIN, the amount of the sale, the currency used, and a description of the transaction, such as the product name. (We provide a sample script that does all these things in Chapter 13.) That's it!

To walk through this process in detail, let's begin a transaction from a customer's point of view:

1. The customer launches a Web browser.

2. The customer accesses a merchant's Web site and selects an item to purchase through the FV Internet Payment System.

3. After filling out the order form, the customer inputs a VirtualPIN into the appropriate blank.

4. The transaction is initiated, and the customer waits for confirmation, an example of which is shown in Figure 8-10.)

Figure 8-10
Confirmation form is sent to First Virtual. ©1996 First Virtual Holdings, Incorporated.

5. After several minutes, First Virtual sends the customer an e-mail regarding the purchase that includes the merchant's name, the item to be bought, the price, and a confirmation request. A sample message is shown in Figure 8-11.

6. The buyer replies *yes,* to confirm the transaction, *no* to deny it, or *fraud* to indicate unauthorized use of the VirtualPIN. If the reply is *fraud,* the buyer's VirtualPIN is immediately canceled, and the customer must reapply for a new VirtualPIN at the First Virtual Web site (see Figure 8-12).

7. If a transaction is confirmed, the buyer's credit card is charged, and the item is shipped, as per the merchant's standard procedure (see Figure 8-13).

8. The confirmation of a user's credit charge is posted (see Figure 8-14).

```
Date: Thursday, 10-Oct-96 04:53 PM

From: FV Commerce Server      \ Internet:  (sgcs-server@card.com)
To:  ed tittel                \ Internet:  (etittel@lanw.com)

Attachment: 00000001.unk Code: 04BCOHC \ Created: Unknown [1 Kb]

Subject: @@@19961010.25799964023@card.com> — transfer-query

Transaction: Desserts from Cyber Sweets!
Cost:        28.95 usd us dollars
Seller-Name: Sherry Isler
Transfer-ID: @@@M1lv41Zs0QcBAAA@infohaus.com>
Server-ID:   @@@19961010.25799964023@card.com> (put this in the "Subject:"
field of your reply)

Sherry Isler has requested that
Ed Tittel should be charged 28.95 (in usd us dollars)
for "Desserts from Cyber Sweets!".

Please reply to this message with the word Yes, No,
or Fraud. Your message should look something like this:

     +————————————————————————
     I
     I   From:   your e-mail address here
     I   To: response@card.com
     I   Subject: Re: @@@19961010.25799964023@card.com> — transfer-query
     I   ——————————————————-
     I   Yes
     I
     +————————————————————————

The message should be addressed to "response@card.com"
and the Subject line should contain your Server-ID:
   @@@19961010.25799964023@card.com>
The body of the message should contain ONE of the following
words: yes (as shown), no, or fraud.

— The Definitions of Yes, No, and Fraud are as follows: —

1) "Yes" - You authorize us to charge your
        credit card 28.95 usd us dollars.

   For information products, a "yes" answer means that
   you successfully received the information product,
   examined it, and feel it is worth paying for.

2) "No" - You decline the request for payment and are
        canceling the sale.

   You may refuse payment if you wish to cancel the
   sale or, in the case of information products,
   you did not receive a satisfactory product.

3) "Fraud" - You are authorizing your VirtualPIN to be
        IMMEDIATELY canceled because you believe
        your VirtualPIN has been STOLEN.

   Calling fraud means that you were unaware of this
   transaction and did NOT request to purchase this product.

   ************* PLEASE NOTE **************
   If you do say "Fraud", we will IMMEDIATELY and
```

```
      PERMANENTLY cancel your VirtualPIN. Just like
      reporting a credit/debit card stolen, this action
      closes your account. You will need to apply for a
      new VirtualPIN to make any future purchases through
      First Virtual.

NEED HELP?

      If your situation does not fit any of the three
      options above, you can respond with the word "Help",
      followed by a brief description of your problem.

      By responding with "Help" and then describing your
      problem, the text that follows the word "Help" will
      be forwarded to a Customer Support Representative
      and personally responded to.

IF YOUR MAIL SYSTEM CANNOT CONSTRUCT SUFFICIENTLY LONG SUBJECT LINES:

Please send a message to response-challenged@card.com  with the first (and
only) lines in the message being the following two lines:

Server-ID: @@@19961010.25799964023@card.com>
Authorization: yes (or no or fraud or help)

Your message should look like this:

    +-----------------------------------
    I  From: your e-mail address here
    I  To: response-challenged@card.com
    I  -----------------------
    I  Server-ID: @@@19961010.25799964023@card.com>
    I  Authorization: yes (or no or fraud or help)
    +-----------------------------------


Use of the First Virtual Internet Payment System is governed by our Terms
and Conditions effective 16 December 1995. When you use your VirtualPIN,
you agree to our Terms and Conditions, so please read them.  To receive a
copy of the TACs pertaining to either buying, selling, or selling as an
InfoHaus merchant, send a blank e-mail message to one of the following
addresses: "fineprint-buyer@fv.com", "fineprint-seller@fv.com", or
"fineprint-infohaus@fv.com". The reply will contain the corresponding docu-
ment.

FIRST VIRTUAL is a servicemark of First Virtual Holdings Incorporated.

Please ignore anything that appears after this line.
```

Figure 8-11
Confirmation e-mail arrives.

```
Date: Thursday, 10-Oct-96 05:16 PM

From: Ed Tittel            \ Internet:   (etittel@zilker.net)
To:   response@card.com    \ Internet:   (response@card.com)

Subject: Re: @@@19961010.25799964023@card.com> — transfer-query

Yes.
```

Figure 8-12
Reply generated by user, confirming transaction.

```
X-Tag: 961010362047 960328889246
Subject: @@@M1lv4lZsOQcBAAA@infohaus.com> — transfer-result
From: FV Commerce Server @@@sgcs-server@card.com>
Comments: generated by via-email.tcl - Enabled Mail (EM) environment for
UNIX
MIME-Version: 1.0
Bcc:
Date: Thu, 10 Oct 1996 17:17:29 -0500
Message-ID: @@@29873.844985849.2@card.com>
Reply-to:    support-transfer-result@card.com
Content-Type: multipart/alternative; boundary=fv

—fv

Transaction: Desserts from Cyber Sweets!
Cost:        28.95 usd us dollars
Buyer-Name:  Ed Tittel
Transfer-ID: @@@M1lv4lZsOQcBAAA@infohaus.com>
Authorization-Result: yes

Ed Tittel has authorized the transfer of
28.95 (in usd us dollars) to Sherry Isler
for "Desserts from Cyber Sweets!".

The buyer's credit card has NOT yet been charged for this purchase.
You will receive payment (reduced appropriately by our service charges),
once the buyer's credit card has been charged, and the Settlement
Date has been reached.

Use of the First Virtual Internet Payment System is governed by our
Terms and Conditions effective 16 December 1995. When you use your
VirtualPIN, you agree to our Terms and Conditions, so please read
them.  To receive a copy of the TACs pertaining to either buying,
selling, or selling as an InfoHaus merchant, send a blank e-mail
message to one of the following addresses: "fineprint-buyer@fv.com",
"fineprint-seller@fv.com", or "fineprint-infohaus@fv.com". The reply
will contain the corresponding document.

FIRST VIRTUAL is a servicemark of First Virtual Holdings Incorporated.

Please ignore anything that appears after this line.

—fv
Content-Type: application/green-commerce; transaction=transfer-result

Buyer-Name:        Ed Tittel
Seller-Name:       Sherry Isler
Amount:            28.95
Currency:          usd us dollars
Transfer-Type:     info-sale
Server-ID:         @@@19961010.25799964023@card.com>
Description:       Desserts from Cyber Sweets!
Transfer-ID:       @@@M1lv4lZsOQcBAAA@infohaus.com>
Authorization-Result: yes

Use of the First Virtual Internet Payment System is governed by our
Terms and Conditions effective 16 December 1995. When you use your
VirtualPIN, you agree to our Terms and Conditions, so please read
them.  To receive a copy of the TACs pertaining to either buying,
```

```
selling, or selling as an InfoHaus merchant, send a blank e-mail
message to one of the following addresses: "fineprint-buyer@fv.com",
"fineprint-seller@fv.com", or "fineprint-infohaus@fv.com". The reply
will contain the corresponding document.

FIRST VIRTUAL is a servicemark of First Virtual Holdings Incorporated.

—fv—
```

Figure 8-13
First confirmation of user approval.

```
Date: Friday, 11-Oct-96 12:04 PM

From: FV Commerce Server      \ Internet:    (sgcs-server@card.com)
To:   ed tittel               \ Internet:    (etittel@lanw.com)

Attachment: 00000001.unk Code: 03TMRVG \ Created: Unknown [2 Kb]

Subject: payin-notification

You, Ed Tittel, previously approved
the following purchases:

  Amount   Seller/Description
  _____   _____

    28.95 Sherry Isler
          Desserts from Cyber Sweets!

We have NOW billed your credit card for these PREVIOUSLY APPROVED pur-
chases, for a total of 28.95 (USD).

YOU DO NOT NEED TO REPLY TO THIS MESSAGE.

We suggest that you save a copy of this message as a receipt. It provides an
itemized list of your purchases which will appear as one line on your
credit card bill.

This line charge may be identified as "99765233" on your  credit card bill.

If you would like to discuss any of these transactions, please contact  the
seller of the item(s). If there is something you need to discuss  which is
specific to the First Virtual Payment System, please send  a message to:

          support-payin-notification@card.com

Use of the First Virtual Internet Payment System is governed by  the Terms
and Conditions effective 16 December 1995.  To receive a  copy of the TACs
document pertaining to either buying, selling,  or selling as an InfoHaus
merchant, send e-mail to one of the following  addresses: "fineprint-
buyer@fv.com", "fineprint-seller@fv.com", or  "fineprint-infohaus@fv.com",
and the reply will contain the  corresponding Terms and Conditions. If you
have not read and accepted  and agreed to be bound by these Terms and Condi-
tions, do not proceed  with this or any other First Virtual transaction.

FIRST VIRTUAL is a servicemark of First Virtual Holdings Incorporated.

Please ignore anything that appears after this line.
```

Figure 8-14
Final confirmation of user credit charge.

That's it! The buyer is out of the loop for most of the transaction, other than initiating and confirming it. This simplicity drives First Virtual's appeal—there are no complex programs, complex cryptography methods, or room for fraud, because the buyer is in control of the purchase at all times.

From the merchant's side, things are more onerous. First, the merchant builds a script into their Web site that generates an e-mail to First Virtual for every purchase. This e-mail must contain specific information that meets rigorous format requirements that includes the customer's VirtualPIN, the merchant's VirtualPIN, the amount of the sale and currency used, and the names of the items purchased.

Here, we follow the transaction life cycle from a merchant's point of view:

1. The buyer initiates a transaction.

2. The merchant's script builds an e-mail with the appropriate information and sends it to First Virtual.

3. After some length of time (up to a month) the buyer is required to respond to First Virtual, confirming or denying the purchase. The merchant is out of the loop during this phase of the transaction and must wait patiently for the process to conclude. If the buyer does not respond within a month, the transaction is voided.

4. Once buyer confirmation is received, First Virtual sends an e-mail, called a transfer result, to the merchant that confirms the transaction as valid.

5. Next, the merchant must wait again, for up to ninety-one days, before receiving a direct deposit from First Virtual to the merchant's bank account.

Merchants interested in faster payment systems should consider other third-party services, or try setting up their own credit card verification system through appropriate parties.

Applying: user

To apply for a Buyer VirtualPIN, customers must have a valid e-mail address and a Visa or MasterCard account. The application can be found at the First Virtual Web site, and includes only general contact information and the requested VirtualPIN number. Credit card and bank account numbers are not transmitted over the Internet for any First Virtual transaction. After sending the application form, the buyer will receive an e-mail message with a 12 digit application code and instructions to call an 800 number. From an automated system, the user enters credit card information over a touch-tone phone. The buyer then receives a second e-mail message confirming the activation of the First Virtual account.

Buyers can apply at First Virtual's Account Application page:

```
http://www.fv.com/newacct/ .
```

The cost for a First Virtual Buyer's Account is two dollars per year. This gives the buyer free access to several thousand merchants that deal in everything from soft goods, such as digital images and cryptography programs, to hard goods, such as CDs and T-shirts. The world of Internet commerce is open: Go out there and buy!

Applying: merchant
To use First Virtual's payment system as a seller, you must have a bank account that accepts direct deposit and a valid e-mail address. Merchants must then fill out the same form (at the URL previously listed). Once a confirmation e-mail is received, the merchant must call the First Virtual 800 number to give bank account information. After this, all that remains is to pay the various fees and set up a Web site to begin taking First Virtual payments. The fee for setting up a Seller's VirtualPIN is currently $10. Sellers are charged 29 cents per transaction, plus 2 percent of the value of the items sold. In addition, there is a $1 charge for processing payments and depositing funds into the seller's account. This may seem like a steep fee schedule, but it is a bargain compared to stand-alone credit card verification systems, that not only charge similar fees, but also charge for server software, setup, and licensing fees, on top of the costs for any special hardware that may be required to implement and maintain such systems. By comparison, First Virtual is competitively priced for the services offered.

Conclusion
Although First Virtual's system is simple, the merchant's side of the transaction can be cumbersome because of the three-month lag before receiving payment. Please note, however, that such long delays apply only to merchants who do not wish to submit to a more ordinary, but time-consuming (and expensive) commercial credit check. If you're willing to undergo the same credit checking process required to establish a relationship with a merchant bank or credit card processing company, First Virtual will offer payment on the same terms they do (in as little as one or two days, in other words).

Some small companies or organizations choose not to spend the money (up to $1,000) or do the work (lots of forms and credit history information to fill out), and they can still conduct commerce through First Virtual without having to jump such hurdles. That's the real reason why First Virtual can sometimes take such a long time to pay. They wish to protect buyers and credit card companies from fraud, and to protect themselves from buyer-contested charges after payments have already been issued to merchants.

First Virtual's ideal merchant is one who deals in "try-before-you-buy" electronic information products, such as shareware. This, in First Virtual's opinion, "is the most compatible with the unrestricted flow of information that now governs the Internet," and they claim that this philosophy will expose more consumers to a company's product. They also maintain a system for tracking users who habitually abuse the goodwill of First Virtual merchants, and guilty buyers will find their VirtualPINs canceled. With these checks and balances in mind, a merchant that wishes to use a third-party verification system should evaluate First Virtual and compare this system to other options, and more important, evaluate its fit with their business model. First Virtual is the simplest form of Internet payment system and definitely the most secure. In many ways, it is also the cheapest.

Summary

In this chapter, we've examined two of the more popular implementations of digital cash, an electronic analog for currency. We've also explored the First Virtual Internet Payment System, which cleverly manages to use credit cards without ever transmitting any sensitive information over the Internet. Along the way, we hope you've observed that these technologies offer some interesting approaches for vendors to establish a commercial presence on the World Wide Web. In the next chapter, we'll turn our focus to integrated commerce solutions, where a number of technology and service providers have created fully fledged commerce solutions that need only to be installed, configured, and turned loose on the world!

CHAPTER NINE

INTEGRATED SOLUTIONS

W hen shopping in a mall, or even over the phone, most people rarely worry about the security of using credit cards, debit cards, or writing a check. The idea of transmitting credit card information over the Web, however, often strikes fear in even the most plastic-oriented consumers. Many people have heard horror stories in the media about 13-year-old hackers running up millions of dollars in stolen credit card charges. The fact that some of these stories are true is a good reason to exercise caution when saying "charge it" online. Even some of the biggest online vendors, such as the Internet Shopping Network, can't guarantee the security of credit card transactions, and post unsettling warning messages such as these on their sites:

- You should remember that purchases under major credit cards including Visa, MasterCard, and American Express are insured and limited in liability.

- If you receive notification of an order that you did not place, notify Customer Service immediately.

Although the Internet Shopping Network allows consumers to charge purchases, its transactions are not formally verified, and it lacks a complete security solution. Thousands of people have safely purchased goods over Web sites such as the Internet Shopping Network, but given the Net's mutable character, no guarantee exists that unverified transactions will be viable in the future. See what you think about the Internet Shopping Network's system by surfing to its home page at the following URL:

```
http://www.internet.net/ .
```

The simple truth is that the Web can be an insecure place to use credit cards. When security breaches occur, they can involve great amounts of information, and thereby affect millions of dollars. Although using credit cards, ATM cards, debit cards, and even phone cards offline involves risk as well the Internet's financial arena is largely an unproved one. Major industry players, including Netscape and Microsoft, recently addressed security concerns to create SSL encryption standards that ensure the protection of sensitive data. You can read more about SLL and other encryption techniques in Chapter 2.

In this chapter, we investigate integrated solutions for electronic transactions. An integrated solution is one that combines a number of software applications to provide an almost complete security solution. Many of these packages use a secret-key cryptography that's designed to provide a secure environment for you to conduct electronic transactions over the Net. Since key-based environments make it easy for merchants to process safe credit card orders, they're garnering much attention from companies scrambling to get online. In the upcoming pages, we examine the structures and features of several different systems, and discuss the benefits and drawbacks of the various integrated solutions.

What Are Cryptography Keys?

Cryptography keys are used for security in "symmetric" systems; systems that have one basic decryption key (several of the environments we examine incorporate more complex security measures in addition to this key, though). This key is used to encode information on the sender's side, and then decode it at the other end.

Cryptography keys, or crypto keys, work like the combination to a padlock, which is why it's important that the keys are not lost or destroyed. If essential information is encrypted, and the key to decrypt them becomes unavailable, the information could simply be irretrievable—unless, that is, a backup key exists. Therefore, when crypto keys are used, it's important that backups of the keys are made, just as backups of regular data need to be made.

Key escrow

The use of cryptography keys and backup key systems provokes the question of who has access to the key and backup data. Key escrow (also called escrowed encryption) is a concept that places a third party (or parties) in charge of keeping backup keys. Its use would assure that no untraceable anonymity or absolute individual privacy exists. Third parties could be commercial key holders who are bonded, private organizations, or they could be governmental agencies (this is an area in which standards are only beginning to emerge). For more current information about encryption and the question of government involvement in key escrow, investigate Dorothy Denning's cryptography site at:

```
http://guru.cosc.georgetown.edu/~denning/crypto/index.html .
```

Although key systems based on key cryptography are fundamentally secure, the manner in which the Internet transmits the encrypted data can weaken their security. Under the Net's vast packet-switching network, information may travel through forty or fifty ports before reaching its final destination (see Figure 9-1). And even if modes of transmission are secure, using a key-based system portends the risk of having the key fall into unintended hands. In addition, if the system on which the encryption was generated is broken into, it may be possible for the invader to read information from plain-text files, memory contents, or other sources, and procure information that would compromise the security of the cryptography key.

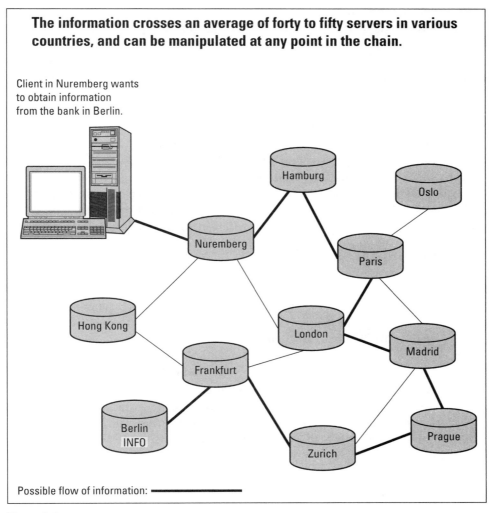

The information crosses an average of forty to fifty servers in various countries, and can be manipulated at any point in the chain.

Client in Nuremberg wants to obtain information from the bank in Berlin.

Possible flow of information: ▬▬▬▬▬▬▬

Figure 9-1
This diagram shows how data can hit many places as it is transferred across the Web.

The key appeal

Key-based security solutions offer a certain simplicity and efficiency. They don't involve complicated, expensive hardware to be installed or moved between CPUs, like hardware-based security systems may. Since they're software-based, they can be quickly and easily updated. These solutions operate within the infrastructure of banks that have been established for years, and since they often employ transaction systems that operate in the familiar credit card transaction paradigm, banks don't have a difficult time adjusting to their implementation. Because encryption solutions play up point-of-sale (POS) benefits, they play upon consumer's immediate gratification impulses—it's more fun to "click and buy" than picking up the telephone or (heaven forbid) filling out a snail mail order form.

The Web's seductive way of linking information is also perfect for POS impulse buying, especially in conjunction with a facile, plastic-oriented interface like those offered by integrated solutions. Since the online world is also perfectly suited to providing excellent customer product information, online merchants have the added ability to offer extensive technical product assistance, juicy graphical representations of goods, and even chat rooms to talk about electronic purchases.

Because credit cards are a major means of the public's purchasing power, vendors are pushing to make credit card purchases a true online option. Key-based cryptography solutions offer a very credit card friendly structure, which is why this technology has garnered so much attention. Considering that it's easier to get plastic credit than ever before, and that millions of Americans have eagerly taken full advantage of the credit they've been offered (whether or not they have the "real" money to back it up), it's easy to see why businesses are so aware of security software's appeal.

INFORMATION, PLEASE

Merchants also like simple key solutions for the customer information they're so good at capturing. When an anonymous payment solution such as NetCash is used, the vendor loses all sorts of useful information about who is purchasing the products. However, because an integrated solution is nearly all-encompassing, the merchant receives a plethora of information that can be used to propitious marketing advantage in the future.

By monitoring transactions, merchants can use feedback about how users responded to online ads, what elements of the site merited attention, and how much time transpired during the purchasing process. Environments that assign identification codes to their users can also track customer purchases (and tendencies) with great accuracy, so that customers may be presented with a certain type of good or information when they enter the site that's been selected according to their past purchases.

The SET Protocol—Future Security?

The main impediment for electronic transaction solutions to date has been an insecurity complex. Truly secure systems for transmitting delicate information (such as your

Visa number that sports a $10,000 line of credit, for example) haven't really emerged—at least, not sufficiently to make the average Web user feel comfortable about online purchases. However, the Secure Electronic Transaction (SET) protocol is indubitably going to have an effect on secure transaction environments. SET, developed by Master-Card, Visa, IBM, VeriSign, GTE, and Microsoft, is being hyped as the most viable security plan to date, and one that will be the successor to Netscape's SSL (Secure Socket Layer), the current protocol of choice.

SET goes beyond secret key encryption and protects its data with a combination of public key encryption and digital signatures. From the customer's end, a SET transaction has the familiar feel of a credit card transaction—customers select goods and then indicate what credit card they'd like to use for the purchase. SET takes the transaction data and encrypts it with a randomly generated symmetric encryption key, which is in turn encrypted with a public key held by the recipient of the message. This packet of data, called the "digital envelope," is sent to the recipient along with the encrypted message. Upon receiving the message, the recipient uses the private key to obtain the randomly generated symmetric key—then employs the symmetric key to decode the original message.

SET also works in conjunction with a digital signature and third-party CAs that lend extra trust and credibility to the transaction. Before sending SET messages to merchants, credit card holders have to register with SET and establish that they're worthy customers. Although SET will probably be in widespread use by the time you read this, as this book goes to press, it hasn't yet been released. However, that hasn't prevented some of the solutions we examine in this chapter from preparing to integrate it.

With its massive base of industry support, it's likely that SET will be propelled into becoming accepted as a standard. It's already slated to be incorporated into Web browsers and Internet e-mail packages from Oracle, Microsoft, and Netscape. Also, LivePayment, Netscape's integrated solution we examine in this chapter, is already primed to embrace SET as well. For more information about SET, flip back to Chapter 2, or hit the following URL:

```
http://www.visa.com/cgi-bin/vee/sf/set/intro.html .
```

Some Different Integrated Environments

Now that we've covered the basics of integrated solutions, we take a look at what several different companies offer in this area. Although these integrated solutions vary in scope and style, they all employ important security applications at some layer of their electronic commerce environment.

CyberCash

As mentioned in Chapter 8, CyberCash created its system around the idea that the POS contact is crucial, so the ideal technology encourages customers to say "charge it" at the moment they see a product, and feel safe and secure in doing so.

With CyberCash (see Figure 9-2), you can shop the Web with whatever browser appeals to you. If you come across an item you'd like to purchase, you can do so with your credit card through the CyberCash Secure Internet Payment Service by pushing the "PAY" button. CyberCash's structure features instantaneous secure communications between consumers, merchants, and the bank's processor. By functioning within existing paradigms of financial transactions, CyberCash's setup is definitely convenient for merchants.

Figure 9-2
The CyberCash logo can be seen on many Web shopping sites.

This is the URL for the CyberCash home page:

`http://www.cybercash.com/` .

A listing of merchants accepting CyberCash can be found at the following URL:

`http://www.cybercash.com/cybercash/shopping/` .

HOW CYBERCASH WORKS

When a consumer makes a CyberCash transaction (which normally lasts fifteen to twenty seconds), three components are at work (for ease of paradigm shifting, these parts are crafted from traditional metaphors of financial transactions):

- CyberCash Wallet
- Secure Merchant Payment System (SMPS)
- CyberCash Gateway Servers

Figure 9-3 depicts the CyberCash Administration window.

Figure 9-3
Consumers can perform functions such as changing their password in the CyberCash Administration window.

CYBERCASH WALLET The CyberCash wallet is the software that lets the consumer make payments over the Internet. It's available for both Windows-based and Macintosh platforms. The size of the Windows wallet is approximately 500KB compressed—when it's decompressed and installed, it takes up about 1MB of hard drive space. For more information on the various CyberCash elements, refer back to Chapter 8.

The Macintosh version of the wallet is 800KB compressed for 68000s, 900KB for PowerPCs, and 1.5MB for both 68000s and PowerPCs. Nearly half a million CyberCash wallets have been distributed for use.

When you hit the "PAY" button at a site that accepts CyberCash, the wallet is automatically opened. If the consumer does not have sufficient funds to cover the transaction, the authorization process rejects the order. After the transaction is complete, the wallet stays on the computer, ready for purchases anytime the consumer hits a CyberCash vendor. The wallet can be downloaded free from the CyberCash home page or retrieved directly from this site:

```
http://ftp.cybercash.com/cgi-bin/download .
```

Merchants who offer CyberCash transactions often offer wallet downloads at their sites as well. The CyberCash wallet is also bundled with Web browser software, and often in a CD-ROM accompanying a book about the Internet. Companies such as Checkfree and CompuServe also distribute the CyberCash wallet, and banks have the option of distributing the wallet software under their own name (as they do with credit cards).

After downloading the CyberCash wallet software, consumers are asked to establish a CyberCash wallet ID, as shown in Figure 9-4. This ID becomes connected to the customer's existing credit card numbers (as well as any new ones). Although at the present time, the wallet can only contain credit cards, plans are underway for it to also accept debit cards, electronic checks, and electronic cash.

Figure 9-4
The CyberCash wallet window asks the customer to create a wallet ID.

SECURE MERCHANT PAYMENT SYSTEM (SMPS) Secure Merchant Payment System (SMPS) is the glue that connects the three components of CyberCash. While the wallet stays on the user's computer, the SMPS lives on the merchant's server. When the consumer hits the magic CyberCash "PAY" button, the SMPS scuttles off with the transaction information. It's the SMPS that administers the details of secure credit card processing—it authorizes transactions, handles voids and returns, and provides receipts. SMPS also lets merchants process orders from 1-800-number telephone calls, e-mail, and faxes.

The SMPS software was clearly designed with merchants in mind—it easily integrates with merchant Web sites. The SMPS interfaces that accomplish merchant administrative functions also have a familiar browser-based look to them.

CYBERCASH GATEWAY SERVERS The CyberCash Gateway Servers act as a secure link between merchants and customers on the Internet, as well as between merchants and banks. CyberCash helps minimize the risks banks incur in electronic transactions by serving as a bridge between the Internet and the bank. With CyberCash as the intermediary, a bank that uses CyberCash never needs to truly extend to the Internet. For this reason, banks may use CyberCash to save time and money, as well as reduce the risk of corruption. CyberCash is easy for banks to deal with as well, since the transactions processed through CyberCash arrive at the bank in the same way as traditional credit card transactions.

A STEP-BY-STEP CYBERCASH TRANSACTION
Now that we've covered the building blocks of the CyberCash framework, let's examine the sequence of events in a CyberCash transaction (the entire transaction takes approximately fifteen to twenty seconds). This sequence may be familiar to you from Chapter 3, where we covered the process of a transaction using CyberCoins.

1. The Web user sees something worth buying at a site that accepts CyberCash. If the user has already downloaded the CyberCash wallet, the Web browser knows to open the wallet when the "PAY" button is activated (see Figure 9-5).

2. The customer decides how to pay. This choice is restricted to different credit cards today, although the wallet's contents will eventually be able to extend to debit cards, electronic checks, and electronic cash (see Figure 9-6).

Figure 9-5
PAY button for CyberCash.

Figure 9-6
Use a credit card.

3. When the customer sends the payment information for the transaction and confirms the purchase amount, it sets the transaction in motion, launching the request for approval for the charge. Table 9-1 shows a typical purchase.

TABLE 9-1: SUMMARY OF A TYPICAL ELECTRONIC PURCHASE

ITEM	COST
No Code (Pearl Jam)	$15.99
S&H	2.00
Tax	1.49
Total:	19.48

```
Encrypted credit card info
 `/(#``#__P``%AD``!4```#K!P``__
```

4. The merchant is then sent an encrypted charge payment message. This message is accompanied by the customer's order information, although the merchant can't see the customer's credit card information (see Figure 9-7).

5. The confirmed payment message and order information is received by the merchant's SMPS software, which then adds its own merchant identification information before passing the payment request to the CyberCash Gateway Server. This payment information is digitally signed and encrypted with the merchant's private key (see Figure 9-8).

Figure 9-7
Customer order information is sent to the merchant.

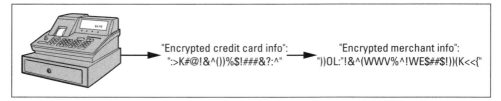

Figure 9-8
Encrypted merchant information.

6. The CyberCash Gateway Server's firewall system then decides whether to accept the charge authorization request. If it accepts, it takes the transaction off the Internet, and decrypts the message with a hardware-based crypto box (see Figure 9-9) .

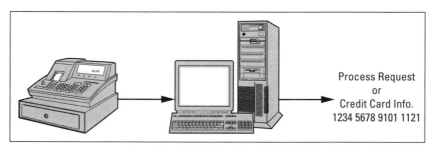

Figure 9-9
Processing the charge authorization request.

7. The CyberCash gateway sends the request, as shown in Figure 9-10.

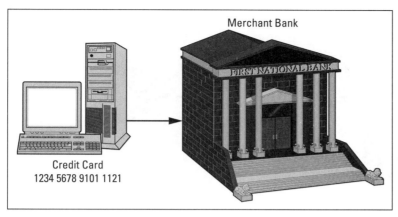

Figure 9-10
Sending the request via the CyberCash gateway.

8. The authorization request is then forwarded by the merchant's bank to the bank that has issued the credit card, or to American Express or Discover. The approval (or denial) is sent to CyberCash (see Figure 9-11).

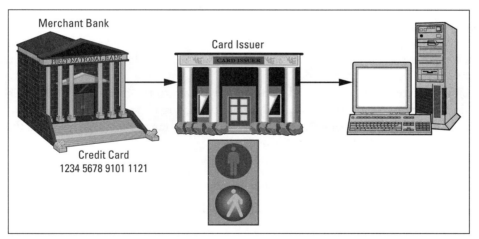

Figure 9-11
Merchant forwards request to issuing bank. Issuing bank sends approval/denial code.

9. CyberCash returns the resulting approval or denial code to the merchant. The merchant then sends it to the consumer (see Figure 9-12).

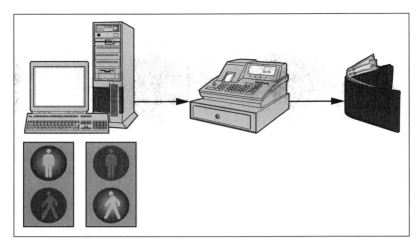

Figure 9-12
Merchant forwards approval/denial code.

CYBERCASH'S SECURITY AND ENCRYPTION

All communication that transpires among CyberCash's assorted elements (the wallet, the merchant, and the gateway server) is done so through the standard HTTP protocol. CyberCash uses full-strength 56-bit DES encryption technology when its card information is passed to the merchant and the server. The unique key it employs for each transaction is protected by 768-bit RSA public key technology (which is approved by the U.S. government for 1024-bit).

Since the customer's credit card number isn't visible to the merchant, CyberCash provides the customer with considerably more privacy than some of the other solutions. In the case of an emergency (such as a fraudulent transaction), the bank has the option of being supplied the card information.

For a look into how CyberCash can be used, voyage to the NetLink Web page at:

```
http://www.netlink.net/cybernet/cybernet.htm .
```

At the NetLink site, consumers can brandish a "virtual shopping cart" that automatically creates an invoice for the items thrown into it. When a consumer is through with their shopping spree, the virtual shopping cart's checkout stand automatically figures the sales tax and shipping fees. It then produces the grand total and asks how the customer would like to pay. If they don't already have the CyberCash wallet, they have the option to download it at that time. When the consumer indicates his or her form of payment, CyberCash begins sending its series of encrypted automatic messages. If everything is approved, the order will be sent out.

CDI's Self Serve Software

Commerce Direct International created an integrated environment that uses a "Digital Envelope Solution" (DES, to avoid confusion with the Digital Encryption Standard, we'll refer to it throughout as "CDI's DES") to ensure privacy for customers. The term "digital envelope" can be used to refer to a cryptographic block of data whose authenticity is protected by a shroud of encryption. CDI's DES works by employing a certificate of authorization, which is based on order processing, as well as a signature process, which is coded and "key-verified." MasterCard, Visa, American Express, and Discover cards can all be used with CDI's DES.

CDI's integrated structure allows the customer to remain unaware of its inner workings. The customer only has to complete the Self Serve Software online order processing form, which already includes the vendor's Internet address (and phone number, for direct connection). Padded with a 32-bit multithreaded, synchronous communication operating system, the Self Serve Software prides itself on its security, but also stresses that its order processing is a transparent, hands-off way for customers to use electronic commerce. As far as CDI is concerned, the most important thing is that the customer feels safe using their products, and that they return for future transactions.

The DES is part of CDI's suite of products that incorporate VBScript, Microsoft's ActiveX, and CDI's Self Serve Software. It's the Self Serve Software that CDI's service bureau uses to register customers and encrypt their credit card transactions. When the customer is ready to pay for services or products, CDI's encryption-based, secret-key processing system takes over the reins. It processes the order and renders the payment in a single step.

Self Serve Software is currently available for Windows 95 and NT platforms only, with versions for Macintosh and UNIX machines promised for the near future. You can read more about CDI at its home page, CDINet, where you can also register as a CDI consumer. CDINet can be found at:

```
http://www.cdi.net/times.cgi .
```

Before registering, however, it is important to understand that CDI has an aggressive attitude toward capturing consumer data—they advertise that they're not just collecting data for merchants, they're helping them build a customer "cyber-base" that will allow for tightly targeted direct marketing. From a consumer's perspective, this can be somewhat daunting. From the merchant's perspective, however, it is a marketing dream come true.

CDI'S SECURITY: RANDOM SAFETY

To outwit the fastest hacker minds, CDI uses a proprietary encryption algorithm process that goes beyond the standards of RSA (a public-key cryptosystem for both encryption and authentication invented in 1977 by Ron Rivest, Adi Shamir, and Leonard Adleman) and PGP (a freeware, high-security RSA public-key encryption application that stands for Pretty Good Privacy).

Rather than remaining stagnant and therefore predictable, the encryption standard is applied in a constantly changing way. CDI uses its synchronous channels in a random manner to accomplish this feat; by processing data packets in a wholly unpredictable order, it's difficult for malicious intruders to discern what parts would be most useful to intercept. The only way to identify a packet's contents is by applying the secret key, to which only two parties (CDI and the customer) have access.

CDI also boasts a key-verified signature process that automatically verifies that goods purchased from the vendor are originals, not illegal copies (this is particularly pertinent in dealing with software transactions, a CDI specialty). Self Serve Software is also capable of incorporating the code-signing key technologies that have been proposed by Microsoft in the hopes of furthering security.

CDI says that its method of continually changing the algorithms and methods of delivery makes it impossible to decipher the message or compromise the transaction. We'd advise them to never say never, but acquiesce that the system's randomization does give it a definite security advantage.

Netscape's LivePayment

LivePayment is an extension to Netscape's server platform that exists to support payments over the Internet. Supported by a bevy of leading financial institutions and banks, LivePayment acts as a type of terminal for POS interactions. By adding the LivePayment software to their sites, companies enable their Web sites to accept credit card transactions that are safeguarded through a high-grade encryption scheme. LivePayment can be used both for online display of wares and to collect payment for electronic content.

When Netscape originally debuted its LivePayment structure, it was under the name Netscape CashRegister. LivePayment is actually just one cog in Netscape's vision of an entire Netscape commerce platform, which features a suite of commerce-related server software (Netscape SuiteSpot) and corresponding extensions (Netscape Commerce Extensions). LivePayment is the first Netscape Commerce Extension to be released.

The following are some of LivePayment's most important characteristics:

- Offers an immediate payment option—it features an application that can instantly verify the customer's ability to pay, and transmits charges to the bank the minute the purchasing process has been completed.

- Uses JavaScript or command-line utilities to integrate payment functionality into Web sites.

- Can clear transactions by communication with bank card gateways.

- Supports multiple platforms and Web browsers.

- Features configuration and administration controls that provide flexibility in logging reports.

- Offers POS simplicity—LivePayment embeds a "paynow" tag in a Web document.

■ Provides security—it uses high-grade encryption technology that is based on RSA public key/private key algorithms, and also relies on SSL and SET to assure safe delivery of payment information.

■ Supports MasterCard, Visa, American Express, Discover, and Diners Club cards.

As a product from Netscape, LivePayment was predictably developed with a keen eye toward browser considerations. LivePayment has great browser-related benefits such as payment instructions that appear directly inside Web pages. However, it's not biased toward Netscape Navigator—it was carefully developed for use with a variety of browsers.

Check Netscape's Products page, found at the following URL, for up-to-date information about LivePayment:

```
http://www.netscape.com/comprod/products/iapps/client.html .
```

THE COMPONENTS OF LIVEPAYMENT

LivePayment is composed of the following elements:

■ A payment processor

■ A set of LiveWire commands

■ An administrative interface

■ A set of utility commands

LIVEWIRE   LiveWire is an "online development environment" that enables the construction of an interactive Web page. It does so through extensions to the Netscape HTTP server—these extensions are responsible for triggering JavaScript statements buried in HTML documents. There is a set of LiveWire objects that deal specifically with handling online electronic payments.

HOW LIVEPAYMENT WORKS

With LivePayment, a Web entrepreneur can create a Web page that works much as a bank card authorization system (another phrase for that small gray box through which credit cards are swiped). Figure 9-13 provides an overview of LivePayment's payment procedure. The page can ask the consumer for credit card information, verify the received data, and then send the transaction to the bank. It's relatively simple for developers to add LivePayment to their pages by embedding server-executed JavaScript code in HTML pages. This code is written using the HTML <SERVER> and </SERVER> tags. The JavaScript statements send requests to the LivePayment Card Processor, which is responsible for communication with the bank that processes the card.

When consumers indicate that they want to buy something with LivePayment, the Web browser will prompt them for their credit card information (as well as other information, such as their address). The consumers enter this information either into a SET-compliant application (like Netscape Navigator) or an SSL-secured form.

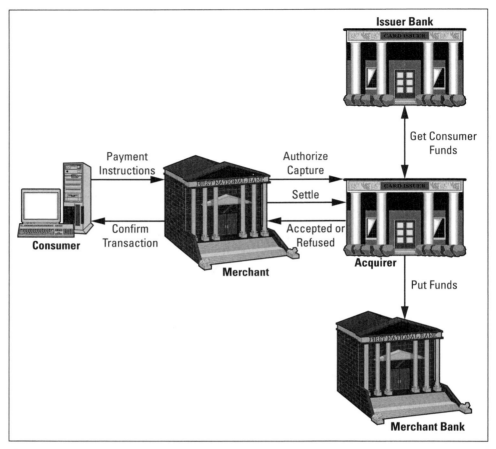

Figure 9-13
This graphic demonstrates LivePayment's payment procedure.

If the customer is using the SET option, the credit card information goes into the electronic form of a credit card receipt, called a slip. This slip, which is both encrypted and electronic, is what's sent off to the merchant. If the customer is using SSL, one of LivePayment's LiveWire extensions will create a slip for him or her.

When the merchant company receives this slip, it may send it to an "acquirer" institution for authorization. The acquirer is the financial institution that operates the payment gateway used by the customer. The merchant company may also act as its own acquirer. This acquiring institution holds the power to authorize or refuse the transaction.

If the transaction is authorized, the next step is a "capture," which takes the authorization information and charges the credit card. It's possible that a time lag may occur between the authorization and the capture, since the merchant shouldn't capture until the desired goods can be shipped. The transactions that transpire are accumulated into a batch, where they're confirmed. After the batch settling has occurred, the acquirer sets the transfer of funds from the consumer's bank(s) into the merchant's bank.

HOW MERCHANTS CAN USE LIVEPAYMENT

If you're a merchant, the process of signing up for LivePayment is similar to signing up for a card-swipe device. As with the other technology, the merchant's bank arranges for an acquirer (such as NaBanCo or FDC) to take care of the processing demands. The acquirer gives the merchant whatever identification information is necessary, and configures its Internet banking gateway to accept the merchant's transactions. To guarantee secure communications (and accurate identification), the merchant also must apply to a certificate authority for a digital certificate.

LIVEPAYMENT BENEFITS

LivePayment is a well-developed, complex payment environment. One of LivePayment's strongest selling points is its support—it's backed by leading banks and prominent financial institutions such as First Data Corp., MasterCard, Wells Fargo Bank, GE Capital Retailer Financial Services, CyberCash, and VeriFone.

LivePayment is armed with the tools to help you add it to your Web site (including templates). Its cross-platform abilities are also a positive attribute—it runs on UNIX and Windows NT operating environments. The sample applications that LivePayment offers are also useful, as is its JavaScript tutorial. LivePayment also gains strength by being a part of Netscape's wide-reaching environment for electronic commerce.

THE FUTURE OF LIVEPAYMENT

At the time of writing, LivePayment was working on creating an exportable SET version of LivePayment for use in foreign countries. Look for LivePayment to accept a wider variety of payment forms (including debit cards and electronic checks), as well as micro-payments. Netscape also plans to expand LivePayment with server-side Java applications.

For more information about LivePayment, refer to the LivePayment FAQ, found at the following URL:

```
http://www.netscape.com/comprod/products/iapps/platform/
livepay_faq.html .
```

The LivePayment White Paper can be viewed at the following site:

```
http://www.netscape.com/comprod/products/iapps/platform/
livepay_white_paper.html .
```

Open Market

Open Market heralds itself as "the only software available that offers companies a complete back-office infrastructure for secure Internet commerce." Its software solution is regarded as one of the most viable for businesses wanting to establish an online commerce presence. It provides solutions for business-to-consumer transactions as well as business-to-business transactions. One of OM's greatest selling points is the fact that it functions with all types of browsers, all varieties of payment types, and all security protocol formats.

Open Market offers three commerce products: OM-Transact, OM-Axcess, and OM-Securelink.

OM TRANSACT

OM-Transact is an extensive commerce application that provides companies the ability to offer secure payment, order management, and online customer service over the Internet. OM-Transact boasts that it features a "unique distributed architecture" (see Figure 9-14) that separates its shared services from content servers. By separating these entities, Open Market Transact lets companies focus separately on the content and the transaction infrastructure. This architecture wins points for its flexibility and ease to update, since either the "front end" or "back end" of the structure can change without affecting the other.

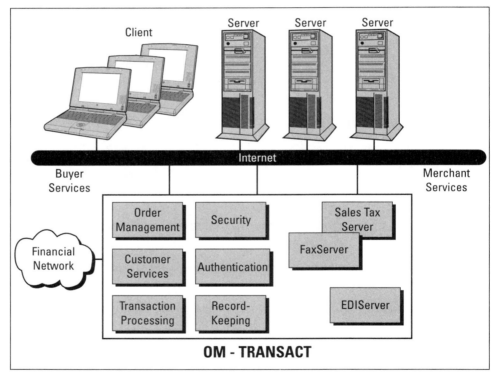

Figure 9-14
This illustration provides an overview of the Open Transport architecture.

Customers can either use OM-Transact for a one-time purchase, or establish an account for future shopping. If a customer is using OM-Transact to shop among multiple Web stores, they can grab a "shopping cart" that lets them conveniently combine your orders. With OM-Transact, merchants can offer the option of installment payments and subscription payments.

OM-Transact features some "optional modules" that can be included with the environment. There's a sales tax server that can automatically compute tax, as well as a fax server that will fax hard copies of transaction reports to merchants.

Some of the client standards Open Market's OpenTransact supports include the following:

- VRML (Virtual Reality Modeling Language)
- Java
- HTML (Hypertext Markup Language) 3.0
- Multipurpose Internet Mail Extensions (MIME) types

And some of the server standards it supports include the following:

- HTTP 1.0
- HTML documents
- Standard image formats (including GIF and JPEG)
- S-HTTP and SSL security protocols
- Acrobat/PDF document formats
- Common Gateway Interface (CGI)

OM-AXCESS

OM-Axcess allows companies to decide who can access its information over the Internet. It is used for EC Web applications' management and reporting needs. OM-Axcess centrally manages the authorization and authentication of end users, providing single sign-on access to private data that's distributed across the Web. Companies employ OM-Axcess when it's necessary to exchange information in a monitored, secure environment, or collaborate in controlled settings. OM-Axcess' architecture is scalable, and its support of multivendor servers arms it with a useful flexibility.

OM-SECURELINK

OM-SecureLink allows you to assure that users pay for subscriptions or goods that they're accessing from your Web site. It does so by generating a "digital receipt" that every user must have to prove their purchase. Without this receipt, which contains a unique keyed message authentication code (MAC), customers simply don't receive the goods. OM-Transact works in conjunction with OM-Axcess by verifying each MAC to make sure that the transaction is valid.

The following is the URL for the Open Market home page:

```
http://www.openmarket.com .
```

WebMaster Inc.'s CommerceRoom

WebMaster Inc.'s CommerceRoom is an electronic commerce software option that runs with Windows NT-based servers. Released in July, 1996, CommerceRoom is aimed at merchants who want to use automated servers to conduct their electronic commerce transactions and process credit and debit card information without human intervention. CommerceRoom works as a plug-in to Web servers, employs RSA certification (merchants are required to obtain RSA certification to use CommerceRoom), and uses ICVERIFY as its credit card verification network. For more information about ICVERIFY, see the section entitled "Benefits of ICVERIFY" later in this chapter, or turn to Chapter 10.

CommerceRoom has a familiar feel to it because it uses a Microsoft Windows graphical interface—WebMaster's specialty lies in creating Window NT-based Web and Internet server solutions. It's billed as a user-friendly package designed for non-computer professionals to handle and maintain with ease, and offers full telephone and e-mail support options.

The CommerceRoom software is currently available for Intel and MIPS CPUs, with versions for Digital Alpha AXP and PowerPC scheduled for imminent release. CommerceRoom is authorized by credit card processing organizations including Visa, MasterCard, Discover, and American Express.

At the time of writing, licenses for CommerceRoom cost approximately $649 per server. This price includes a manual and all the necessary software. CommerceRoom operates with relational database systems, including Microsoft's BackOffice, Microsoft Access, Microsoft SQL Server, Informix, and Oracle. You can check out current prices, as well as much more information about CommerceRoom at its Web site at:

```
http://www.webmaster.com/high/products/commerceroom/ .
```

HOW COMMERCEROOM WORKS

CommerceRoom uses the Internet to collect the customer's credit card information, so when customers want to buy something through CommerceRoom, they enter order information into their (form-enabled) Web browser. Although similar security environments make the merchant pay a transaction fee for each credit card use logged, CommerceRoom doesn't require this surcharge (this fee is forgone due to CommerceRoom's use of the Net rather than proprietary forms software to collect its information).

CommerceRoom's use of standard HTML for its interface also means that it receives information in a simple form post. It can be extended to work with database applications or CGI scripts as well. In addition, CommerceRoom is compatible with Microsoft's BackOffice.

The CommerceRoom software adds POS capabilities to a Web catalog. When CommerceRoom receives information about what the customer would like to buy and the selected form of payment, it processes the information either immediately, in real-time mode, or waits to process it as part of a larger, queued batch. Whether the transaction is processed (and authorized) immediately or is postponed, the customer will ultimately receive an e-mail confirming the purchase. Because CommerceRoom stores the transaction information in a secure area of the merchant's system, the transaction details are only accessible from the console, not from the Internet.

Anacom's SecurePay and SecureForm

Anacom's SecurePay and SecureForm are offerings in another environment that uses encryption security. Any Web browser that supports SSL can be used in conjunction with SecurePay and SecureForm, which were designed as a security solution for smaller businesses that can't afford to pay many thousands of dollars to design and implement a hardware-based system. Anacom offers merchants the ability to use encryption security for a monthly subscription fee, which starts at $29.95 per month plus 20 cents per transaction. The initial setup fee for SecurePay is $149 if it's used with the SecureForm service (both of which are explained later), and $249 if used with a merchant's own order taking system.

By using SecurePay, merchants have the ability to accept order information in a wholly secure, encrypted environment. Since the user's Web browser indicates that this support exists, Anacom hopes that its logo inspires sufficient confidence to generate orders.

Anacom already announced that it will automatically upgrade its server software for emerging standards and encryption technologies (including SET).

SECUREPAY

Instead of requiring a wallet or membership identification for purchases, SecurePay verifies and clears credit card charges as the customer orders. SecurePay doesn't have access to the funds—the funds go directly into the merchant's account. This method relieves the merchant of having to deal with clearing the credit card data, and is also ideal for transactions that require real-time speed (such as granting user access to a site after the entrance fee has been paid).

SECUREFORM

Anacom's SecureForm allow merchants to create their own product order forms, which are then linked to their sites. A merchant can contract Anacom only to use SecureForm, in which case they assume responsibility for processing the credit card transaction, and must therefore retrieve the payment and order information (this is the $249 setup option). Anacom is authorized as an ICVERIFY reseller, so merchants who want to process their own transactions can purchase ICVERIFY from Anacom at a discount. However, Anacom also offers the option of using SecureForms in conjunction with the SecurePay system (which requires only the $149 initial setup fee).

As the receptacle for credit card and other important information, SecureForm can be tailored to the merchant's needs through a program called FormBuilder. Form-Builder allows merchants to create customized order forms through simple fill-in-the-blank techniques. The merchant has free access to the FormBuilder, so that products and prices can be updated at any time.

SecureForm calculates tax, summarizes order information (including shipping and cost information), and can offer up to five shipping options. It can also list up to 50 different products and capture credit card information.

HOW THE SECUREPAY SYSTEM WORKS

Anacom's link to the secure server is displayed on sites where it is employed. When a customer wants to make a purchase, clicking on the link to the Anacom server will produce the customized order form. When the customer completes the order form, having entered all necessary credit card and payment information, a confirmation request will appear in the browser. When the confirmation is activated, the order confirmation is sent via e-mail to the merchant. If the merchant is using the SecurePay service, the credit card information is automatically processed through the merchant account. If the merchant is using solely the SecureForm service, they're responsible for handling the payment and order information, and have to process the credit card transaction.

The SecurePay and SecureForm systems may be an ideal option for merchants' initial foray into the realm of cyberbusiness, since they don't require any software to be housed at the merchant Web site. Whatever information that customers provide in the purchasing process is kept on Anacom's secure server, alleviating direct security risks for the merchants.

BENEFITS OF ICVERIFY

Both CommerceRoom and SecurePay have the capacity to use ICVERIFY. One of the reasons for ICVERIFY's widespread use is that, unlike many of the fresh start-up companies, ICVERIFY has a history of use outside as well as inside the Internet, and provides access to over ninety-nine percent of U.S. banks. On a multi-user system, ICVERIFY also functions more quickly than an individual VeriFone terminal. As long as there are transactions in the queue, ICVERIFY can keep the line open indefinitely, which can results in transaction times of only five to seven seconds.

CommerceRoom employs ICVERIFY with such enthusiasm and ease because ICVERIFY Inc. is one of its co-creators—WebMaster was the other half of the development team.

For more information about ICVERIFY, keep reading—it's the subject of the next chapter. You can also check out the ICVERIFY home page at:

```
http://www.icverify.com/ .
```

The Future of Integrated Solutions

In this chapter, we've covered several prominent integrated security solutions. Within a few years, or possibly even months, a significant chunk of what we've discussed may be laughably outdated, for many of these technologies are still decidedly in their infancy. There's been lots of buzz surrounding integrated solutions—and expect more to come, especially with the MasterCard and Visa marketing machines pushing SET.

Upcoming months or years will see security solutions become better, more sophisticated, and more widely used. However, even if they emerge into prominent use in the next few years, they may not be the best ultimate technology for the job. Many people argue that integrated technologies are little more than a stepping stone to a more secure security system, since software can be broken by other software, making all software-based security solutions fatally flawed. Hardware, on the other hand, can be used in a closed environment, which makes it fundamentally more secure. Hardware chips can have different circuits in each chip, meaning that each user can have a unique identification—what the folks at MeCHIP define as a "digital DNS."

MeCHIP—tomorrow's security solution?

The MeCHIP is a hardware solution that, according to the vendor, ensures secure online electronic interactions. Created by ESD (Information Technology Entwicklungs GMBH), the MeCHIP creates a "digital identity" for each of its users. Consumers are inextricably connected to this identity, much more than they would be to a single credit card number, since it could be used for *all* electronic transactions. The MeCHIP uses coding technology based on the internationally acknowledged DES and RSA methods, and although it can use existing payment methods such as credit cards or DigiCash, it doesn't create a new payment system. Rather, it serves as an identifying device to further secure the transmissions in these transactions.

Since the MeCHIP's code would be the online identity a customer would have to assume to purchase anything, it has to be portable and removable. At the present time, the semiconductor wizards at Fujitsu are the primary manufacturers of the MeCHIP. ESD makes the hardware available to its customers at production cost (the price varies according to production quantity).

The following three sections cover the three designs ESD provides for the MeCHIP.

PARALLEL PORT VERSION

The parallel port version has an exterior connection from the PC's standard printing port to the printer. The advantage of this version is that the PC doesn't have to be open for the MeCHIP to be removed, making the MeCHIP easily portable.

PCMCIA PLUG-IN CARD

The plug-in card sports a credit card-like format. You insert the card into the PCMCIA slot (this acronym stands for Personal Computer Memory Card International Association, a standards-creating body), which is becoming ubiquitous on most portable PCs, and being implemented into regular computers as well. This option is targeted toward hardcore laptop users who would be lost without a digital identity at their fingertips.

ISA PLUG-IN CARD

ISA's plug-in card is built into the PC's ISA interface. This card is geared toward PC manufacturers who want to include the pre-installed technology with their machines, as well as PC dealers who want to provide customers with a pre-installed option.

Is Big Brother watching?

The MeCHIP's ability to identify consumers won't be restricted only to electronic commerce. Hypothetically, that identity could accompany the owner anywhere they went online, popping up whenever they tried to download, purchase, or sell anything. If the scenario of being barred from certain sites due to the lack of a digital identity makes you think of George Orwell's *1984,* maybe it's not a coincidence.

Privacy is a big issue on the Internet, and many people think that electronic commerce will be a watershed for determining many privacy issues. Integrated environments are not conducive to privacy like Net cash solutions (discussed in the previous chapter) may be. When a consumer uses a credit card at a restaurant or store today, the transaction information is captured, and often used by the merchant. Customers may sometimes receive a catalog in the mail from information that the merchant has gleaned about their buying habits based on information captured from their credit card transactions.

Information that can be captured about customers when they're surfing and charging, though, may be much more accurately targeted. If a consumer has a chip or even an electronic wallet containing information about past purchases, buying habits, and so on, this information can be used to pinpoint buying and surfing habits with remarkable accuracy. To merchants, the ability to capture such information is a wonderful advancement, because they will be able to target the consumer one-on-one based on their tendencies. Customers who prefer to remain anonymous, however, will have an opposite reaction.

For the latest ideas in online privacy, refer to the Internet Privacy Coalition's Golden Key campaign site, located at:

```
http://www.privacy.org/ipc/ .
```

Summary

As the global economy becomes increasingly dependent upon electronic commerce, the security of electronic transactions will be essential. If the types of solutions mentioned in this chapter don't provide the maximum in security, their use will probably be restricted, or eliminated, perhaps to be replaced by something such as the MeCHIP. On the other hand, if these solutions prove to be reliable, safe, efficient, and cheap, they could become so ubiquitous that it's difficult to imagine life online without them. The success (or failure) of SET will have a great impact on integrated environments. One thing is for sure, although the precise details of how electronic commerce transactions will become a common part of online life may still be enveloped in mystery, there's no doubt that it will in fact become so.

Expect integrated development to be an active field in upcoming months and years. Because they're software-based, key-based systems always have to stay one step ahead of the punch, riding the brisk rate of the software development wave. If you want to keep abreast of new electronic payment mechanisms, the following sites contain links to many types of payment solutions:

```
http://ganges.cs.tcd.ie/mepeirce/project.html .
http://www.pitt.edu/~malhotra/elecomm.htm .
```

CHAPTER TEN

ICVERIFY AND OPEN CREDIT CARD AUTHORIZATION

ICVERIFY is one of the most powerful and open credit card authorization packages available, and is used in every imaginable retail situation. It was the first PC-compatible credit card authorization application to hit the market. Developed as ICVERIFY Inc.'s first product, its goal was to supplant electronic payment terminals such as those manufactured by VeriFone and other companies. ICVERIFY describes its product as:

> *A software package that provides Credit Card Authorization/Draft Capture, Check Guarantee, and Debit/ATM card authorizations functions on open-platform, Point-Of-Sale/business systems worldwide.*

In this chapter, we discuss what ICVERIFY is, what it does, and how to install and configure it. The background you obtain from this chapter will be useful to you in Chapter 14, where we actually incorporate ICVERIFY into a Web commerce solution.

Running ICVERIFY for Internet Commerce

Let's look at how to run ICVERIFY for Internet commerce. We take a look at how appropriate ICVERIFY is for Internet commerce, how to run it for a Web commerce site, and how to begin development for it.

165

How it stacks up

In our opinion, ICVERIFY is one of the most versatile pieces of credit card transaction software available, and can be easily integrated into a Web commerce environment. Others agree. WebMaster, Inc., uses ICVERIFY as the transaction-processing back-end of CommerceRoom, their turnkey Web commerce product for Windows NT. We found that ICVERIFY rates quite well when it comes to the three requirements for Internet commerce we delineated in Chapter 4: fast, open, and secure.

FAST

One of ICVERIFY's slogans is: "From zero to verified in seconds." Indeed, it does only take approximately twenty seconds for a transaction to occur. ICVERIFY can detect the existence of a request file and place a call within one to three seconds. And an answer can come back within another fifteen seconds. This kind of speed is definitely needed in the fast-paced world of Web commerce, in which hundreds of consumers from around the world could visit your site within an hour.

OPEN

ICVERIFY can be considered "open" in many ways. First, ICVERIFY is accepted by many of the major processors, banks, and check guarantors. It stays away from creating proprietary standards or attempting to force its own standards. Instead, it morphs itself to fit the mold of individual processors.

In addition, ICVERIFY can be driven by simple quote and comma delimited text files. ICVERIFY is completely open about the format of these files and what the fields mean. The "request" file is what actually initiates a transaction and feeds the transaction information to the processor. The request file can be generated by a copy of ICVERIFY or a program created by you, the user. The "answer" file contains the authorization data received from the processor, which can also be interpreted by a program written by you.

SECURE

Because ICVERIFY uses an external modem to dial directly into the processing network, it doesn't have the security problem authorization over the Internet has. Of course, ICVERIFY's openness is a double-edged sword: Because it doesn't encrypt request or answer files, development is made easier; but, it leaves the files open to be readable. You can, of course, implement your own scheme to encrypt ICVERIFY's request directory. It's ultimately up to you as the Webmaster to ensure the security of your site and ICVERIFY server. We look at ways you can do this in Chapter 14.

Features of ICVERIFY

ICVERIFY contains all of the features you would expect from a well-rounded credit card processing solution—and then some. Because of its venerability in the electronic commerce world, ICVERIFY has the benefit of years of experience as well as customer requests to assist in the direction of its product. The following lists some of the functions ICVERIFY performs:

- Processes VISA, MasterCard, American Express, Discover, Diners Club, Carte Blanche, JCB, and private cards

- Authorizes and settles cards in real-time

- Archives up to nine years of transaction information

- Supports PIN pads for ATM/debit card transactions

- Supports magnetic stripe readers for credit cards, driver's licenses, checks, and ATM/debit cards

- Generates transaction reports that can be printed or viewed

- Exports transaction data into plain text, which can then be imported into a spreadsheet or database

For more information about what ICVERIFY can do, or order ICVERIFY, contact ICVERIFY, Inc., at the number listed in the Vendor's List at the back of this book, or visit the ICVERIFY Web site at:

```
http://www.icverify.com .
```

The Anatomy of ICVERIFY

When ICVERIFY was created, there were already point-of-sale (POS) systems based around PC architecture, many of which ran POS software on top of the DOS operating system. For most of these, credit card transactions were processed either by an external electronic payment terminal or by proprietary software. ICVERIFY saw the need for a credit card processing application that could run on top of any POS system or be easily integrated into almost any back-office retail environment.

Platforms and requirements

ICVERIFY began as a DOS-based product, but now, there are also versions for Windows 3.1, NT, and 95 systems, as well as a handful of UNIX flavors. The DOS version requires a 386 computer with at least 2MB of available memory, running DOS 3.x or later. If you're running the DOS version under Windows, your system should have enough resources to run your version of Windows.

A native Windows version of ICVERIFY is now available, and allows access to ICVERIFY functions through a Dynamic Link Library (DLL). This means that POS software developers can easily include ICVERIFY functions in their programs, making interoperability with storefront and back-office applications easier. There is also great potential to use this DLL in CGI applications for Web commerce. The package now includes an OLE interface as well, so that it can be linked with other OLE-compatible applications.

On UNIX platforms, ICVERIFY is available for SCO UNIX, HP UNIX, Sun

Solaris, and IBM's AIX. ICVERIFY, however, has recently redoubled its UNIX efforts, building from its original emphasis on Windows 95 and NT as the emerging platforms of choice.

All versions of ICVERIFY require a 100 percent Hayes-compatible modem for communicating with the processing networks. They suggest that you have at least a 300 baud modem, but these days, you're unlikely to find anything under 14.4 Kbps except at a junk sale. Many of the processing networks, however, are still using 300, 1200, or 2400 baud modems on their end.

To use ICVERIFY's card reading functions, you must have a two-track capable magnetic stripe reader or better. In fact, ICVERIFY manufactures two- and three-track readers (the latter can read new U.S. driver's licenses with magnetic stripes). This, of course, will only be useful if you have walk-in business, and aren't taking orders exclusively over the phone or over the Internet.

Single-user configuration

The single-user version of ICVERIFY runs as a pop-up Terminate and Stay Resident (TSR) program on a DOS POS workstation with a modem. All sales, authorizations, and settlements occur on this single system. This setup is fine for a retail store, but won't handle Internet payment schemes unless they're done by hand. This is because the only way to enter information into a single-user copy of ICVERIFY is to bring up the pop-up by way of a user-defined hot key, and type the card information into the fields. An automated Internet payment system requires some way to pass the information to a running copy of ICVERIFY, which is where the multiuser configuration comes in handy.

Multiuser configuration

ICVERIFY's multiuser configuration was originally intended to be a method for networked POS workstations running a "slave" copy of ICVERIFY to send information to a "master" copy. Only the master computer requires a connected modem, with which it calls into the credit card processing network. Figure 10-1 shows a sample master/slave setup.

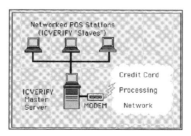

Figure 10-1
This is an ICVERIFY setup with slave POS workstations and a master ICVERIFY server, typical in a retail environment. © 1996 ICVERIFY, Inc. All rights reserved.

In a multiuser configuration, the slave stations are linked to a shared directory on the master ICVERIFY server. The slave stations run a copy of ICVERIFY in "slave" mode. Whenever a transaction is entered into a slave copy of ICVERIFY, the slave dumps the information (in the form of a request file) into the shared directory. The master station constantly runs a copy of ICVERIFY in "master" mode—in other words, it's not running as a TSR pop-up. The master ICVERIFY polls through the shared directory for request files, and uses the information to call up the processing network and authorize transactions.

If you understand this process, the benefit of the multiuser ICVERIFY configuration to Internet commerce becomes clear: The master ICVERIFY station doesn't require human attention—it processes transactions automatically. Automated transactions are essential to Web commerce, where sales can take place at any time of the day. Additionally, the transaction information is sent to the master station as a file. Once we understand the format of this file, we can generate the automated transactions with our own CGI programs, and have the ICVERIFY master copy process them. This is exactly what we'll be doing when we set up our own payment server.

Installing ICVERIFY

Installing ICVERIFY is a fairly straightforward process. The product is shipped on a floppy diskette for the DOS, Windows, and UNIX versions. The big question, however, is where you should install it. Since you will probably use ICVERIFY for Web commerce, you should install it on a server on which directories can be shared and mounted by your local systems. Which network operating system you choose depends on what protocols your local systems use: TCP/IP, IPX, or NetBIOS. For Web commerce, we suggest you install ICVERIFY on a system that is accessible by other machines on your local area network, but totally or partially firewalled from the Internet. We discuss this in further detail in Chapter 14.

DOS/Windows installation

The installation process for both DOS and Windows is essentially the same. Simply insert the floppy disk into the appropriate drive and run the "Install" program from the MS-DOS Command Prompt, through File Manager or Windows Explorer.

The installation program asks you on which drive and directory you would like to install ICVERIFY. The default selection is C:\ICVERIFY. If possible, don't install ICVERIFY on the C: partition where the operating system is. This way, you won't have to wipe-out ICVERIFY (and all of its transaction data) if you're forced to reformat C: and reinstall the OS. It's also important to put ICVERIFY in a secure location—preferably where most users don't even have Read Only access to—and one that is far out of reach from "guest" or "anonymous" accounts.

The installation program examines your computer to find the serial ports, and attempts to detect if modems are connected to them. If it discovers modems, then it will also concoct a dial string for them and give you the opportunity to accept or change it. It then asks you if you're required to dial a number (such as "9") to obtain an outside line. Finally, it gives you the serial port and dial string it has chosen. Write this information down—you'll need it later. After installation, ICSETUP runs automatically.

UNIX installation

To install ICVERIFY on a UNIX system, you must be logged on as "root" or a "super-user." Make a directory in which to place ICVERIFY. The directory "/usr/icverify" should be fine. The *tar* command is used to extract the contents of the floppy into that directory. Running the "./install" program immediately kicks you into "icsetup," which is discussed in the next section.

What's most surprising about the UNIX version of ICVERIFY is how much it resembles the DOS version. The UNIX version looks like a direct port of the DOS code. Most of the setup screens are the same, the directory structure is the same, and the filenames follow the 8.3 (eight characters preceding the "dot" with a three-charac-ter extension) naming convention. However, it still takes some UNIX savvy to properly configure and run ICVERIFY. For instance, you must understand the concepts of UNIX devices (such as /dev/ttyS1) and file permissions.

Speaking of file permissions, limit the number of people who will have access to the ICVERIFY directory and can run "icsetup" and view merchant information. It's advis-able to make the owner of "/usr/icverify" and its subdirectories "root" create a group for users allowed to execute ICVERIFY, and also give this group read, write, and execute ("rwx") permissions.

Configuring ICVERIFY with ICSETUP

Once ICVERIFY is installed, you must run ICSETUP before ICVERIFY may be run. ICSETUP (or "icsetup" under UNIX) configures ICVERIFY with your processing net-work's information, and also sets up local information.

Required information

To complete an ICSETUP configuration, you must obtain both your processor infor-mation and an ICVERIFY validation code.

PROCESSOR INFORMATION

The processor information you're required to enter in ICVERIFY depends greatly on what information your processor expects ICVERIFY to know when dialing in. The manual that comes with ICVERIFY lists what information is required from each pro-cessing network, but the amount of information needed and the terminology used varies from vendor to vendor. Table 10-1 gives you an example of the information needed from two of the major processing networks. It's up to you to call your processor and obtain this information.

VALIDATION CODE(S)

To activate ICVERIFY, you must obtain a validation code from ICVERIFY Inc. The validation desk at ICVERIFY will need the following in order to provide you with a code: your company name and address, your ICVERIFY serial number (found on the disks and package), and the information codes you received from your processing network. If you're running a multimerchant setup, then you must obtain a separate validation code for each merchant using ICVERIFY. Validation codes may be obtained from the ICVERIFY validation desk via phone, fax, or e-mail, Monday through Friday, from 8 a.m. until 5 p.m., Pacific time. Complete contact information for ICVERIFY is included in Appendix A.

TABLE 10-1: INFORMATION NEEDED BY ICVERIFY FROM TWO SAMPLE PROCESSING NETWORKS

PROCESSOR	INFORMATION CODES
GENSAR-L	Merchant Number, Terminal Number, Network Routing, Optional Serial Number, ISO ID Number, American Express SE Number
FIRSTUSA-S	Merchant Number, Terminal Number, BIN Number, Terminal Type 50 or JO, Store Number, Category/SIC/MCC Code, Country Code, City or Zip Code, Time Zone Differential, Terminal ID, Network Login String, Application ID

Setting up ICVERIFY

Once you have the required information, you can configure ICVERIFY with ICSETUP. ICSETUP is automatically run after installation, but you can also execute it directly from the ICVERIFY directory (\ICVERIFY\ICSETUP under DOS and /usr/icverify/icsetup under UNIX).

PROCESSOR SETUP

The first portion of ICVERIFY to configure is your processor information. After executing ICSETUP, you'll see a screen similar to Figure 10-2, where you're asked to select your Credit Card processor, your Debit Card processor, and your Check Guarantee processor. Since we're only concerned about credit card payment for Web commerce, that's the only field we'll concern ourselves with (at this time, you can't have someone enter an encrypted PIN code or give you a check over the Net). The following steps explain the processor setup:

1. Select from over 50 credit card processors supported by ICVERIFY, and enter the corresponding letter in the "Credit Card Type" field.

2. Scroll down to the "OK?" field and enter "Y" for yes. For our example, we chose "L: GENSAR."

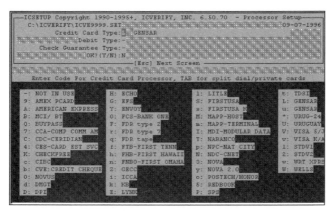

Figure 10-2
The processor setup screen on ICSETUP with a list of letter codes designating each processor.

3. The next screen is where you enter the information codes retrieved from your processor. On our screen (Figure 10-3), we're given fields for the codes that apply to our GENSAR service: Merchant Number, Terminal Number, Network Routing Number, ISO ID Number, and Optional Serial Number.

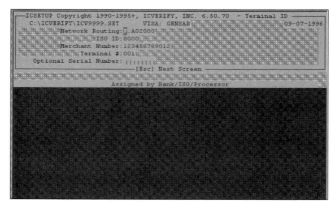

Figure 10-3
ICSETUP screen for entering processor-specific codes.

4. The next screen, shown in Figure 10-4, allows you to enter the data phone numbers ICVERIFY dials for authorization and settlement with GENSAR. This screen also includes GENSAR's requested American Express SE number, and entry points for help desk numbers that you might be required to call by voice.

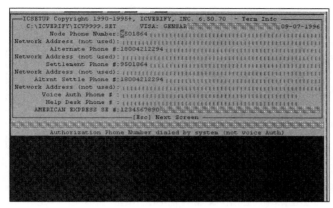

Figure 10-4
ICSETUP's screen for entering processor-specific authorization and settlement numbers.

5. Next, enter the terminal codes for the issued cards we will accept. For credit cards, our choices are VISA, MasterCard, NOVUS (Discover), AMEX (American Express), and DBO (Diner's Club and Carte Blanche). Depending on the processor and how the cards are settled, these codes may all be the same or all different. These codes are obtained from your processor. Also enter here the debit card and check guarantee information, which we'll ignore since we aren't using these features.

6. Finally, the screen shown in Figure 10-5 is where we enter our ICVERIFY serial number and validation code, which we obtained from ICVERIFY's validation desk. If your validation code is wrong, ICVERIFY will let you know.

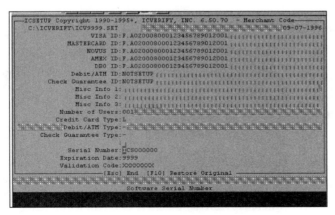

Figure 10-5
ICSETUP's Terminal ID screen for specific cards.

Many processors have their own terminology and data formats. Don't assume that a Terminal Number for Envoy is the same as a Terminal Number for NOVUS. Even within processors, there may be several different sub-networks within the network that require different information. For example, there's NOVA 1.0-3 and NOVA 2.0-y.

It's also important to note that ICVERIFY "configures itself" based on the processor information you enter, so examples you see in this book and other ICVERIFY documentation may not match what you see after you enter your merchant/processor-specific codes.

7. The Merchant Information screen is shown in Figure 10-6. The fields we need to fill out are the merchant name, address, and phone number fields. We call our sample company the Caffeine Consortium and type in the address.

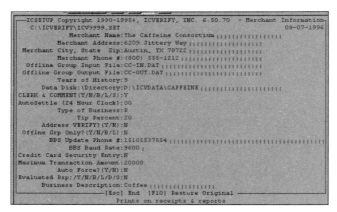

Figure 10-6
ICSETUP's Merchant Information screen.

The other fields in the Merchant Information screen should be set up specifically for Web commerce, so we'll go through them individually, as follows:

1. **Offline/Online Group Input File:** We also need to give the offline batch processing input and output files a name. We call ours "CC-IN.DAT" and "CC-OUT.DAT."

2. **Years of History:** This lets us select how many years historical data is to be kept. We stick to the default of nine years.

3. **Data Disk/Directory:** This is where ICVERIFY's data is located. It should be different from ICVERIFY's program directory, and also different from the

shared directory in a multiuser setup. If you're running a multimerchant setup, then each merchant should have its own directory as well.

4. CLERK & COMMENT: Because we have a multiuser/multimerchant setup, we select "L" to indicate that ICVERIFY will get the information from the request file (otherwise, the information would have to be entered by hand).

5. AutoSettle: This is where the hour (based on a 24-hour clock) of settlement is entered. This is the time that all transactions are settled. Settlement is either initiated by ICVERIFY, or performed by the host at the processing network. If it's done by the host, the time can be set to "00" (our processor supports host-based settlement, so this is where we leave it). Otherwise, enter the time you want settlement to take place.

6. Type of Business: We selected "R" for Retail. What you select (Hotel, Retail, Bar, Travel, and so on) depends on how your processor has you set up. Some processors only have the Retail code type.

7. Address VERIFY: If your processor supports address verification, then you can select "Y". If you want to do address verification, then you'll have to send the address and ZIP code to the processor along with the authorization request.

8. Offline Group Only: This should be selected if you want authorization to take place in batch. Since we prefer real-time authorization, we selected "N".

9. Credit Card Security: If "Y" is selected, then you must enter the last four digits of the credit card number by hand after it has been swiped through a magnetic strip reader. This is to verify that the raised numbers printed on the credit card and the numbers encoded in the magnetic strip are the same. As a Web commerce site, we don't use magnetic strip readers, nor do we have someone who can enter the card numbers by hand. We selected "N".

10. Maximum Transaction Amount: You must come up with your own management practices about maximum transaction amount, based on your agreement with your processor and how much product you think will be sold to each customer.

11. Evaluated Response: This applies to the request and answer files generated by a multiuser ICVERIFY setup. "Evaluated" means that ICVERIFY will generate a simple response from the full response of the processor. If you decide to work with ICVERIFY, you might want to examine their evaluated responses to see if you can glean the data you need, because the full response is chock-full of obscure and potentially confusing messages.

THE CREDIT CARD MENU

The Credit Card Menu, shown in Figure 10-7, allows you to enter specific information for the types of cards you will be processing. You are given a choice of the major card issuers—VISA, MasterCard, Novus, American Express, and DBO—as well as fields for private card issuers, labeled as "Other."

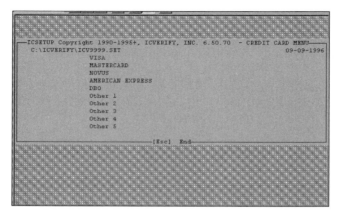

Figure 10-7
ICVERIFY's credit card selection menu shows the major card issuers and "Other" for private label cards.

Once you've selected a card type, the screen such as the one shown in Figure 10-8 appears in which you can enter card-specific information. The entry fields ask for the following information: the merchant number for that specific card type, phone numbers used for authorization, baud rate for the connection, voice authorization and help lines, and card code information unique to your card processor. All of this information is obtained from your processing network.

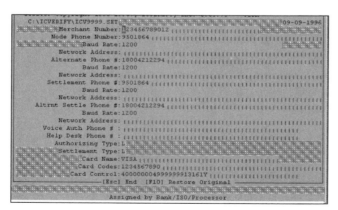

Figure 10-8
Fields for entering card and processor specific information for VISA cards.

After entering the information, you have the opportunity to copy the information for all other card types. This may be acceptable for your processing network, if they only have a single set of information for all cards.

Since we're not providing debit card or check guarantee services on our Web commerce site, we'll skip over those two configuration options and proceed to the hardware.

HARDWARE CONFIGURATION

The next screen that will appear during the ICVERIFY setup contains fields for configuring the hardware we're going to use with ICVERIFY. In our case, the modem is the only piece of hardware we will be using, as we don't have any external PIN pads or receipt printers attached. The ICVERIFY configuration screen is shown in Figure 10-9, and we will go over the items that specifically concern our Web commerce site.

- **Modem Port:** This is the communications port to which your modem is connected. In DOS/Windows, you can access a standard COM port this way, or use a non-standard one by providing the IRQ and IO base address of the port. In UNIX you should use the appropriate device (such as/dev/tty1). On a DOS/Windows system, we suggest that you don't run anything, such as fax software, that may reset the modem or COM port. On UNIX systems, make sure that there aren't any "gettys" running on that device (*uugetty, mgetty, getty*, and so on). "Gettys" are processes that control serial input and output in the UNIX OS. ICVERIFY will want full control of the port, and a getty may interfere with this. For both, we also suggest sticking to a standard communications port, rather than attempting to use a DigiBoard or some other multiport/MUX device. If you end up having problems, these devices will only confuse the issue.

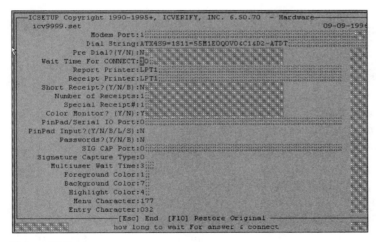

Figure 10-9
ICVERIFY's hardware configuration screen.

- **Dial String:** This field is used to define an initialization string and dial string for the modem. Try connecting to your processor with the one ICVERIFY creates for you. If it doesn't work, hit the Tab key in the Dial String field. This will bring up a list of modems that ICVERIFY has pre-defined init strings for (see Figure 10-10). Select the modem that most closely matches yours. If this still doesn't work, then you'll probably have to tweak it by hand. Most processors and banks still use generic 1200 baud modems, which expect no extra chatting from the modem on the other end (so there's no need for you to invest in a 33.6 Kbps modem!). If you're using a high-speed modem, disable all error correction, compression, and high-speed negotiation functions by modifying the initialization string. Consult your modem's manual and technical support for information about how to do this.

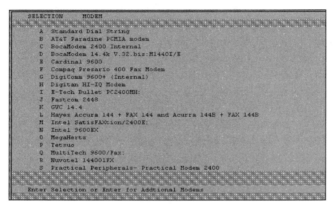

Figure 10-10
ICVERIFY's list of modems with predefined init strings.

■ **Multiuser Wait:** This applies to a multiuser setup such as the one we'll run for Web commerce. This defines how often the master copy of ICVERIFY will "poll" the transaction directory for a new transaction request to process. The default is three seconds, but one time should be fine as well. A setting of "0" causes ICVERIFY to quit after processing the transactions in the directory, so don't use this for real-time Web commerce.

POP-UP SETTINGS

The ICVERIFY pop-up settings apply to the DOS version only. It controls how the pop-up looks, what hot keys call it up, where in memory it resides, and where to "screen-grab" information from a POS workstation. Since we're running a Web commerce site that no clerk will be attending, most of this screen, shown in Figure 10-11, doesn't apply to us, either. There are only a couple of settings we're concerned with, which are as follows:

■ **Memory Resident:** We set this to "B", which causes ICVERIFY to run in the background for a multiuser setup.

■ **Pop-up as window:** This controls how you want an answer from the processor to appear on the station's screen. In our case, we want ICVERIFY to return the response in the form of an answer file, which can be parsed by our CGI programs, rather than a pop-up. To enable this, we selected "B".

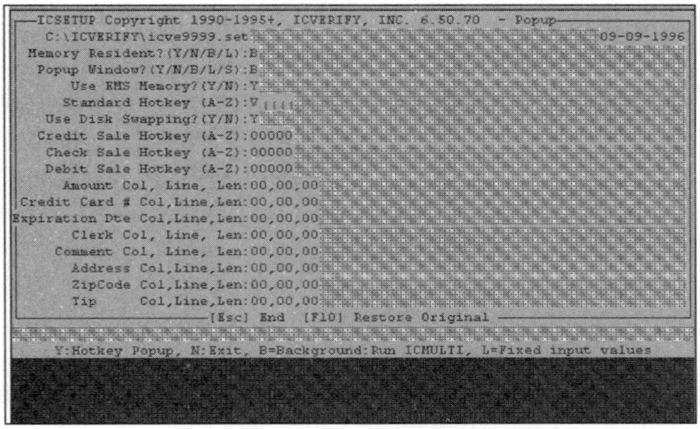

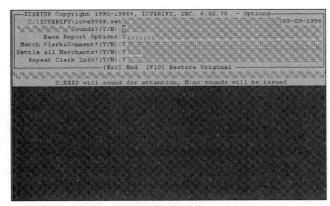

Figure 10-11
ICVERIFY's pop-up menu configuration screen. We'll want to disable pop-up functions for Web commerce.

OPTIONS SCREEN

All other miscellaneous ICVERIFY functions are lumped into ICSETUP's Options screen, shown in Figure 10-12. This screen controls sounds, clerk comments, and other functions. The ones we are most concerned with for our Web commerce site are as follows.

Figure 10-12
ICVERIFY's options screen has a couple of items you must modify for Web commerce.

- **Settle All Merchants:** If you wish to run a multimerchant setup (discussed later in this chapter), then you'll want to set this to "Y". This causes settlements/batches to be closed for all merchants when a settlement is done for any single merchant, and makes things simpler.

■ **Multitrans:** Setting this to "Y" allows you to process multiple transactions in a single dial-up session. Setting it to "N" causes the modem to redial for each transaction. For a Web commerce site, set this to "Y" to save as much time as possible.

Finally, ICSETUP will ask you if you would like to save the setup file you've created. If you don't think there are any problems, go ahead and choose yes.

Multiuser configuration

As we've said, for Web commerce you'll want to run ICVERIFY in its multiuser configuration. In this case, you'll have a server that acts as a dedicated ICVERIFY master and polls for request files generated by a CGI program. It's the station that's actually connected to the modem that will be used to call the processing network. We discuss example configurations in detail in Chapter 14.

All configurations assume that there's a shared directory in which request files will be dropped and answer files will be generated. For our DOS example, we'll call this shared directory C:\REQDIR, and for our UNIX example, simply /services/icverify/reqdir.

DOS CONFIGURATION

If your master ICVERIFY station is a DOS machine, then you'll need to edit your AUTOEXEC.BAT file to add the following lines:

```
LH C:\ICVERIFY\ICMULTI
C:\ICVERIFY\ICVERIFY /M C:\REQDIR
```

where C:\REQDIR is the shared directory for request and answer files. The /M puts ICVERIFY in master mode. When you reboot, ICVERIFY will start automatically in multiuser mode.

WINDOWS CONFIGURATION

The Windows configuration is also quite simple.

For Windows 3.x:

1. Use the New menu item under the File menu in Program Manager to create a new Program Item.

2. Select the Browse button and locate the ICVERIFY.PIF file in the ICVERIFY directory. Make ICVERIFY the description and click OK.

3. Use Window's PIF Editor to edit the ICVERIFY.PIF file.

4. Change the Optional Parameters line to include: /N /M C:\REQDIR. The /N tells ICVERIFY not to run as a memory resident (TSR) program, which you wouldn't need to do on a Windows workstation because it has multitasking capabilities. Memory management under Windows is different as well, so TSR programs don't work well within DOS boxes.

5. Click on the Background checkbox to have ICVERIFY execute in the background.

6. Put a copy of ICVERIFY in the StartUp group.

Windows 95 configuration is even easier:

1. From the desktop, go to the Windows ⇨Start Menu ⇨Programs ⇨StartUp on your computer's hard drive.

2. Go to the File menu of StartUp and select New ⇨Shortcut.

3. Browse for the ICVERIFY.EXE program.

4. Give it the name "ICVERIFY" and Finish the creation.

5. Select the new ICVERIFY icon and hit the right mouse button, then select Properties.

6. After ICVERIFY.EXE in the Command Line Field, enter: /N /M C:\REQDIR (See Figure 10-13). Apply the changes.

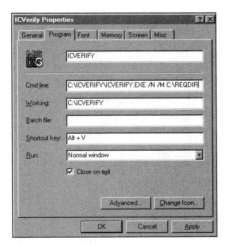

Figure 10-13
Modifying the command line for a Windows 95 multiuser setup.

Note that you don't need to run the ICMULTI TSR when running ICVERIFY under Windows. Windows 3.x, 95, and NT have their own multitasking abilities.

UNIX CONFIGURATION

For UNIX systems, you may run ICVERIFY as a daemon in the background. The best way to do this is to write a script with the following lines and place the script in your system's startup script, or put these lines directly in your startup script (usually "rc.*something*"):

```
cd /usr/icverify
umask 0
nohup ./icverify -m /services/icverify/reqdir < /dev/null >
/dev/null &
```

As you can see, the `-m` is the same as "/m" on DOS systems. The `/dev/null` devices are used to prevent anything from going to ICVERIFY from standard input (stdin) or being dumped from ICVERIFY to standard output (stdout).

Configuring ICVERIFY for multiple merchants

The multimerchant ability of ICVERIFY allows one multi-user copy of ICVERIFY to process transactions for more than one merchant. This setup requires that each merchant has its own merchant ID number, and that there are separate validation codes for each account. In Web commerce, this is especially useful for ISPs or Web presence providers that want to provide a Web commerce solution for customers. As a business, however, it isn't wise to have others use your merchant account and then pay them out of the same account. In fact, most agreements between you and a processor will legally not allow such a thing.

To set up ICVERIFY for multiple merchants, follow these steps:

1. Obtain the new merchant's merchant information from the processor handling the account. (Most likely the merchant will probably have to do this and then give it to you.)

2. With this information, obtain a new ICVERIFY validation code from the ICVERIFY validation desk. These extra merchant licenses cost approximately $100 per merchant.

3. Copy an existing ICVERIFY.SET file to a new name, in the following format: ICVExxxx.SET, where "xxxx" is a unique number you assign to the merchant (for example, copy ICVERIFY.SET ICVE0001.SET).

4. Stop and restart the ICVERIFY master program, which should be running in the background.

5. Use ICSETUP to edit the new SET file: ICSETUP ICVE0001.SET.

6. Set up the merchant with the merchant's processor information, just as you learned how to earlier in this chapter. The Data Disk:\Directory you choose should be unique to the merchant.

7. Enter the new validation code where appropriate. That's it!

Summary

In this chapter, we gave you an overview of the ICVERIFY installation and configuration process. ICVERIFY is an open-ended software package for performing credit card transactions on DOS, Windows, and UNIX systems. We use ICVERIFY in the rest of our credit card transaction examples in this book. In Chapter 14, we cover how to create and read ICVERIFY's request and answer file format. We also use ICVERIFY to create a CGI program-based online credit card payment system.

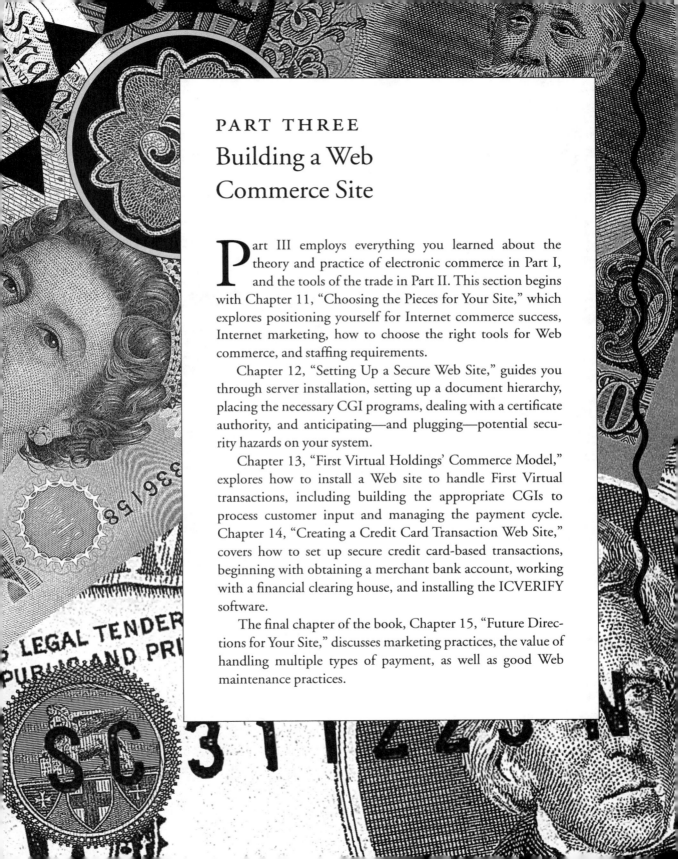

PART THREE
Building a Web Commerce Site

Part III employs everything you learned about the theory and practice of electronic commerce in Part I, and the tools of the trade in Part II. This section begins with Chapter 11, "Choosing the Pieces for Your Site," which explores positioning yourself for Internet commerce success, Internet marketing, how to choose the right tools for Web commerce, and staffing requirements.

Chapter 12, "Setting Up a Secure Web Site," guides you through server installation, setting up a document hierarchy, placing the necessary CGI programs, dealing with a certificate authority, and anticipating—and plugging—potential security hazards on your system.

Chapter 13, "First Virtual Holdings' Commerce Model," explores how to install a Web site to handle First Virtual transactions, including building the appropriate CGIs to process customer input and managing the payment cycle. Chapter 14, "Creating a Credit Card Transaction Web Site," covers how to set up secure credit card-based transactions, beginning with obtaining a merchant bank account, working with a financial clearing house, and installing the ICVERIFY software.

The final chapter of the book, Chapter 15, "Future Directions for Your Site," discusses marketing practices, the value of handling multiple types of payment, as well as good Web maintenance practices.

CHAPTER ELEVEN

CHOOSING THE PIECES FOR YOUR SITE

We've discussed many aspects of Internet commerce in the last ten chapters, from secure Web servers, to myriad payments systems, to security implications. Now is the time to decide what path your Internet commerce dreams will take and time to prove to management that the Internet is really the wave of the economic future. The Internet will make you a millionaire, right? Well, before you buy a yacht stall in the Florida Keys, there are many considerations to mull over.

Positioning for Internet Commerce Success

Before jumping into any business venture, there is a plethora of avenues to explore and decisions to be made. Conducting business on the Internet is unlike business anywhere else in some ways, and exactly like doing business in a standard fashion, in other ways. The main differences are the concept of a truly global market, a level business playing field, and the technological blessings and pitfalls associated with the Internet. Prior to any Internet commerce implementation, these issues must be addressed and plans made to accommodate them.

The two myths of the Internet

About three years ago, the public, and more specifically, the business community, began considering the Internet as a commercial vehicle. At that time, the Web was coming into being at CERN (*Centre European Researche Nucleare*—European Center for Particle Physics), in the form of HTML. Also, the first graphical Web browser, Mosaic, was developed by the National Center for Supercomputing Applications (NCSA). In those days, ninety percent of Internet traffic was confined to a UNIX prompt, which handled e-mail, file transfers, and remote server manipulation (telnet). Obviously, no one but computer scientists were impressed, and not even they saw the potential of a ready vehicle for doing business on the Internet. It was about this time that "Internet Hype Syndrome" began. Now, Internet hype is a part of everyday life, and the two main points that every reporter, journalist, CS professor, and guy next door like to quote are: "The Internet has a global market potential of fifty million consumers," and "The Internet levels the business playing field." Though both are true in theory, nothing could be further from the truth in actuality.

INTERNET MARKETING 101

Both the global market and the level playing field are ideals that are quickly being rescinded, refurbished, and spit back out as the familiar business sound bite, "niche marketing." Could a start-up software company in Charleston expect an overnight global market and an even a chance of selling its database program against software giants such as Oracle? The answer is obvious, Internet or not. Some claim that the Internet is a ripe market of fifty million consumers just slavering at their desktops waiting to buy. This is obviously not true, either.

Internet users are divided and subdivided by their interests, their technological involvement with the Internet, and simply their browsing habits. This creates a million different "little Internets," making it difficult for any company to reach everyone. The Internet marketplace as a whole is built on market niches. To best exploit these niches, a company must provide a place to sell a product effectively to a limited number of people who share a desire for the product. How a business increases desire in its products is a factor of marketing to the right people and qualifying those potential customers to purchase the product, much the same as real-world marketing. The following are a few qualifying factors, and how they apply to Internet commerce:

- **Customer's technology level.** The main qualifying factor to a company doing business on the Internet is whether their existing customer base even has Internet access, and questions in this direction should be included in any marketing survey campaigns.

- **Customer's payment potentials.** If your company is considering Internet payment methods, it will find that these are limited to the seemingly dubious *netcash* variety, or the apparently questionable *secure credit card transaction*. Customers must be convinced that your company and these forms of payment are legitimate. Again, this is a function of effective marketing.

■ **Customer demand.** This is a very obvious and essential assessment to any business venture. Is the product in demand, or can demand be generated? This question reaches another level when you consider the products people will actually buy over the Internet, and is similar to considering a mail-order product strategy. If a company sells homemade pies by mail order, only a small percentage of the customers actually reached by various marketing efforts will even consider buying pies through the mail. The only problem that's left, after factoring in the two previous points, is convincing them that they can actually purchase pies on the Internet.

Additionally, marketing an Internet site is not just marketing the site on the Internet, exclusively. Turn on the television, listen to the radio, open a magazine; URLs are everywhere. Land O'Lakes butter has a Web site. Do they need one? That is a question to be answered by those qualified to sell that product. Do you need a Web site? And, more importantly, should your company actually transact business on the Internet? Again, only you and your management team can answer that question.

The important thing to do, once the decision is made to go to the Web for its commercial potential, is to publish the URL everywhere the company normally advertises. Likewise, hype the capacity to order and pay for a product online. Get the word out through both online and standard marketing channels. Sure, the online channels may reach a few qualified customers across the world, but the standard marketing methods not only increase the "oh wow" factor in an existing client base, but also catch the eyes of Internet-capable potential clients who will notice the URL and read further. The Internet is not a closed system when it comes to marketing and selling a product. It merely offers an alternative, innovative, and often easier way to reach a customer and get them to buy. Knowing how to do this effectively differs little from standard marketing channels.

THE "LEVEL FIELD"

There is no such thing as a level business playing field. This may have been true when the Web was in its inception, and no one knew enough about it to utilize it to its fullest potential. But businesses have reacted to this phenomenon with an appropriate level of funding. Microsoft has a bazillion dollars to dump into its Internet infrastructure in systems, Web sites, products, marketing, and expertise. A small company just now approaching the Internet as a marketing and commerce vehicle has considerably less capital, and like most businesses, is confined to its understanding of the medium, the expertise available, and the resources to utilize both. The best way to position an Internet commerce strategy is to find the niche that will prove the most profitable.

The start-up software company in the earlier example would not take on Oracle in a standard marketing medium, such as print advertising, or TV ads. They wouldn't have the resources, nor would they have the reputation. Why would they think the Internet would be different? It's not. Web sites are relatively cheap, when compared to traditional commerce options. Running a virtual storefront doesn't require fixtures, a host of employees, a splashy marketing run, or other such overhead. But, the cost and effectiveness of the Web site are still the driving factors to the success of the venture, and no one at this point should be fooled by the hype.

Slave to technology

Though most IS managers may be loathe to admit it, the secondary consideration to implementing an Internet commerce plan is applied technology. What do you need to do the job, and how best can these tools be implemented? The answers to these questions vary as widely as the company's marketing plans, and, similarly, depend on the product, the target market, and the expected return on investment. The main considerations are server software, platform, connectivity level, security, and the transaction system. These issues are addressed in detail later in this chapter.

Again, the important thing to remember is that Internet commerce should only be a piece of the overall strategy for doing business. How big that piece is, and how much revenue is generated should determine the investment in Internet infrastructure deployed. After all, when the Internet hype is pushed aside, IS and business managers must take a hard look at the real potential for the Internet as a commercial avenue, and react appropriately. Many companies are jumping on the Internet bandwagon, with expensive Web pages and equally expensive back-end infrastructures, without a definite return on these investments. This is a strategy for disaster, and can be avoided with rational, standard business assessments. Internet infrastructure is an investment like any other, and should be approached as such.

A Game of Questions: Conceiving Your Commerce Web Site

The main question any business should ask before even considering Internet commerce is, can this product sell on the Internet? There are products that won't, obviously. Would someone buy a car, without seeing it first, from some Web site in Nova Scotia? Probably not. Would the same person buy a name-brand watch from a well known mail order vendor? More than likely. Would someone buy an HTML version of this book? Maybe, maybe not. The actual process of marketing the product and the virtual storefront, and qualifying the potential customer differs little from standard business practices. Before any consideration of where to proceed is made, this question should be answered. Subsequent questions should be based on the assessment of the product's Internet marketability. Some of the main questions everyone should consider follow.

What does the site cost?

The cost for an average Web site has been quoted by various sources, and the results are equally varied across the spectrum. Numbers in the range of $20K to $100K have been kicked around in the popular media recently. On average, standard Web sites are much cheaper, though commerce-capable Web sites do incur additional charges. How to determine the effectiveness of the site, and whether the effectiveness of the site is a function of the money spent, are still matters for debate.

So what does a business manager do when building a budget for Internet commerce? Research, research, research! There are sources for Internet consulting, programming, Web page design, connectivity, and a thousand other related services both online and in standard print media. There are evaluations published of product performance, service levels, and a thousand other infrastructure needs found from the same sources. Hopefully, we can dam up some of the flood of research options, by offering a simple trickle of wisdom: The level of investment in Internet infrastructure should be pushed toward the expected areas that will reap the most return.

Necessary equipment

In Internet infrastructure, there is a lot of equipment to consider. This base amount needed to run any site effectively is dependent upon other considerations, such as connectivity requirements, server and platform requirements, and the technical level of the staff, to name a few. Hardware can always find a purpose, but the trick is in buying smart. First, evaluate the capability of the equipment you already have, and then determine what you need to support a commerce site. Overall, the types of commerce Web sites which require consumers to pay for access should not require more hardware than a standard Web site, since sites where people have to pay to access are typically less popular than free ones. Some simple rules should bring this into better focus.

EVALUATE, BUY, EVALUATE, BUY

Put simply, never stop evaluating the needs of the commerce site. Once implemented, the original setup should be reevaluated throughout the site's life cycle.

You may find that three months after the commerce site is up, the traffic levels are much higher than expected. Capacity issues are the usual warning sign that your setup is in need of an upgrade. Regularly generating Web page status reports gives the IS manager a good idea of the number of hits to the site, the level at which transactions are being conducted and carried out, and a lot of other information. When traffic to the site, or other sites co-hosted on the server, begin to impede the commerce site's performance, the company should consider moving the site to their own dedicated server, either hosted on the ISP's backbone, or hosted locally with some connectivity out to the Internet. And this example only covers a very basic, though common setup. The main point here is that a commerce site, like any Internet service, often runs into capacity problems, which require constant monitoring to alert the staff when upgrades in equipment may be necessary. Alternatively, such constant evaluation also lets the IS manager know when to "downgrade," should the site be less popular than expected.

THE RIGHT TOOLS FOR THE JOB

Often, hardware needs are not correctly evaluated when implementing any sort of Internet service, resulting in one of two dangerous scenarios:

■ **We've got to go with the best!** This suggests that an uninformed business manager or an overeager IS department driving the evaluation process. The investment in such an arrangement would be much higher than the expected return, causing the company to play catch up just to cover the cost of overpowered equipment. This is where the constant evaluation process comes into play. If a corporation finds that the equipment implemented far outclasses the commerce site's potential, the hardware should be assigned somewhere else in the operation, or dumped entirely.

■ **Money is tight!** A timid approach to any Internet service, especially Internet commerce, is as bad as overcompensation. The bottom line is, more potential customers will be lost by faulty or inadequate hardware configurations than the actual cost of doing the job right the first time. The initial investment in equipment should reflect not only the expected traffic over the short term, but also over the long term. The choice in such areas as server platform should leave room for quick and easy upgrades, as needed.

Again, the point with equipment purchases is to make the initial evaluation of the commerce site's hardware needs count. And, keep that evaluation process in the forefront.

STAFFING THE WEB SITE

As with equipment, the initial evaluation process should take into account the number of staff and the level of expertise necessary to plan, build, and launch the site. After the site is launched, there is, of course, recurring maintenance to perform, e-mail and other correspondence to which you must reply, orders to fill, accounting to perform, evaluations to review, and a host of other tasks that warrant attention. When hosting a site at an ISP or other Web provider, general maintenance is usually handled by the provider's staff. This includes the actual server, the physical hardware, and the connectivity. All that's left are the Web pages themselves and their associated functions, such as CGIs, logs, and reports. In this scenario, one or two people well-versed in the technological and business end of the operation could easily run a small or even medium commerce site.

For large on-site operations, the number of administrators needed could be much higher. Not all of these people need be computer engineers; however, as with a commerce site, there are all facets of business-related functions to perform. Accounting, customer service, content management, and general management are among those needed, depending on the volume of transactions and the number of customers.

Web commerce sites require more work than standard Web sites for the obvious reason that sales and customers are involved. All the positions that a standard business would expect to need are likewise required for virtual businesses. The following is a list of general areas of expertise that are necessary to run any size Web commerce site. Personnel can multitask as needed to cover more than one area.

■ **Site engineering.** This is a general heading for the person or people responsible for the technological side of the Web site. This would include hardware, software, and connectivity planning, procurement, and maintenance, including the general set up of the commerce software and systems. If the site is hosted on an ISP's server, much of this job function should be included with the hosting arrangement.

■ **Webmasters (or -mistresses).** One or more people should be responsible for the Web site itself, including the design, construction, and maintenance of the HTML pages, programming of any CGI scripts, and general maintenance of the Web site. In most cases, very little of this would be handled by an ISP. If the page design is outsourced to a Web developer, there should still be a person in charge of interacting with the developers.

■ **Accounting.** Businesses live on money, thus there is a need for accountants and other accounting staff. Accounts receivable and payable positions must be filled. You also need a person to prepare the taxes or act as the main contact to an outside accounting agency.

■ **Business management.** Business managers drive the direction of the company and ensure that employees' work gets the company where it needs to be. Of course, small operations may have only one or two people, but one or both still need to think in business terms about the history, current status, and future potential of the Web commerce venture.

■ **Customer service.** A big catch-all category of persons responsible for keeping the customer happy. This could include technical support for products that require it; handling customer complaints; and other such day-to-day responses to customer needs. As it applies to a Web commerce site, this category of personnel need not be technically proficient, because little interaction with the technology, other than phone and e-mail, is required.

■ **Marketing and advertising.** Getting the word out, generating leads, and building the corporate identity are crucial to the success of any business. With Web commerce, the company has to face both online and standard advertising hurdles, as well as giving the customer peace of mind that the company and its products are legitimate. Again, these types of functions can also be outsourced to third-party advertising agencies.

WHAT DOES IT REALLY COST TO OFFER ONLINE PAYMENT?

The cost to implement online payment for products or services varies according to the size of the operation, the payment method implemented, and the volume of transactions. Internet commerce companies that use credit card verification systems are considered by merchant banks to be mail-order businesses, which typically carry the highest fees. This is obviously to cover the cost of fraud and misuse. So, Web site entrepreneurs should be aware of these charges, both obvious and hidden, when pricing products for sale from a Web site.

There is an initial cost for obtaining and setting up the commerce package, which could include the commerce software, a secure Web server, and any development costs for integrating the two. Additionally, with a merchant bank, which is required for clearing credit card transactions, there is a fee for setting up an account. Normally, commerce software, like ICVERIFY, only requires a one-time licensing fee to use the copy for a single merchant. In the case of an ISP that wishes to offer credit card payment services for its customer's Web sites, an additional copy of the software must be licensed for each merchant.

Recurring charges are generally low. A monthly service fee is sometimes required from the merchant bank, which clears credit card transactions, and is always necessary from the third-party payment organization for validation of virtual money. Some hidden charges such as monthly maintenance fees and statement generation fees (for sending you a monthly statement!), are not uncommon. Those looking into merchant bank accounts are advised to read all the fine print and ask specific questions about associated fees.

Other recurring costs, such as transaction fees, are usually derived as a percentage of the company's monthly volume, in addition to a flat charge for each transaction. The volume expected is typically claimed up front when a merchant applies for a credit card merchant account at a financial institution, and may vary with the card issuer. Thus, if a company applies for a merchant account with Joe's Bank & Trust, the company must specify what it expects the total volume to be for the account. Joe's Bank then generates a schedule of charges by percentage of volume from each credit card company. This percentage varies from card issuer and merchant bank, and is affected by the "class" of business applying for the merchant account. As stated earlier in this section, Internet commerce merchants are considered the highest risk business class, and thus incur the highest fees for volume percentages and per transaction.

WHAT'S THE TOTAL COST BREAKDOWN?

Table 11-1 denotes the total cost for three generic sites. These numbers will obviously vary by individual setup, and are meant as a general idea of what it costs to implement a commerce Web site. A more detailed description of each site is provided after the table, addressing components from which the costs listed were derived. When reading the following sections, remember to refer back to this table.

TABLE 11-1: A SUMMARY OF WEB COMMERCE SITE COSTS

	SMALL SITE	MEDIUM SITE	LARGE SITE
HARDWARE	Initial: $600	Initial: $1,200	Initial: $3,300
	Recurring: N/A	Recurring: N/A	Recurring: N/A
SOFTWARE	Initial: $200	Initial: $395	Initial: $1,000
	Recurring: N/A	Recurring: N/A	Recurring: N/A
DEVELOPMENT	No significant cost	Initial: $500	Initial: In-House
		Recurring: N/A	Recurring: N/A

	SMALL SITE	MEDIUM SITE	LARGE SITE
COMMERCE PACKAGE	Initial: $10	Initial: $700	Initial: $700
	Recurring: $30	Recurring: $140	Recurring: $600
CONNECTIVITY	Initial: $100	Initial: $300	Initial: $800
	Recurring: $50	Recurring: $600	Recurring: $1,200
MARKETING	No significant cost	Initial: $600	Initial: $2,000
		Recurring: $300	Recurring: $1,000
PERSONNEL	Initial: $200	Initial: N/A	Initial: N/A
	Recurring: N/A	Recurring: $2,000	Recurring: $13,000
TOTALS	Initial: $1,100	Initial: $3,695	Initial: $7,800
	Recurring: $80	Recurring: $3,040	Recurring: $15,800

SMALL SITE CONFIGURATION

In Figure 11-1, the merchant would host the actual Web commerce site on an ISP's Web server, and use First Virtual's payment system for transacting business. Connectivity to the merchant's location is kept at a minimum (28.8 Kbps modem), and likewise, personnel, marketing, and hardware costs are minimal.

This type of site is geared either toward the small business just getting into Internet commerce, or an established virtual business with a limited array of products. For our example in Figure 11-1, we chose to host the site on an ISP's server, using a third-party payment system (such as First Virtual), with minimal organization connectivity, personnel, and marketing. The site would be developed in-house and marketed only on the Internet. Expected volume for this account is $500 and fifty transactions per month. The basic infrastructure follows:

HARDWARE A minimal amount of hardware is required for a small commerce site, as the Web pages are actually hosted on an ISP's secure Web server. A 28.8 Kbps modem and a personal computer are the only hardware requirements.

SOFTWARE There is no need for a secure Web server or commerce software package, because the site is hosted on the ISP's server and uses First Virtual's third-party payment system. Web development tools, Internet client software, and some sort of accounting software would cover the needs of a small site.

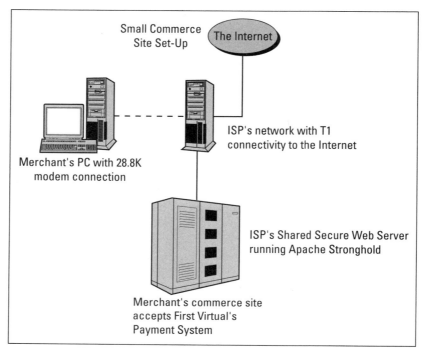

Figure 11-1
This diagram depicts a simple configuration for a small commerce operation.

DEVELOPMENT Because development is handled in-house, the cost is only in time, pay, and overhead for the developers.

COMMERCE CHARGES First Virtual charges a tiny setup fee ($10), and a basic recurring charge, based on the monthly transaction volume (29 cents plus 2 percent of the monthly transaction volume). In addition, First Virtual charges $1 to process and deposit payments to the merchant's bank.

CONNECTIVITY Connectivity to the merchant's site and the actual Web page is hosted at the ISP's site. Here, we've given the merchant a dial-up modem connection to the Internet, and the ISP account includes a secure Web page hosting service. Of course, these costs are variable from region to region and ISP selected.

PERSONNEL Because a small site is easily run by one or two people, the charges for personnel should be minimal. A nominal charge has been included in the table to cover any outside consulting that may be required.

MARKETING The site would be marketed on the Internet itself, which is practically free. Some announcements in appropriate newsgroups, adding the site to Web directories, such as Alta Vista, and maybe some sort of linking arrangement with other Web sites are sufficient.

MEDIUM SITE CONFIGURATION

The sample Web site shown in Figure 11-2 is still hosted at the ISP's location, except that it resides on a dedicated server owned by the merchant. Connectivity to the merchant's LAN is ISDN on demand, providing high-speed digital connections for each workstation, through an ISDN router. Hardware and personnel costs rise somewhat with this configuration, with the purchase of the ISDN router and the Web server. ICVERIFY and a merchant bank are used to clear credit card transactions, which incur considerable costs initially, but are manageable recurring charges.

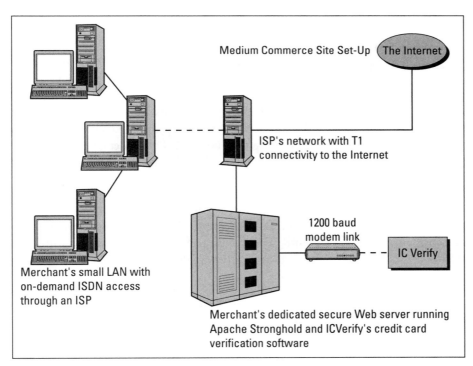

Figure 11-2
This is a typical medium commerce site configuration.

Typically, this sort of site would be fielded by a small- to medium-sized business with a certain level of on-site expertise, and a need for a more expansive setup. Though there are several options available as far as connectivity and hosting arrangements go, we've chosen to host the site on a company owned server at an ISP's site. In this example, ICVERIFY is the commerce package used, along with a generic merchant bank. Expected revenue per month is estimated to be less than $4,000 per month on forty transactions. Connectivity and personnel are still kept at a minimum, but we have included a modest marketing budget for both online and traditional print media sources.

HARDWARE This organization has a small LAN of four computers, and requires network connectivity on-demand via ISDN. Thus, the site needs an ISDN router. The actual network is not taken into account in the preceding cost estimate, assuming it is already in place. On the ISP's site, the company provides a medium-powered personal computer for use as a secure Web server. ICVERIFY's commerce software requires a dedicated 1200 baud modem, which can be picked up for a couple of dollars from a computer chop shop.

SOFTWARE The company's server, hosted at the ISP's site, is running a Stronghold: Apache-SSL secure Web server on a Linux platform. Necessary local software includes some high-powered Web development tools and accounting software for tracking transactions. ICVERIFY's credit card clearing software is covered in the "Commerce charges" section that follows.

DEVELOPMENT Development is handled in-house, with some of the CGI scripting outsourced to a third party. In-house development costs are covered in the "Personnel" section that follows, because developers in a medium-sized business require salaries.

COMMERCE CHARGES ICVERIFY charges $449 for its Internet commerce software. The generic merchant bank charges $300 to set up the merchant account, 30 cents per transaction, and a 3 percent charge on the monthly transactions volume. Add to this the $10 per month charge for processing and producing a monthly statement of charges.

CONNECTIVITY On-demand ISDN connectivity to the organization's site is quoted here at about $200 for a network connection per month. Actually hosting the server at an ISP's site runs about $400 per month. There are usually setup fees involved with both types of accounts. These prices vary widely and have been quoted here at $300 for both accounts.

PERSONNEL The cost of employees to both develop and provide ongoing support for the site is probably the most expensive aspect of doing Web commerce, as with any business. For this example, we've provided for one technical person to handle Web page development, as well as hardware and software procurement and management. Two other employees would handle the business end of the Web commerce venture, keeping track of accounting, marketing, and customer service. We assume they are self-managing. Although the cost listed in the table does not necessarily reflect monthly salaries for three people, our example takes into account that these employees are just assigned these tasks as a portion of their overall jobs within the organization.

MARKETING Because a medium site has such a high overhead due mostly to capacity and personnel, a solid marketing plan is needed, both on and off the Internet. Online marketing costs are kept to a minimum; however, print media advertising and other standard promotional campaigns can easily become very expensive. We've allotted a modest budget for this.

LARGE SITE CONFIGURATION
Commerce costs stay the same to set up, but recurring costs rise as the number of transactions and monthly ticket totals rise. T1 connectivity is expensive, but the example in Figure 11-3 takes into account that this connection is shared with the rest of the organization. Several persons are also needed to cover such areas as site engineering, customer service, accounting, and general management.

A large commerce site entails considerable costs. Typically, the commerce server is hosted locally, and depending on how many commerce Web sites are present, may span several servers. On-site connectivity, development staff, and other personnel are also required and expensive. In this example, we've opted for T1 connectivity to a large LAN, a single secure Web server running O'Reilly's WebSite Professional, and an adequate development staff. The marketing budget for the site itself is considerable, still relying on both online and traditional media, only more expansive. All development, support, and administration is handled by on-site employees, as well. By our estimates, this site would need to generate over $18,000 with about 180 transactions per month just to reap a modest profit.

HARDWARE For T1 connectivity, a basic Cisco router ($2,500) and CSU/DSU ($800) is included in the cost. Other ancillary servers, such as a mail or news server, are not included, as they are considered to be non-essential to the operation of the commerce site. The Web server is dedicated to the commerce site and is a high-end PC running Windows NT.

SOFTWARE O'Reilly's WebSite Professional is a secure, feature-rich Web server, and a solid commerce solution. High-end Web development and programming tools are essential to the success of the site, as well as some applications developed in-house for logging and reporting transactions and feeding them into a custom accounting system.

DEVELOPMENT Web site development costs are covered in the "Personnel" section that follows, because it is done totally in-house.

COMMERCE CHARGES This setup doesn't actually change from the medium site. ICVERIFY is well-suited for a medium to large Web commerce operation, and the same merchant bank statistics from the example Figure 11-2 were used. Obviously, the recurring transaction fees and percentages of monthly volume would be higher.

CONNECTIVITY The price for T1 level connectivity is actually much higher than the numbers we quoted, but we are not suggesting that the T1 be dedicated to the Web commerce site alone. The price estimate reflects an average usage by the site and its personnel to total about 40 percent of the total bandwidth usage over the course of a month.

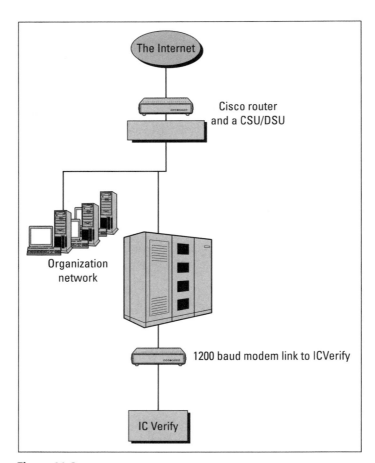

Figure 11-3
The large commerce site configuration is obviously the most expensive.

PERSONNEL A site of this size requires a dedicated technical person to handle both hardware and software issues, as well as provide technical support to the other staff members and general maintenance on the site itself. A connectivity engineer must devote some time to the commerce venture just doing standard network administration. A dedicated business manager, some of the IS manager's time, and about five employees dedicated to customer service and accounting are also a basic requirement. One person is needed to handle marketing the site.

MARKETING A splashy marketing and advertising budget is quoted here, including print media, online advertising space, and some television and radio advertising. As with other points in this large-site cost breakdown, only a percentage of an overall advertising budget is used, as proportional to the Web site itself.

How much revenue will the site return?

With all the infrastructure and recurring charges for the site, in addition to the stringent application process for the many varieties of online payment, companies approaching Web commerce for the first time are understandably leery. The medium is all but untried, the polls are still out on the effectiveness of Internet marketing, and an overall stigma surrounds security and the Internet. As an added roadblock, popular consensus is that the common consumer either does not have Web access or does not realize that the technology exists to transact secure commerce over the Internet. So, the question is, how do you make money on the Internet? Few people can answer that question with any certainty, but the following sections describe a few common-sense guidelines for generating income with a commerce site.

RIGHT SIZE

The key to reducing overhead related to any Internet service, and especially with a Web commerce site, is to start off with adequate capacity. When potential customers cannot access a busy or downed site, they probably will not come back. Likewise, overpowered equipment and a top-heavy organization will take away profits in sizable initial and recurring costs. As previously mentioned, constant assessment of the performance of the site is necessary to react to increased demand. Upgrading as needed insures the commerce site's capacity always slightly exceeds demand.

RIGHT PRODUCTS

There are no ready guidelines for suitable products to sell over the Internet. A good model to follow is the mail order marketplace. There are, admittedly, many different products available through mail order, but the most successful items are non-perishable, easy to mail, and have reliable quality. Items such as clothes, books, music CDs, software, and the like are well-suited to Internet commerce. Flowers, travel agency services, and shareware were among the first and most successful products marketed and sold online. Adult-oriented services are also surging across the Internet, such as the sale of access to X-rated images. The main product of the Internet, however, is still information. Real time stock-quoting services, research firms, and other such information vendors enjoy across-the-board success, because information is the nature of the Internet.

SMART MARKETING

Selling products and services, through any medium, requires smart marketing. On the Internet, this is essential. There are hundreds of Web pages popping up every day that sell advertising space. Newsgroups, Internet indexes, and other high-traffic sites are usually free to add links, or post announcements. Traditional media sources are usually expensive and ineffective unless approached with a big budget. However, putting together public relations sessions disguised as free seminars, press releases, and the like are always cheap options. The two important points to include in any marketing effort are the URL to the site and the fact that it is Internet-commerce capable. For existing customers with Internet access, the benefit to purchasing products online is great. For potential clients, the added value of convenience and reputation may be the deciding factor in a purchasing decision.

RELIABILITY

Unreliable businesses are not so for long. Never is this more true than when conducting Internet commerce. Consumers are approaching Web commerce timidly, with good reason. Credit card numbers are safeguarded against fraud in everyday life, and still such activities are rampant. Overbilling, untimely product delivery, or a for-pay service that is not available because of overloaded or downed servers, all bring the integrity of the merchant into question, and hurt return and referral business. This is another reason why constant monitoring and assessment of the systems involved, both electronic and organizational are essential. Merchants with numerous customer credit card complaints could find their merchant accounts revoked.

SUMMARY OF GUIDELINES

Again, making money in any business venture requires the information outlined previously, except that with Web commerce, the obstacles are more of an impediment. As consumer and financial institutions become better acquainted with the concept of the Internet and its potential for transacting business, Web economies will surge. The companies, both large and small, which establish themselves early in the online market will see greater rewards as new consumers venture forth onto the Internet. Not only will they have honed their systems and procedures to the electronic business world, they will also have established a reputation for being among the first companies to develop the Internet commerce arena.

What are the security implications?

The Internet and credit card numbers. It sounds like a hacker's dream. Security is thus a number one priority when dealing with Internet commerce. Although it is not impossible to intercept and retrieve credit card numbers or other sensitive data from public e-mail, the practice is not exactly common knowledge. Likewise, with data encryption techniques currently being fielded across the Internet, secure transmission of data is a present reality.

Secure Web servers enable users to input credit card numbers in payment for goods and services using data encryption technologies. Consumers, merchants, and financial institutions are still shy when it comes to Internet commerce, and the main reason is, they do not understand the technology. The same consumer that would balk at buying a $20 book using a credit card through a secure Web page will turn around and read out their card number to a travel agent in payment for airline tickets.

Although most of the fear of using a credit card on the Internet is unfounded, a threat does exist. A company wishing to do business over the Internet should research the most secure method that suits the product and the company's overall Internet commerce strategy. Secure Web servers enable customers to type their credit card numbers into a form, which, when transmitted, is encrypted using RSA data encryption technology. Thus, while the various packets of information zoom across the Internet, they are protected by this encryption—not from interception, but from being read. Once at the destination, a special key decrypts the transmission, and the merchant's Web site processes the request.

Secure Web site software is usually fairly expensive and requires expertise to set up. So what's a merchant to look for in alternative Web payment solutions? Chapter 3 covers third-party Internet payment systems and details how to handle security in a variety of ways. Two of the three systems presented in this book use RSA encryption techniques with backup verification processes, which either notify the user of confirmation of a transaction, or give the customer an adequate chance to dispute any charges.

First Virtual works in the open, by giving the user and the merchant a VirtualPIN, which is an alias of either the consumer's credit card number or the merchant's bank account number. Each transaction is individually verified via e-mail to the customer, who replies either "Yes" to validate the transaction, "No" to decline it, or "Fraud" to indicate that some unauthorized person is using the consumer's VirtualPIN. These insecure e-mail messages all go to First Virtual's network, where, behind a firewall, their back-end verification system processes the transactions over private bank networks, returning an accepted or declined message to the merchant and the customer. These payment methods are equally valid for doing electronic commerce, and offer equally secure alternatives to often expensive credit card verification systems.

The commerce server will only be as secure as it appears to be to the prospective consumer. If the site is unprofessional or prone to faulty operation and frequent downtime, the customer reaction will be one of mistrust. This will impede business more effectively than actual security breaches. A Web commerce company lives and dies on its reputation, which can only be gained and maintained by professional dealings in all aspects of the operation.

The Web site should be professionally designed and easy to use, especially the secure areas where customer's actually purchase products. Shipments of products should be timely and insured, to prevent delays, mix-ups, and lost parcels. If information or other online services are the main products, these services should be operational at all times, with mirror sites on other servers; nightly data backups of such information as users who have registered and paid for recurring services; and ordering and shipping information. Internal professionalism in procedures also ensures that employees, contractors, or other business associates do not take advantage of insecure data, giving the company a bad name. Again, the reputation of the Web commerce company cannot be overstressed. This reputation draws or repels customers more readily than the online payment methods used or the products sold.

Summary

The preceding chapters have given a good indication of what areas need to be developed in an online commerce business plan. Planning and implementing a Web commerce site is a lot of work, requiring expertise that may be above the casual Internet user. Likewise, companies less than two years old or companies with a nebulous product, may find it hard to actually obtain a merchant account through a financial institution or third-party payment organization. Thorough research, wise consulting, and benchmarking other Web commerce sites are three key actions that improve the chances of a commerce site's success.

Magazines, books, newspapers, and online sources also offer insight into the often confusing options available for Internet entrepreneurs. Given all of this attention, however, one can expect that Internet commerce will be as common as mail ordering a sweater, paying for plane tickets by telephone, and simply driving to the store and shopping for groceries.

SETTING UP A SECURE WEB SITE

Setting up a secure Web server is the first step you need to take when setting up a Web commerce site. It will provide the peace of mind that your customers desire before doing any type of commercial transaction online. In this chapter, we discuss issues you should consider before setting up your commerce server, such as how to deal with a certificate authority, and how to install and configure our secure server of choice—Stronghold: Apache-SSL.

Stronghold Is Our Choice

Of all of the secure Web servers we've investigated, we chose Stronghold: Apache-SSL. There are several reasons for this:

- It's similar to NCSA, the mold from which practically every other Web server is made; therefore, issues that apply to NCSA (and Stronghold: Apache-SSL) apply to many other Web servers as well.

- Its installation process is very hands-on, meaning that you can learn quite a bit about how secure servers work by installing it.

- It has very few frills to confuse the major issues.

- Its low price makes it one of the most accessible of all the Web servers for consumers.

The version of Stronghold we focus on is 1.3 (still beta at the time of this writing), the major features of which were covered in Chapter 5 of this book. Since Stronghold is available only for UNIX, we also focus on that platform—specifically the Linux flavor (though most everything will apply to the other versions of UNIX as well). If you have UNIX, we suggest that you visit the Stronghold Web site at:

```
http://stronghold.c2.net .
```

Download the evaluation copy of Stronghold and follow along with us.

If you don't use UNIX, you'll find that much of what we cover will apply to your secure Web server as well, be it on Windows NT or Macintosh. Where appropriate, we also make comments about the differences in other platforms which we feel are important.

Considerations Before Starting

There are a few basic topics to investigate when setting up a secure server. The following sections detail these considerations.

Security and accessibility issues

Where you place your Web server, both the physical machine and the Web server software, is the most important concern to anyone setting up a secure Web site. Should it be behind a firewall? Who should have access to the information? What other services should it run? What good is it to have a $2,000 piece of software and military-grade encryption technology at your disposal when the Web server it's running on is publicly accessible through other means and has little or no access control lists?

In this section, we don't go through the numerous security and configuration issues pertaining to secure servers one-by-one and piece together what you should do. Instead, we explore three scenarios in which secure servers are most often deployed—intranet manager (low accessibility), Web merchant (medium accessibility), and Internet Service provider (high accessibility), and tackle the problems with which a webmaster in each situation should be most concerned.

THE INTRANET MANAGER

Someone running a secure server at an intranet site definitely has something they don't want the outside to know about. A secure intranet Web server typically houses the proprietary information and intellectual property of the company running the server. The type of information you might find includes employee records, client leads, sales reports, and engineering specifications. Finding any of this information in a rival's hands wouldn't be very pleasing. Consequently, a secure intranet Web server should be the least accessible server of the three scenarios we examine. It's also the secure Web server upon which the other scenarios will be based. When it comes to Web server security, you want to build the tightest and thickest brick wall you possibly can, then decide where to put the doors and windows.

FIREWALLS Firewalling an intranet server can be extremely simple or distressingly difficult, depending on how your organization is structured. For most corporate intranets, there are four different firewall situations, ranging from easiest to most complex:

1. **No Internet connectivity.** In this instance, you would not connect your LAN to the Internet at all. If you don't have Net connectivity, nobody can get in. Of course, it seems unlikely that any company employing intranet technology would not have some type of connectivity to the greater Internet.

2. **LAN access only.** "No LAN is an island" once it's connected to the greater Internet, and it's up to the network manager to keep intruders out. The best way to do this is through access control lists on a firewall-capable Internet router, such as a Cisco or an Ascend MAX. Ideally, you would block all traffic from that machine from leaving your LAN's IP subnetworks, and block any access to it from other than your LAN. This solution is best for companies with smaller LANs.

3. **LAN/WAN access only.** This solution incorporates "LAN access only," but also allows access from IP subnetworks which are directly connected to the LAN via some type of WAN technology. Examples would include a leased T1 line to a corporate division, ISDN connectivity to a branch office, or a dial-up modem pool for remote access users. Access to the Internet would still be completely blocked.

4. **Internet access.** It has become more common for companies to use the Internet as a medium for their intranet. Depending on the scale of your remote access solution, paying an ISP $20 per month can sometimes be cheaper than maintaining a modem pool. The security, however, can be jeopardized. If you have an employee who needs to use an ISP to access your intranet, then try to find one that has an account with a fixed IP address. Then modify your firewall to allow his or her IP address to get through, but keep everyone else out!

Another way to limit access is via the Web server itself. Most Web servers allow you to do this, either through the administration utility (as in Netscape), or through a configuration file (as with Apache). Both ways work using deny/allow lists, which restrict the systems that can access your Web server by domain, subnet, or machine. On NCSA and Apache (including Stronghold), this is done with an access.conf file. The disadvantage of using the Web server's access lists is that it's less reliable than a true router-level firewall. The advantages are that you don't have to be too TCP/IP network savvy to configure it, and you can restrict access within your own LAN.

For further reading on network security, we suggest *Building Internet Firewalls* by Chapman and Zwicky (1995, O'Reilly & Assoc., Inc.). For more information on Web server security, we suggest the "Web Server and CGI Security" chapter of *The CGI Bible* by Tittel, Gaither, Hassinger, and Erwin (1996, IDG Books Worldwide), or your Web server's documentation.

USER AUTHENTICATION User authentication is an HTTP feature that allows you to protect document trees with password security. In other words, to access protected areas of your server, the user must have a user name and password in your Web server's authentication database, and must log in to retrieve the data (similar to an FTP log in).

It's important to remember that HTTP user authentication isn't the same that as the client/server authentication that takes place during an SSL or S-HTTP session, and the user name and password being sent isn't encrypted in-transit unless you're using a server and browser that support one of these protocols.

The nice thing about user authentication is that it allows you to provide an extra layer of security for certain areas where you would like to restrict access, making it a must for intranet environments. For instance, there's no reason why your phone reps should need access to your prototype engineering specs. Likewise, the engineers shouldn't need to modify your client database.

Like access control, every Web server allows for some sort of user authentication. On Apache and NCSA servers, you put an .htaccess file in the directories to which you want to restrict access. Each .htaccess file has its own information on what users are allowed in and what password file to use.

ACCESSIBILITY VIA OTHER TCP/IP SERVICES If you're concerned enough about the data on a particular Web server to run a secure server on it, then chances are you probably don't want people touching it in other ways, either. Telnet, FTP, and other services should, therefore, be highly restricted. If you are using a UNIX system, then you may want to consider running the TCP Wrapper package (tcpd) that comes with Linux and many other UNIX distributions to block access to these services except to certain hosts. If you're running a system other than UNIX, such as Windows NT, it might be best not to install extra services (such as Telnet) in the first place.

It's also wise to restrict these services through your router's firewall. Telnet, FTP, TFTP, and Finger are services you should watch out for in particular. If you don't care about sending mail from the server, then also restrict or turn off the sendmail application. If you're running Windows NT, 95, or OS/2, you should also restrict the Net-BIOS over TCP/IP service ports of 137, 138, and 139.

It's a good idea not to run your secure Web server as anything else. For instance, don't also make it a mail or news server. The money you save by glomming servers together isn't worth risking your sensitive data. The ultimate truism of system security is: If you don't think you'll use a service, then don't even run it.

FILE PERMISSIONS If you do allow people other than yourself to access your system via services other than the Web server, then you'll want to set file permissions appropriately. In most cases of an intranet server, there's a small group of people maintaining it, so this shouldn't be a problem. Still, it's best to follow these simple rules:

■ Only allow people who need to update pages to have a log in account on the server.

- Don't have a guest account on the server.
- Don't allow any of the secure documents to be world readable. Running a secure server won't matter if someone with an account can FTP in and read all of the data because your document root and all the files in it are world readable.

We go over file permissions and other security issues in more depth in the "Tightening the Holes" section of this chapter.

THE WEB MERCHANT

A Web merchant is a company that is running its own Web commerce server, as opposed to sharing a server with others at an ISP. The Web merchant is a company that has an ISDN connection (or faster) to the Internet and has the server sitting in its office. From this server, the merchant sells products or information online, and maintains it from its location. The data that is housed on the server and transferred to and from the server is typically financial information (such as a buyer's credit card number), and products (if the products are transmittable over the Internet).

Like the intranet manager, only people within the company need to have access to update the server, but people on the outside also need to be able to retrieve data from the Web server with their browsers. The need to have the server partially open makes securing it a little harder and riskier than in an intranet situation.

FIREWALLING Unlike the intranet secure Web server, the Web merchant's secure server *must* have some type of Internet access. For most Web merchants, this means that they won't restrict HTTP access to their secure Web server at all, as potential buyers could be coming from practically any IP address. The exception to this would be merchants that know where their clients are coming from. For instance, if the clients are a handful of banks, a merchant can open up the server only to people coming from the banks' domains.

USER AUTHENTICATION The Web merchant can employ user authentication to its advantage as well. Some of the products for sale on the Internet today aren't material items, but information or services of some sort available directly on the Web site, such as graphics, financial news, or online stock trading. User authentication provides a convenient means to block off the portion of your site that's for sale, requiring that the buyer purchase the user name and password from you for access.

ACCESSIBILITY VIA OTHER TCP/IP SERVICES When it comes to other TCP/IP services, the Web merchant should follow the example of the intranet manager: Only the people within the Web merchant's company who need to update files on the Web server should have access to it via other TCP/IP services. It's best to completely block off these other services from the Internet using your router's firewall software—possibly pigeon-holing it if one of the people updating the site uses an ISP account with a fixed IP address. Also, the Web merchant should not run the secure server as anything else, such as a news or mail server. Doing so would be asking for problems.

FILE PERMISSIONS Again, the Web merchant should follow the same rules as the intranet manager when it comes to file permissions: Only people within the company whose job it is to update pages should have any type of permission to read, create, or modify the secure data.

THE INTERNET SERVICE PROVIDER (ISP)

The ISP is sort of a special case when it comes to running a secure server. By ISP, we don't necessarily mean someone who provides Internet access, rather an Internet *presence* by allowing individuals and companies to operate and maintain a Web site on their Web servers. This presents a number of security and accessibility issues:

- Since the ISP may not be providing the connectivity for the person updating the site, that person could be coming from *anywhere* on the Internet. You can't guarantee what IP address they'll have, because they may come from an account that assigns them dynamically.

- When you run a Web site on an ISP's Web server, you're typically sharing that Web server with dozens (or even hundreds) of that ISP's other customers. Each customer should get their own directory for their pages, one to which no other customer has access.

- The ISP's customers will probably require that their potential buyers be able to get to their site from anywhere on the Internet.

The goal of an ISP offering a secure Web site is to allow each of its customers to act as a Web merchant, but all on the same server. It has to be highly accessible, but protected enough to give each customer a sense of security. This makes the ISP's secure Web server the most complex one to manage, and the most risky to operate.

Between a jewelry warehouse and a jewelry store, which one is more likely to be a victim of theft? The warehouse has a security system that's on 24 hours a day, a limited number of employees are allowed to enter, it's closed to the public, and it has a complex shipping and receiving log. The store keeps its security system off during business hours, there's a high employee turnover rate, it's open to the public, and merchandise is constantly changing hands. It doesn't matter that the warehouse has millions of dollars more in jewelry than the store. The store survives on its openness, which also makes it an easier target for shoplifting or employee theft. Now think of the warehouse as an intranet site and the store as an ISP site and you'll see the unique challenges that the ISP faces.

FIREWALLING Firewalling for an ISP is rather simple. You basically can't firewall most of your server if customers from elsewhere on the Internet are going to be updating their sites there. The best thing to do is firewall the entire server from the Internet with your router, then start opening holes in TCP/IP service ports that people need to access. Here are the main ones that will have to be open to the entire Internet:

- **Telnet** for customers to access shell accounts and manipulate files in their site (This one's actually optional, as you may be able to allow only FTP.)

- FTP for customers to upload files to their sites
- HTTP **port 80** for the ability to allow people to access the insecure Web server
- HTTP **port 443** for access to the secure Web server
- **Ports greater than 1023** for FTP

All other ports should be closed to the rest of the Internet, as long as you're not running any other services on the secure Web server.

USER AUTHENTICATION An ISP generally doesn't deal with user authentication, because their customers will decide what directories in their hierarchy need to be protected. The ISP should, however, encourage and facilitate the use of user authentication for their customers, because it provides a convenient means of tracking who's accessing the server.

ACCESSIBILITY VIA OTHER TCP/IP SERVICES Anyone running an Internet server will try to use that server for as many Internet services as possible to keep costs down. It's not unusual to find a single server acting as a primary DNS server, a WWW server, an anonymous FTP server, and a mail server. ISPs are no exception to this rule.

When it comes to a Web server, however, an ISP should try to keep it acting only as a secure or insecure Web server, and nothing else. The fewer services you have running on the server, the less vulnerable it will be to attacks through these services.

If the ISP doesn't allow UNIX shell accounts, then you may want to consider not allowing access via Telnet, either. Most functions that people need to update a Web site, such as creating directories, changing permissions, and so on, are available through modern FTP clients. Telnet can easily be blocked through a firewall or TCP wrapper.

FILE PERMISSIONS File permissions may be the most important tool that an ISP has, because it's the one where the ISP can exercise the most control. Each of the ISP's customers has a directory in which to put the data they want to serve. The permissions for each of these directories must follow three conditions:

1. The owner of the directory needs to be able to read from and write to that directory to place files there.

2. The Web server software needs to be able to read from the directory to serve retrieved files.

3. Other customers with accounts should not have any access to the owner's directory. For example, the webmaster from company A, after updating the files in her directory, should not be able to download the files in company B's directory with her FTP client.

Dealing with Certificate Authorities (CA)

If you're going to run a secure Web server, you're going to have to use a CA. It's the nature of both S-HTTP and SSL to require that your server's public key be digitally signed by some trusted party. Your CA can either be one of the large Internet CAs, or your own organization. The following sections outline the pros and cons of internal and external CAs in detail.

INTERNAL CAS

In an intranet situation, it may be advantageous for you to run your own certificate authority. In the case of an internal CA, you have a system that signs certificates for the secure Web servers at your site, thus verifying they are who they say they are. One advantage of the internal CA is that sensitive information never has to leave your site and end up in the hands of a third-party CA. The disadvantages are that your certificate will be less flexible, not accepted by default by any browsers, and not accepted on the Internet. Netscape 2.0 and later has an option that lets it accept certificates besides those signed by VeriSign or the other popular CAs, shown in Figure 12-1.

Figure 12-1
With Netscape, you can accept a certificate signed by a private CA.

Even though your certificate authority signs certificates only for servers on your network, you'll still want to assure your network users (and yourself) that the information is secure. It's therefore necessary to keep your CA's private key completely secret. Most security experts agree that a large CA should take the following measures:

- Do not connect the CA to a network.
- Restrict physical access to the system and log who uses it.
- Allow log in privileges only to authorized personnel.
- Shield the system from radio frequency (RF) surveillance.
- Have a security expert evaluate your CA.

You're also going to need some CA tools. Stronghold comes with some basic CA tools for intranet applications, and X-Cert software has a plug-in module that allows for more advanced CA features. Because becoming your own CA is more a concern of intranet managers, we won't cover it further here in this commerce book. You can, however visit the Apache-SSL Web site to learn more.

Depending on the size of your organization, the number of certificates you're the CA for, and the sensitivity of your information, you'll want to protect your CA system appropriately.

EXTERNAL CAS

We suggest using an external CA when you are engaging in electronic commerce or have a secure site that's being accessed from multiple places on the Internet. Not for technical reasons, as it would be just as easy for someone to accept a certificate signed by your organization, but for peace of mind between you and your customers. Having an external CA act as a trusted third party ensures a client that the data being sent from your Web server is actually by who it says it is, and that it isn't being forged—even by someone within your organization. Choosing a CA that's trusted by many people (and many browsers) means that clients won't have to put up with the hassle of deciding whether or not the certificate is real, as in Figure 12-2. For example, the Netscape browser already knows that a certificate signed by VeriSign is true and correct.

VERISIGN'S CA PROCESS VeriSign, Inc., started by RSA, Inc., has the honor of being the first certificate authority on the Internet to sign digital IDs. Because of this, VeriSign has the most experience on how the process works, and they are one of the most secure and most widely accepted CAs around. In addition, experience has taught them how to make their process simple to complete.

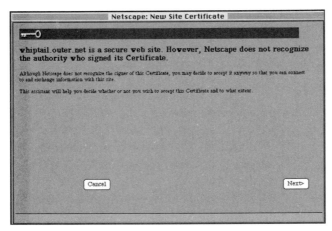

Figure 12-2
VeriSign can sign certificates for a plethora of secure servers.

A REAL AND ELECTRONIC PAPER TRAIL   There are four steps you must complete
to have your secure Web server signed by VeriSign:

1. **Enrollment.** This is completed through an online registration form. To
complete this form, you need the fully qualified domain name (FQDN) of the
secure Web server; the organization name; the organization unit (such as the
department or division) running the server; the organization's city, state, and
country; authorized billing and technical contacts; the secure Web server
package you're running; and payment information (check, purchase order, or
credit card). Other information, such as your Dun & Bradstreet number, will
help VeriSign determine the financial status of your organization and speed the
processes along.

2. **Generate a certificate request.** A certificate request is typically generated
and sent to VeriSign by your secure Web server package. Because of the
venerability of VeriSign, most secure server packages are able to generate a
request for a signed certificate from them.

3. **Order completion.** Once VeriSign has your enrollment form and certificate
request, they will process your order. To do so, they may check with third-party
sources to determine the health of your organization. If you are a relatively new
company (in business for less than six months), you should also fax or mail
them your articles of incorporation or other appropriate charter documents. If
they need more information, they will contact you.

4. **Install your certificate.** Once your order is complete, you will receive your
signed certificate within three to five business days. It's then up to you to install
the certificate on your secure server. We'll cover how to do this with Stronghold.

EVERY STEP IS IMPORTANT! VeriSign suggests you follow each of these steps in sequential order, and try not to leave any out. Like the InterNIC (and many other Internet businesses and organizations) VeriSign is experiencing explosive growth. They've tripled the number of secure Web server vendors they sign certificates for just in the first six months of 1996! Because of this, you'll want to stick close to their process, and not leave a step out. Also, keep track of your order and be sure to contact VeriSign if you don't receive your signed certificate within a week. Finally, be prepared to spend some money, depending on your required level of service and authorization. Individuals will pay up to $24 a year for an ID, while servers or businesses will pay anywhere from hundreds to thousands of dollars a year, depending on their particular requirements. Visit the Digital ID Services area at `http://www.verisign.com` for the details.

Installing and Configuring Stronghold

Compared to some UNIX Web servers, including the Apache server upon which it's based, Stronghold is fairly simple to install. A shell script guides you through most of the installation process, including the creation of your certificate and sending the certificate request off to a certificate authority. In this section, we guide you through the installation process, warning about potential problems along the way.

Note: Because Stronghold is a secure server, it is assumed that you have full authority to install and configure new software packages on the server. The CA you choose will also assume that you have full authority to operate the server for which you're requesting a signed certificate. It's suggested, therefore, that you don't even attempt to install Stronghold unless you have superuser access to the machine on which you're installing it.

Extracting the archive

Once you've obtained the archive appropriate to your platform, you'll need to GNU unzip and untar it. Unlike its cousins NCSA and Apache, Stronghold isn't distributed as a full HTTP server directory hierarchy. Instead, it's an installation package which you run to create the *httpd* server and SSL directories.

Once you've downloaded the archive appropriate to your platform, move the GZIPed tar file to a directory where you normally put the installation package for new software. Something like */usr/src* might be a good choice. When the package is extracted, it will be placed in a directory called *./ApacheSSL* wherever you unarchive the package.

The Stronghold platform we downloaded is for the Intel processor version of Linux kernels supporting ELF binaries. To extract the archive, we run the following:

```
tar -zxvf "apachessl_us-1.1.1+1.2+1.3b2-i386-unknown-
linux(ELF).tar.gz"
```

After doing so, you should see the ./ApacheSSL hierarchy being created.

Installing the server

After the package has been extracted, you can begin the server installation. Stronghold comes with an installation shell script called *INSTALL.sh* that helps you through the majority of the installation process.

A word to the wise: The installation process requires that certain environment variables be set for SSLeay to generate your certificate. To make your life easier, go ahead and set them up before you run the install script. For csh, enter the following lines (or add it to your .cshrc):

```
# setenv SSLTOP /usr/local/ssl
# setenv PATH /usr/local/ssl/bin: . . . the rest of your PATH . . .
```

For Bourne shell, use the following (or add it to your .profile):

```
$ SSLTOP=/usr/local/ssl
$ PATH=/usr/local/ssl/bin: . . . the rest of your PATH . . .
$ export SSLTOP PATH
```

Once this is set, go ahead and run INSTALL.sh from the ./ApacheSSL directory:

```
/usr/src/ApacheSSL [32 ] # INSTALL.sh
```

This will begin the installation process, which consists of a series of prompts for information.

The whats and wheres of installation

To help prepare you for the questions which INSTALL.sh will ask you, we go through each question here, and explain what you should enter.

1. The first question you'll be asked is which platform you're running. Unless you downloaded the archive that contains all of the available platforms, you'll more than likely only have one choice, which you should enter at the prompt.

```
Available platforms:
i386-unknown-linux(ELF)
Pick your platform > i386-unknown-linux(ELF)
```

2. The next portion of the installation questions you on which directories you wish to install the SSLeay and Stronghold packages. For SSLeay, the default directory, /usr/local/ssl, should be fine, unless you have some other personal preference. For security reasons, it may be a good idea to keep it in /usr, though, as opposed to a structure like /home. If it fails due to permission problems, it will let you know.

```
Where do you want to install SSLeay? [/usr/local/ssl]
Testing permissions...done
Installing SSLeay...done
```

3. The next question asked is where you would like to place the ServerRoot, which is the main directory hierarchy for the server. Servers such as NCSA and

Apache often come preconfigured for installation in a /usr/local/etc/httpd directory, and it's up to you to change your configuration files if you place them anywhere else. For most first-time installations, the default /usr/local/apache ServerRoot directory should be sufficient. Likewise, going with the default /usr/local/apache/logs directory for your server's logs will keep them separate from your other log files. If you decide on other locations, however, the installation program will conveniently update your configuration files for you.

```
Where would you like to locate the ServerRoot?
[/usr/local/apache]
Where would you like to locate the logs? [/usr/local/apache/logs]
```

4. Next, you'll be prompted for the name of your server. The installation script selects as the default the output it receives from the UNIX hostname command. Many people running Web servers, however, have one actual name for the server and one or more canonical names as well. For instance, it may be called *whiptail,* but also have a canonical name of *www.* In this line, put the popular name you want your server known as, as well as what you want to send to your CA. For our example, the whiptail name is fine.

```
What's the name of your server? [whiptail]
```

5. You'll also be prompted for the e-mail address of the server administrator. It will default to "webmaster@*hostname*" but you should specify the well-known e-mail address of your webmaster or administrator.

```
What is the email address of the server admin? [www@outer.net]
```

6. The next questions deal with which TCP/IP ports on which you want to run the server. Stronghold's *httpsd* can listen on two ports simultaneously—one for SSL HTTP and one for non-SSL HTTP delivery. The well-known port for SSL HTTP is 443, and the one for non-SSL HTTP is 80. Stronghold will use both of these as defaults. If you are running an Internet commerce server, these are definitely the ports you should use, as most browsers will default to them. If your server is an intranet server, you can run the server at other ports of your choosing (usually above 1023). This will afford you a little extra security, as your server won't be running on the well-known ports.

```
What port do you want to run for SSL? [443]
What port do you want to run for nonSSL? [80]
```

7. The user and group your server runs as is quite important. Keep in mind that when you run a server as a certain user, the server will gain all the rights and privileges of that user, in addition to any CGI programs that a client executes. In other words, it's best not to run the server as anyone with any power, especially *root.* The default user *nobody* is a good choice. For the group,

however, you should create a group called *httpd,* rather than the default *nogroup.* We'll explain why later in the section entitled "Tightening the Holes."

```
What user should the server run as? [nobody]
What group should the server run as? [nogroup] httpd
Installing Stronghold...done
Configuring Stronghold...done
```

At this point, everything should be installed. Now begins the process of generating a key, a certificate request, and a temporary test certificate.

Generating a key and certificate pair

Before SSLeay generates your key and certificate pair, it will remind you to add the SSLTOP variable and /usr/local/ssl/bin path in your environment. Don't worry about it: We've already added this and it will say this regardless of whether or not you actually have them in your environment. If you didn't take our advice and make these changes, go ahead and do it now.

```
Now add SSLTOP=/usr/local/ssl to your environment.
Also add /usr/local/ssl/bin to your PATH.

Edit your .cshrc, .login, or .profile appropriately:

csh:
> setenv SSLTOP /usr/local/ssl
> setenv PATH/usr/local/ssl/bin:/bin:/usr/bin:/usr/ucb:

sh:
$ SSLTOP=/usr/local/ssl
$ PATH=/usr/local/ssl/bin:/bin:/usr/bin:/usr/ucb:
$ export SSLTOP PATH
```

Next, you have to choose whether you want to convert an existing Netscape commerce server key/certificate pair or generate a new one. We assume this is your first time setting up a secure Web server, so this sample is for generating a new key/certificate pair.

```
Now you need to install a key/cert pair.
A) Convert an existing Netscape Commerce key/cert pair
B) Generate a new key/cert pair
Choose [A/B] B
The key will be called whiptail.key.
The certificate will be called whiptail.cert.
They will be stored in /usr/local/ssl
```

```
Hit return:
******** READ ME *************
You are now generating a new key and key request. The key request
will be sent to the CA of your choice and the keyfile will reside in
/usr/local/ssl/private/whiptail.key.

If you have already sent off a key request for this server before,
makesure you aren't overwriting your old key which is awaiting a
corresponding certificate from your CA.

If they key generation fails, move the file
/usr/local/ssl/private/whiptail.key to a backup location and try
again.
******** READ ME *************
```

Next, you'll be asked for the size of your key, between 384 and 1024 bits. A size of 768 is a good average size for most electronic commerce transactions. Keys of less than 512 bits could be easily cracked, while 1024 is military-grade security and could cause your server to run slowly. It will also ask you for some random keystrokes, the timing of which will give SSLeay more random bits to work with.

```
Choose the size of your key. The smaller the key you choose the
faster your server response will be, but you'll have less security.
Keys of less than 512 bits are trivially cracked, while for high
security applications you probably don't want a key of less than
1024 bits. Choosing an appropriate keysize is your responsibility.
   How many bits of key (384 minimum, 1024 maximum): 768
   Now we will generate some random data, using the truerand library
developed by Matt Blaze, Jim Reeds, and Jack Lacy at AT&T.
   This may take some time.
   Generating 1536 bits of
randomness...........................................
   Now we generate more random data, from keystrokes. We need to
generate 1536 random bits. This is done by measuring the time
intervals between your keystrokes. Please enter some random text on
your keyboard until you hear the beep:
   1536
```

Next, it will ask you to choose some files which contain random bits of data. Practically any log file will work. We've chosen *syslog, messages,* and *wtmp.*

```
   Finally, choose some files with random bits, to complete our
random number seed generation. You might want to put in logfiles,
utmp, wtmp, etc.
```

```
Once the key is generated you will be asked to enter a PEM pass
phrase.
This is the pass phrase used to encrypt the key on the disk.

     -DO NOT LOSE THIS PASS PHRASE-

Enter colon-seperated list of files:
/usr/adm/messages:/usr/adm/syslog:/usr/adm/
wtmp
Now we are generating the key. This may also take some time. Be
patient.
The passphrase you enter here is very important. Do not lose it.
2150016 semi-random bytes loaded
Generating RSA private key, 768 bit long modulus
....+++++
.+++++
e is 65537 (0x10001)
```

Finally, you are asked to enter a passphrase. This passphrase is used to DES encrypt your private key in its storage space on disk. You must keep and remember this pass phrase, as you have to enter it when the server starts up.

```
Verifying password. Enter PEM pass phrase:
Key generated
```

Sending the certificate request to a CA

Now that the key and certificate is generated, it needs to be sent off to your certificate authority of choice. Stronghold lets you choose between VeriSign, Thawte, and a generic CA request. Because we plan on running a commerce server, we want to use the authority that's most widely accepted in North America—VeriSign.

After you've chosen VeriSign, the Stronghold installation package reminds you to visit the VeriSign Web site and complete the enrollment form (if you haven't already done so), before sending off the certificate request. It's best to follow this advice, as sending off the request before the enrollment gets there can cause confusion.

```
Would you like to send a Certificate Request to a CA? [Y/N] Y
Please choose the CA you would like to use:
A) VeriSign
B) Thawte
C) Other
Choose: A
Before you continue here, please visit VeriSign's Digital ID
Center. Use your favorite SSL-enabled browser to view
http://www.verisign.com/apachessl-us/index.shtml. Complete the
```

enrollment form at the Web site there. Once you've finished the form
at the VeriSign Web site, return here and finish filling in the
appropriate fields.

Next, you must fill in information for the certificate request. This form is similar to
the enrollment form, but doesn't include the billing information. Instead, it includes the
e-mail address and phone number of the webmaster. The e-mail address to send an
Apache-SSL request to VeriSign, `apachessl-us-request-id@verisign.com`, appears
as default.

```
Now we will generate the certificate request.—
Enter PEM pass phrase:
You are about to be asked to enter information that will be
incorperated into your certificate request.
What you are about to enter is what is called a Distinguished Name
or a DN.
There are quite a few fields but you can leave some blank.
For some fields there will be a default value.
If you enter '.', the field will be left blank.
—
Country Name (2 letter code) [US]:
State or Province Name (full name) [California]:Texas
Locality Name (city, town, etc.) [Springfield]:Austin
Organization Name (company) [Random Corporation]:OuterNet
Connection Strategies, Inc.
Organizational Unit Name (division) [Secure Services
Division]:Network Operations Center
Common Name (webserver FQDN) [www.random.com]:whiptail.outer.net

Webmaster email: www@outer.net
Webmaster phone: 512-206-0527
Hit return to send the CSR to the default CA address...
Send certification request to [apachessl-us-request-
id@verisign.com]:
```

The following is the format for the certificate request e-mail that's sent to VeriSign,
just so you'll know what's going on behind the scenes:

```
From charlie@news.outer.net
Date: Sun, 28 Jul 1996 15:02:13 -0500
From: "Charles H. Scott" <charlie@news.outer.net>
To: apachessl-us-request-id@verisign.com
Subject: Key certification request
```

```
Webmaster: www@outer.net
Phone: 512-206-0527
Server: Apache-SSL-US

Common-name: whiptail.outer.net
Organization Unit: Network Operations Center
Organization: OuterNet Connection Strategies
Locality: Austin
State: Texas
Country: US

—BEGIN CERTIFICATE REQUEST—
MIIBmDCCASICAQAwgZ4xCzAJBgNVBAYTA1VTMQ4wDAYDVQQIEwVUZXhhczEPMA0G
A1UEBxMGQXVzdG1uMS0wKwYDVQQKEyRPdXR1ck51dCBDb25uZWN0aW9uIFN0cmF0
ZWdpZXMsIE1uYy4xIjAgBgNVBAsTGU51dHdvcmsgT3B1cmF0aW9ucyBDZW50ZXIx
GzAZBgNVBAMTEndoaXB0YW1sLm91dGVyLm51dDB8MA0GCSqGSIb3DQEBAQUAA2sA
MGgCYQCxdaTuq7/CRkLOfKB49A4mSxTuZxOAtr1ZEoy8aO4vxdJ7VdQLi9y918qV
IovkOOBwvbfHHC1SH5YUIn6Mg/2TEDIH/GP6wha3w41Y2MExTkG/bgegfEp5j7aF
Ia9abOUCAwEAATANBgkqhkiG9w0BAQQFAANhAGYhcxIAQC4v5aT7q6KOkmA1zaxT
aISrg+GKUwjwyeS9ktVCx1XqxcjEwj7x0aXN5Ouec+fbIJbX08wToKfYsDV9dZ4Y
BZg2LciRV8Q7iztx1YzgD7zcoUA1WFvM9pOIJg==
— -END CERTIFICATE REQUEST— -
```

The top portion is the information you filled out, and the portion delimited by the ——CERTIFICATE REQUEST—— headers is the actual certificate itself, or in other words, a public key.

Next, the installation process will self-sign your certificate for you, to act as a test certificate until your CA-signed certificate comes back. You basically fill out the same information you filled out for your original request, then INSTALL.sh will install the test certificate and start the Stronghold server.

```
Country Name (2 letter code) [US]:
State or Province Name (full name) [California]:Texas
Locality Name (city, town, etc.) [Springfield]:Austin
Organization Name (company) [Random Corporation]:OuterNet
Connection Strategies, Inc.
Organizational Unit Name (division) [Secure Services
Division]:Network Operations Center
Common Name (webserver FQDN) [www.random.com]:whiptail.outer.net
—COMPLETE—
Your key has been generated and a test certificate has been
installed
—COMPLETE—
Starting the server...
```

After three to five days, you should receive the signed certificate back from VeriSign. When you do, it's a simple process to install it with a program called *getca* that comes with SSLeay. Save the CA's response into a temporary file (called something like */tmp/ca-cert*), and run the program with this syntax:

```
$ getca hostname < /tmp/ca-cert
```

In our case, for instance, we would want to run:

```
$ getca whiptail < /tmp/ca-cert
```

Then restart your server. That's it! You're now ready to run your secure server.

Tightening the Holes

It's not over yet. Just because your secure server is up and running doesn't mean it's the safest thing in the world. You need to make some changes to your configuration to make your server even more Net-safe.

Separating the secure from the insecure

Chances are, you don't want secure documents or CGI programs accessible from the same directory hierarchy as insecure documents. What's the use of making them secure if there's a way to get around it because both documents are in the same document root? We suggest making separate directories for your secure documents. Create a directory called *./ssldocs* in your server root for your secure documents, and one called *./cgi-ssl* in your server root for secure CGIs. Then edit the *./conf/httpd.conf* file and find the section that's delimited by the following tag:

```
<VirtualHost *:443>
```

Stronghold runs the SSL portion of the server as a separate VirtualHost, meaning that you can specify a unique DocumentRoot and ScriptAlias for someone accessing your server on that port. You should also change the paths in the <Directory> tag lines of the VirtualHost section, as in our example:

```
DocumentRoot /usr/local/apache/ssldocs
ScriptAlias /cgi-bin/ /usr/local/apache/cgi-ssl/

<Directory /usr/local/apache/ssldocs>
Options Indexes FollowSymLinks
AllowOverride None
</Directory>

<Directory /usr/local/apache/cgi-ssl>
AllowOverride None
Options None
</Directory>
```

Now, when someone accesses our site with the URL

```
https://whiptail.outer.net/
```

they will retrieve documents from the /usr/local/apache/ssldocs directory.

File permissions for document root

You can also protect the documents in your document root using file permissions, so that only the owner of the documents can update them, and only the Web server can read them. This is why we wanted you to create an *httpd* group earlier. The simple way to set this up is to use the following command to change permissions on the ssldocs document root:

```
$ chown root /usr/local/apache/ssldocs
$ chgrp httpd /usr/local/apache/ssldocs
$ chmod 2750 /usr/local/apache/ssldocs
```

This will give you the following permissions on ssldocs:

```
drwxr-s—- 2 root  httpd  1024 Jul 29 17:19 ssldocs/
```

As you can see, *root* is the owner of this directory, and has write permissions, meaning that only *root* can create files there. (Actually, *root* has read, write, and execute permission, as indicated by the *7* in the *2750* in the chmod <argument>). The *httpd* group, under which the Web server runs, has read permission for this directory, so the Web server can serve documents from it (as indicated by the *5* in the *2750* in the chmod <argument>). No one else has permission to do anything in that directory (as indicated by the *0* in the *2750* in the chmod <argument>). The *2* in *2750* makes any file that root places or creates in ssldocs inherit the same group permissions as the directory itself, so that only the *httpd* group can read from that directory, no matter what appears within it. That's also why the *2* is sometimes called the group ID bit. Setting the group ID bit is a good solution for any ISP where multiple customers update pages, each of whom doesn't want other customers to see what they have, or what they've done.

Summary

In this chapter on secure servers, we examined the circumstances under which one might run a secure server, what you should be concerned with when doing so, and how to install our server of choice—Stronghold. Now that we've got our security set up, we can start doing electronic commerce. In the next chapter, we start out simple with the Net cash solutions!

FIRST VIRTUAL HOLDINGS' COMMERCE MODEL

C hapter 8 introduced the First Virtual Internet Payment System (FVIPS) from First Virtual Holdings, Inc. FVIPS is a trusted third-party payment system, in which buyers and sellers use Personal Identification Numbers (PINs) to interact with each other and First Virtual—no *real world* financial information travels across the Internet. Only First Virtual Holdings knows the bank account number of the seller and the credit card number of the buyer, and charges the buyer's card and deposits funds into the seller's account appropriately. All this is done without the need for encryption, and can be performed using standard Internet technologies such as e-mail—no special software is (necessarily) needed.

In this chapter, we actually put First Virtual's commerce model into practice using their Application Programming Interface (API). By the end of this chapter, you should be able to implement the First Virtual payment system on your Web site. For information on how to set up a seller's account, refer to Chapter 8.

Why We Chose First Virtual

We chose to cover First Virtual as an example for implementing a trusted third-party payment system for the following reasons:

- **Ease of use.** There are easy-to-use APIs available which can easily be integrated into CGI programs.

- **No special client software.** Though it does require that the buyer have a PIN, no special client software is required (as there is with Cybercash and others). This means that a buyer can use their FV account from any system, running any platform, at anytime.

- **Versatility.** Although we're concentrating on Web commerce, FV's commerce model doesn't require that you use the Web. Transactions can even be carried out in an e-mail message.

- **The API is free.** You don't have to pay for software licensing on the server-side.

Of all the trusted third-party payment systems, only First Virtual meets all of these criteria. That's not to say that Cybercash, Ecash, and others aren't excellent paradigms, but rather that First Virtual is the easiest to demonstrate of all the well-accepted payment systems.

Implementing First Virtual on a Web Site

There are many ways in which First Virtual can be implemented on a Web site. You could have a form that packages a request in e-mail format, which is then sent to FV for processing. You could store all of the form information in a file, and then send the entire file to FV. By far, the fastest way to process a transaction is to implement the First Virtual API in a CGI program, which is what we cover in the rest of this section.

The First Virtual API (FV-API)

First Virtual created an API which makes it easier to implement the Green Commerce Model into your own programs. The FV-API is a versatile collection of programs which can perform any transaction with a First Virtual Transaction server. The FV-API actually includes two APIs: one for C and one for shell programming. Both are created at the same time when you build the FV-API.

The C API is called *libfv.a*, and is a library which can be compiled and linked to any C program you create that uses First Virtual API calls. Using this library can be pretty complex, and requires a good knowledge of C programming.

The shell API is a C program called *fv*, which must be compiled on your system. The fv program is a command-line utility which can perform almost all of the First Virtual transaction functions. Though it's called a shell API, it can be used as a system call in almost any program.

Instead of delving into the depths of making calls from C libraries and linking libraries with your programs, we concentrate on the simpler solution—the invocation of the fv utility in a CGI program. More specifically, we incorporate fv into a CGI program written in Perl.

Currently, the FV-API Makefile only supports Linux, Solaris, and SunOS. If you're familiar with the *make* utility and C compiler on your particular flavor of UNIX, you can probably also get it to compile with modifications. The FV-API isn't supported at all on non-UNIX platforms, though First Virtual plans to port it to other operating systems in the near future.

OBTAINING THE FV-API
FV-API is available as a UNIX tape archival (*tar*) file from First Virtual's FTP site. Within this tar file is the source code for building the API. The easiest way to get it is from the following page:

```
http://www.fv.com/tech/fv-api.html .
```

Or go directly to the FV FTP site at:

```
ftp.fv.com .
```

Then change to the /pub/code/fv-api directory. You'll see the following files:

```
fv-api.tar
fv-api.tgz .
```

The tar file is just a regular UNIX tar file, while *.tgz* is a tar file that has been GNU zipped with the gzip utility for better compression.

COMPILING THE FV-API
Once you've downloaded the fv-api.tar file, extract its contents into a directory, such as /usr/src/fv-api, where you can build it. Place the tar file into this directory and extract it with the command *tar -xvf fv-api.tar* (if you downloaded the gzipped tar file, be sure to *gunzip* it first).

Once extracted, you should have almost three dozen files which are used to compile fv. The first step is to edit the file called *Makefile*. You must *uncomment* the lines which apply to your particular version of UNIX. In our case, we're using Linux, so we'll uncomment the following:

```
#Uncomment the following for GCC under Linux
CC=gcc
STATIC=-static
CFLAGS=-O2 $(STATIC) -DANSIHEADERS -DPROTOTYPES
CFLAGS=-g $(STATIC) -DANSIHEADERS -DPROTOTYPES
RANLIB=ranlib
```

This sets up our C compiler (*gcc*) with the appropriate flags for compiling fv under UNIX.

If you're not using Linux, SunOS, or Solaris, you may be able to compile fv on your system anyway by experimenting and finding the appropriate flags for your compiler.

You can then run *make* on the command line to build the program. Just running *make* will build fv and place it in the directory in which you're building the API. Running *make install* will compile fv and copy it into the /usr/local/bin directory, its ultimate home. If your system doesn't have /usr/local/bin, then you can either make it, or specify a different directory in the install target of the Makefile.

FV AND ISPS

> If you're a user on a system run by your ISP or system administrator, you may not have the authority to execute the make utility or the C compiler, and you definitely don't have permission to copy fv into the /usr/local/bin directory. After compilation, you have to modify one of the UNIX system's network configuration files, which, typically, only someone with superuser access can do.
>
> Check with your ISP before compiling and installing fv. They may already have it set up, or may be willing to install it for you. If you are an ISP, you may want to consider installing it for your customers as a value-added service for your virtual Web host accounts.

WHAT FV DOES

The fv utility can be used to perform a variety of functions against a First Virtual account. It can be used to validate an account, charge an account, and check files that are configured to cost a certain amount. It can be used to sell access to a Web site, hard goods, or even files.

When invoked properly, it opens up a socket connection (the default is 440) with a First Virtual payment server using the Simple Green Commerce Protocol (SGCP). It takes the command line arguments given to it and translates them into the equivalent Green Commerce commands. When it gets a response back from the server, it turns this response into a simple word or phrase, such as *active* for a valid FV account and *ok* if the charge goes through.

THE COMMAND LINE INTERFACE Running fv directly from the command line should give you a pretty good idea of how it works. If it's compiled correctly, you should see a list of acceptable commands for fv.

```
fv usage:
  To check the status of an FV Account-ID:
    fv [-f .$] check 'First Virtual Account ID'
    fv checkat server_address 'First Virtual Account ID'
      (Returns invalid/seller-only/active/suspended/unavailable)
  To find out how much a file is configured to cost:
    fv [-f .$] costof filename
  To submit a bill for the contents of a file:
    fv [-f .$] chargefor filename 'FV Account ID' ['Description']
  To submit a single charge (a bill):
    fv [-f .$] bill buyer seller amount 'Description'
      (Returns ok/unavailable/error)
  To submit an arbitrary transfer-request transaction
```

```
     fv trstdin [serverip emailaddr emailprog xferpref] <packet
>result
```

```
  Either /.$ or ./.$ must exist and be properly formatted
   for initialization purposes, or use the -f option.
```

The *-f* flag requires that the full path to an fv configuration file be specified. This file can contain information which directs the fv program on how to perform operations. The *.$* is a specialized Payment File which can be placed in a directory which contains files that a user must purchase before downloading. This hidden file contains information specific to that directory, such as how much to charge per file (or per *x* number of KB), who should be paid, and so on. This is useful for anonymous FTP sites that charge for the data they house.

Although there's much that can be done with payment files and the fv program, we're only going to work with a couple of functions of that program: *fv check* and *fv bill*.

Incorporating FV into a CGI Program

Rather than show you how to implement one of First Virtual's precooked CGI programs into your Web site, we'll show you how to build a Web commerce application from scratch. One way to do this would be to implement the Green Commerce Model and communicate with an FV transaction server directly using the Application/Green-Commerce MIME type and the Simple Green Commerce Protocol. Although FV provides much of the information you would need to do this on its Web site, it will mean getting much more involved in the process than required. Instead, we'll use the FV-API. That's what it was made for, after all.

Not for the timid

FV's "Software for Automating Sales" page, which lists all of its CGI programs, attaches this warning to the FV-API:

> *The First Virtual API is a complex set of utilities for creating a highly customized environment. The much simpler Websale will meet the needs of virtually all Webmasters selling Information products; we strongly suggest trying Websale before considering the full API.*

It seems that they would like to steer you away from using the FV-API. Although it's true that FV's Websale CGI is more ready-to-wear, it's also more limited. If you're comfortable with CGI programming, there's no reason why you can't implement the FV-API in your own programs. To someone who's already familiar with Perl or shell programming, as well as executing utilities within these programs, the FV-API won't seem as complex as First Virtual makes it sound.

Running fv on your server

For fv to run on your server, you must create a configuration file and make a couple of changes on your UNIX system to allow it to work.

CREATING A CONFIGURATION FILE

A configuration file (or *payment file*) needs to exist in order to run fv. Information on the commands this file can be found in the API documentation at:

```
http://www.fv.com/tech/fv-api-spec.html.
```

Each command within this file is in standard e-mail header format—a keyword, followed by a colon, followed by the value. We're only concerned with one of the possible commands—*SERVER-IP.* This command specifies the IP address or fully qualified domain name of the First Virtual transaction server that should be contacted for PIN checking and billing. If the configuration file is empty, then it defaults to card.com. It can, however be changed, with the following command:

```
SERVER-IP: card.com
```

We call our configuration file *fv.conf* and place it in our /www/conf directory. We left ours empty, so that we're just using the default server of card.com.

EDITING THE SERVICES FILE

You must edit the /etc/services file on your UNIX system to allow the SGCP traffic to take place. It's probably best to stick with the default port of 440 unless you're already using it for something else. If you want to change it, just specify a different port in the services file. Here's an example of what the line in your services file should look like:

```
sgcp          440/tcp
```

TESTING FV

The easiest way to test fv is to run it from the command line. First, you may want to ping card.com to ensure you have connectivity. If you can't ping it, then you may want to check your Internet connection, or attempt to trace the connection with traceroute, ping -r, or a similar utility to see if there may be a problem along the way.

If you can reach card.com, then try running fv from the command line with the following options:

```
fv -f /www/conf/fv.conf check first_virtual_account_id
```

The first_virtual_account_id is a buyer's VirtualPIN. If the check is successful, you should get an *active* response from fv. Even if you don't have a buyer's PIN, you can check by putting in a random number, such as *99999.* You should get an *invalid* response from fv. If you get an *unavailable* response, the card.com server is either not running, you don't have SGCP configured in your /etc/services file, or you're running a firewall that's preventing the SGCP traffic.

Our sample CGI program

For our sample CGI program, which implements the First Virtual API, we'll go back to an example that may be familiar to readers of *Web Programming Secrets with HTML, CGI, and Perl* (1996, IDG Books Worldwide)—the Perl hacker t-shirt. The Perl hacker t-shirt is just a regular t-shirt that comes with cappuccino and pizza stains. It's also curved inward at the stomach to match the posture of a Perl programmer hunched over a keyboard!

In that book, the Perl hacker t-shirt CGI was a self-contained Perl program which included an HTML form, the code to parse the form data, and the code to call and log the FV-API transactions. Here, we've taken the same code and made it more generic for you, so that it may be implemented with other types of sales more easily.

Because the FV-API hadn't changed in the year since the CGI program was written for the last book, we found no need to change our code drastically. This is one of the benefits of using the First Virtual Internet Payment System. While technologies like SET are in flux, FVIPS has been stable and providing secure transactions since its inception. This keeps webmasters from having to constantly update the payment system with new versions.

FV FORM.HTML

Our order form for the Perl hacker t-shirt is called *fv_form.html*. It's a standard HTML 2.0 form, with fields for purchaser information, First Virtual account number, and radio buttons for t-shirt size. Figure 13-1 shows you how this looks. This information (included on the CD-ROM) is sent to our CGI program that actually calls the FV-API called *fv_generic.pl*.

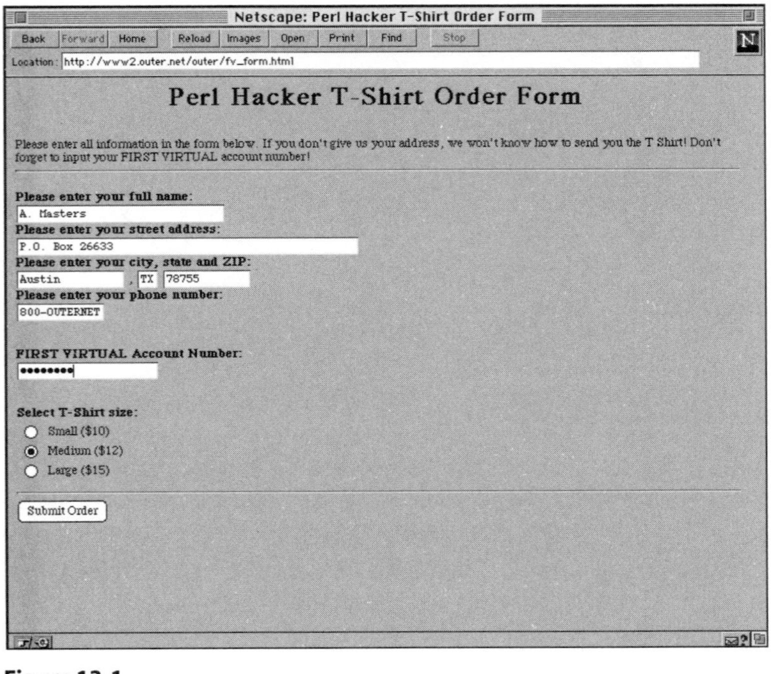

Figure 13-1
The Perl hacker t-shirt order form for First Virtual payment.

```
<!DOCTYPE HTML PUBLIC "-//IETF//DTD HTML 2.0//EN">
<HTML>
<HEAD>
<TITLE>Perl Hacker T-Shirt Order Form</TITLE>
</HEAD>
<BODY>
<H1 ALIGN="Center">Perl Hacker T-Shirt Order Form</H1>
<BR>
<P>
Please enter all information in the form below. If you don't
give us your address, we won't know how to send you the T
Shirt! Don't forget to input your FIRST VIRTUAL account
number!<BR>
<HR ALIGN="Center">
<B>Please enter your full name:</B><BR>
<FORM METHOD="POST" ACTION="http://www2.outer.net/cgi-
bin/fv_generic.pl">

<INPUT TYPE="text" NAME="FullName" SIZE="30"  MAXLENGTH="50" >
<BR>
<B>Please enter your street address:</B><BR>
<INPUT TYPE="text" NAME="StreetAddress" SIZE="50"  MAXLENGTH="60"
>
<BR>
<B>Please enter your city, state and ZIP:</B><BR>
<INPUT TYPE="text" NAME="City" SIZE="15"  MAXLENGTH="20">,
<INPUT TYPE="text" NAME="State" SIZE="2"  MAXLENGTH="2" >
<INPUT TYPE="text" NAME="Zip" SIZE="12"  MAXLENGTH="12" >
<BR>
<B>Please enter your phone number:</B><BR>
<INPUT TYPE="text" NAME="Phone" SIZE="12"  MAXLENGTH="12" >
<BR>
<P><BR>
<B>FIRST VIRTUAL Account Number:</B><BR>
<INPUT TYPE="password" NAME="FVAcct" >
<BR>
<P><BR>
<B>Select T-Shirt size:</B><BR>
<TABLE>
<TR>
<TD ALIGN=RIGHT>
<INPUT TYPE="radio" NAME="" VALUE="Small" CHECKED></TD>
<TD>Small ($10)</TD>
```

```
</TR>
<TR><TD ALIGN=RIGHT>
<INPUT TYPE="radio" NAME="" VALUE="Medium"></TD>
<TD>Medium ($12)</TD>
</TR>
<TR><TD ALIGN=RIGHT>
<INPUT TYPE="radio" NAME="" VALUE="Large"></TD>
<TD>Large ($15)</TD>
</TR>
<TR>
</TR>
</TABLE>
<HR ALIGN="Center">
<TABLE>
<TR>
<INPUT TYPE="submit" NAME="Submit" VALUE="Submit Order"><BR>
</TR>
</TABLE>
</FORM>
</BODY>
</HTML>
```

FV-GENERIC.PL

The Perl script fv_generic.pl is tailored for the Perl hacker t-shirt, but is designed to be flexible enough for easy modification for other products. The code itself (included on the CD-ROM) is heavily commented, so you should be able to follow along and see what's going on.

In a nutshell, this program verifies the buyer's virtual PIN using fv. If it's invalid or the FV server is unavailable, it lets the buyer know. It also logs all transactions with the FV server in a user-defined log file. If the PIN is approved, then it charges the buyer's FV account for an amount specified in the $CHARGE variable, and logs all of the buyer's contact information in a user-defined order database.

```
#!/usr/local/bin/perl
#
# fv_generic.pl — A generic CGI Interface for First Virtual
transactions.
#
# Copyright (C) 1995,1996
#   Charlie Scott (charlie@outer.net)
#   Mike Erwin (mikee@outer.net)
#
# All rights reserved.
```

```
#
#
# FIRST VIRTUAL (TM) and the FIRST VIRTUAL logo are service marks
# of First Virtual Holdings Incorporated.
#
# Redistribution and use in source and binary forms, with or
without
# modification, are permitted provided that: (1) source code
distributions
# retain the above copyright notice and this paragraph in its
entirety, (2)
# distributions including binary code include the above copyright
notice and
# this paragraph in its entirety in the documentation or other
materials
# provided with the distribution, and (3) all advertising
materials mentioning
# features or use of this software display the following
acknowledgment:
# THIS SOFTWARE IS PROVIDED ''AS IS'' AND WITHOUT ANY EXPRESS
# OR IMPLIED WARRANTIES, INCLUDING, WITHOUT LIMITATION, THE
# IMPLIED WARRANTIES OF MERCHANTABILITY AND FITNESS FOR A
# PARTICULAR PURPOSE.
#
#   fv_generic.pl
#
# Created:     Wed Dec 20 22:06:52 CST 1995
# Made Generic: Mon Sep 23 22:47:34 CDT 1996
#
#   Revision History:
#
#   Version 1.0    Script Created.
#
# PURPOSE:         This script provides an HTML form interface
for a
#                  generic First Virtual Sale. When posted, it
extracts the
#                  entered data and checks the user's First
Virtual
#                  account information. If valid, it adds the
user's
#                  information to an order file and charges their
```

```
#                     First Virtual account.
#
# INSTALLATION:       To configure this script, edit all of lines in
the next
#                     section that have a "#!" as a comment to their
immediate
#                     right. This script need to be installed in
your web
#                     servers binary directory, typically "cgi-bin".
You will
#                     also need the First Virtual API "fv" to use
this script,
#                     available at ftp://ftp.fv.com. You will also
need to
#                     create a file called fv.conf, which will
contain the
#                     configuration information.
#
# USAGE:      This script is called directly by the user's Web
#                     browser.
#
#######################################################################

$| = 1;               # output NOT buffered

chop ($datestr = 'date');

$THIS_SCRIPT = "http://www2.outer.net/cgi-bin/fv_generic.pl";

#! The location of the fv app itself
$FV        = "/usr/local/bin/fv";
#! Your FV Config File for www transactions
$FV_CONFIG  = "/www/conf/fv.conf";
#! The Seller's FV Account Number
$FV_SELLER = "12345678";
#! A full report of each invokation herein
$LOGFILE    = "/tmp/web_fl.log";
#! The location of your input html
$INPUTPAGE  = "/www/httpdocs/outer/fv_form.html";
$OURORDERDB = "/home/charlie/tmp/perl_hack_tshirt.orders";

open(LOGGER,"> $LOGFILE");
```

```perl
###########################################################################
#
# parse_environment
#
# Basically this sifts through the @ENV for things of note.
#
###########################################################################

sub parse_environment {

    $host = $ENV{SERVER_NAME};
    $ENV{SCRIPT_NAME} =~ s/([a-zA-Z0-9\.\-_]+)$//;
    $program = $1;
    $scriptpath = $ENV{SCRIPT_NAME};

    ## formlib stuff.

    if (($ENV{REQUEST_METHOD} eq "POST") &&
        ($ENV{CONTENT_TYPE}   eq "application/x-www-form-
urlencoded")) {

        # extract form data - borrowed heavily from
        # Brigette Jellinek's formlib.pl

        read(STDIN,$input,$ENV{CONTENT_LENGTH});

        foreach (split("&", $input)) {
            /(.*)=(.*)/;
            $name = $1;
            $value = $2;

            $value =~ s/\+/ /g ;
            $value =~ s/%(..)/pack('c',hex($1))/eg;
            # unescape characters

            if (defined $in{$name}) {
                $in{$name} .= "#" . $value
            }
            else {
                $in{$name} = $value;
            }
        }
        return (1);      # If this is a POST return true
    }
```

```
        return (0);           # else return false and just fall through
    }


    #####################################################################
    #
    # get_variables
    #
    # Gets various variables and puts them into easier to deal with
handles.
    #
    # Based on your input fields in you "$INPUTPAGE" you will need to
make
    # some modifications to this method.
    #
    # It is IMPORTANT to remember that the "$FVAcct" variable can't be
changed
    # as this script is reliant on it to process the whole
transaction.
    #
    #####################################################################

    sub get_variables {

        $FVAcct = $in{FVAcct};           #! This must be here and in the
$INPUTPAGE!

        $FullName = $in{FullName};
        $StreetAddress = $in{StreetAddress};
        $City = $in{City};
        $State = $in{State};
        $Zip = $in{Zip};
        $Phone = $in{Phone};
        $FVAcct = $in{FVAcct};

        $Small = $in{Small};
        $Medium = $in{Medium};
        $Large = $in{Large};
    }


    #####################################################################
    #
    # check_fv_account
    #
```

```
# Runs fv and checks the first virtual account before we do
anything.
#
###########################################################################

sub check_fv_account {
    chop ($FV_CHECK = '${FV} -f ${FV_CONFIG} check ${FVAcct}');

    ($FV_CHECK, $Remainder) = split("\r\n\t\ ", $FV_CHECK, 2);

    return ($FV_CHECK);
}


###########################################################################
#
# log_report
#
###########################################################################

sub log_report {
    local($result_string)= @_;

    print LOGGER "$datestr: $result_string";
}


###########################################################################
#
# process_order
#
# Here you will use the variables that you set up in your
"$INPUTPAGE" and
# have parsed into local variables with the "get_variables"
function above.
# Much of your processing should be done here. You could e-mail a
copy of
# the order to your shipping department, which will take care of
delivery.
# You can perform any database lookups or updates that need to
occur here
# as well.
#
# In our rather simplistic example, we merely update a file located
at:
```

```perl
# $OURORDERDB, which we will then mail to our order processing
department
# via a cron job processed nightly. You can certainly see the need
to
# flesh this our for your own application needs.
#
# Finally, a very important thing to process in this function is
the determination
# of the final billing price of the products or services. We take
care of
# this a simply as possible just to illustrate.
#
#
#################################################################

sub process_order {

    # First we calculate the $CHARGE variable so the we know how
much to
    # make the FV transaction for.

    if ($Small) {
        $CHARGE = 10;
    }
    elsif ($Medium) {
        $CHARGE = 12;
    }
    elsif ($Large) {
        $CHARGE = 15;
    }

    open (ORDERS,"> ${OURORDERDB}");
    print ORDERS "$FullName\t";
    print ORDERS "$StreetAddress\t";
    print ORDERS "$City\t";
    print ORDERS "$State\t";
    print ORDERS "$Zip\t";
    print ORDERS "$Phone\t";
    print ORDERS "$FVAcct\t";
    print ORDERS "\$$CHARGE\t";
    close(ORDERS);
```

```perl
        print STDOUT "<TITLE>Your Order Has Been
Processed</TITLE>\n";
        print STDOUT "<H1>Your Order Has Been Processed</H1>\n";
        print STDOUT "<P>";
        print STDOUT "Your <B>FIRST VIRTUAL</B> account will be
charged \n";
        print STDOUT "<B>\$$CHARGE for this transaction. Your T-Shirt
\n";
        print STDOUT "is on its way!\n";

        # Charge the account
        system("fv -f $FV_CONFIG bill $FVAcct $FV_SELLER $CHARGE \"T-
Shirt\"");
    }


#############################################################################
#
# FV System is not responding.
#
#############################################################################

sub is_unavailable {
    print "<TITLE>First Virtual Transaction Failed</TITLE>\n";

    print "<H1>FV Server Unavailable!</H1>\n";
    print "The First Virtual Commerce Server is unavaiable.\n";
    print "Please try again later.\n";

    &log_report("$FVAcct:   $CHARGE:   FV Server Unavailable\n");
}


#############################################################################
#
# Account is suspended for invalid use or non-payment.
#
#############################################################################

sub is_suspended {
    print "<TITLE>First Virtual Transaction Failed</TITLE>\n";
    print "<H1>FV Account Invalid</H1>";
    print "The First Virtual Account you entered is not valid\n";
    print "for online purchases at this time.\n";
```

```perl
        print "Your account has been suspended due to a \n";
        print "backlog of purchase queries that need \n";
        print "your attention!\n";

        &log_report("$FVAcct:   $CHARGE:    FV Account Suspended\n");
    }


#############################################################################
#
# Account is granted seller privs only. No purchasing at this
time.
#
#############################################################################

    sub is_seller {
        print "<TITLE>First Virtual Transaction Failed</TITLE>\n";
        print "<H1>FV Account Invalid</H1>";

        print "Your account is not authorized for \n";
        print "purchases. You need to activate it \n";
        print "as a Buyer account with First Virtual.\n";

        &log_report("$FVAcct:   $CHARGE:    FV Seller Account
Only\n");
    }


#############################################################################
#
# Typically, the conditional falls through to here if the account
is invalid.
# Usually this is due to an incorrect FV account number or a typo.
#
#############################################################################

    sub is_other_error {
        print "<TITLE>First Virtual Transaction Failed</TITLE>\n";
        print "<H1>FV Account Invalid</H1>";

        print "If you entered it correctly, please\n";
        print "contact First Virtual about your \n";
        print "account's status.\n";
```

```
        &log_report("$FVAcct:    $CHARGE:    FV Invalid Account
Number\n");
    }


###################################################################
#
# This function redirects the output of an HTML file to the
browser.
# This is the fall through condition for the entire application.
It assumes
# that if the user just stumbled across things or has seriously
fubared
# things, something intelligent can come up.
#
# You can also note that the location of the $INPUTPAGE can be
called
# from the browser directly if you choose.
#
###################################################################

    sub print_form {

        print STDOUT "<FORM ACTION=\"${THIS_SCRIPT}\"
METHOD=\"POST\">";
        open (FORM, "$INPUTPAGE");
        while (<FORM>) {
            print STDOUT;
        }
        close(FORM);
    }


###################################################################
#
# MAIN-  Here's where everything starts.
#
###################################################################

    {
        print STDOUT "Content-Type:\ttext/html1\n\n\n",
                    "<!DOCTYPE HTML PUBLIC \"-//IETF//DTD HTML
2.0//EN\">\n";
```

```
    $post_action = &parse_enviornment();

if ($post_action) {
    &get_variables();
    $fv_status = &check_fv_account();

    if ($fv_status eq "active") {
        &process_order();
    }
    elsif ($fv_status eq "unavailable") {
        &is_unavailable();
    }
    elsif ($fv_status eq "suspended") {
        &is_suspended();
    }
    elsif ($fv_status eq "seller-only") {
        &is_seller();
    }
    else {
        &is_other_error();
    }
}
else {
    &print_form();
}

    close (LOGGER);
}
```

First Virtual and firewalls

If your Web server is sitting behind a firewall, you should make sure that the firewall allows both inbound and outbound traffic to port 440 (or whatever SGCP port you choose) for your server. Otherwise, you won't be able to communicate with the First Virtual transaction server. An *unavailable* response from fv may be an indication that this is happening.

First Virtual and encryption

Although First Virtual's Green Commerce Model is designed to avoid the need for encryption, that doesn't mean that you can't implement it. There's no reason why you can't put your payment form (fv_form.html) and CGI (fv_generic.pl) on a secure server. This will assure the buyer that all of the information they've entered into the form is being securely sent across the Internet, so that their First Virtual PIN can't be intercepted and read. The communication between the First Virtual transaction server and the Web server running fv, however, isn't encrypted, so some risk still exists. If the buyer's PIN is intercepted and used by someone else, they would still have to hack into the buyer's e-mail account as well to acknowledge the transaction when the First Virtual verification e-mail comes. In short, First Virtual's Green Commerce Model is a good way to avoid spending a chunk of money on secure servers and digital IDs, but if you already have a secure server, then the warm, fuzzy feeling it gives the buyers can't hurt.

Summary

First Virtual Holding's Green Commerce Model is one of the simplest trusted third-party Internet payment systems available. It's a prime candidate to deploy on your commerce site because it doesn't require special software on the client end. On the server end, it can either be implemented using existing Internet technology (such as e-mail) or through a freely available API. This API can be easily integrated into a Perl CGI program to provide a simple online payment solution.

Now that we've seen how to implement a trusted third-party Internet payment system, let's move on to taking credit cards directly on the Internet using the Stronghold secure server and the ICVERIFY credit card processing software.

CREATING A CREDIT CARD TRANSACTION WEB SITE

I n this chapter, we'll start to put together some of the pieces you've been learning so far: merchant banks, credit card processing networks, secure Web servers, and ICVERIFY. By the end of this chapter you should have a good idea of how to navigate through the merchant ID application processes, as well as set up and protect your credit card transaction site.

Working with a Merchant Bank and Processor

This section is an extension of Chapter 4, where we covered the basics of credit card transactions. In this section, we detail how to obtain a merchant number, how to choose a merchant bank and processor, and the initial and recurring costs involved in doing so.

Obtaining a merchant number

As we stated in Chapter 4, there are three main things you need to do to be able to accept credit card transactions:

1. Establish a commercial bank account.
2. Obtain a merchant ID number from a merchant bank.
3. Create a relationship with a credit card processing network.

Setting up a bank account should be familiar to most of you. Just go to your local bank and open up a commercial bank account for your company. Depending on your type of business, you need to bring along the appropriate tax and financial paperwork. If you're a corporation, you need your corporate charter, tax ID number, and a corporate resolution specifying that the person opening the account is authorized to do so.

CHOOSING A MERCHANT BANK

Although the world of Internet commerce is new, credit card transactions in which a merchant and a customer aren't face-to-face have been common for years. Credit card transactions over the Net fall under the hubris of *non-traditional retail* in the lingo of merchant banks and processing networks. Other types of non-traditional retail transactions are phone sales, mail order, and electronic kiosk sales.

THE NET CAN BE RISKY BUSINESS Because the merchant and customer never meet, and often a signature isn't obtained from the card bearer, non-traditional retail sales are considered by merchant banks and processors to be riskier than storefront sales. The chance of someone using a stolen card with anonymity is increased because no other form of identification is required. The chances of fraudulent chargebacks are also increased. (A fraudulent chargeback is when an unscrupulous customer purchases something, claims it was never received or that the transaction was never made in the first place, and demands that their card account be credited.) In the case of chargebacks, the merchant not only doesn't receive payment for the merchandise, but also must pay chargeback fees to their processor. The signature helps protect the merchant by validating that the customer did indeed receive the goods or services, and that they agree to the obligations of paying their card issuer.

BANKS MAY NOT BE THE BEST BET For credit card services, many retailers and service businesses go directly to the bank where they have their bank accounts. Why not? Most large banks offer credit card merchant services, and it keeps the number of players involved to a minimum.

Banks, however, are not inclined to take what they perceive as unnecessary risks, so they're not as likely to accept non-traditional retail merchants. Internet sales may seem especially dangerous to them. You may want to go ahead and approach your bank about processing your Internet sales, but don't feel bad if they're not interested in this business.

MERCHANT BANKS TAKE RISKS One of the reasons that merchant banks exist is that they're willing to take risks that traditional banks won't. Their sole purpose is to grant merchant ID numbers and to set merchants up with processing networks. Most of the processing networks themselves are married to one merchant bank or another. Phone or mail order businesses often have to go through merchant banks. Businesses wishing to do Internet sales usually have to go through a merchant bank as well.

INTERNET-FRIENDLY MERCHANT BANKS It has taken a while for merchant banks to catch on to the Internet as a vehicle for commerce. They often consider Internet sales to be akin to phone or mail order business, and so they don't always have a structure in place for the particular needs of an Internet business, or they make assumptions that it's like other types of retail. They might assume, for instance, that you want an electronic payment terminal and offer to provide it as part of the package, when in fact you probably don't need one.

In 1994, one of the authors of this book called a merchant bank in an attempt to get a merchant account for the Internet service provider that employed him. One of the requirements of the application process was to obtain trade references from companies his employer did business with. At one point, the agent from the merchant bank asked the author to get a trade reference from The Internet. That would be quite a task! The point is, the merchant bank didn't know what the Internet was, and in the end they were afraid to provide a merchant account for use on the Internet.

Thanks to the media explosion since then, there are very few people who don't know what the Internet is today. Merchant banks are also recognizing the commercial possibilities of the Internet, and are taking Internet businesses more seriously. Whether or not you're able to get a merchant account will depend more on how long you've been in business and your annual sales, than whether or not you're Internet-based. Web commerce has gained almost equal footing with mail and phone order businesses. Today, there are even merchant banks that specialize in electronic commerce.

Overall, you should look for a merchant bank that's Internet friendly. It doesn't necessarily have to provide the complete solution, but it should be familiar enough with the Internet to understand what an Internet sale entails. A list of merchant banks which are Internet-friendly is in Appendix B of this book.

MAKE SURE THEY ACCEPT YOUR SOFTWARE It's important to ensure that your merchant bank/processing network will interoperate with your credit card transaction software. In our case, it's ICVERIFY. Because it's compatible with 80 processors, ICVERIFY is rarely a problem. Remember to let the processing network know that what software you choose.

"Bad credit? No Credit? No problem!" Promises such as this from credit card issuers that are willing to give cards to people with poor or no credit records are familiar to credit seekers these days. These cards often charge the highest possible interest rates, in addition to a high annual fee. Similar services exist for merchants who want to make credit sales. Some merchant banks specialize in high risk companies—typically those that are new, or have poor payment histories —that may otherwise have a hard time obtaining a merchant ID. These "merchant banks of last resort" often charge higher fees all around. If you find you're unable to obtain a merchant ID, and feel like you must use one of these services, you'll have to pay the price!

LET THE MERCHANT BEWARE!

WHEN TO APPLY FOR A MERCHANT ID

If you're venturing into Internet commerce, chances are your company is in one of four situations:

1. You already have a relationship with a merchant bank/processor, already do phone or mail order business, and are venturing into Internet sales.

2. You already have a relationship with a merchant bank/processor, don't already do phone or mail order business, and are venturing into Internet sales.

3. You've been in business for a while, but don't have any relationship with a merchant bank/processor, and wish to do Internet credit card sales.

4. You're a new business seeking a merchant bank/processor for Internet sales, perhaps for other types of transactions as well.

If you already have a merchant account and are already doing mail or phone order business, conducting Internet commerce should be no problem. In fact, chances are you won't even need to tell your merchant bank or processor that you're doing Internet sales. Just let them know that you wish to use ICVERIFY to process transactions.

If you already have a merchant account but aren't doing mail or phone order business, then you'll want to contact your merchant bank about doing Internet commerce. Chances are, the agreement you signed with them stipulates that you can only perform transactions where a signature will be obtained. There may also be limits on the types of electronic equipment you may use. You may have to re-negotiate your discount rates and fees based on the addition of Internet commerce to your monthly sales.

If you've never done credit card business before, and don't have a merchant ID or processor, then you're going to have to apply to a merchant bank for that privilege.

THE APPLICATION PROCESS

How involved the application process gets will depend on how long your company has been in business, its financial standing, and the number and size of transactions you think you'll need to accept. Chances are, it will entail providing the following information:

- Merchant information
- Bank references
- Trade references
- Owner's/officer's information
- The cards you wish to honor, transaction size, and volume
- Site survey

All except the site survey are part of the application paperwork that must be completed. Not all merchant banks require all of this information, and some scrutinize it more than others. In the following sections, we go through each of these items individually, to give you a feel for the application process. The type of information remains consistent across applications at different merchant banks, though the grouping may differ from ours.

MERCHANT INFORMATION You must provide the legal name of your company, including a DBA. You must also provide the physical address of your company, the number of locations, and the phone number. The bank also requires company information such as the type of ownership, tax ID number, and the number of years in business under the current management and/or ownership. If you've been in business less than two years, you must provide a previous employer or business name and contact information. The bank also needs to know what percentage of the time you plan to accept credit card payments over the phone, through the mail, or online.

The merchant bank may ask for other specific information to give them an idea of the number of chargebacks you may receive, or if you plan to process recurring transactions. Typical questions in this category include: "How long must your customers wait for your product or services after purchase?" and "Do you offer any warranties, subscriptions, or memberships?" Because delays, warranties, or other ongoing business relationships entail increased risk of chargebacks, such business transactions will be more expensive to conduct online.

The merchant bank also needs to know if your company has accepted credit cards before, and if so, whether or not the other merchant bank or processor terminated that relationship. The final question is whether any of the officers or owners of your company have ever filed for personal or business bankruptcy.

BANK REFERENCES The merchant bank requires all bank references for the past two years. They may ask for a specific contact name and phone number, as well as your account number. This information is used to obtain a financial history of your company.

TRADE REFERENCES You need to provide trade references from companies from which you purchase goods or services. Preferably the ones you spend the most money with, have good terms with, and tend to pay on time. Before listing these companies, you should ask them if they are actually willing to give out your information to the merchant banks. Some businesses make it a policy not to divulge such information.

OWNER'S/OFFICER'S INFORMATION The merchant bank will want to know personal information about some of the owners or officers. For instance: Where they live, how long they've lived there, whether they rent or own their dwelling, and so on. They also require personal bank references, dates of birth, and social security numbers, from which to obtain credit histories on the owners or officers.

THE CARDS YOU WILL HONOR This is simply a list of the types of cards you wish to process: Visa, MasterCard, American Express, Diners Club, Discover, JCB, and others. The merchant bank also asks you to estimate the average transaction amount and your estimated total annual volume (in dollars) of credit card sales. All this information is used to help the merchant bank and processor determine the percentage for their discount rate. The higher your volume, the lower the discount rate (subject to their assessment of risk).

SITE SURVEY A site survey typically occurs only if yours is a new business with a limited credit history. For a site survey, an agent of the merchant bank visits your location and makes a visual survey of the property. The agent evaluates the condition of the property, makes sure that it looks appropriate for the type of business you operate, and makes sure you have a business permit or license. He or she may even take a few photos of signage, merchandise, or equipment. This is just to ensure that you're actually a business, and not a fly-by-night operator temporarily leasing space from which to conduct a credit-card scam.

THE COSTS INVOLVED

Becoming a credit-card-accepting merchant isn't free, or even especially cheap. There are several costs that you must bear. First is the application fee. Almost all merchant banks will charge an application fee of between $75 and $150. For some merchant banks, this fee is nonrefundable whether you're accepted or declined. In addition, there may be an installation fee, no matter what type of processing equipment you wish to use. The amount of that fee depends on the type of equipment you use. For ICVERIFY service, it should run between $50 and $150. You end up paying your merchant bank and processor between $200 and $400 to get things started. ICVERIFY itself also costs you between $350 and $450, depending on where it's purchased. Individual merchant banks vary greatly in their initial charges. What they don't take from you at setup, they may recover during processing. Overall, you should expect to pay between $500 and $1,000 just to begin processing credit cards.

You also have the option of buying additional equipment, such as a credit card imprinter or an electronic payment terminal. Having these might prove useful if your primary means of authorizing cards (ICVERIFY) fails. If you choose any of these, those costs should also be factored in to your setup charges as well. It's not unusual to spend between $2,000 and 3,000 for startup fees.

WHAT YOU GET

If you get through the application process and pay the appropriate fees, your merchant bank gives you merchant ID numbers for the cards you wish to process. Typically, MasterCard and Visa have the same numbers, while American Express and Discover may have different ones. You also get the phone numbers to the modem banks at the processor, which you'll dial in to authorize your customers' credit cards.

Your Monthly Statement

When you first glance at the monthly statement from your merchant bank and see how much money is actually being taken *out* of your account for you to process credit cards, you may wonder if it's all worthwhile.

For each day of the month, you see the total number of batches, the number of gross sales, the number of credits, and the adjustments for that day. Gross sales is the total number of dollars charged that day. Credits are the total number of dollars which were credited to cards that day. Adjustments are either funds that are being or have been held from deposit into your account, chargeback fees for disputed charges, or rejected cards. Next to these numbers is the total discount rate for all cards applied to that day. Finally, there's the net deposit, which is gross sales, minus credits, and plus or minus adjustments. You also see the discount rates and money you're being charged for each individual card you honor.

Depending on your merchant bank, there may be other charges that you incur. Some banks charge you a fixed fee per transaction and per batch. Most also charge you for voice authorizations on a per-transaction basis. Some services have a minimum monthly discount, just in case your transactions don't add up to much. Many merchant banks that don't have a minimum monthly discount will have a *statement fee,* which they charge you for the service of generating and sending your monthly statement.

Implementing a Credit Card Transaction Web Site with Stronghold and ICVERIFY

For our example of a credit card transaction Web site, we use the two pieces of software we consider best for doing electronic commerce: The Stronghold: Apache-SSL server and the ICVERIFY credit card transaction software. But wait—our Stronghold server runs Linux, and there doesn't happen to be a version of ICVERIFY for Linux. What are we going to do?

Simple. We're going to continue to run our secure server on Linux, but run ICVERIFY on a Windows 95 system! This illustrates the well-known fact that a Web server environment doesn't have to be homogenous. In fact, some Web server environments use multiple servers running on various platforms, each performing its appointed task.

In the sections that follow, we explain how to select, install, and configure the individual components that went into constructing our own environment. This should give you plenty of inspiration for creating your own unique commerce solution.

Keeping the servers separate

Calling this a Web commerce *site* may not be the most appropriate terminology. That's because we suggest you don't make your secure Web server and your ICVERIFY master server the same machine. There are several reasons we believe this is best:

■ **Performance.** Web servers can be hit with quite a load. Files are constantly being accessed and copied across the Net. CGI programs are being run, stealing CPU cycles. Serial I/O on a PC, such as over a modem, requires that the CPU be interrupted briefly in order to take care of the hardware access request. This can cause a slowdown on your Web server, or interfere with the modem.

- **Reliability.** This is also related to the performance issue. Because busy Web servers can be a drain on resources, they can interfere with how quickly a system is able to access it's serial buffer. Serial buffer overflow may cause your modem to drop the connection. Also, if your system is unable to send request file information quickly enough to a processor after connecting because it's too busy sending a GIF to someone over the Net, the processor might time-out and hang up.

- **Security.** Having separate servers also makes things more secure. It lessens the chances of someone accessing or changing critical ICVERIFY information, such as the SET files. If you're an ISP that has customers who can upload and download their content from your Web server, you're especially at risk of someone stumbling onto this information. Also, in multimerchant setups, you wouldn't want one merchant finding out what another's gross credit card sales are from the ICVERIFY history files.

If having two servers isn't economically or technically feasible for you, then go ahead and run one server, but you may want to keep card transactions to a minimum.

WHICH SERVER DOES WHAT?

In our suggested two server setup, one server acts strictly as the secure Web server and the other acts as the ICVERIFY master server.

The secure Web server

- serves up an HTML form for the secure entry of credit card information.

- delivers the completed form to a CGI program that it runs. The CGI program generates an ICVERIFY request file that contains credit card and sales information.

- deposits the ICVERIFY request file into a directory that it's sharing through a file sharing protocol.

The CGI program then looks for the ICVERIFY answer file in the shared directory and parses it. If it sees an approval from the processor, it places an order for the customer. If the card is rejected, it tells the customer so.

The ICVERIFY master server

- is mounted/connected to the shared directory on the secure Web server.

- is running a multiuser copy of ICVERIFY, which is polling the shared directory.

- calls the processor via a modem connected to the ICVERIFY master server whenever it sees a request file in the shared directory (which was generated by the secure server's CGI).

- generates an answer file from the processor's response, and places it in the shared directory.

Directory placement

There are five directories which come into play in a secure credit card transaction Web site: secure HTTP directory, secure CGI directory, ICVERIFY program directory, ICVERIFY data directory, and a shared ICVERIFY REQ/ANS file directory. Note that by "secure HTTP directory" we don't necessarily mean one using the S-HTTP protocol, but one that contains documents only accessible from a secure server. Likewise for the secure CGI directory.

Each of these directories lives on either the secure Web server or the ICVERIFY master server. The only one accessible by both is the ICVERIFY REQ/ANS file directory. Table 14-1 shows which server each directory should live on, a sample name, user group, and permissions. For naming, we use our choice of a UNIX server for the secure server and a Windows 95 system for the ICVERIFY master.

TABLE 14-1: WEB COMMERCE SITE DIRECTORY PLACEMENT AND PERMISSIONS

DIRECTORY	SERVER	SAMPLE NAME	USER GROUP	PERMISSIONS
Secure HTTP	Secure Web Server	/www/ssldocs	(owner).*httpd*	rwxr-s——
Secure CGI	Secure Web Server	/www/cgi-ssl	(owner).*httpd*	rwxr-s——
ICVERIFY program	ICVERIFY master	D:\ICVERIFY	n/a	n/a
ICVERIFY data	ICVERIFY master	D:\DATADIR\ICV	n/a	n/a
ICVERIFY request	Secure Web Server (but shared)	/home/icv	icverify.httpd	rws-wx—— *chmod* 4730

DIRECTORY PERMISSIONS

On the UNIX server, we created a user name called *icverify* which belongs to the group *icv*. This user has ownership of the ICVERIFY request directory. When the ICVERIFY program accesses this shared directory, it accesses it as the icverify user. This user has ownership of the request directory. The set user ID bit is also turned on in that directory, so that files generated in that directory are also owned by icverify. The *httpd* group has write and execute permission in the request directory. This means that while our CGI programs can write and delete files in that directory, they can't even peer inside. The secure server directories were described in Chapter 12. In our case, the ICVERIFY program and data directory owners and permissions don't apply, because we're running it on a Windows 95 system.

SHARING THE REQUEST DIRECTORY

When running two servers, one as the ICVERIFY master and one as the secure server, you have to share a directory on the secure server that the ICVERIFY master server can access. Depending on the platforms of the servers you're running, this can be done one of three ways: NFS for TCP/IP, Windows file sharing with NetBEUI, and Windows file sharing with NetBEUI over TCP/IP. Let's look at each in detail.

NETWORK FILE SYSTEM (NFS) FOR TCP/IP   NFS has long been a way for UNIX systems to share directories with each other using TCP/IP. An NFS server exports a directory, which other machines can mount, making it appear that that directory exists on the mounting host.

On UNIX systems, the directory you wish to export and the machine you want to access it should be stored in the exports file, which is usually kept in the /etc directory. Here's a sample line:

```
/home/icv  -access=icv.outer.net,root=icv.outer.net
```

In this example, a directory called *services/icverify* is being exported. Access to this directory is only being granted to a machine called *icv.outer.net*. icv.outer.net would access this directory using the *mount* command, which would have a format similar to this:

```
mount -t nfs www2.outer.net:/home/icv /services/icverify
```

While *-t nfs* means that the file system type is NFS (on UNIX, *mount* can be used to mount file systems of different types), *www2.outer.net:/home/icv* means to mount the /home/icv directory on www2.outer.net. The final *services/icverify* is the mount point which exists on icv.outer.net.

There are also versions of NFS available for Windows systems, both commercial and free. Examples of free NFS servers for Windows are SOSS NFS for Windows NT and Tropic NFS for Windows 3.x. Both can be found at the WinSite archive:

```
http://www.winsite.com/info/pc/winnt/netutil/sossntr4.zip/
    index.html
http://www.winsite.com/info/pc/win3/winsock/trnfs15.zip/
    index.html .
```

These packages are functional, but a UNIX user would find them more comfortable than the average Windows user. For better support, a commercial version of NFS for Windows and Macintosh systems, called ChameleonNFS, is available from Net-Manage. For more information, visit their Web site at:

```
http://www.netmanage.com .
```

The benefit of NFS is that it's available on the most platforms. You could even have a Macintosh WebStar SSL server running ChameleonNFS as your secure server, and a Windows 3.1 system also running ChameleonNFS as your ICVERIFY master server.

WINDOWS FILE SHARING WITH NETBEUI Windows for Workgroups, Windows 95, and Windows NT Workstation and Server can all perform file sharing using the NetBEUI protocol. Encapsulated within the NetBEUI protocol are Server Message Blocks (SMB), which contain information about the source and destination machines, plus the data that's actually being transferred.

In order to do Windows file sharing with NetBEUI, you need to be running the NetBEUI protocol, the Client for Microsoft Networks, and File and Printer Sharing for Microsoft Networks. Windows 95 and Windows NT systems that have a network card can install these automatically.

All sharing functions under Microsoft Networks can be performed using the File Manager. Connecting to a shared directory can be done through the File Manager, the Network Neighborhood tool under Windows 95, or through the NET USE command line.

If both your secure server and ICVERIFY master server can do Windows file sharing with NetBEUI, then you may want to *only* run the NetBEUI protocol on your ICVERIFY master server and have the two systems communicate that way. The advantage of this is that NetBEUI is not a protocol routed over the Internet, so you're less likely to have intruders from the Net.

WINDOWS FILE SHARING WITH NETBEUI OVER TCP/IP Windows file sharing with NetBEUI over TCP/IP operates in the same fashion as Windows file sharing with NetBEUI. The only difference is that the NetBEUI packet and SMB is encapsulated within a TCP/IP packet. This is enabled automatically whenever a Windows 95 or NT system has both NetBEUI and TCP/IP installed, as well as the Client and File and Printer Sharing for Microsoft Networks. This is useful when you want to route NetBIOS traffic, which isn't normally routable.

When running a nifty system utility on your UNIX system called *Samba*, it also becomes useful as a means to enable Windows systems to access shared UNIX directories without NFS. Samba is free source code which can be compiled for over 30 UNIX flavors. It can be obtained from:

```
ftp://nimbus.anu.edu.au/pub/tridge/samba/
```

Samba includes services such as NetBEUI name server support (nmbd), sharing resources for other NetBEUI systems to access (smbd); and an FTP-like client to access resources that are shared via NetBEUI (smbclient).

Sharing resources through Samba's smbd program is done through a configuration file called *smb.conf.* For each resource you specify the share name a comment (if desired), a path, whether or not the share is publicly readable, writable, or printable, and what users or groups can access it. Conveniently, Samba uses the UNIX *passwd* and *group* files, so you don't have to maintain separate user and group lists. Here is a sample setup:

```
[icv]
    comment =
    path = /services/icverify
    public = no
    writable = no
    printable = no
    read list = @icv
    write list = @icv
```

The [icv] field designates that the share name is icv. We didn't put in a comment. This is for security reasons. You can often browse Windows networks and see the shares available as well as their comments. The less you say about the share, the more likely someone will ignore it. If you put something like "Credit Card Authentication Dir," you might as well add "HACK HERE!!!" to the end of it. The *path* is to the directory we're sharing. Here it's */services/icverify*. We turned off all public accessibility, and to the read list and write list we only added the icv group, of which our icverify user is a part.

Firewall considerations

Firewalling your secure Web server and ICVERIFY master server is essential. Just by announcing that you're running credit card transaction services will make your site a prime candidate for hacking.

   If nothing else, on your Web server you should block every service besides insecure and secure Web services (TCP/IP sockets 80 and 443, respectively) from being accessed from the greater Internet. This can usually be done at your own router, or at your ISP's Internet gateway router, if it supports access lists of some kind. Windows NT Advanced Server 4.0 also supports access restrictions at a service level. If you're allowing the anonymous download of files from your server, or if you're an ISP and have Web host clients that come in through other providers who need to upload their pages, then you can also open up FTP—keeping in mind that this can also be a good entry point for hackers.

   You should also block *any* type of traffic from the greater Internet from accessing your ICVERIFY master server. ICVERIFY uses a modem rather than the Internet to communicate with a processor, therefore the *only* machine that should ever need to access it for file transfers is the secure Web server itself.

DIFFERENT PHYSICAL AND LOGICAL NETWORKS

If you have the expertise and can obtain the equipment, here's a configuration that offers even more security: Place the ICVERIFY master server on a different physical network from the Internet router, and make each network use different logical TCP/IP networks.

   This configuration requires that you have two Ethernet cards installed in your secure Web server. One card connects to the Ethernet where your Internet gateway router is connected. The other connects to the Ethernet to which only the ICVERIFY master server is connected (you'll also need to obtain the appropriate cabling, hubs, and such).

We've greatly simplified our discussion of Internet firewalls in this chapter. A detailed description of firewall options and how they work would require a book in itself, and there are many excellent ones out there, such as John Vacca's *Internet Security SECRETS,* from IDG Books Worldwide, and Brent Chapman's *Building Internet Firewalls,* from O'Reilly and Associates.

Firewalling is a complex topic, requiring in-depth knowledge of the behaviors of the protocols and services you're trying to control. The best advice is to leave firewalls to the professionals: your network administrator or your ISP. If you are an administrator or ISP, or just want to start manipulating firewalls on your own router, read the literature on firewalling concepts, the protocols and services you run, and access controls on your particular router. Then start testing on equipment *other than* your Internet gateway router. A single typo can cause serious problems, or even deny you from accessing your router from your own LAN!

A NOTE ON FIREWALLS

Figure 14-1 gives an example. We don't cover the TCP/IP addressing, subnetting, and routing issues in-depth here. Instead, we simplify them this way: The secure Web server can assume that the ICVERIFY master is directly connected to it via the Ethernet 1 card, and the ICVERIFY master server can also assume that the secure Web server is connected to it via its Ethernet card. The secure Web server also knows how to get to the rest of the world through its default gateway: The Internet gateway router, which the server assumes is connected to its Ethernet 0 card. The Internet gateway router, however, doesn't know that traffic destined for the ICVERIFY master should go through the secure Web server, because it doesn't have know that route exists. Likewise, the ICVERIFY master server doesn't have a default gateway route, so it doesn't know it should go through the secure Web server to talk to the rest of the world. This effectively isolates the ICVERIFY master from any communication with the Internet.

This description is greatly simplified, but anyone familiar with TCP/IP routing should understand the figure. There are also other issues that may need to be handled. For instance, protocols help routers learn routes from other machines and routers should be turned off on at least the secure Web server. An example of this is the Routing Information Protocol (RIP). If the gateway router, the secure Web server, and the ICVERIFY master server all run RIP, the gateway router could learn from the secure server how to get to the ICVERIFY master, and the ICVERIFY master could learn that it should go through the secure Web server to get to the rest of the world. In this case, that's highly undesirable!

As with firewalls, routing is something that you might want to have your network administrator or ISP handle, especially if it's an unfamiliar topic. Remember to use caution. Even a small change to routing tables can affect hundreds of machines!

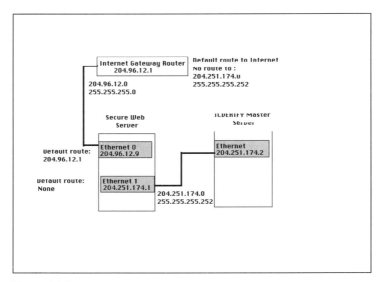

Figure 14-1
A more secure method of restricting access to the ICVERIFY master: two physical and logical networks.

Development with ICVERIFY

As we've said, ICVERIFY includes an open transaction system that makes it easy to build software that includes its capabilities. All authentication request and answers take the form of ASCII text files that can be generated and parsed by CGI programs. These files are known as *request* and *answer* files.

In a typical ICVERIFY setup, a POS workstation running a slave copy of ICVER-IFY or custom software would generate a request file and place it into a shared directory. The ICVERIFY master copy polls this shared directory, and upon seeing the request file calls the processor for authentication. ICVERIFY communicates with the processor and sends the processor merchant-specific information, plus the credit card number, expiration date, and purchase amount. ICVERIFY takes the processor's response and generates an answer file, containing an answer and authorization code.

THE REQUEST AND ANSWER FILE FORMAT

ICVERIFY request files have the filename extension *REQ,* while the answer files have the filename extension *ANS.* This must always be the case, as it's how ICVERIFY knows what to do with the files. It also makes it easy for our CGI program to decide what do with the file.

ICVERIFY REQ/ANS files are always plain ASCII text, with no embedded control characters. There's always one request per line, and they can have unlimited length.

Data fields on each line are delimited by quotation marks and commas, with each field being within double quotation marks and separated by commas. For instance:

```
"C1","WWW","Killer Java applet","5237710000427592","9805","9.55"
```

In a request line, such as the one preceding, the first field is always an ICVERIFY command. In this case, the command *C1* denotes a sale. Other ICVERIFY codes for the retail industry are shown in Table 14-2. The other arguments are clerk (*WWW* in this case for our Web server), comment (we're selling Java applets), account number, expiration date, and amount.

TABLE 14-2: ICVERIFY COMMAND CODES FOR THE RETAIL INDUSTRY

CODE	MEANING
C1	Sale
C2	Void sale
C3	Credit/return
CR	Credit void
C5	Force sale
C6	Pre-auth/auth only (means that authorization will be performed, but not a sale)

As you may remember from Chapter 10, ICVERIFY is capable of creating a full response answer file, or one which it has evaluated and regenerated into a consistent simple response that contains essential elements. Choose the format you wish in the Evaluated Response field of the Processor Setup screen.

THE FULL RESPONSE ANSWER FILE   The long response answer file generated typically by ICVERIFY contains two lines. The first line is an echo of the request, and a second is another quotation mark/comma-delimited line which contains the date, time, and response from the processor. For example:

```
"09-14-96","13:27:23","APPROVED 772885 38567188","A","","000001"
```

The first two fields are the date and time. The third is the processor's response—in this case the transaction was *APPROVED*. In the same field are the six-digit authorization code, and an eight-digit reference number. The other fields are a null response and a sequence number.

The full response file gives you quite a bit of information. In most cases, all you're concerned about is whether or not the transaction is approved, and what the authorization and reference numbers are. A CGI program which parses a full response file will have to pull out this information. The program could also use the extra information for its own tracking purposes.

Parsing the full response file is fine if you're doing authorizations with one processor. The problems start to occur in a multiprocessor or multimerchant setup, where you might dial into two or more processing networks. Each processor has its own response. For instance, instead of *APPROVED,* you might see *Good, AP,* or *OK.* Your CGI program would have to be able to understand every string a processor might return.

THE SIMPLE RESPONSE ANSWER FILE If you elect to have an evaluated response, then ICVERIFY parses and distills the processor's answer for you. Unless you absolutely want the date, time, and sequence information, we suggest that you use a simple response without an echo of the request. It makes your programming job much easier!

The format for the simple response answer file is a single character value, followed by the six-digit authorization code, followed by an optional eight-digit reference number. There are no spaces or other characters between this information. For example:

```
"Y77288538567188"
```

The *Y* indicates that the transaction was approved. *772885* is the authorization code, and *38567188* is the reference number. Both of these numbers are used for the merchant and processor's records.

If authorization is declined, then the answer file will only contain the reason for the denial. For instance:

```
"NHOLD CARD"
```

This indicates that the authorization was declined, and the card issuer asks that the card be held by the merchant (it may have been stolen). In a Web commerce setting where there's no physical contact with the card bearer, of course, there's no way to take the card from them. What your CGI program should do is disregard everything but an approval response. You can log all transactions, and report fraudulent attempts to the card issuer.

TESTING A CGI PROGRAM WITH ICVERIFY
ICVERIFY is very developer-friendly. Rather than provide a complete proprietary POS solution, their goal is to be the credit card transaction piece in anyone's POS system. Consequently, they make it easy for small shops and even individuals to develop for ICVERIFY. Their documentation includes a description of the request and answer file formats, as well as instructions for capturing data from a POS screen.

They also include two methods for developers to test ICVERIFY with their programs. The first is a set of demonstration setup files for a variety of processors that come with pre-validated test merchant numbers. These demonstration files are named *DEMO01.SET* through *DEMO20.SET.* Choose one for the processor you wish to test for (a table is included in the documentation), and copy it to ICVERIFY.SET. Then run ICSETUP against the ICVERIFY.SET file, and double-check the modem dial string and phone numbers. Also make changes to the data drive/directory if need be. You can then run ICVERIFY using this SET file, and have it processes information.

You can also use your own SET file and merchant information when running ICVERIFY with the /D option (*-d* under UNIX). This will cause ICVERIFY to run, but not dial your processor. Instead, dialing will be simulated, as will authorization, answer files, and settlement.

A simple one-off credit card payment system

In this section, we'll cover a simple one-off card payment system. It consists of two CGI programs written in Perl. The first, *oneoffcard.pl*, is a form which contains fields for entering credit card and ordering information for a product. The second, *charge.pl*, actually authorizes the card and e-mails the card-bearer that the card has been charged.

These programs will charge a single card a single time, and are mostly to provide an example and test. They can be expanded upon to integrate into your online commerce system. There are also modifications and error-checking routines which should be implemented before putting this code into production.

Note that charge.pl also uses formlib.pl. formlib.pl is a Perl library containing HTML form-handling subroutines. It's written by Brigitte Jellinek and can be obtain from her Web page (as well as the included CD):

```
http://www.cosy.sbg.ac.at/www-doku/tools/bjscripts.html

#
#!/usr/local/bin/perl
#
#
# Copyright (C) 1996 Mike W. Erwin <mikee@outer.net>
# All rights reserved.
#
# Redistribution and use in source and binary forms, with or
without
# modification, are permitted provided that: (1) source code
distributions
# retain the above copyright notice and this paragraph in its
entirety, (2)
# distributions including binary code include the above copyright
notice and
# this paragraph in its entirety in the documentation or other
materials
# provided with the distribution, and (3) all advertising
materials mentioning
# features or use of this software display the following
acknowledgement:
# THIS SOFTWARE IS PROVIDED "AS IS" AND WITHOUT ANY EXPRESS
```

```
# OR IMPLIED WARRANTIES, INCLUDING, WITHOUT LIMITATION, THE
# IMPLIED WARRANTIES OF MERCHANTABILITY AND FITNESS FOR A
# PARTICULAR PURPOSE.
#
#  oneoffcard.pl
#
#  Revision History:
#
#  This script creates the ssl page required to input credit card
information
#
# PURPOSE:   The purpose of this script is to put together an on
the
#        fly HTML page the will be sent back to a browser giving the
#        use a list of form boxes to fill out and a button to
#        initiate the authorization of the credit card system.
#
# INSTALLATION: Merely put the script in your secure servers cgi-
bin directory,
#        and edit the "CHARGE_CGI" variable below. This will need
to be
#        localized for your specific site.
#
#
# USAGE:  https://www.YOURSITE.com/CGISSLDIR/oneoffcard.pl
#
#
###################################################################

$CHARGE_CGI = "https://www.YOURSITE.com/CGISSLDIR/charge.pl";

{
  print STDOUT "Content-type: text/html\n\n";
  print STDOUT "<HTML><HEAD>\"
<TITLE>Credit Card Clearing House</TITLE>\
<CENTER>\
<H3>\
Online Credit Card Clearing (Realtime)<BR>\
One Off Credit Card Transaction Screen<P>\
</H3>\
</CENTER>\
<HR>\
</HEAD>\
```

```
<BODY>\
\
<BLOCKQUOTE>\
Please enter your credit card information below:\
<P>\
<B>Customer Information</B>\
<P>\
<FORM ACTION=\"${CHARGE_CGI}\" METHOD=\"POST\">\
<PRE>\
 First Name: <INPUT TYPE=\"text\" NAME=\"First_Name\" SIZE=40>
\
     Last Name: <INPUT TYPE=\"text\" NAME=\"Last_Name\" SIZE=40>\
     Street Address: <INPUT TYPE=\"text\" NAME=\"Street_Address\"
SIZE=40>\
     City: <INPUT TYPE=\"text\" NAME=\"City\" SIZE=40>\
     State-Province: <INPUT TYPE=\"text\" NAME=\"State_Province\"
SIZE=14>\
     Zip: <INPUT TYPE=\"text\" NAME=\"Zip_Code\" SIZE=15> \
     Country: <INPUT TYPE=\"text\" NAME=\"Country\" SIZE=14>\
     Phone Number: <INPUT TYPE=\"text\" NAME=\"Phone_Number\"
SIZE=40>\
     Email Address: <INPUT TYPE=\"text\" NAME=\"Email_Address\"
SIZE=40>\
              (Email is REQUIRED, Confirmation is sent via mail)\
     </PRE>\
     <B>Credit Card Information</B>  (Don't include spaces or
dashes)\
     <PRE>\
     Card Number: <INPUT TYPE=\"text\" NAME=\"Account_Number\"
SIZE=40> \
     Expiration Date: <INPUT TYPE=\"text\" NAME=\"Expiration_Date\"
SIZE=4> \
     (In the form \"MMYY\")\
     </PRE>\
     <B>Product Purchase Information</B>\
     <PRE>\
     Product: <INPUT TYPE=\"text\" NAME=\"Product_Description\"
SIZE=40 \
             VALUE=\"YOUR PRODUCT OR SERVICE HERE\">\
     Total Sale: <INPUT TYPE=\"text\" NAME=\"Sale_Price\" SIZE=20>\
     </PRE>\
     </BLOCKQUOTE>\
```

```
<HR>\
<INPUT VALUE=\"Authorize Transaction\" TYPE=\"SUBMIT\">\
<HR>\
</FORM>\
</body></html>";
}
charge.pl
#!/usr/local/bin/perl
#
#
# Copyright (C) 1996 Mike W. Erwin <mikee@outer.net>
# All rights reserved.
#
# Redistribution and use in source and binary forms, with or
without
# modification, are permitted provided that: (1) source code
distributions
# retain the above copyright notice and this paragraph in its
entirety, (2)
# distributions including binary code include the above copyright
notice and
# this paragraph in its entirety in the documentation or other
materials
# provided with the distribution, and (3) all advertising
materials mentioning
# features or use of this software display the following
acknowledgement:
# THIS SOFTWARE IS PROVIDED "AS IS" AND WITHOUT ANY EXPRESS
# OR IMPLIED WARRANTIES, INCLUDING, WITHOUT LIMITATION, THE
# IMPLIED WARRANTIES OF MERCHANTABILITY AND FITNESS FOR A#
# PARTICULAR PURPOSE.
#
#  charge.pl
#
#  Revision History:
#
#
#
# PURPOSE:   This script will take the inputs from the form
generated by
#         the oneoffcard.pl script that goes along with this one and
#         will parse out the relevant information and create an
#         appropriate request file in a directory that ICVerify
sees.
```

```
#       The script will also wait for a response from the credit
#       card processor and will return an HTML page with the
results
#       of the transaction.
#
# INSTALLATION: Install this script along with the oneoffcard.pl
script in
#       the cgi-bin directory of your SSL server.
#
#
# USAGE:  This script needs to be called from a form that has the
#       fields a defined in the "get_web_fields" function below.
#       The calling form may be generated by another script or
#       it can be a flat file.
#
#
##############################################################################

##############################################################################
#
# Setup some variables from the ones passed from the web server's
environment
# variables and include all the the PERL libs that might be
needed.
#
##############################################################################

##############################################################################
#
# Here we use the formlib.pl script to parse out the environment
variables.
#
##############################################################################

require "/www/cgi-bin/formlib.pl";

&GetFormArgs();    # parse arguments passed from FORM (now in %in)
$ENV{PATH_INFO} ne '' && &GetPathArgs($ENV{PATH_INFO});

# This is where ICVerify looks for new requests
$REQ_DIR = "/home/icv/requests";
# This is used to log the transactions
$LOG_DIR = "/home/icv/logs";
$datestr = `date '+19%y%m%d%H%M%S'`;
```

```perl
chop($datestr);

#############################################################
#
# This function is used to parse out the environment variables
into some
# easier to use ones. This is for convenience only and does
nothing to
# provide a faster or better algorithm.
#
#############################################################

sub get_web_fields {
  $First_Name        = $in{First_Name};
  $Last_Name        = $in{Last_Name};
  $Street_Address    = $in{Street_Address};
  $City             = $in{City};
  $State_Province    = $in{State_Province};
  $Zip_Code         = $in{Zip_Code};
  $Country          = $in{Country};
  $Phone_Number     = $in{Phone_Number};
  $Email_Address    = $in{Email_Address};
  $Account_Number   = $in{Account_Number};
  $Expiration_Date   = $in{Expiration_Date};
  $Transaction_Type  = $in{Transaction_Type};
  $Product_Description = $in{Product_Description};
  $Sale_Price       = $in{Sale_Price};

  $Account_Number =~ s/\-//;
  $Account_Number =~ s/\ //;

  $Expiration_Date =~ s/\-//;
  $Expiration_Date =~ s/\ //;

  $trans_type = "C1";     ## This forces the transaction to be a
sale.

  if ($Email_Address) {
    $mail_good = 1;      ## Make sure an e-mail address is specified.
  }
}


#############################################################
#
```

```perl
# Here is where the most of the credit card processing takes
place.
# This function will create a file called "ICVER001.REQ" which
will contain
# The appropriate fields for ICVerify to process the transaction.
#
##############################################################

sub run_card {

    $newfile = $REQ_DIR."/ICVER001.REQ";

    #
    # Need a hazard breakout loop counter here. This is example code
and
    # should not be put into production as it has no condition for
exit.
    #
    while (( -e $REQ_DIR."/ICVER001.REQ" ) || ( -e
$REQ_DIR."/icvr001.hld") ||
          ( -e $REQ_DIR."/icvr001.ans")) {
    }

    open(NEW_TRANSACTION,"> $newfile");
    print NEW_TRANSACTION
"\"${trans_type}\",\"\~0001\~\",\"${Product_Description}\",\"${Acco
unt_Number}\",\"${Expiration_Date}\",\"${Sale_Price}\"";
    close (NEW_TRANSACTION);

    system("chgrp -f icv $newfile");
    system("chmod 660 $newfile");
}


##############################################################
#
# This is the counter-part to the "run_card" function. Once the
request is
# made, this function will wait until it sees a response. PLEASE
NOTE THAT
# THIS FUNCTION SHOULD NOT BE PUT INTO PRODUCTION WITH
# MODIFICATION. As the "run_card" function above, we make no
assumption
# about how long to wait for a response to appear. In other words,
if the ICVerify
```

```perl
# process is broken or not responding correctly, this process
will zombie.
#
###############################################################

sub get_answer {
  $answerfile = $REQ_DIR."/icver001.ans";
  $logfile = $LOG_DIR."/${datestr}.transaction";
  $done = 0;

  #
  # Need a hazard breakout loop counter here. This is example code
and
  # should not be put into production as it has no condition for
exit.
  #
  while (! $done) {
    if ( -e $answerfile ) {
      $done = 1;
    }
  }

  system("mv $answerfile $logfile");   # Once done, copy the
completed trans
                     # to a log dir for later collection.


}


###############################################################
#
# Here we output an HTML page if the transaction was made
correctly.
#
###############################################################

sub print_response {
  print STDOUT "Content-type: text/html\n\n";
  print STDOUT "<HTML><HEAD>\
  <TITLE>Credit Card Clearing House</TITLE>\
  <CENTER>\
  <H3>\
  The Credit Card Transaction has been processed.<BR>\
  </H3>";
```

```perl
    $answer_val = `tail -1 $logfile`;
    chop($answer_val);
    $answer_val =~ s/\"//g;

    @answer_split = split("",$answer_val);

    if ( $answer_split[0] eq "Y" || $answer_split[0] eq "y") {
      $approval_code = join('',@answer_split[1..6]);
      $reference_code = join('',@answer_split[7..14]);
      print STDOUT "<h3>The transaction has been
approved.</h3><HR>";
      print STDOUT "<h3> Approval Code: $approval_code</h3>";
      print STDOUT "<h3> Reference Code:
$reference_code</h3><HR><h4>";
      print STDOUT " Card Number: $Account_Number<BR>";
      print STDOUT " Transaction: $Transaction_Type<BR>";
      print STDOUT " Amount: $Sale_Price</h4>";
    }
    if ( $answer_split[0] eq "N" || $answer_split[0] eq "n") {
      $elements = $#answer_split;
      $deny_code = join('',@answer_split[1..($elements)]);
      print STDOUT "<h3>The transaction has been denied \
                   for the following reason:</h3><HR>";
      print STDOUT "<h3> Deny Code: $deny_code</h3><HR>";
    }
  }


#####################################################################
#
# Here we output an HTML page if the transaction was NOT made
correctly.
#
#####################################################################

  sub print_retry_response {
    print STDOUT "Content-type: text/html\n\n";
    print STDOUT "<HTML><HEAD>\
    <TITLE>Credit Card Clearing House</TITLE>\
    <CENTER>\
    <H3>\
    The Card was NOT Processed. Some field was left blank or the
e-mail\
    address was somehow invalid.<P>\
    E-Mail address: $Email_Address\
```

```
    </H3>";
    }


#############################################################
#
# Finally we send some e-mail to the user to verify what just when
on.
    #
#############################################################

sub wrap_up {
    open (ACKMAIL, "| /bin/mailx -s 'Credit Card Charge Receipt'
$Email_Address");
    print ACKMAIL "\n\nYour credit card has been charged by YOUR
COMPANY.\n";
    print ACKMAIL "for the following goods and services:\n\n";
    print ACKMAIL "$Product_Description\n\n";
    print ACKMAIL "Type of Transaction:\t\t$Transaction_Type\n";
    print ACKMAIL "Amount of Transaction:\t\t\$ $Sale_Price\n\n";
    print ACKMAIL "Thank you,\YOUR COMPANY.
(billing@outer.net)\n\n";
    close (ACKMAIL);
    }



#############################################################
#
# MAIN- Everything starts here.
#
#############################################################

{
  &get_web_fields();

  if (! $mail_good ) {
    &print_retry_response();
    exit();
  }

  &run_card();
  &get_answer();
  &print_response();
  &wrap_up();
}
```

INSTALLING THE CGI PROGRAMS

Let's go through the setup and installation of these CGI programs step-by-step.

1. Obtain formlib.pl from the CD-ROM and place it into your CGI directory. In our case, it's */www/cgi-bin.* Make sure that permissions are set correctly to enable the Web server to execute it. Also, check the require statement and charge.pl, and change the location of formlib.pl if you need to.

2. Obtain oneoffcard.pl and charge.pl from the CD-ROM. In oneoffcard.pl, edit the $CHARGE_CGI variable to reflect the URL of charge.pl on your system. In our case it's *https://www2.outer.net/cgi-ssl/book/charge.pl.* Note the https as a protocol designator to use the SSL port.

3. In oneoffcard.pl, where you see the following line of code:

```
Product: <INPUT TYPE=\"text\" NAME=\"Product_Description\"
SIZE=40 VALUE=\"YOUR PRODUCT OR SERVICE HERE\">\
```

input the name of your product or service in the VALUE field. In our case, it's *Web Commerce Book.*

4. Edit the $REQ_DIR and $LOG_DIR variables in charge.pl. Put the name of your request and logging directories here. For ours, it's */home/icv/requests* and */home/icv/logs,* respectively.

5. Place charge.pl and oneoffcard.pl in the secure CGI directory on your server. In our case, it's */www/cgi-ssl.* Make sure that permissions are set appropriately to execute them (refer back to Table 14-1).

6. Create the icverify user and icv group on the secure server.

7. Create the request directory /home/icv and the subdirectories /home/icv/requests and /home/icv/logs. Set permissions as per Table 14-1.

8. Share the directory with Samba or export it with NFS. In our case, we'll share it as icv, using Samba.

9. Mount or connect to the secure server's shared request directory from the ICVERIFY master server. Because we're using a Windows 95 machine, we'll use the NET USE command in a batch file. For example:

```
NET USE I: \\WWW2\ICV
```

10. Run ICVERIFY on the master server. Refer to Chapter 10 on how to configure ICVERIFY. In our case, we'll run it with the command line options:

```
ICVERIFY /N /M I:\requests
```

If you don't have a validated copy, you can still run it with the DEMO sets.

11. Access oneoffcard.pl through your Web browser.

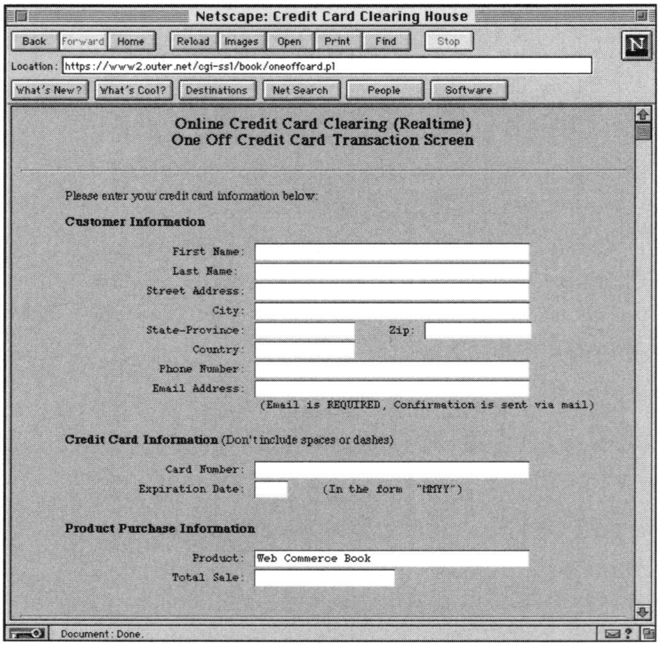

Figure 14-2
The information entry page for oneoffcard.pl.

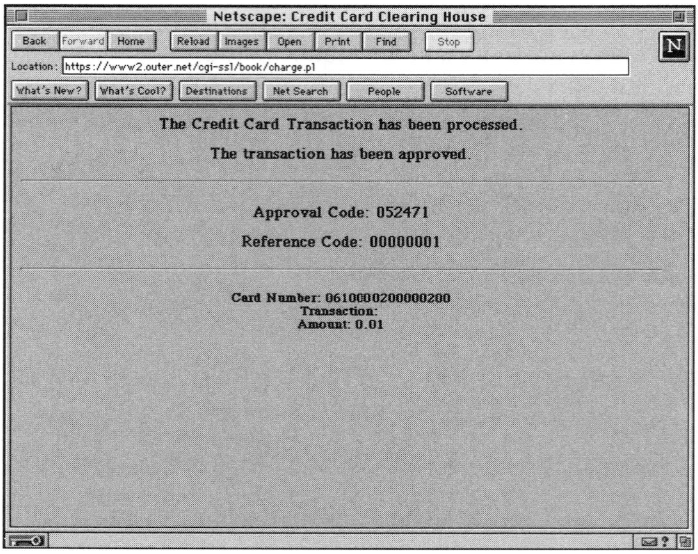

Figure 14-3
charge.pl reporting a successful card authorization.

That's it! If you've set everything up correctly you should see a form such as the one in Figure 14-2. If you enter a credit card number to process a transaction and it's approved, you'll see a page such as Figure 14-3. If it's declined for some reason, you'll see a page telling you why, as in Figure 14-4.

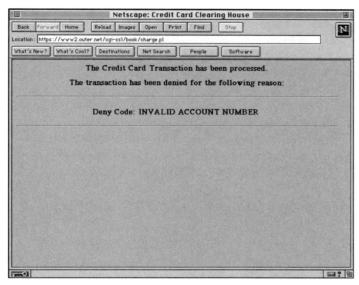

Figure 14-4
charge.pl reporting an invalid account number.

Summary

The information in this chapter should help you begin processing credit cards. We've taken what you've learned in the chapters on credit card payment, secure servers, and ICVERIFY, and applied it. We've gone through setting up a merchant account and what kind of charges to expect from them. We've also explored different scenarios for firewalling a commerce site. Finally, we've covered developing CGI programs for ICVERIFY and provided you with example CGI programs which can be bolstered and expanded for use in your own site. Where do we go from here? Future directions are what we cover in the next chapter!

CHAPTER FIFTEEN

YOUR SITE'S FUTURE

As with all Web-related work, the temptation to rest on your laurels and bask in your achievements will be nearly irresistible once you've designed, built, tested, and deployed your commercial site. But resist that impulse! This is actually when the real work begins, because it's only when you open your doors to the public that you'll truly start to understand what's really required, how well things are working for your customers, and what kinds of assumptions you've made that turned out to be less than accurate, if not downright misguided.

In this chapter, we cover some important points to ponder once you've made it past the initial hurdles of establishing a commercial site, and are beginning to deal with the aftermath. Along the way, we discuss the importance of soliciting—and acting on—user feedback; marketing what you have to sell; handling multiple types of payment; and how to handle payment problems. We also cover some of the key issues involved in keeping your Web site secure and up-to-date. Finally, we conclude with some ruminations on the future direction of Web commerce, and some strategies you might consider to help you keep up with these rapidly changing times and technologies.

Ask for Feedback!

There's an old joke about the restaurant business that concludes what a great job waiting tables would be, if only there weren't any customers to deal with. But of course, since customers are the very lifeblood of any business, the real humor in the joke is that without customers, the business couldn't exist. Funny or not, the same thing is true of your own business, and also of your commercial presence on the Web.

It really doesn't matter how great you think your Web site might be, or how attractive and intelligible you find your own order forms and the other appurtenances necessary for conducting business of the Web. The only thing that really matters is what your customers think—so why not ask them?

But if you're not careful about what and how you ask for feedback, you might not get the information you need most, which boils down to "How well does this site work for my clientele?" If you don't think about it much, you might conclude that an e-mail address or mail to URL on your pages is all you'll need to open the door for customer feedback, and the rest will flow from there.

We disagree, and what's more important, so do many direct marketing experts. Likewise, those Web sites that have set up proactive means to solicit feedback from users, or even provide inducements for that purpose, tend to enjoy higher sales and stronger growth than those who do not.

For one thing, it's important to understand that your customers may not know exactly how to articulate their wants and needs so that you can instantly understand them. This is as true of their reactions to what you're selling (your products or services) as it is to how you're selling them (through your Web site, order forms, and other channels). It's therefore up to you to give your customers a hand with feedback forms, nicely worded requests, and a thank-you note via e-mail whenever you do get feedback (regardless of whether it's positive or negative). You'll definitely get e-mail when your Web site doesn't work like it should, or when server or e-mail problems interfere with communications. You'll even learn to appreciate the occasional pat on the back that can come from your customers—albeit too rarely.

Build your own report card

If you aren't getting feedback, something isn't right. If you already have a feedback form on your site, you want to ask some peers or colleagues to take a look, and tell you what they think about it. If you don't have a feedback form, by all means build one right away! There's nothing like giving customers a chance to grade you to bring out their likes and dislikes. One of the better ways of deciding what kind of feedback form to use is to look around the Web for forms that you like, and imitate them without copying directly (to avoid potential copyright infringement). Unless they're built on Java applets, or by CGI programs with no sense of style, you can learn a lot by viewing their source HTML, as well as by looking at them on your display. Just for your edification, here's a list of some of our favorite feedback forms that you can use as a source of inspiration:

- Netscape bug-reporting

    http://cgi.netscape.com/cgi-bin/auto_bug.cgi

- Yahoo! feedback (see Dead Link and Fix the Listing)

    http://www.yahoo.com/text/suggest.html

- Real Audio (includes contact information and a feedback form)

    http://www.realaudio.com/reachus.html

- Macromedia (includes a good master list with great sub-pages)

    http://www.macromedia.com/macromedia/contact.html

A simple text form on a page of its own for users to copy or download, fill in, and e-mail back to you is much better than nothing. A real CGI-backed HTML form, with questions and response boxes is better still. Although it's important to be specific in your requests for information, be sure to leave space for general comments. Sometimes, the problems you don't anticipate, or the requests that have never occurred to you, can lead to the best results. For the same reason, open-ended queries like "What kinds of other products would interest you?" or "What are the three most important needs our products or services don't fulfill?" can also be extremely informative.

Serious feedback

If you really want details, ask about specific topics in your feedback form. Tell customers that you're considering developing a new product or changing an existing one, and ask them to tell you what they think. Have a contest in which you give prizes to the people who submit the best or worst features of your products or services and also tells you why. Get your customers involved in your business, and you'll all benefit. Here are some specific methods you can use to solicit more feedback, or improve the quality of the feedback you're getting.

FOCUS GROUPS

If you're serious about reaching out to your customer base with your Web site, you may want to consider a focus group approach, used very successfully by marketing and advertising companies. This activity is similar to beta testing software in that it involves providing access to your materials to outsiders specifically to obtain feedback, although focus groups are usually more structured, and aimed at select groups of target customers.

To build your own focus group online, try to select a small group (5 to 10 is the usual range) of customers that represent your customer base. E-mail each prospective group member a request to participate. Provide group members with a special URL to view your pages, and be sure they understand how things work, and how to get their feedback to you. Many companies find that for such purposes, it's a good idea to schedule a phone call, and conduct an in-depth interview with each focus group member.

This will usually be more of a marketing exercise than a form of Web page testing, but it can be very important to you and your business. You may, therefore, want to involve your marketing department or an advertising consultant in the planning process and in creating the questionnaires for your focus group. (The same advice holds true for building feedback forms as well.)

ESTABLISH AN ONLINE PRESENCE

Whatever your market niche may be, there are probably related newsgroups and mailing lists you can join. If you don't know about any, allow us to recommend a couple of excellent sources to check:

Publicly Accessible Mailing Lists:

`http://www.NeoSoft.com/internet/paml/`

Liszt: Searchable Directory of Mailing Lists:

`http://www.liszt.com/`

When you find these online convocations, don't just lurk in the background, PARTICIPATE! Make online friends with the folks who are in-the-know. Answer as many general technical queries asked in the newsgroup as possible. This gives you credibility. Make yourself known as someone who understands the market and knows how to play the game online. Put an auto-signature at the end of your postings, listing your name, title, and WWW address for the company. The more people know about you and your company, the more customers will visit your Web site.

Finally, try to figure out a way to add value to your Web site, so people will get something out of their visits there. Some techniques to create value that we've seen work well include conducting an industry survey, taking a poll, or analyzing market trends and data, and then using the Web site to publicize the results. Regular updates even give visitors a reason to return on a regular basis, and help improve your organization's credibility.

DON'T JUST LISTEN, DO SOMETHING!

When your customers do respond with feedback, thank them immediately via e-mail. It's okay to set up an autoresponder to generate an initial reply, but make sure the message it delivers says you're grateful for their feedback, and that you'll pay attention to what they say. Then use their feedback to alter your Web pages, your content, and your sales techniques as much as makes sense. The best thanks you can give your customers for their feedback is when they see you put their ideas to use, or respond to their critiques, in a timely manner.

The bottom line for your commercial Web site is to understand how things look in the eyes of your customers, and to make sure that they look as good as possible from that point of view. If you can succeed in this quest, you'll get the kind of results you no doubt hope for.

Marketing Your Wares Online

It's not enough simply to build a brand-new Web site and wait for the world to beat a path to your door. The same is true for the grand opening of your electronic commerce capabilities on the Web, even if you already have a Web site. Unless you get the word out, it's hard to expect the kinds of throngs you want flocking to your site to show up.

Consequently, we have a few tips to dispense about publicizing your capabilities. We assume you already know the importance of publicity, and that you know how to work with the trade press and trade shows for your industry. Forgive our narrow point of view, but we'll stick to some pointers about getting the word out online.

Make some noise!

To begin with, you should have an electronic copy of an information release announcing your newly minted commercial capabilities ready to mail. If you maintain your own electronic mailing list, you'll want to send a copy to your partners, your customers, and representatives of the trade press. If you have any targeted e-mail lists, you might mail to them as well, but be sure to sanity-check your message with some Internet old-timers before sending to someone you've never done business with before (see the Sidebar entitled "Never Spam a Stranger" later in this chapter).

Create a one-page announcement that's brief to the point of terseness (brevity improves the chances that its recipients will actually read it). Make sure you cover the following points, but not much more:

- Indicate who owns the Web site, be it a company or corporation, a person, an association, or some other kind of legal entity. Be sure to include traditional contact information and a contact name to call or e-mail.

- Indicate what you're selling, and what kinds of payment systems you support.

- Don't announce anything until the site is ready for public access, and you're ready to take orders. If you can't fulfill the demand you create, somebody else will.

- Be sure to highlight your URL so that interested customers can find your Web site.

- Summarize the content of your pages, emphasizing the value and interest of the materials, and of your products or services.

Your announcement should identify itself clearly, highlight your Web site's URL, and stress content. If it manages to suggest some commercial aspirations, rather than taking a hard-sell approach, it'll fit the prevailing ethos of the Internet audience much better. Remember, this is traditionally an audience where crassly commercial motives are regarded with disdain, and should be clearly secondary to information and content.

Getting the word out

There are lots of ways to publicize your new online commerce center, from posting information on "What's New" pages around the Internet, to placing subliminal messages in your e-mail. Here are a few that are worth pursuing:

- Send the announcement to the moderated newsgroup `comp.infosystems.www.announce`. Make sure your subject line includes a brief, meaningful description of the site, not just an unadorned URL.

- If the magazines in your market niche have Web sites, visit them and find out if they have a What's New submission procedure, or a cross listing of industry vendors.

- Advertise your site in the WWW Yellow pages at `http://www.bigbook.com/`.

- Send descriptions of your site and URL to "Cool Site of the Day" at `cool@infl.net` or "Spider's Pick of the Day" at `boba@www.com`.

- What's New (WN) listings worth pursuing include:
  - Mosaic WN: `whats-new@ncsa.uiuc.edu`
  - Yahoo! WN: `suggest-picks@yahoo.com`
  - c|net's "Best of the Web" at `http://www.cnet.com/Content/ Reviews/ Bestofweb/feedback.html`

- Register your URL with a search engine, as follows:
  - For Yahoo!, look for the "Add URL" selection at `http://www.yahoo.com`.
  - For Webcrawler, look for the "Submit URL" selection at `http://www. webcrawler.com`.
  - For Alta Vista, check out their recommendation for use of the META HTML tag in the Help section from their home page at `http://www. altavista. digital.com/`; you'll also find an "Add URL" link at the bottom of this page.
  - For mass coverage of an impressive list of search engines, newsgroups, and mailing lists visit "Promote-It!," a compendium of the Internet's best publicity tools at `http://www.cam.org/~psarena/promote-it.html`. It includes excellent pointers to free and for-a-fee publicity opportunities. It also provides a convenient, one-stop location from which to send your information, or to locate others who can do it for you.

Ready for searching

If you get your site properly indexed by the major search engines, then you have created a conduit for customers trolling the Internet to find your site. The best tip we can give you here is to use the META HTML tag in the <HEAD> section of your home page to provide pointers for users to find you. If your company makes reverse-threaded widgets for Throckmorton assemblies, it's probably a good idea to add a tag like the following to your home page:

```
<META HTTP-EQUIV="Keywords"
 CONTENT="reverse-threaded widget,
 Throckmorton assembly">
```

In your travels on the Web, or in your e-mail box, you may occasionally run into companies that promise to send your e-mail message to millions of readers online, for an absurdly low price. Don't fall for this ploy! While it's true that large numbers of readers will see your information, it may lead to fear and loathing on their part, because these so called *direct e-mail* companies don't exercise much restraint when deciding where to send their messages. Some of them simply send a copy to every Usenet newsgroup or to every mailing list they know of. This kind of indiscriminate mailing is called *spamming* in Internet-speak, and is universally reviled.

Most of these newsgroups and mailing lists won't care about your widgets anyway. Likewise, many of these venues have strict rules about posting, including injunctions against advertising. If you do decide to do business with a direct e-mail vendor, please solicit and check references before giving them your business. It's been said that any publicity is good publicity, but you may think otherwise if one of the slimier outfits makes your company name a synonym for something unmentionable!

NEVER SPAM A STRANGER!

This will tell any search engines that pass by, in the most explicit possible way, what you have to offer to potential visitors to your site. It also helps to guarantee that when someone uses the search term "reverse-threaded widget" on a particular engine, that your company's URL will show up in the results for that search.

Another good tip is to make sure to make the text assigned to the HTML <TITLE> tag clear and descriptive for all your pages. Most search engines search and index these as well, so they can be a powerful beacon to those in need of what you have to offer— but only if you consider this when creating them in the first place!

If you take the right steps to let the world know what you have to sell, and keep your customers' needs in mind as you lead them through your online materials, you shouldn't have any trouble making the Web a useful sales tool for your business. Properly approached, the Web can be the foundation of a business all by itself.

Handling Multiple Payment Systems

Even though the examples in Part III of this book concentrated on single system solutions for your Web pages, there's no reason why you can't broaden your potential customer base, and build order or payment forms that can accept payment from multiple payment systems. If this sounds like an appealing way to increase your online sales, we encourage you to investigate your options. But first, here are some points you need to ponder before adding more buttons, bells, or whistles to your Web pages.

Consider the costs

Each payment system has its own particular requirements, as you've already learned. The best of all possible worlds would be to learn that your merchant bank or credit card processor supports multiple payment systems, and add one or more additional systems to what you already have. This may mean that another application fee and credit check won't be necessary, or that additional hardware won't be required, either. But in many cases, there will be additional costs up-front to add more capability to support another system, and there'll certainly be added processing costs for the second system.

Trading market share against customer convenience

In some markets, multiple payment systems coexist, with none owning a compelling market share. To reach a broader audience, you may well feel compelled to add support for those other systems that reach a sufficiently large portion of that audience to make it worth your while. Just remember, though, that you're adding complexity to your Web pages and costs to your bottom line, just to be able to reach out and include this audience. It's a trade-off that must be fully explored to determine whether the added revenue potential is worth the added complexity, cost, and maintenance efforts.

Measuring customer impact

Adding some payment systems may require that you add another entire Web server to your mix of hardware and software, since that's a requirement for some of the options you'll be considering. It's important to understand what impact, if any, this might have on your customers. If you can keep two or more payment systems basically disjoint, then long waits or problems with one system will have little or no impact on others. This is a good thing. If your payment services are not properly separated from each other, on the other hand, a wait on approval or validation from one payment service might make everybody wait their turn thereafter. This will add to potential bottle-necks, rather than alleviate them.

Managing the maintenance burden

Supporting multiple payment systems means multiplying the number of maintenance tasks related to upgrades, enhancements, and API changes by the number of systems supported. If you've got an in-house programmer or access to a cheap source of programming talent, this will be less of a concern than if you have to pay market rates for CGI programmers to maintain your pages for you. (The typical hourly rate for this service are upwards of $50 per hour in the U.S.; we've paid as much as $125 per hour for such services on occasion.)

As you work your way through these various points and the issues that surround them, you should be able to work out the pros and cons of supporting multiple payment systems on a single Web site. We haven't seen that many sites on the Web yet that are quite so ambitious, but with the expected proliferation of electronic commerce on the Web, and the number of payment systems available, it's not unreasonable to expect that this may become a way of separating large, sophisticated vendors from smaller, less well-heeled ones. Most of the sites we've worked on currently support only one payment scheme, but the potential is clearly there to expand, given sufficient expectation of increasing revenues.

Handling Payment Problems

Disputed charges are a fact of life in commerce of any kind. The electronic variety appears to be particularly prone to this phenomenon, possibly because customer and vendor usually interact with one another without face-to-face contact. Whatever the cause, handling disputes is something you have to be prepared for if you plan to conduct commerce online.

Your expectations may be that some kind of reasonable resolution is possible, based on both parties presenting their version of the facts to some kind of arbitrating authority, which then decides who is liable and assesses charges accordingly. Unfortunately, such expectations run afoul of the credit laws, which have been deliberately constructed (at least in the U.S.) to protect the rights of the consumer above all else.

When it comes to credit card transactions, consumer liability is limited by law to $50. Unfortunately, this puts the onus on the merchant, who is usually liable for the entire amount of whatever purchase is involved, because the processor is entitled to keep the $50 as a fee for its involvement in the dispute. In addition, most credit card processors will assess a chargeback fee to a vendor involved in a dispute. That means there will be extra costs involved, in addition to whatever losses are incurred as a result of the disputed charge.

This, of course, explains why the notion of nonrepudiatability is so important in electronic commerce. Nonrepudiatibility means that a transaction cannot later be rejected as specious or fraudulent; that is, it gives buyers the ability to prove voluntary involvement of the merchant in a fraudulent transaction, and vice-versa. For merchants, the good news here is that various forms of liability insurance are available to help defray losses from certain claims. It's also useful to understand that around 1 percent of all charges are disputed, so it's a good idea to arrange for coverage, or a reserve fund, to cover the inevitable losses that will be involved.

The details about handling disputed charges, along with related liabilities, chargebacks, and resolution procedures should be clearly spelled out in any contract that you sign with a credit card processor, merchant bank, or other payment system provider. Be sure to have an attorney look over this part of the contract, and apprise you of your rights and obligations thereunder. It's absolutely essential to understand what liability attaches to you and what kinds of coverage or reserves you'll need in order to handle your end of this bargain. Most companies that offer such contracts maintain detailed statistics on disputed charges. Ask them to share this information with you, because it is an essential ingredient in determining the risk that's involved. You might, indeed, be compelled to raise prices to cover a reserve if the gap between coverage (which almost always has a deductible element to overcome) and loss means that you'd end up paying for most of the charges anyway (as is often the case).

Managing Site Security

Given that a commercial site offers goods or services that are valuable enough to pay for, and funds are collected from the purchase of these goods and services, a server that handles such transactions must be considered a prime target for system hacking. Someone sufficiently sophisticated could conceivably make off either with your merchandise, your proceeds, or both. That's why so much effort has been expended, and so much technology developed, for ensuring secure transactions and protecting their contents. But the same degree of attention and care is not always lavished on the systems that service commercial applications. That's why we make these general recommendations to help you stay out of trouble, followed by specific recommendations for the platforms we covered in Chapters 5–7.

A general prescription for safety and security

The following approaches to system design, partitioning, and security will help maintain your system's inviolability—and your peace of mind—a great deal. These recommendations do have their costs, but go down easiest if they're evaluated as a form of insurance against theft or malfeasance.

SEPARATE COMMERCE FROM CONTENT

Even if it's just a matter of establishing a separate directory structure, with the most stringent access controls and file protections your platform will allow, we strongly recommend that you situate your commerce-related Web documents differently from your purely informational or content-specific ones. This means placing the pages, graphics, and CGI programs for commerce pages in a separate directory tree from all the others. Actually, we've found it to be useful to run commerce pages and related code on a separate server, because it not only provides added security and protection, but also guarantees that users who wish to conduct business won't be affected by the load on the general server that handles everyone else passing through a Web site.

TAKE ALL REASONABLE SYSTEM PRECAUTIONS

Every platform has its own well-known back doors, loopholes, and entry points. Even if you don't know all of them yourself, you are advised to learn them and block them off, or hire someone else to do the job for you. (We cover the best-known ones and their solutions in the sections that follow.) Likewise, keep prowling robots away from your commerce pages. (Check Martijn Koster's "World Wide Web Robots, Wanderers, and Spiders" page at `http://info.webcrawler.com/mak/projects/robots/robots.html` for more information about robots.)

It's also worth researching any of a variety of security programs for your commerce server. Such programs can monitor system activity and respond instantly to well-known patterns that often presage a break-in attempt. Haystack Labs' WebStalker software is a particularly powerful program of this type. Check it out at `http://www.haystack.com`.

KEEP THE DETAILS ON A NEED-TO-KNOW BASIS

Chances are good that even in the smallest organizations with commercial Web sites there are more employees at the company than need to be involved in the details of the site's configuration, operation, and capabilities. If you restrict these details to only those people responsible for the server or who are directly involved with it, this will also help to limit the potential for break in or compromise.

PROTECT YOUR COMMERCIAL ASSETS

It's a sad fact of life that less than half of the servers in daily use worldwide are backed up at all, not to mention regularly. Since a commerce server is by definition an important business tool, we strongly recommend that it be made as available and reliable as possible. Among other things, this means the following:

- Use an uninterruptible power supply (UPS) to help assure maximum uptime. No power ordinarily means no server. A UPS can overcome this problem, at least long enough to shut down the server gracefully and close out pending transactions. Otherwise, an abrupt departure from the Internet can be fraught with peril.

- The only good backup is a fresh backup. You should perform incremental backups on your commerce system nightly if a complete backup isn't possible, and full backups at least every weekend. Practice restoring from a backup once a quarter or so, so you'll be prepared to do it for real in case the system fails.

- A fallback arrangement will keep you in business in case of disaster or a prolonged system outage. If your commerce server holds even a fraction of your receipts, loss of service can mean a loss of revenue. Investigate potential sources of services should your system be out of commission for any length of time, be it at your ISP, a disaster recovery company, or a vendor from whom you can purchase system resources and Internet access on demand.

If you follow these reasonable precautions, chances are good that you won't have to deal with the aftermath of a system break-in, or the costs of successful fraud. Once again, the costs involved and contortions required to satisfy these precautions should be considered as a form of insurance against potentially dire results.

Understanding UNIX security

In addition to the server itself, the CGI programs that reside on a host machine can also be viewed as possible sources of system penetration or compromise. The misconfiguration or unintentional misuse of certain CGI programs could lead to site-wide havoc, or perhaps even a completely hacked-apart Web server.

Most HTTP servers operate as a collection of separate processes on a UNIX host. Here, CGI programs operate as the core of the Web system. They provide system administrators with the ability to configure and program their Web servers, and allow the Web system to interact with other aspects of the host machine. When you allow other applications to control the system with a CGI, it stands to reason that the security of the CGI and how it is used should be carefully guarded. Since commerce systems essentially require the implementation and deployment of CGI programs, this advice is particularly poignant for a UNIX commerce server.

Here are some potential UNIX points of entry or compromise to understand and block as much as possible:

- *httpd* **configuration file.** Here, we recommend that you set up a special group under which *httpd* runs, and strictly limit access and permissions. We also recommend using a non-standard port address for secure transactions; since these are not obvious to hackers, they're much harder to break into.

- **UNIX Internet daemon (inetd).** Run the Web server from inetd to add an additional level of system protection

- **Server Resource Map file.** Edit the Server Resource Map file (named srm.file, if applicable) to set the scope of the DocumentRoot strictly within a particular directory tree. This will keep individuals who enter your site through the Web server bottled up within a small part of the server's file system rather than granting them broader access.

On a UNIX system, the best thing you can do for your Web server's security is to understand file permissions and ownerships, and to make sure that they've been properly applied for your particular circumstances. It's also important to understand other access controls, such as IP address filtering, and password control for Web pages (through the access.conf configuration file, and .htaccess control file). These, too, can help keep the unauthorized away from sensitive information or off-limits areas on your UNIX Web server.

For a complete discussion of these topics and more UNIX-related security information, please consult Chapter 32, "WWW Server and CGI Security," in *The CGI Bible*, (1996, IDG Books Worldwide).

Walling off Windows NT

When it comes to managing access to your Windows NT Web server, there are three fundamental areas that you want to control:

1. Those who have the right to view your information.

2. Those who have the right to update or change your information.

3. Those who control the presence and location of Web sites, determine what programs and facilities they can use, and manage the content that the site contains.

It's typical for most Web pages and documents to be readable by anyone, with perhaps a few documents or areas that are password-controlled. This lets the public view, but not change, what's visible on your site. Likewise, it's common for individuals with responsibility to update or change information on a Web site to have only mediated

CHAPTER FIFTEEN: YOUR SITE'S FUTURE

access to that site—in other words, they can make copies of materials, make changes to those copies, and then deliver the changed versions to someone who has the right permissions to add or alter files in the directories from whence the Web server obtains its documents, graphics, and programs. Even more stringent must be the control over who establishes and maintains a Web presence. Typically, this is someone with administrator-level access to the system. Such access is nearly always tightly controlled.

Nevertheless, it's often surprisingly easy for hackers to break into even well-run, well-organized systems. That's why it's so important to perform regular security reviews, and why you'll hear so many experts preach the importance of using the same tools that hackers use, BEFORE they can use them, to test the strength of your system's defenses.

Based on a set of recommendations compiled by Randall Golhof on his "NT Security" Web page (http://www.telemark.net/~randallg/ntsecure.htm), we feel confident that the following elements will help improve your NT server's security:

- **Manage passwords.** Make sure administrators and users follow some kind of disciplined approach to picking hard-to-guess passwords. Nearly all system break-ins result from bad password choices, according to Golhof.

- **Disable NetBEUI over TCP/IP.** NetBEUI provides many more back doors and break in opportunities. Disable this capability on any commerce server.

- **Assign a password to the GUEST account and severely restrict its system access.** The GUEST account is one of two well-known points of NT entry. Be sure to close it off.

- **Rename the ADMINISTRATOR account.** This account has rights to everything, yet is another well-known point of entry. Rename it to something non-obvious and hackers will have to guess the account name as well as the password!

- **Remove Share permissions and network access for EVERYONE.** This closes the final well-known point of entry for would-be NT hackers.

- **If you use PERL for CGIs . . .** never put perl.exe into the Web server's cgi-bin directory. Otherwise, it is possible for Web users to upload malicious programs to your site and then execute them, possibly trashing the server.

- **If you must use the FTP service . . .** put it in its own disk partition so that users cannot access any other parts of the NT file system. Otherwise, disable it altogether.

- **If you use RAS for dial-in . . .** check out Golhof's recommendations on protecting that service. We don't recommend that you run RAS on a commerce server, nor that you make it available for RAS connections.

- **Check the security log regularly.** In User Manager/Policies/Audit Policy select all failure events, and successful Logon and Logoff, User and Group Management, Security Policy Changes, and Restart. If you see anything untoward, it will be a warning of break-in attempts.

■ **Run the C2 configuration manager.** Even if you don't need C2 level security on your system, it will provide all kinds of useful information about potential points of entry, password problems, and so on. For more information about C2 and how it applies to NT, visit Microsoft's C2 page at:

```
http://www.microsoft.com/NTServer/c2bltn.htm .
```

Also be sure to check out Frank Ramos's NT security materials, available from his company, Somarsoft, at:

```
http://www.somarsoft.com/security.htm .
```

Not much worry with Macintosh

Other than protecting file system access, and keeping the Perl interpreter from easy access (that is, out of the cgi-bin directory or wherever else you store your CGI programs), the Macintosh does not offer any well-known back doors or points of entry. To prove this point, Jon Wiederspan and Jeff Evans, with financial backing from Apple, offered a $50,000 prize to anyone who could crack their Apple Web server on the Internet. Although this invitation was issued in December, 1995, no one has managed to collect that prize. Therefore, as long as you don't deliberately leave the system's doors open, the Macintosh is about as safe as it gets for a commerce server!

When it comes to system security, your best bet is to read the system logs and audit trails if any are available. Also examine your Web server's error and activity logs regularly. When hackers come a-knockin' at your door, it's nearly impossible for them to do so without leaving some telltale signs behind. If you're on the lookout, you can usually head them off at the pass.

Stay Current—or Go Stale!

Beyond the threats that hackers and thieves may pose for your site, there's an even more insidious enemy to consider—boredom! It's absolutely essential to revisit your site on a regular basis, to make sure that things are current and fresh, or you risk losing your audience (your customers, that is) to someone else who offers valuable content and keeps that information just this side of the leading edge of the industry.

The best thing you can do for your Web site is to make its care and feeding somebody's job. The title *webmaster* is becoming more familiar in corporate America, and is even a recognizable job description these days. We suggest you hire or appoint someone to that position, and that you make their number-one responsibility an increase in traffic on your site. Of course, the only way to achieve this goal is not only to flog the highways and byways of cyberspace to bring the public to your electronic doorway, but also to keep the content on the Web site fresh and ever-changing, to give your customers an ongoing reason not to visit your Web site just once, but on a regular basis.

As we suggested at the outset of this chapter, the temptation to rest on your laurels can be nearly irresistible after getting past building, testing, and soliciting user feedback on your Web site in general, and your commerce pages in particular. It's amazing how quickly after a "short rest" you can go back to your Web pages and exclaim "Boy, has this stuff really been there since last *March*?" That's why another important aspect of the webmaster's job is constantly refreshing at least part of the content on your site, as well as keeping current on everything else that's out there, ready to make a change as soon as it's justified.

With that attitude in mind, here are some specific recommendations for Web site maintenance:

- **Check in on your pages regularly**. Make it a part of your webmaster's job to perform regular, scheduled maintenance.

- **Keep your content current**. Make sure "What's New" lives up to its name. Review all site content in light of recent market news and events, and make sure your stuff keeps up with the times.

- **Check those links**. The beauty of hypertext is that it will let you point to third-party products that enhance your own, industry associations you support, and sources of good information about your industry and market niche. The Web's a shifting landscape, and nothing changes more than links do. Get an automatic link checker, and run it at least once a week. Fix broken or stale links promptly!

- **Keep up with technology**. Is everybody else using Internet Explorer 3.0 and Navigator 3.02, while you're still building your pages for 2.2? Does your HTML support the DTD in force two generations back? Technology changes just like content. Make sure your site changes with it!

Web site maintenance isn't just a job; it's a way of life. If you make Web activities a part of the regular daily grind, and keep checking in on your site, its content, and your commercial capabilities, you won't be left behind in the relentless charge of the marketplace into the future. Making Web maintenance a part of the regular routine means you'll know how to budget for the work involved, and when to lay on extra help to deal with launching a new product, adding support for new HTML capabilities, or upgrading your payment system to the latest version. But don't forget—when things change is also when they're most likely to break. Be sure, therefore, to plan and schedule for extra testing and feedback whenever the wheels of progress turn more quickly than usual.

Coming Soon to a Web Site Near You

Finally, it's essential to keep in touch with the times and trends in electronic commerce. In general, this means following the trade rags and watching for new developments in this rapidly growing area. When new standards and technologies emerge, you need to be ready to evaluate your current circumstances in this new light, and decide whether to stick with what you already have, or move on to something newer and possibly more exciting.

In particular, this means touching base with your chosen payment system vendor and your transaction processing company (especially if they're not one and the same), to keep up with current developments on their end. Many such vendors won't support more than one or two versions of software at the same time. If a change to the APIs or underlying systems is in the wind, you need to find out before the crunch is at hand. We suggest cultivating a good working relationship with the vendor representatives that handle your account and show regular interest in what's new and interesting— that's the most reliable way to find out when changes are in the offing. Face it: The sooner you find out that your systems need to change, the more control you have over the changes.

Looking at the state of today's electronic commerce marketplace, we think that watching for upcoming developments and standards from the SET initiative is particularly important. We gave some pointers on SET in Chapter 2. We recommend putting those URLs in your bookmarks and visiting those sites at least twice a year (or whenever you see signs of activity in the trade press). With MasterCard and Visa behind this initiative, and Microsoft, GTE, and Terisa Systems involved, among others, anything that emerges from this group will bear watching. Someday, it may even be worth evaluating, if not adopting outright.

If your products are primarily digital, or easily delivered in electronic format, we'd suggest keeping tabs on the various micropayment systems currently available and under development. This kind of payment system is particularly appealing to information and content providers of all kinds, but may well have ramifications for software developers as well, and therefore bears watching. In particular, we think DEC's Millicent is worth tracking, because it appears to offer the most usable approach to true micropayment technology.

It's absolutely true as well that within the next year, there will probably be other options worth tracking that haven't even seen the (public) light of day yet. That's why you should keep your eyes and ears open for news on the electronic commerce front. Join some newsgroups. Read the trade press. Stay in touch with your vendors. You won't be sorry—you'll be plugged in, instead.

Summary

In this chapter, we've picked up the inevitable loose ends that begin to unravel immediately after the successful deployment of a commercial Web site. If you pay attention to your site, protect it from the digital elements, keep it fresh, and stay in tune with recent developments in the marketplace, we predict your commercial Web site will be a success. Throughout this book, we've tried to arm you with approaches, resources, and information to help you deal with this shifting landscape successfully. Hopefully, you'll have something to share with us in exchange, as you deploy and maintain your own commercial presence on the World Wide Web. Welcome to the twenty-first century!

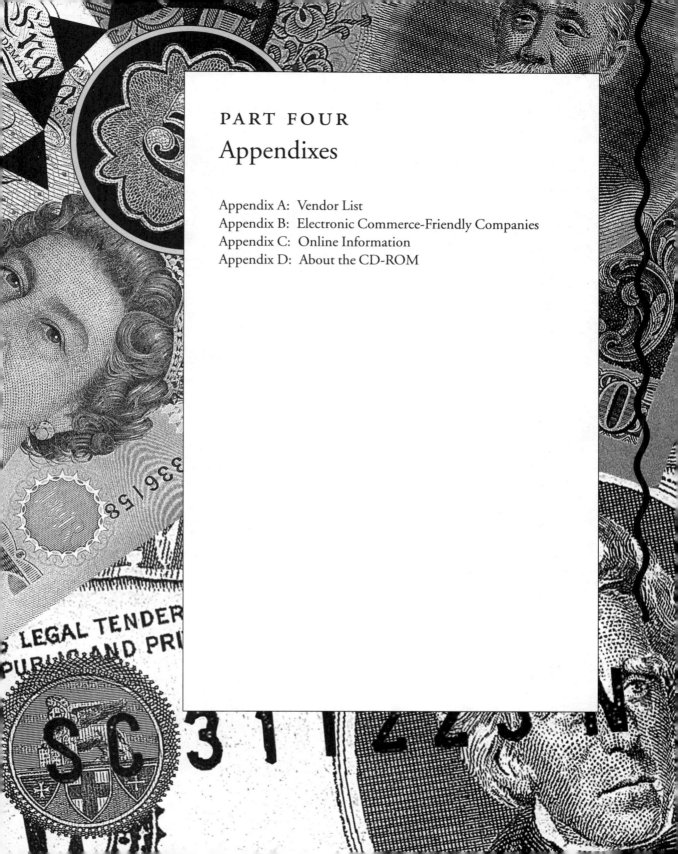

PART FOUR
Appendixes

APPENDIX A

VENDOR CONTACT INFORMATION

The following list includes all of the vendors we mentioned throughout this book. We tried to provide as many points of contact for each vendor as possible, including mailing address, phone number, fax number, and URL address. In some cases, we were not able to provide all of these items; our apologies for any inconvenience this may cause.

Please send e-mail to webmaster@lanw.com if you find any inaccuracies in this information. We'll be sure to incorporate all verified changes in the next edition. Thanks for your assistance!

Anacom General Corp.
(Computer Products Division)
1244 S. Claudina St.
Anaheim, CA 92805-6235
TEL: 714-774-8080
FAX: 714-774-7388
http://www.anacom.com

Apple Computer Corp.
1 Infinite Loop
Cupertino, CA 95014
TEL: 800-776-2333 or 408-996-1010
http://www.apple.com

CERN
(*Centre European Researche Nucleare*—**European Center for Particle Physics**)
CH - 1211 Geneva 23 Switzerland
TEL: +41 22 767 6111
FAX: +41 22 767 6555
http://www.cern.ch/

Clickshare Corp.
75 Water St.
Williamstown, MA 01267-0367
TEL: 413-458-8001
FAX: 413-458-8002
http://www.clickshare.com/clickshare

Commerce Direct International
205-591 Bernard Avenue
Kelowna, BC
Canada, V1Y 6N9
TEL: 604-861-3217
FAX: 604-861-3266
http://www.cdi.net

Community ConneXion
1212 Broadway, Suite 905
Oakland, CA 94612-1802
TEL: 510-986-8770
http://www.c2.net

CyberCash, Inc.
2100 Reston Pkwy.
Reston, VA 22091
TEL: 800-9CYBER1 or 703-620-4200
Direct sales: 415-594-0800
FAX: 703-620-4215
http://www.cybercash.com

DigiCash
55 East 52nd St. 39th Floor
New York, NY 10055-0186
TEL: 212-909-4092 or 800-410-ECASH (800-410-3227)
FAX: 212-318-1222
http://www.digicash.com

Digital Equipment Corp. (DEC)
146 Main St.
Maynard, MA 01754-2571
TEL: 800-344-4825 or 508-493-5111
FAX: 508-493-8780
http://www.dec.com

Enterprise Integration Technologies (EIT)
800 El Camino Real
Menlo Park, CA 94025
TEL: 415-617-8000
FAX: 415-617-8019
http://www.eit.com/

ESD USA, Inc.
3000 N. Atlantic Ave., Suite 207
Cocoa Beach, FL 32931
TEL: 800-313-6334 or 407-783-6332
FAX: 407-783-6394
http://www. l-n.net/esd

First Virtual Holdings, Inc.
11975 El Camino Real, Suite 300
San Diego, CA 92130
http://www.fv.com

IBM
Old Orchard Rd.
Armonk, NY 10504
TEL: 800-426-3333 or 914-765-1900
http://www.ibm.com

ICVERIFY Corp.
473 Roland Way
Oakland, CA 94621
TEL: 510-553-7500
FAX: 510-553-7553
Tech support: 800-382-5535
http://www.icverify.com

Internet Engineering Task Force (IETF)
c/o Corporation for National Research Initiatives
1895 Preston White Drive, Suite 100
Reston, VA 22091
TEL: 703-620-8990
http://www.ietf.org

LANWrights, Inc.
5810 Lookout Mountain Dr.
Austin, TX 78731
FAX: 512-452-8018
http://www.lanw.com

Microsoft, Corp.
One Microsoft Way
Redmond, WA 98052-6399
TEL: 800-426-9400 or 206-882-8080
http://www.microsoft.com

National Center for Supercomputing Applications (NCSA)
605 E. Springfield Ave.
Champaign, IL 61820
TEL: 217-244-3473
http://hoohoo.ncsa.uiuc.edu

NCR Corp.
1700 S. Patterson Blvd.
Dayton, OH 45479-0001
TEL: 800-447-1124 or 513-445-5000
Direct sales: 800-637-2600 (AT&T Direct Connect)
FAX: 513-445-4184
http://www.ncr.com

Netscape Communications Corp.
501 E. Middlefield Rd.
Mountain View, CA 94043
TEL: 800-NETSITE or 415-254-1900
FAX: 415-528-4124
http://home.netscape.com

Novell, Inc.
1555 N. Technology Way
Orem, UT 84757
TEL: 800-453-1267 or 801-222-6000
FAX: 800-NOVLFAX
http://www.novell.com

O'Reilly & Associates
103A Morris St.
Sebastopol, CA 95472
TEL: 800-998-9938
http:// www.ora.com

Open Market, Inc.
215 First St.
Cambridge, MA 02142
TEL: 617-621-9500
FAX: 617-621-1703
http://www.openmarket.com

Oracle
500 Oracle Parkway
Redwood Shores, CA 94065
TEL: 415-506-7000
http://www.oracle.com

Pacific Coast Software
11770 Bernardo Plaza Court, Suite 462
San Diego, CA 92128
TEL: 619-675-1106
FAX: 619-675-0372
http://www.pacific-coast.com

Quarterdeck
50 Pico Blvd.
Santa Monica, CA 90405
TEL: 800-354-3222 or 310-392-9851
http://www.quarterdeck.com

RSA Data Security, Inc.
(subsidiary of Security Dynamics, Inc.)
100 Marine Pkwy., Suite 500
Redwood City, CA 94065-1031
TEL: 800-782-5453 or 415-595-8782
FAX: 415-595-1873
Tech support: 415-595-7705
http://www.rsa.com

Spry
(Internet Division of CompuServe, Inc.)
3535 128th Ave., SE
Bellevue, WA 98006
TEL: 800-SPRY-NET or 206-957-8000
FAX: 206-957-6000
Tech support: 206-447-0958
Tech support BBS: 206-447-9060
http://www.spry.com

Spyglass
1230 E. Diehl Rd.
Naperville, IL 60563
TEL: 800-647-2201 or 630-505-1010
http://www.spyglass.com

Sun Microsystems
2550 Garcia Ave.
Mountain View, CA 94043-1100
TEL: 415-960-1300
http://java.sun.com/

Tellan Software, Inc.
2670 S. White Rd., Suite 281
San Jose, CA 95148
TEL: 800-483-5526 or 408-274-1110
FAX: 408-274-8392
http://www.tellan.com

Terisa Systems, Inc.
4984 El Camino Real
Los Altos, CA 94022
TEL: 415-919-1750
FAX: 415-919-1760
http://www.terisa.com

TradeWave Corp.
(subsidiary of SunRiver Corp.)
3636 Executive Center Dr., Suite 100
Austin, TX 78731
TEL: 512-433-5300
FAX: 512-433-5303
http://www.tradewave.com

VeriFone, Inc.
Three Lagoon Dr.
Redwood City, CA 94065-1561
TEL: 415-591-6500
Direct sales: 800-545-5557
FAX: 415-598-5504
Tech support: 800-654-1674
http://www.verifone.com

VeriSign, Inc.
2593 Coast Avenue,
Mountain View, CA 94043
TEL: 415-961-7500
FAX: 415-961-7300
http://www.verisign.com

WebMaster, Inc.
1601 Civic Center Dr., Suite 200
Santa Clara, CA 95050
TEL: 408-345-1800
FAX: 408-297-9372
http://www.webmaster.com

World Wide Web Consortium (W3C)
Massachusetts Institute of Technology
77 Massachusetts Ave.
Cambridge, MA 02139
TEL: 617-253-2613
FAX: 617-258-5999
http://www.w3.org

ELECTRONIC COMMERCE-
FRIENDLY COMPANIES

In this Appendix, we provide information about all of the companies we discovered by trolling the reaches of cyberspace looking for vendors with stated interests in electronic commerce. Since we didn't have time to interview each company and assess their relative capabilities, services, and pricing, a few caveats are in order.

When looking for partners in commerce, a certain amount of due diligence is required. Because these companies will either be handling your money, or providing goods and services to help you handle your own money, it's important that you research and understand whomever you plan to partner with. It's also important to understand what kinds and levels of service you can expect from your partners, and what will happen if and when problems arise. Finally, it's absolutely essential to understand how much your credit-handling arrangements will cost, from top to bottom.

With these general recommendations in mind, here is some specific advice, which we gleaned from conversations with several company operators who specialize in this market, and were willing to share their experiences with us, strictly "off the record." We emerged from these conversations a bit shaken, because there are so many opportunities for hidden costs or after-the-sale charges to make what may seem like a great deal turn out to be merely mediocre, if not an outright rip-off.

That's why we strongly recommend that you take this advice to heart, and try to learn as much about the vendors you'll be involved with as you possibly can.

■ Always ask for references from any company that may be a candidate for a commercial credit relationship. Don't just ask for this information, either—be sure to follow up with calls to at least two or three of the accounts that are furnished in response to your request. Ask them questions about anything that concerns you, but try to touch on the rest of the points we mention here as well.

■ When considering credit-handling costs, there are many factors that contribute to the total costs of a relationship. Here are some of the things you're going to want to get down on paper before signing any kind of agreement, or otherwise obligating yourself to a credit handling company:

• What is the discount rate (the percentage of funds collected that the credit handler takes off the top)? How does this change with volume or activity in your account (it should become less expensive as your business activity increases)?

• What kind of audits or other reports does the vendor offer? What happens to returns or contested purchases? Ask them to explain how they solve problems, deal with discrepancies, or resolve disputes. Are there any special handling charges associated with returns or fraudulent transactions?

• How much do they charge for transaction handling? What other kinds of monthly fees do they charge? How do these fees change with respect to volume (or the discount rate)?

• How much will they charge for up-front costs? Try to get a total figure, because these costs will often include charges for application fees (to establish creditworthiness and set up and account), equipment (PIN pads, magnetic strip readers, and so on), programming fees (setting up your account information, and customizing transaction-processing software for your organization, etc.), and installation (sending a person on-site to install and test equipment and software)? What other up-front costs might occur?

■ What kind of service after the sale can you expect? Do they offer 24/7 live technical support? Is it a toll call, or do they have an 800/888 number? Is there a charge for technical support? How do they handle software upgrades and equipment change-outs? How quickly can they respond to equipment problems, or supply loaner units? What kinds of fees may be involved? Are such services always for a fee when rendered, or can you obtain a yearly support contract, with monthly or yearly payments? What will this add to your bottom line?

■ How long does it take for the vendor to disburse your funds? How are the funds delivered to your account? How will your earnings be reported, along with associated charges or chargebacks?

■ Most contracts with credit handling companies will have terms of 24 to 48 months, yet the typical life of the equipment involved is 72 to 96 months. Be sure to amortize the costs of your credit relationship over the life of the lease, but also over the longer term of your equipment's effective life as well.

■ What happens if you're not happy with your relationship with a vendor? What grounds for termination of the contract apply to you? What are the possible implications of termination on your creditworthiness? (Note: You should definitely get some legal advice on whatever contract your credit vendor asks you to sign; at that point, be sure to review and understand the termination clauses for both sides of the agreement.)

All of the operators we approached for advice likened the electronic commerce marketplace to the wild frontier of the nineteenth century, where con artists and genuine operators worked shoulder to shoulder in the field. Apparently, this is such a wide open market, with such tremendous potential, that there's room for fly-by-night or unscrupulous operators to get a share of the market that may not benefit from their partnership. That's why it's so important to research any credit relationship with care and caution. We certainly don't mean to suggest that any of the operators in this list would qualify in this regard, but only you can take the steps that are necessary to protect your revenues, especially when they're moving through some other organization's hands.

One final word of warning: many of the commerce handling companies, especially those that offer package deals including magnetic strip readers, PIN pads, and receipt printers, along with their other services, set some of their prices deliberately low to attract potential customers. Careful research will determine that their overall costs are on a par with other vendors—or even higher, in some cases. That's why it's so important to research all the costs and amortize them over the term of the contract (and the life of the equipment). It's the only way to be sure of how much things really cost!

The Commerce-Friendly Vendor List

The following list includes numerous vendors that we judged to be commerce-friendly, based on extensive surfing on the Web. Wherever possible, we tried to provide as many points of contact for each company as possible, including its snail mail address, its phone and fax numbers, e-mail address, and URL. In some cases, we were not able to provide all of these items; our apologies for any inconvenience this may cause.

Please send e-mail to webmaster@lanw.com if you find any inaccuracies. We'll be sure to incorporate all verified changes in our next edition. Thanks in advance for your assistance!

A2i, Inc.
1940 Cotner Ave.
Los Angeles, CA 90025
TEL: 310-479-6767
FAX: 310-478-4770.
info@a2i.com
http://www.A2i.com/

A2i creates and produces interactive electronic catalogs and order entry systems as powerful sales tools for distributors, manufacturers, and publishers.

Advanced Procurement Systems
TEL: 800-448-0760
aps@bga.com
http://www.realtime.net/aps/

APS develops PC- or LAN-based software with full-function purchasing, inventory, and Electronic Data Interchange modules.

AdventureDirect
TEL: 609-953-8282
FAX: 609-953-9205
mikee@voicenet.com
http://www.adventuredirect.com/

AdventureDirect is an online order taking service that lets prospects request information or place orders without calling an 800-number or interrupting their session.

Amercian Banking Systems, Corp. (ABS)
8000 S. Orange Ave. Suite 102
Orlando, FL 32809
TEL: 407-888-9091
FAX: 407-888-9092
BBS: 407-888-9093
sales@absbank.com
http://www.absbank.com/

American Banking Systems Corporation specializes in designing, developing, marketing, and implementing software and service payment solutions for businesses of all types and sizes.

Anacom General Corp.
(Computer Products Division)
questions@anacom.com
http://www.anacom.com/

Anacom provides low-cost order processing and payment solutions to merchants. Their products allow customers to create and maintain product order forms and accept credit card payments on-line in a secure environment.

For more contact information, please see Appendix A: Vendor Contact Information.

Apple Computer Corp.
webmaster@apple.com
http://www.apple.com/

Apple participates in the CommerceNet Consortium, a nonprofit organization that supports electronic commerce activities on the Internet. Apple also focuses on giving the Internet Protocol suite more plug-and-play capabilities, as AppleTalk has now, and increasing security, so that the Internet can realize its potential to become the Information Superhighway.

For more contact information, please see Appendix A: Vendor Contact Information.

Applied Business Consultants Ltd.
101460.2221@COMPUSERVE.COM
http://ourworld.compuserve.com/homepages/abc/

ABC are developers and suppliers of an electronic point-of-sale (EPOS) and stock management system/retail solution.

Atomic Software
2837 Peterson Place
Norcross, GA 30071
TEL: 770-849-0107
FAX: 770-849-0533
info@atomic-software.com
http://www.atomic-software.com/

Atomic Software is a developer and marketer of Electronic Payment Software for the retail, mail/phone order, Internet, grocery, fast food, and practice management markets.

Barclays Bank PLC
54 Lombard Street
London EC3P 3AH, 0800-400170 UK
purchase.online@barclaycard.co.uk
http://www.barclays.co.uk/purchaseonline/

Barclays has developed PurchaseOnline, a secure service for businesses wanting to buy and sell goods using the Internet.

Big Hairy Dog
3205 Ramos Circle
Sacramento, CA 95827
TEL: 916-368-3939 or 800-377-7776
FAX: 916-368-1411
bhdinfo@mother.com
http://www.bighairydog.com/

BHD is a brand distributor for many point-of-sale products including computers, peripheral hardware, and software.

Bohemian Net
P.O. Box 1147
Mill Valley, CA 94942
TEL: 415-381-3668
FAX: 415-381-3669
71035.1603@compuserve.com
http://www.bohemiannet.com/home.htm

Bohemian Net is a server and browser software suite for online sales of products and services. It contains a server module with authoring features and automated order taking. A browsing module is included which can be distributed royalty free.

Business Systems Communications, Inc.
81 Vincentown Road
Pemberton, NJ 08068
TEL: 609-894-0300
FAX: 609-894-0033
inquiry@bop.com
http://www.netaxs.com/people/bsc/index.html

Business Systems Communications, Inc. is an open systems vendor offering a Windows-based total point-of-sale software solution for retailers.

Calido Software, Inc.
Box 357, 3-11 BelleRose Drive
St. Albert, Alberta, Canada T8N 5C9
TEL: 800-558-4431
FAX: 403-973-3131
http://www.calido.com/

Calido has created CashPro, the newest point-of-sale (POS) software system designed for any type of business, from retail stores, restaurants and gas stations to golf courses, ski areas, and recreation facilities.

CERN
(*Centre European Researche Nucleare*—European Center for Particle Physics)
www.support@cern.ch
http://www.cern.ch/

CERN is the European Laboratory for Particle Physics, located near Geneva in Switzerland and France and the birthplace of the World Wide Web.

For more contact information, please see Appendix A: Vendor Contact Information.

GC Tech
155 Ave of the Americas
New York, NY 10013
TEL: 212-989-7182
FAX: 212-989-209
info@gctec.com
http://www.gctec.com/

GC Tech is a software company whose business is to develop technology solutions for secure payment systems and intermediation services on the Internet and intranets.

CheckFree Corp.
P.O. Box 2168
Columbus, OH 43216-2168
TEL: 800-532-9696
FAX: 614-825-3279
info@checkfree.com
http://www.checkfree.com/

CheckFree is an automated monthly payment and electronic funds transfer package that includes consumer payment services.

CheckMaster Corp.
3157 Skyline Drive
Oceanside, CA 92956
TEL: 619-757-6635
FAX: 619-757-6699
info@internetchecks.com
http://www.checkmaster.com/internetchecks/

InternetChecks provides a means for vendors to collect money for purchases using checks (drafts) printed by CheckMaster or locally on a laser printer.

Cleo Products

4203 Galleria Drive
Loves Park, IL 61111-8616
TEL: 800-233-2536
FAX: 815-654-8294
cleo@interaccess.com
http://www.rock.cleo.com/

Cleo Products is a major supplier of communications solutions to the Electronic Data Interchange (EDI) and Electronic Commerce marketplace.

Commerce Direct International

USA@cdi.net, Canada@cdi.net, UK@cdi.net
http://www.cdi.net/

CDI operates a proven and secure service bureau. The bureau is currently available to the many companies that wish to sell their products through the new world of Internet commerce. CDI's secure Digital Envelope Solution guarantees customer privacy and also efficiently manages the clients catalog of products. The Digital Envelope Solution uses a certificate of authorization based on an order processing and coded "key-verified" signature process.

For more contact information, please see Appendix A: Vendor Contact Information.

Compass Software, Inc.

Seven Fawn Ridge Road
Lebanon, NJ 08833
TEL: 908-236-2334
FAX: 908-236-2109
compass@blast.net
http://www.fawnridge.com/

COMPASS Software, Inc., is a solution-based company that provides a complete system for business both large and small.

Concord Systems, Inc.

stakutis@www.sgi.net
http://www.tiac.net/users/stakutis/csi.html

Concord Systems (CSI) specializes in quick, low-cost, solid interfacing to the nation's leading automatic payment processor, Checkfree, which provides online real-time credit card authorizations, credit card charges, settlements, voids, and credits, batch-mode via FTP processing, and systems integration.

Connect, Inc.
515 Ellis Street
Mountain View, CA 94043-2242
TEL: 415-254-4000
FAX: 415-254-4800
info@connectinc.com
http://www.connectinc.com/

Connect, Inc. is a supplier of state-of-the-art technology, wide area e-mail, bulletin boards, and electronic commerce solutions.

Creative Consultants
PO Box 633
Olathe, KS 66051-0633
TEL/FAX: 913-764-0112
Creative@TFS.NET
http://www.tfs.net/~creative/

Creative Consultants specializes in retail/wholesale point-of-sale solutions.

Creative Digital Technology (CDT)
PO Box 788,
Narrabeen, NSW, 2101 Australia
TEL: 02-9999 2340
FAX: 02-9999 2767
info@creative.com.au
http://www.creative.com.au/

CDT has developed an open and extendable online shopping system. It has full shopping cart functionality and runs on any UNIX or NT platform compatible with any standard Web server.

Crichlow Data Sciences, Inc.
5925 Imperial Parkway, Suite 227
Mulberry, FL 33860
TEL: 800-678-4535
bob@loki.thegeneralstore.com
http://www.thegeneralstore.com/

Crichlow produces The General Store point-of-sale solution.

CyberCash, Inc.

info@cybercash.com
http://www.cybercash.com/

CyberCash is focused on providing Secure Financial Transactions Services over the Internet, including secure credit card transactions electronic checks and micro transactions.

For more contact information, please see Appendix A: Vendor Contact Information.

CYBERManagement, Inc.

151 Bloor Street West, Suite 470
Toronto, ON M5S 1S4 Canada
TEL: 416-929-1014
FAX: 416-929-1552
cyber@cybermanagement.com
http://www.cybermanagement.com/cyber/

A management consulting firm specializing in Internet strategy, market research, publishing and Internet electronic commerce.

Data Transfer Associates, Inc.

2700 S. River Rd. Suite 402
Des Plaines, IL 60018
TEL: 800-318-3282
dta1jr@aol.com
http://www.datatransfer.com/

Data Transfer Associates, Inc., provides merchants with the tools they need to accept credit cards in person or over the Internet.

DigiCash

info@digicash.nl
http://www.digicash.com/

DigiCash develops and licenses payment technology products, such as chip card, software only, and hybrid.

For more contact information, please see Appendix A: Vendor Contact Information.

Digital Delivery, Inc.

TEL: 617.275.3830.
sales@digitaldelivery.com
http://www.digitaldelivery.com/

Digital Delivery, Inc., produces software publishing tools for distributing hard goods and digital products. CatalogBuilder and TitleBuilder use encryption technology for secure transaction and content control.

Digital Equipment Corp. (DEC)
http://www.dec.com/

For more contact information, please see Appendix A: Vendor Contact Information.

DynamicWeb
TEL: 800-356-8560
sales@dynamicweb.com
http://dynamicweb.com/

DynamicWeb Transaction Systems develops, markets, and supports electronic commerce solutions which enable businesses to tighten their marketing and distribution relationships with their trading partners.

EES Companies, Inc.
Vernon St. Suite 404
Framingham, MA 01701
TEL: 508-653-6911
FAX: 508-650-1872
http://www.posoe.com/

EES provides business software for point of sale/order entry, credit card processing, accounting, inventory, control, sales tracking internet products and services, and more.

Enterprise Integration Technologies (EIT)
info@eit.com
http://www.eit.com/

EIT is responsible for two electronic commerce initiatives—the CommerceNet Consortium and Secure HTTP. EIT was instrumental in the formation of CommerceNet, an industry consortium that promotes electronic commerce and developed and commercialized Secure HTTP, which is rapidly becoming the de facto security standard for information processing on the World Wide Web.

For more contact information, please see Appendix A: Vendor Contact Information.

Europay International S.A.
Chauss_e de Tervuren 198 A, B-1410
Waterloo, Belgium
TEL: 32/2. 352 5936
FAX: 32/2. 352 5718
http://www.europay.com/

Europay International offers the widest possible range of payment products and services on both a European and worldwide basis.

First Virtual Holdings, Inc.
everly@fv.com.
http://www.fv.com/

The First Virtual Internet Payment System provides a simple, secure and safe method for buying and selling over the Internet. No special hardware, software or encryption is required, just e-mail.

For more contact information, please see Appendix A: Vendor Contact Information.

Flexicom, Ltd.
32 Lower Leeson St
Dublin 2 Ireland
TEL: +353-1-676-6188
FAX: +353-1-676-6199
info@flexicom.ie
http://www.flexicom.ie/

Flexicom, Ltd., provides client/server solutions including new generation electronic payment solutions and end-to-end card management systems.

Gemtronics, Inc.
105 Planters Rd.
Toney, AL 35773
Sales@gemtronics.com
http://www.gemtronics.com/

Gemtronics, Inc., develops point-of-sale system for small and home businesses.

Global Business Alliance (GBA), Inc.
TEL: 800-537-IBEX
ibex@globalx.net
http://www.ibex-gba.com/index.html

GBA produces IBEX, and electronic commerce trade product which will help businesses find, qualify and negotiate with prospective business partners worldwide.

HOME Account Network, Inc.
info@homeaccount.com
http://www.homeaccount.com/

HOME Account Network, Inc., provides comprehensive electronic commerce solutions for financial institutions.

IBM

askibm@info.ibm.com
http://www.ibm.com/

IBM solutions teams are organized into groups that specialize in particular kinds of businesses, with teams dedicated to helping customers across all industries.

For more contact information, please see Appendix A: Vendor Contact Information.

iCAT

1420 Fifth Avenue, Suite 1800
Seattle, WA 98101-2333
TEL: 206-623-0977
FAX: 206-623-0477
moreinfo@icat.com

iCAT Europe Ltd.

Kinetic Centre
Borehamwood WD6 4PJ UK
TEL: 44-0-181-387-4070
FAX: 44-0-181-387-4073

iCAT Japan

c/o Trans Cosmos Inc.
Sumitomoseimei Akasaka Building
3-3-3, Akasaka, Minato-ku, Tokyo, 107 Japan
TEL: 81-3-3586-2880
FAX: 81-3-3584-6079
keys@trans-cosmos.co.jp
http://www.icat.com/

iCat has developed software for instant electronic commerce that allows creation of compelling interactive catalogs, and transaction processing from any internet server.

ICVERIFY Corp.

http://www.icverify.com/company/talk.html
http://www.icverify.com/

A provider of cost-effective, credit authorization/draft capture, check acceptance and ATM debit card authorization software for the emerging PC Point-Of-Sale industry.

For more contact information, please see Appendix A: Vendor Contact Information.

Internet Engineering Task Force (IETF)
ietf-web@ietf.org
http://www.ietf.org/

The protocol engineering and development arm of the Internet, the IETF is a large open international community of network designers, operators, vendors, and researchers concerned with the evolution of the Internet architecture and the smooth operation of the Internet.

For more contact information, please see Appendix A: Vendor Contact Information.

Internet Transaction Services, Inc.
3724 NE 72nd Terrace
Gladstone, MO 64119
TEL: 816-436-4148
FAX: 816-436-3137
sales@itrans.com
http://www.itrans.com/

Internet Transaction Services (iTrans) is a company dedicated to providing automated authentication and accounting services for Internet applications.

InterTrust Technologies Corp.
460 Oakmead Parkway
Sunnyvale, CA 94086
TEL: 408-222-6100
FAX: 408-222-6144
info@intertrust.com
http://www.intertrust.com/

InterTrust Technologies Corporation has been inventing and implementing a general-purpose architecture for secure electronic commerce and digital rights management.

ISOCOR
420 Ocean Park Blvd.
Santa Monica, CA 90405-3306
TEL: 310-581-8100
FAX: 310-581-8111
http://www.isocor.com/

ISOCOR develops backbone software for electronic information exchange over the Internet and other value added networks.

Killen & Associates, Inc.
1212 Parkinson Ave.
Palo Alto, CA 94301
TEL: 415-617-6130
FAX: 415-617-6140
info@killen.com
http://www.killen.com/

A market research and consulting firm specializing in electronic commerce and banking; develops multiclient studies and video seminars.

LANWrights, Inc.
etittel@lanw.com
http://www.lanw.com/

LANWrights, Inc., is an Austin, TX, company that specializes in network-oriented writing, training, and consulting.

For more contact information, please see Appendix A: Vendor Contact Information.

Magic Control Systems, Inc.
TEL: 707-586-4777
FAX: 707-586-4774
mcs@ap.net
http://www.magicpos.com/index.html

Magic Control Systems, Inc., is a business management solutions corporation providing state of the art, point of sales systems.

Majestic Link Corp.
Ann Arbor, MI
TEL: 313-663-9506
cjw@majesticlink.com
http://www.majesticlink.com

Majestic Link Corporation specialize in creating Electronic Commerce applications that enable companies to conduct business over the Internet.

Marketplace Solutions
24361 Indoplex Circle
Farmington Hills, MI 48334
TEL: 810-473-5900
FAX: 810-473-5933
info@marketplacegroup.com
http://www.marketplacegroup.com/

Marketplace Solutions has extended their point-of-sale expertise into the area of
Internet Commerce Solutions, implementing secure Internet ordering solutions for a
variety of companies and developing a suite of software products to facilitate the
development and management of Internet stores.

Mercantec, Inc.
3033 Ogden Ave., Suite 203
Lisle, IL 60532
TEL: 630-305-3200
FAX: 630-305-6065
sales@mercantec.com
http://www.mercantec.com/company/index.html

Mercantec develops and markets SoftCart, a virtual store front application.

Microsoft
http://www.microsoft.com/

Microsoft's online banking goals include: the cooperative development of a truly open
specification for Internet banking, available to all financial service providers and client
software developers; creating a network of premier third-party solution providers to
build and implement home banking solutions, based on this specification, for financial
service; and rapid development of client-side product support from Microsoft, including
Microsoft Money, Microsoft Investor, and a set of Web-based banking controls for banks
to "private label" and use on their own transactional Web sites.

For more contact information, please see Appendix A: Vendor Contact Information.

Mind The Store, Inc.
121 Willowdale Ave., Suite 100
North York, Ontario, M2N 6A3 Canada
TEL: 416-226-9520
FAX: 416-226-9527
webfeed@mindthestore.com
http://www.mindthestore.com/

Mind the Store, Inc., has developed a real-time, integrated electronic commerce
application with Virtual Store Builder, inventory and customer management, secure
online payment processing, and order fulfillment.

National Center for Supercomputing Applications (NCSA)

webdev@ncsa.uiuc.edu
http://www.ncsa.uiuc.edu/

The National Center for Supercomputing Applications has evolved into a scientific research center built around a national services facility. NCSA is developing and implementing a national strategy to create, use, and transfer advanced computing and communication tools and information technologies. These advances serve the center's diverse set of constituencies in the areas of science, engineering, education, and business.

For more contact information, please see Appendix A: Vendor Contact Information.

NCR Corp.

info@ncr.com
http://www.ncr.com/

NCR is dedicated to being a world-class provider of computer products and services to customers in all industries. The company is also leveraging its expertise and market presence to provide computer solutions to three targeted industries—Retail, Financial, and Communications.

For more contact information, please see Appendix A: Vendor Contact Information.

NetBank from Software Agents, Inc.

mailto:help@agents.com
http://www.netbank.com/~netcash/

Software Agents develops commerce applications that allow merchants and their customers to conduct and conclude cash transactions over the Internet in an easy, natural, and secure way.

NetCart

TEL: 800-334-9746
Info@NetCart.com
http://www.netcart.com/

NetCart offers an electronic commerce ordering and catalog solution for the World Wide Web.

NetCheck Commerce Bureau

776 Canyon Rd.
Springville, UT 84663
TEL: 801-491-8185
netcheck@netcheck.com
http://www.netcheck.com/

The NetCheck Commerce Bureau was established to promote ethical business practices worldwide and to increase consumer and corporate confidence in purchasing products and services on the Internet.

NetCheque by USC/ISI's GOST Group
4676 Admiralty Way, Suite 1001
Marina del Rey, CA 90292-6695
TEL: 310-822-1511
FAX: 310-823-6714
NetCheque@isi.edu
http://nii-server.isi.edu/info/NetCheque/

The NetCheque payment system is an electronic payment system for the Internet developed at the Information Sciences Institute of the University of Southern California.

NetConsult Communications, Inc.
mailto:info@netconx.de
http://www.intershop.de/

NetConsult is dedicated to leading the development of a full breadth of online shopping solutions.

Netscape Communications Corp.
moreinfo@netscape.com
http://home.netscape.com/

Netscape Communications Corporation develops, markets, and supports open client, server, and commercial applications software that enables information exchange and commerce over the Internet and private Internet Protocol networks.

For more contact information, please see Appendix A: Vendor Contact Information.

NetX Clearing Corp.
2200, 700 - 9 Ave. S.W.
Calgary, AB T2P-3V4 Canada
TEL: 403-543-3570
FAX: 403-543-3573
info@netx.ca
http://www.netx.ca/

NetX is creating an independent buying group on the Internet by combining the customer purchasing power of multiple leading Internet Service Providers (ISPs).

Northwest Network Solutions, Inc.
18529 S.E. Yamhill Circle
Portland, OR 97233 Canada
TEL: 800-570-5509
FAX: 503- 669-7183
trs@nwns.com
http://www.nwns.com/~trs/

Northwest Network Solutions is a point-of-sale software design company.

Novell, Inc.

prodinfo@novell.com
http://www.novell.com/

Novell defined the networking operating system marketplace, with close to 15 years of experience serving over 55 million users worldwide. Today, as the fourth largest software company in the world and the networking leader, Novell is bringing its knowledge and expertise to the intranet, providing you with the services you need to evolve your network into an intranet.

For more contact information, please see Appendix A: Vendor Contact Information.

O'Reilly & Associates

software@ora.com
http://website.ora.com/

O'Reilly & Associates is aleading publisher of books for UNIX, X, the Internet, and other open systems, as well as a pioneer in online publishing.

For more contact information, please see Appendix A: Vendor Contact Information.

OnLineCHECK Systems

TEL: 800-967-7033
accorp@ix.netcom.com
http://www.onlinecheck.com/

OnLine CHECK Systems offers echecks for call centers and merchants via telephone, fax, and/or the internet. OnLine CHECK Systems was the first company to allow internet merchants to accept checks via the Internet for purchases in a secure environment.

Open Market, Inc.

support@openmarket.com
http://www.openmarket.com/

Open Market provides software products that are used to develop the infrastructure for Internet commerce.

For more contact information, please see Appendix A: Vendor Contact Information.

Oracle

sales@oracle.com
http://www.oracle.com/

Oracle Corporation is the world's largest vendor of information management software, with annual revenue of over $4.2 billion. Oracle software runs on almost every computer in the world, from personal digital assistants to supercomputers, managing everything from personal information to global information networks.

For more contact information, please see Appendix A: Vendor Contact Information.

Outreach Communications Corp.
9101 Burnet Rd., Suite 207
Austin, TX 78758
TEL: 888-280-9999
FAX: 512-832-8901
feedback@outreach.com
http://www.outreach.com/

Outreach Communications' mission is to provide the highest possible performance, accessibility, reliability, and ease-of-use for your commerce Web site at the lowest possible cost.

Pacific Coast Software
info@pacific-coast.com
http://www.pacific-coast.com/

Pacific Coast Software provides professional tools for interactive catalog publishing on the World Wide Web.

For more contact information, please see Appendix A: Vendor Contact Information.

PC America
TEL: 914-267-3500
FAX: 914-267-3550
72642.702@compuserve.com
http://www.pcamerica.com/pcan.htm

America's leading distributor of POS software and equipment.

Point of Sale Technology, Inc.
2104 North Highway 81
Duncan, OK 73533
TEL: 405-255-4324
FAX: 405-255-4437
postech@postech.pair.com
http://postech.pair.com/

Point of Sale Technology, Inc. provides quality point of sale systems by integrating innovative product design with the latest features.

Portland Software

1000 SW Broadway, Suite 1850
Portland, OR 97205
TEL: 503-220-2300
FAX: 503-220-8504
home@portsoft.com
http://www.portsoft.com/

Portland Software is proud to be a co-founder of eTRUST, an organization designed to create certified security and privacy ratings for electronic transactions, in order to improve online business practices and build public confidence in Internet commerce.

Posse Systems Corp.

1700-1111 West Georgia Street
Vancouver, B.C. V6E 4M3 Canada
TEL: 604-687-6303
FAX: 604-689-3348
Gordon_Fleming@msn.com
http://www.possoeasy.com/

Posse Systems is a distributor of point-of-sale software.

Profile Systems, Inc.

330 Whitney Ave.
Holyoke, MA 01040
413-536-2499
info@profilesys.com
http://www.profilesys.com/

Profile System's mission is to maintain and strengthen a leadership position in the development, sales, and successful implementation of standardized SAIM (Supplier Assisted Inventory Management) and related business software.

Quarterdeck

webmaster@quarterdeck.com
http://www.quarterdeck.com/

Quarterdeck Corporation is a developer and marketer of utilities and Internet software for small business, home office, corporate, government, and individual personal computer users.

For more contact information, please see Appendix A: Vendor Contact Information.

Release Software Corp.
200 Middlefield Rd., Suite 202
Menlo Park, CA 94025
TEL: 800-210-5517
FAX: 415-833-0213
info@releasesoft.com
http://www.releasesoft.com/

Release Software Corporation is changing the way software sells by letting software developers create applications that actually sell themselves.

RSA Data Security, Inc.
(subsidiary of Security Dynamics, Inc.)
info@rsa.com
http://www.rsa.com/

RSA Data Security, Inc. is a well knownbrand name for cryptography, with more than 75 million copies of RSA encryption and authentication technologies installed and in use worldwide.

For more contact information, please see Appendix A: Vendor Contact Information.

Shift4 Corp.
5190 S. Valley View Blvd., Suite 104
Las Vegas, NV 89118-1779
TEL: 702-597-2480
FAX: 702-597-2499
sales@shift4.com
http://www.shift4.com

Shift4 Corporation is a software development company that develops, markets, and supports a line of products which facilitates the authorization, auditing, settling, and archiving of credit card transactions for end user merchants who use credit cards in their daily business, utilizing the power of the PC.

SLM Software, Inc.
100-2489 Bloor Street West
Toronto, Ontario M6S 1R6 Canada
TEL: 416-767-8884
FAX:416-767-3557
sales@slmsoft.com
http://www.slmsoft.com/

SLM's Electronic Switching Platform (ESP-Link) family of products enable people to use local and remote applications to exchange information in a cooperative and efficient way within and between organizations anywhere in the world.

SoftCare Electronic Commerce Solutions
4240 Manor St., Suite 211
Burnaby, BC V5G 1B2 Canada
TEL: 604-434-7638
FAX: 604-434-9611
sales@softcare.com
http://www.softcare.com/

Since 1989, SoftCare has been an EDI/Electronic Commerce software provider to hundreds of clients worldwide.

Software Design Group, Inc.
5400 Orange Ave., Suite #111
Cypress, CA 90630
TEL: 714-816-0380
FAX: 714-995-6984
sales@sdgi.com
http://www.sdgi.com/

Software Design Group provides installation, design, and support services for Internet and intranet implementations of EDI software and electronic commerce solutions.

Southern DataComm, Inc.
19345 US Highway 19 North, Suite 200
Clearwater, FL 34624
TEL: 813-539-1800
FAX: 813-535-7971
webmaster@protobase.com
http://www.protobase.com/

Southern DataComm products address transaction processing and extended data requirements for a number of vertical markets.

Spry
(Internet Division of CompuServe, Inc.)
feedback@sprynet.com
http://www.spry.com/

SPRY, CompuServe Internet Division, is a worldwide leader of Internet access, services and software for the home and business markets.

For more contact information, please see Appendix A: Vendor Contact Information.

Spyglass, Inc.
sales@spyglass.com
http://www.spyglass.com/

Spyglass, Inc. licenses World Wide Web client and server technologies.

For more contact information, please see Appendix A: Vendor Contact Information.

SSDS, Inc.
6595 S. Dayton St., Suite 3000
Englewood, CO 80111
TEL: 303-790-0660
FAX: 303-790-1663
info@ssds.com
http://www.ssds.com/

SSDS creates business-driven technology solutions; designing, planning, implementing, and managing information infrastructures that assist their clients in gaining a competitive advantage.

St. Paul Software
1450 Energy Park Dr.
St. Paul, MN 55108
TEL: 612-603-4400
FAX: 612-603-4403
info@spedi.com
http://www.spedi.com/

St. Paul Software is a full service provider of Electronic Commerce/Electronic Data Interchange (EDI) products and services.

Star Development Group, Inc.
135 Beaver St.
Waltham, MA 02154
TEL: 617-893-5700
FAX:617-894-9226
info@stardev.com
http://www.stardev.com/

A consulting firm in the area of electronic distribution for brokerage and financial services firms.

Sterling Commerce, Inc.
4600 Lakehurst Court
Dublin, OH 43016
TEL: 614-793-7000
FAX: 614-793-7092
info@stercomm.com
http://www.stercomm.com/

Sterling Commerce is a leading, global provider of electronic software products and network services that enable businesses to engage in business-to-business electronic communications and transactions.

Subscription.Com, Inc.
TEL: 613-747-8289
FAX: 613-747-7035
busint@ibm.net
http://www.subscription.com/

TeleSubscription, a product of Subscription.Com, offers a rich catalog of products and services, complemented by an end-to-end subscription management service.

Sun Microsystems
webmaster@java.sun.com
http://java.sun.com/

An industry leader in new technology development in the areas of hardware and software.

For more contact information, please see Appendix A: Vendor Contact Information.

Tellan Software, Inc.
info@tellan.com
http://www.tellan.com/

Tellan's primary thrust has been in the area of large mainframes and communications, more recent activity has been developing PC and Apple Macintosh Sales and POS software.

For more contact information, please see Appendix A: Vendor Contact Information.

**TelPay, a company of Telenium,
a division of CTI ComTel, Inc.**
298 Garry St.
Winnipeg, Manitoba R3C 1H3 Canada
TEL: 204-947-9300
FAX: 204-947-2591
sales@TelPay.Ca
http://www.telpay.ca/

TelPay pioneered automated bill payment service in Canada in 1985 by accepting multiple payment instructions from customers over the telephone.

Terisa Systems, Inc.
info@terisa.com
http://www.terisa.com/

Terisa Systems creates the technologies that make electronic WWW commerce possible.

For more contact information, please see Appendix A: Vendor Contact Information.

TradeWave Corp. (subsidiary of SunRiver Corp.)
info@tradewave.com
http://www.tradewave.com/

TradeWave is a leader in providing industrial-strength, enterprise-wide Internet security solutions for intranets and electronic commerce.

For more contact information, please see Appendix A: Vendor Contact Information.

Transactions Systems Architects, Inc.
330 South 108th Ave.
Omaha, NE 68154
FAX: 402-390-8992
corpcom@tsainc.com
http://www.tsainc.com/

Transactions Systems Architects, Inc. is the parent company of Applied Communications, Inc. (ACI) and U.S. Software, Inc. (USSI). ACI develops electronic payments software for the Tandem computer platform.

Transecure, Inc.
TEL: 800-871-9320
aa@transecure.com
http://www.transecure.com/

Transecure is a new online consignment system allowing individuals and small businesses to complete their transaction securely.

Triad Data Processing
22 West Main St.
New Concord, OH 43762
TEL: 614-826-7678
FAX: 614-826-4324
info@easyorder.com
http://www.easyorder.com/

Triad is the premier provider of materials management systems for the extended care industry.

TSI International
45 Danbury Rd.
Wilton, CT 06897
TEL: 203-761-8600
FAX: 203-762-9677
webmaster@tsisoft.com
http://www.tsisoft.com/

TSI International is a software leader in areas critical to success in the new age of electronic commerce with a focus on the integration of electronic data, in all of its forms, with business applications.

Type III Technologies
4454 Rosebank Dr.
La Cañada, CA 91011
TEL: 818-249-7198
FAX: 818-249-5836
webmaster@type3.com
http://www.type3.com/

Type III Technologies is a Southern California based company that specializes in providing our clients with a wide variety of high quality, state-of-the-art products and services.

Universal Shopping Service
P.O. Box 190
40 East Union Hall Plaza
Union Hall, VA 24176
TEL: 540-576-3555
FAX: 540-576-1792
ushop@ushop.com
http://www.ushop.com/

A creation of Universal Shopping Service, Inc., Cyber Shopping with U-Shop creates the world's first borderless shopping mall.

VentureTech
TEL: 800-488-7151
webmaster@vteh.com
http://www.vteh.com/

VentureTech, Inc. is a high technology investment and finance company with several wholly-owned leading edge technologies under its control, and is currently negotiating new acquisitions.

VeriFone, Inc.
webmaster@verifone.com
http://www.verifone.com/

VeriFone designs, manufactures, markets, and supports Transaction Automation solutions, including transaction computer system platforms; local-area and wide-area network systems; printers and other peripherals; security products such as PIN pads and chip-card reader/writers; operating systems, programming languages, development tools, and application software; software products for client-server networking; retail payment systems integration, labor management, and Internet commerce; flexible financing; and customer support services.

For more contact information, please see Appendix A: Vendor Contact Information.

VeriSign, Inc.
info@verisign.com
http://www.verisign.com/

VeriSign, Inc., is the leading provider of digital authentication services and products for electronic commerce and other forms of secure communications.

For more contact information, please see Appendix A: Vendor Contact Information.

VL Virtual Logistics Inc./ VL Logistiques Virtuelles, Inc.
4030 St. Ambroise, Suite 436
Montreal, Quebec, H4C 2C7, Canada
TEL: 514-935-2700
FAX: 514-935-2016
rhsmith@virtlogic.ca
http://www.virtlogic.ca/

VL Virtual Logistics developed the foremost EDI integration software package on the market today.

WebMaster, Inc.
info@webmaster.com
http://www.webmaster.com/

A software engineering, publishing, and consulting company, WebMaster, Inc.'s unique emphasis is on providing software and services for server-centric Internet and Intranet solutions.

For more contact information, please see Appendix A: Vendor Contact Information.

World Wide Web Consortium (W3C)
khudairi@w3.org
http://www.w3.org/

The W3C is an industry consortium which seeks to promote standards for the evolution of the Web and interoperability between WWW products by producing specifications and reference software. Although W3C is funded by industrial members, it is vendor-neutral, and its products are freely available to all.

For more contact information, please see Appendix A: Vendor Contact Information.

APPENDIX C

ONLINE INFORMATION

Chapter 1 URLs

Microsoft
http://www.microsoft.com

Novell
http://www.novell.com

Sun Microsystems
http://www.sun.com

Securities and Exchange Commission (SEC)
http://edgar.stern.nyu.edu

KiwiClub at the University of Texas
http://kiwiclub.bus.utexas.edu/

L.L. Bean
http://www.llbean.com/

San Diego Business Journal
(article discussing electronic commerce)
http://www.businessite.com/Entry/BusinessNet/bj/bjinwells.html

Amazon.com
http://www.amazon.com/

Computer Literacy Bookstores
http://www.clbooks.com/

CDNow
http://www.cdnow.com

CD Universe
http://www.cduniverse.com/

Alligator Bob's Gourmet Alligator
http://www.gatorbob.com/

Godiva Chocolatier
http://www.godiva.com

Pepper Plant Hot Sauce
http://www.pepperplant.com/

Amazing Arrangements
http://www.durhamnews.net/~amazing/

The Ultimate Thought, Inc.
http://www.walrus.com/~tut/

Internet Shopping Network
http://www.internet.com

Buy IT Online
http://www.buyitonline.com/

The Catalog Site
http://www.catalogsite.com/

Egghead Software
http://www.egghead.com/

CompUSA
http://www.compusa.com/

CMP's software site
http://www.software.net/

Shareware.Com
http://www.shareware.com/

Infohaus
http://www.infohaus.com/

Chrysler Corporation
http://www.chryslercars.com

Clickable Systems International, Ltd.
http://www.clickable.com/cars.html

CyberCar
http://www.cybercar.com

Dealernet
http://www.dealernet.com

Delco Electronics
http://www.delco.com/

Ford Motor Company
http://www.ford.com

Financial Aid Matching Service
http://plan.educ.indiana.edu/~www/famatching.html

Silverplate Matching Service
http://www.compumedia.com/~eugene/

Career Matching Service
http://www.imagenetworker.com/public_html/career/career.html

Chapter 2 URLs

Information on DES
http://www.quadralay.com/Crypto/source-books.html

DOS version of PGP
http://www.pgp.com/

VeriSign
http://www.verisign.com/

RSA Encryption
http://www.rsa.com

Netscape
http://home.netscape.com/

SSL mailing list
ssl-talk@netscape.com

CommerceNet Consortium
http://www.commerce.net

S-HTTP e-mail
shttp-info@eit.com

S-HTTP draft specification
http://www.eit.com/creations/s-http/draft-ietf-wts-shttp-00.txt
ftp://ds.internic.net/internet-drafts/draft-ietf-wts-shttp-03.txt

TradeWave VPI WhitePaper
http://galaxy.tradewave.com/tradewave/products/vpiwp.html

TradeWave
http://www.tradewave.com/

The SET specification
http://www.mastercard.com/set/set.htm

JEPI information from the W3C
http://lists.w3.org/Archives/Public/

Chapter 3 URLs

Participating Ecash banks
http://www.digicash.com/Ecash/Ecash-issuers.html

VeriSign
http://www.verisign.com

First Virtual
http://www.fv.com

Clickshare
http://www.clickshare.com

CyberCash
http://www.cybercash.com

NetBill
http://www.netbill.com/

NetBill documentation
http://www.ini.cmu.edu/netbill/pubs/CompCon.html

Millicent
http://www.research.digital.com/SRC/millicent/papers/millicent-w3c4/millicent.html

Chapter 4 URLs

VeriFone
http://www.verifone.com

NCR
http://www.ncr.com

Tellan
http://www.tellan.com

Pacific Coast Software
http://www.pacific-coast.com

ICVERIFY
http://www.icverify.com

MasterCard
http://www.mastercard.com

Chapter 5 URLs

Stronghold: Apache SSL
http://apachessl.c2.org

Netscape Communications Corp.
http://www.netscape.com

Open Market
(site for the OpenMarket Secure Server)
http://www.openmarket.com/servers/

Apache
http://www.apache.org

SSLeay
http://www.psy.uq.oz.au/~ftp/Crypto/

The trials and tribulations of creating a public version of SSL
http://petrified.cic.net/~altitude/ssl/ssl.saga.html

Community ConneXion
http://www.c2.org

The Netcraft survey of current and historical survey data from their Web site
http://www.netcraft.co.uk/Survey/Reports/

Apache FAQ
http://www.apache.org/docs/FAQ.html

To report bugs you find in the Apache server, e-mail
apache-bugs@mail.apache.org

USENET
(a group where a number of Apache developers can be found)
comp.infosystems.www.servers.unix

Thawte's Sioux
(a cheap secure server solution that's similar to Stronghold)
http://www.thawte.com/products/sioux/

Community ConneXion
(Apache-SSL FAQ and documentation)
http:// stronghold.c2.net/faq.html

To report bugs in Stronghold, e-mail
apachessl-bugs@c2.org

For Stronghold technical support, e-mail
apachessl-support@c2.org

FastCGI
http://www.fastcgi.com/

Chapter 6 URLs

Sun Microsystem's Web site:
http://java.sun.com

WebSite Central
http://website.ora.com

David Strom's WebCompare
http://www.webcompare. iworld.com/

Chapter 7 URLs

Netscape, which may be found at this URL:
http://www.netscape.com

Download a demo version of WebSTAR/SSL
http://www.starnine.com/webstarssl/webstarssl.html

Chapter 8 URLs

Cybercash
http://www.cybercash.com

A mini-mall merchant list page is available at
http://www.cybercash.com/cybercash/shopping/

Ecash participating banks
http://www.digicash.com/ecash/ecash-issuers.html

Mark Twain bank
http://www.marktwain.com/ecash.html

First Virtual Holdings, Inc.
http://www.fv.com

First Virtual's Account Application site
http://www.fv.com/newacct/

Chapter 9 URLs

Internet Shopping Network
http://www.internet.net/

Dorothy Denning's cryptography site
http://guru.cosc.georgetown.edu/~denning/crypto/index.html

The SET specification
http://www.visa.com/cgi-bin/vee/sf/ set/intro.html

CyberCash
http://www.cybercash.com/

Merchants that accept CyberCash
http://www.cybercash.com/cybercash/ shopping /

CyberCash Wallet
http://ftp.cybercash.com/cgi-bin/download

NetLink
http://www.netlink.net/cybernet/cybernet.htm

Commerce Direct International
http://www.cdi.net/times.cgi

Netscape's Product page
(contains up-to-date information about LivePayment)
http://partner.netscape.com/comprod/products/iapps/client.html

LivePayment FAQ
http://www.netscape.com/comprod/products/iapps/platform/livepay_faq.html

LivePayment White Paper
http://www.netscape.com/comprod/products/iapps/platform/livepay_white_paper.html

Open Market's OpenTransact
http://www.openmarket.com

CommerceRoom
http://www.webmaster.com/high/products/commerceroom/

ICVERIFY
http://www.icverify.com/

Internet Privacy Coalition's Golden Key Campaign
http://www.privacy.org/ipc/

These sites contain links to many types of payment solutions
http://ganges.cs.tcd.ie/mepeirce/project.html
http://www.pitt.edu/~malhotra/Elecomm.htm

Chapter 10 URLs
ICVERIFY
http://www.icverify.com

Chapter 11 URLs
No URLS

Chapter 12 URLs
Stronghold
http:// stronghold.c2.net/
VeriSign
http://www.verisign.com

Chapter 13 URLs
FV-API
http://www.fv.com/tech/fv-api.html
FV-API documentation
http://www.fv.com/tech/fv-api-spec.html

Chapter 14 URLs
WinSite archive
http://www.winsite.com
Netmanage
http://www.netmanage.com
Samba
ftp://nimbus.anu.edu.au/pub/tridge/samba/

Chapter 15 URLs
Netscape bug-reporting
http://cgi.netscape.com/cgi-bin/ auto_bug.cgi
Yahoo feedback
(see Dead Link and Fix the Listing)
http://www.yahoo.com/text/suggest.html
Real Audio includes contact information and a feedback form
http://www.realaudio.com/reachus.html
Macromedia has a good master list with great sub-pages
http://www.macromedia.com/macromedia/contact.html
Publicly Accessible Mailing Lists:
http://www.NeoSoft.com/internet/paml/

Liszt: Searchable Directory of Mailing Lists:
http://www.liszt.com/

WWW Yellow pages at
http://www.yellow.com/cgi-bin/online/

Cool Site of the Day
cool@infi.net

Spider's Pick of the Day
boba@www.com

Mosaic What's New
whats-new@ncsa.uiuc.edu

Yahoo What's New
suggest-picks@yahoo.com

c|net's "Best of the Web"
http://www.cnet.com/Content/Reviews/Bestofweb/feedback.html

Yahoo!
http://www.yahoo.com

Webcrawler
http://www.webcrawler.com

Altavista
http://www.altavista.digital.com/

Promote-It!
http://www.cam.org/~psarena/promote-it.html

World Wide Web Robots, Wanderers, and Spiders
http://www.info.webcrawler.com/mak/projects/robots/robots-html

Haystack Labs
http://www.haystack.com.

NT Security Web
http://www.telemark.net/~randallg/ntsecure.htm

Microsoft's C2
http://www.microsoft.com/NTServer/c2bltn.htm

Somarsoft (NT security)
http://www.somarsoft.com/security.htm

APPENDIX D

ABOUT THE CD-ROM

The CD-ROM included with this book contains trial and demonstration software mentioned in the text, as well as a URL hotlist, code fragments from the text, and electronic commerce documentation. Any operating system capable of supporting long filenames (Macintosh, UNIX, Windows 95/NT) will be able to easily access every file on this CD. If you have Windows 3.1 or an operating system that is limited to 8.3, these long filenames will be truncated by your system (for example, WINCYBER.EXE-2.0 may be truncated to WINCYB~1.EXE).

Additional Utilities

The files included in the directory on the CD are all archived and compressed. You may need a decompression tool to extract the original files from these archives. All of the following tools can be located quickly using the search engine at c|net's Shareware.Com, which is located at:

```
http://www.shareware.com
```

To use this excellent software search tool, select your platform type from the initial pick list, and then use the name of the program (for example, PKZip or WinZip) for your database search. Locate the download area that's geographically closest with the largest number of stars, and you'll be able to grab what you need.

Windows

Most of the Windows software is archived with PKZip. You can use the original PKWare PKZip program to extract these files, or a newer GUI package called WinZIP. The latest version of PKZip is 2.04G with a filename of "pkz204g.exe." Copy the PKZip file into an empty directory then execute it to extract the files. There is a detailed manual and readme file that explains how to use the software. The latest version of WinZIP can be downloaded from `http://www.winzip.com`. Complete installation and use instructions are available online and in the self-extracting file you will download.

Macintosh

All of the Macintosh archives are BinHexed (hqx) and/or StuffIt archives (sit). You can download the BinHex 4.0 software from `ftp://ftp.bio.indiana.edu/util/mac/binhex.bin`. This file is a Mac-executable program. You can download the StuffIt Expander 4.0.1 from `http://www.aladdinsys.com/`. Complete installation details are available on the Aladdin Web site.

UNIX

There is only one UNIX compression file on this CD and it is a TAR file. Most UNIX OSes include a built-in un*tar* utility. For detailed instructions on the use of TAR, read the manual page by typing `man tar` at any prompt. If your system does not display the TAR page, contact your system administrator. Without access to a working installation of the TAR utility you will not be able to access this archive.

Installation Tips

The following are a few things we highly recommend when installing new software:

- Back up your system.
- Reboot your machine.
- Move the file to be unarchived into an empty directory.
- Test the extracted files for viruses before installation (Note: We have performed a thorough virus test on all of the software on the CD. This step is included as a recommendation for any software you attempt to install.).
- Read all of the instructions before attempting to install.
- Before the installation, unload any TSR programs—especially anti-virus, memory managers, and high-end graphic drivers (this may require you to reboot again).

Contents

We've laid the contents of the CD out in the form of a large table here, where each file or directory name is accompanied by an explanation of its contents (and significance, where applicable).

FILE/DIRNAME	EXPLANATION
Root level	the following files appear at the root level of the CD
ec.htm	the first document you should load in your Web browser
urls.htm	a menued list of URLs from the text
code/	contains code fragments from the text, grouped by chapter
software/	contains all EC software from vendors
software/cybercsh	CyberCash software and materials
wallet1.2.1-68k.bin	CyberCash Wallet for Macintosh 680X0, binary (Mac)
wallet1.2.1-68k.hqx	CyberCash Wallet for Macintosh 680X0, BinHex (Mac)
wallet1.2.1-fat.bin	CyberCash Wallet for Macintosh in FAT format, binary (Mac)
wallet1.2.1-fat.hqx	CyberCash Wallet for Macintosh in FAT format, BinHex (Mac)
wallet1.2.1-ppc.bin	CyberCash Wallet for Power PC, binary (Mac)
wallet1.2.1-ppc.hqx	CyberCash Wallet for Power PC, BinHex (Mac)
WINCYBER.EXE-2.0	CyberCash Wallet for Windows (Win)
software/fv	contains First Virtual software and materials
fv-api.ps	installing and using the First Virtual API utilities (PostScript)
fv-api.txt	installing and using the First Virtual API utilities (text)
fv-api-spec.ps	First Virtual's shell and C Application Programming Interface (PostScript)
fv-api-spec.txt	First Virtual's shell and C Application Programming Interface (text)
green-model.ps	the Green Commerce Model (PostScript)
green-model.txt	the Green Commerce Model (text)
smxp-spec.ps	the Simple MIME eXchange Protocol (SMXP) (PostScript)

FILE/DIRNAME	EXPLANATION
smxp-spec.txt	the Simple MIME eXchange Protocol (SMXP) (text)
software/fv/code	First Virtual code
fv-api.tar.bin	First Virtual API
fv-api.tgz.bin	First Virtual API
orderform.tar.bin	First Virtual Tcl CGI script for an online order form
websale.tar.bin	First Virtual C CGI script for a Web sale page
software/icverify	ICVERIFY software and materials
setup.exe	ICVERIFY Windows demo (Win)
software/icverify/d_devkit	ICVERIFY DOS Development Kit v.6.60.00 (DOS)
software/icverify/w_devkit	ICVERIFY Windows Development Kit v.1.0 (Win)
software/oreilly	O'Reilly & Associates software and materials
setup.exe	installation for WebSite 1.1 (Win)
readme.1st	readme file for WebSite 1.1
software/oreilly/chapters	installation chapters from O'Reilly's *Building Your Own Web Site* in HTML format
ws11ch01.thm	Why Publish with WebSite?
ws11ch02.htm	Before You Start
ws11ch03.htm	Installing WebSite
website11e.exe	WebSite 1.1 (Win)
software/qdeck	Quarterdeck software and materials
README	Quarterdeck's WebStar README
webstar.sea.hqx	Quarterdeck's WebStar Web server for Macintosh (Mac)
software/tellan	Tellan software and materials
MacAuthorizeDemo.hqx	Tellan's Credit Card Authorization demo (Mac)
PCAuthD.EXE	Tellan's Credit Card Authorization demo (Win)

Installation

In the sections that follow, you'll find the installation instructions for each piece of software as provided by the respective vendors.

CyberCash

Macintosh: Launch the `.bin` file, follow the prompts (if you use a `.hqx` you will need to de-BinHex first).
Windows: Execute the self-extracting archive, run setup, then follow the prompts.

First Virtual

Read the associated text files and the heading information in the scripts. Configuration, alteration, and installation details are contained in those areas as well as on the FV Web site.

ICVERIFY

Windows Demo: Execute and follow the prompts.
DOS Development Kit: Execute install, follow the prompts.
Windows Development Kit: Execute install, follow the prompts.

O'Reilly

Read the documentation in the `chapters` subdirectory with a Web browser. Start with the wsch11ch01.htm file. Execute setup.exe, follow the prompts.

Quarterdeck

Read the README file with a text editor. Visit the Quarterdeck site to obtain a trial serial number. Launch the installer script, follow the prompts.

Tellan

Macintosh: De-BinHex, then execute the extracted file, follow the prompts.
Windows: Execute the `.exe` file, then follow the prompts.

Fine Print

The copyright for each of these software products is held by its respective vendor. Any restrictions on use or re-distribution is detailed in each vendor's license agreement, which is either included with the software or available from the vendor. IDG Books Worldwide, Inc., and the book's authors, make no additional claims, nor provide any additional warranties or guarantees about these software products including their use or misuse, or their fitness for any purpose, experimental or commercial.

GLOSSARY

access control. The process of determining who is allowed access to a computer system, including what that user is and is not allowed to access.

algorithm. A step-by-step, programmatic "recipe" for producing a certain set of results in a computer program.

aliasing. The process of using a name or a label to reference someone or something.

API (Application Programming Interface). A set of interface subroutines or library calls that define the methods for programs to access external services, such as hardware devices, telephony systems, or specialty applications.

architecture neutral. The ability to execute a program under a number of computer architectures without requiring recompilation or code changes.

ARPANET (Advanced Research Projects Agency NETwork). A Department of Defense data network, developed by ARPA in the 1970s, on which the Internet was based.

ASCII (American Standard Code for Information Interchange). A coding method used to represent standard alphabetic, numeric, and other keyboard characters in computer-readable, binary format.

asymmetric cryptography. An encryption scheme in which data is encoded with a public key and can only be decoded by the intended recipient with a specific private key.

authentication. User and server certificate data will be examined by authorization software to establish and confirm both sender's and receiver's identities.

authorization. The verification process that allows access to a computer system. Also used in association with the transaction approval of a credit card.

back-office. Refers to products that are key to the superstructure of an organization's information system, such as network operating systems, publication tools, or databases.

bandwidth. The amount of information that can be sent across a network. If you think of a network connection as a pipe with water flowing through it, the amount of water that flows is the amount of *bandwidth*.

Bourne shell. UNIX machines typically have one native command interpreter or shell. On many machines, this is the Bourne shell, named after S.R. Bourne in 1975. The Bourne shell is part of the standard configuration for every flavor of UNIX.

Bps (bits per second). (or Kbps, Mbps, etc.) a measurement of data transfer rate, one kilobit equals 1,024 bits, one megabit equals 1,024 kilobits or 1,048,576 bits.

browser. See *Web browser*.

C. A programming language developed by some of the founders of UNIX, Brian Kernighan and Dennis Ritchie, still very much in vogue among UNIX-heads.

C++. A programming language developed by Bjarne Stroustrup, *C++* is a successor to the C language. It is an object-oriented (OO) implementation of C.

Certification Authority (CA). A service that provides electronic verification certificates which authenticates a user's client.

CGI (Common Gateway Interface). The parameter-passing and invocation technique and programming specification used to let Web clients and Web servers exchange data.

CGI script. A program that executes on a Web server that contains the steps or actions to be performed on data received from a HTML form from a remote user.

chmod. A UNIX command to change the owner of, or permissions for, files in the UNIX file system.

clearing house. A banking center used for financial transactions between banks or other financial institutions to compare and clear accounts based on the value differences between collections of transactions.

commercial bank account. The account in which the processing network will place the incoming funds from a merchant, and deduct any charges or fees.

contact information. The information about the company that hosts a Web site, this includes the snail mail address, phone number, fax number, and e-mail address. Always provide this information to the users of your site.

credit card discount rate. The percentage per-transaction that a processing network pays itself.

credit card processing networks. A community of credit card institutions that operates similar to a bank clearing house. All transactions are compared, and resultant imbalances are corrected with credit transfers.

cryptography. The process, science, and art of concealing the contents of a message or other data collection from everyone except those possessing the proper decoding key.

cryptosystem. A software or hardware solution that uses cryptography as a standard native security measure.

csh (C-Shell). A possible shell for the UNIX environment, based on the programming language C.

CSU/DSU (Channel Service Unit/Data Service Unit). A device to terminate a digital telephone channel on a customer's premises (commonly used to terminate T1 or higher bandwidth connections).

decryption key. A special value that is used to reverse the encryption process.

DES (Digital Encryption Standard). An encryption algorithm that operates on 8-byte (64-bit) blocks of data, and uses a 56-bit key to perform its encryption.

digital certificate. An electronic public-key directory that has been verified by a certification authority, which is used to verify digital signatures.

digital ID. An electronic identification code assigned to a particular user or client application by a verification authority.

digital signature. An electronic identification device used to positively identify a user, for the purpose of making a financial transaction of some kind. Digital ID and authorization certificates are similar caveats.

DLL (Dynamic Link Library). See *Dynamic Link Library*

document root. The base of a Web server's document tree, the root defines the scope of all the documents that Web users may access (i.e., access is allowed to the root and all its children, but not to any of the root's peers or parents).

Domain Name Service (DNS). An Internet service that maps symbolic names (www.outer.net) to IP addresses (204.96.12.2) by distributing queries among the available pool of computers supporting the service.

Dynamic Link Library (DLL). A Microsoft Windows executable code module which is loaded on demand.

electronic commerce. The process, act, and operation of financial transactions over the Internet or the World Wide Web, thus allowing purchases, monetary transfers, and credit exchanges between two distant parties.

electronic data interchange (EDI). A standard for exchanging transactions electronically.

electronic payment systems. The equipment that calls a processing network through a modem data connection, authorizes a credit purchase, then uploads a batch of all sales and credits to the processing network in the evening.

encryption. The application of a special value to plain text that scrambles the data in a deliberately complex and tortuous process. The resulting data is a set of substituted values, based on the value of the key, plus a rigorously defined set of mathematical operations based on that key and the original plain text.

encryption algorithm. An algorithm used to encrypt data. See *algorithm* and *encryption*.

encryption key. An electronic code that locks or unlocks (encrypts or decrypts) data.

FAQ (frequently asked questions). A list of common questions with their answers, maintained by most special interest groups on the Internet as a way of lowering the frequency of basic technical questions.

firewall. A system that supervises all traffic in and out of a particular network, which only allows authorized traffic to access the computer system or network.

FTP (File Transfer Protocol). An Internet protocol that allows users to exchange large files with other users over the Internet or an intranet.

gateway. A program or service that knows how to convert input from one type of system or network to another type of system or network. It handles inbound raw data from Web clients as an extension of the Web server and returns processed data to those same clients.

.gif (also GIF, Graphics Interchange Format). A compressed graphics file format patented by Unisys and widely used in HTML documents for in-line graphical elements.

GSSAPI (Generic Security Services API). The collection of security and transaction handling subroutine calls that comprise the bulk of the TradeWave's Virtual Private Internet (VPI) environment.

GUI (graphical user interface). A generic name for any computer interface that uses graphics, windows, and a pointing device (like a mouse or trackball) instead of a purely character-mode interface. Windows, MacOS, and X-Windows are all examples of GUI interfaces.

helper applications. Applications invoked outside a Web browser to render, display, or play back data that the browser itself cannot handle (for example, video or multimedia files).

hexadecimal. A form of computer data format where all values are expressed as a sequence of Base 16 digits (0–9, A–F).

hierarchical. A form of document or file structure, also known as a tree structure, where all elements except the root have parents (elements of a higher level), and all elements may or may not have children (elements of a lower level).

HTML (HyperText Markup Language). A descriptive markup language used to create documents accessible through the World Wide Web service.

HTTP (HyperText Transfer Protocol). The TCP/IP-based protocol used to convey World Wide Web information between Web clients and servers.

httpd **(HyperText Transfer Protocol Daemon)**. The listener program that runs on a Web server, listening for and ready to respond to requests for Web documents or CGI-based services.

hypermedia. Any of the methods of computer-based information delivery, including text, graphics, video, animation, sound, and so on, that can be interlinked and treated as a single collection of information.

hypertext. A method of organizing text, graphics, and other kinds of data for computer use, which lets individual data elements point to associated resources; a nonlinear method of organizing information, especially text.

IAB (Internet Architecture Board, formerly Internet Activities Board). The governing body for the Internet, which manages standards, contracts certain aspects of the network's operation, and handles what little administration there is over the Internet.

IANA (Internet Assigned Numbers Authority). The arm of the IAB that assigns new IP address ranges to those who request them (and meet other necessary criteria).

IETF (Internet Engineering Task Force). The technical arm of the IAB responsible for meeting current engineering needs on the Internet, the IETF also has custody of RFC content and related standards status.

image map. An HTML construct identified by the ISMAP attribute of the <IMG> tag, an *image map* is a graphical image that has an associated map file of coordinates that lets users select links by clicking on certain portions of the image. A client-side image map is a similar interactive device where the coordinate information is contained within an HTML document and does not require the server side map file.

Information Services. The information technologies and systems deployed by an organization, usually refers specifically to a network or computer system.

instance. A particular incarnation of an object, item, element, class, or record, an instance includes the data for one single specific item in a data collection.

international standard. In generic terms, an international standard is one that is honored by more than one country; in practice, this usually refers to a standard controlled or honored by the International Standards Organization (ISO).

Internet. The worldwide TCP/IP network used by millions across the globe to exchange information via computers.

InterNIC. The quasi-governmental agency responsible for maintaining a registry of existing IP addresses and domain names on the Internet, and which also handles requests for new addresses and domain names.

IP address. A 32-bit address assigned to every host and node on the Internet. Usually, the number is written in dotted decimal notation (204.96.12.2) instead of the 32-character binary number actually used by computers on the Internet.

ISAPI (Internet Server Application Programming Interface). A Microsoft API that allows browsers to access remote server applications.

ISDN (Integrated Services Digital Network). A digital networking technology that's becoming widely available in the U.S., *ISDN* allows communication over one or more 64-Kbps digital data channels through the telephone system.

ISO (International Standards Organization). The standards organization based in Paris devoted to defining standards for international and national data communications. ISO is a voluntary, non-treaty organization chartered by the United Nations.

ISP (Internet service provider). A vendor of Internet access, *ISPs* typically provide numerous types of communications links (modem, ISDN, T-1) and Internet information services to their customers and let them select the amount of bandwidth and access time that meets their access needs.

Java. An object-oriented programming language and environment from Sun Microsystems. Along with C and C++, Java is compiled into an architecture-neutral binary object and then interpreted like Perl or Tcl for a specific computer architecture.

JavaScript. A scripting language used to provide a simplified method to include dynamic behavior (animations, scrolling marquees) within Web documents. JavaScript and Java are different languages, their similarities reside in their names and common programming syntax.

Joint Electronic Payment Initiative (JEPI). A proposed Internet payment standard which concentrates on data security in four ways: a.) building a standard mechanism for Web clients and servers to negotiate payment; b.) piloting the new negotiation process in a live market environment; c.) publishing the result as an open standard; and d.) submitting the results to a recognized standards body (probably the IETF, under the aegis of the W3C) for change control.

jpeg (Joint Photographic Experts Group, also JPEG). A lossy-compression graphics format designed to handle computer images of high-resolution photographs as efficiently as possible.

Kerberos. A well-known security and access control service used on many TCP/IP-based networks; *Kerberos* can issue security tokens, called tickets, as proof of identity or for use as session-level keys.

key. See *encryption key*.

key generator. A software application that creates and/or modifies encryption keys.

keyword. An essential or definitive term that can be used for indexing data, for later search and retrieval.

late binding. Also called delayed binding, the action of waiting as long as possible before defining environmental variables in order to maximize the compatibility and completeness of a particular application.

latency. The time interval between when a network node (any device on a network) seeks access to a transmission channel (a pathway to send and/or receive data) and when access is granted or received.

link. A basic element of hypertext, a *link* provides a method for jumping from one point in a document to another point in the same document, or another document altogether.

link checker. An application that searches through a collection of HTML pages, verifying that all hyperlinks are working properly.

linking. The act of creating a hyperlink that ties one resource with another.

log file. A document or database where all actions, occurrences, errors, and transactions are recorded. Often a log file is used to provide a 'paper trail' of electronic events.

mailing lists. A TCP/IP-based e-mail service that collects all messages from individuals who post to a specific address, and broadcasts those messages to everyone who subscribes to the list. Mailing lists make excellent information distribution tools on just about any subject.

mainframe. A supercomputer (or similar high-end computer) that is used in a host-terminal networking environment, as the central main host.

merchant bank. A banking facility that handles corporate (merchant) transactions.

merchant ID number. The unique number that designates your company to the merchant banks and the processing networks, and is used in any transactions between these entities. This ID number is obtained through a validation service, bank institution, or directly from a distribution service.

message integrity. The guarantee that message contents do not change between sender and receiver.

MIME (Multipurpose Internet Mail Extensions). Extensions to the RFC822 mail message format to permit more complex data and file types than plain text. Today, MIME types include sound, video, graphics, PostScript, and HTML, among others.

mirrored servers. Heavily used file archives, Web servers, or other network servers may be copied to other machines located around a network, to lower the demand on any one such server and to reduce long-distance network traffic. Whenever one server acts as a full copy of another, the second server is said to be a *mirror* of the first.

modem dial-up authorization. Currently, most processing networks require you to dial-in to them via modem.

multihoming. When more than one domain name and Web site exists on a single server machine and distributed by a common Web server software.

multimedia. The combination of numerous forms of media (such as text, graphics, audio, and video) in the communication of information.

multithreaded. A process that lets a multitasking operation system, such as Windows NT, multitask threads of an application. Multitasking is the method of CPU usage where numerous separate computing tasks are performed simultaneously.

multiuser configuration. The setup or parameters of an application that allow more than one user to interact with or gain access to the main system, service, or program.

navigation. The act of finding one's way around the World Wide Web.

NetBEUI. The NetBIOS Extended User Interface is a transport layer driver used by Windows NT (and other operating systems) to deliver information across a network.

NetBIOS. A programming interface that allows I/O requests to be sent to and received from a remote computer.

netiquette. The societal and cultural behavioral code of the Internet. Indicates what is acceptable within a specific service, group, or network. Often the netiquette of a group is well defined in a readily available FAQ written by one or more group members.

newsgroup. A named, publicly available mailing list service that belongs to the Internet-based USENET news hierarchy, *newsgroups* focus around particular topics and can often deliver valuable technical or support information. Today, there are over 7,000 newsgroups accessible through the Internet.

NFS (Network File System). A distributed file system originated by Sun Microsystems that's in wide use in TCP/IP networking environments today. NFS lets users access remote file systems as if they were an extension of their local hard drives.

NNTP (Network News Transfer Protocol). A protocol by which articles from USENET newsgroups are transferred.

non-repudiatability. The use of digital signatures or other positive applications of a party's private key to demonstrate their active involvement in a transaction, thereby proving their complicity. This characteristic is important to ensure that all parties to an electronic transaction will uphold their parts of the bargain involved.

object-oriented. A programming paradigm that concentrates on defining data objects and the methods that may be applied to them.

open. A popular term used to describe Internet technologies. Its primary meaning is that it describes a technology that's not proprietary, and doesn't require the payment of royalties to use it. For instance, Netscape's SSL specification is free to use, but you must pay Netscape to use one of the SSL servers.

Open Database Connectivity (ODBC). A database access API controlled by Microsoft, which provides a standard interface for various database programs and systems, thereby enabling a single application or interface to communicate with a database engine, such as SQL Server, FoxPro, and Access.

Open Transport. The native Macintosh TCP/IP network protocol implementation that enables communication with the Internet and other TCP/IP networks.

payment terminals. These devices consist of a numeric keypad with special function keys, a magnetic stripe reader, a modem line, a port for connecting to a sales slip printer, and a port for connecting to a POS system. The advantage of the payment terminal over sales slips is that transactions are processed much faster by the network; consequently, the merchant receives its money sooner.

payment vendor. A company that provides payment system services for electronic merchants.

PDF (portable document format). A pre-formatted document file type developed by Adobe that maintains a document's original layout, style and fonts across multiple platforms, whether it's viewed or printed.

Perl. An interpreted programming language developed by Larry Wall, *Perl* offers superb string-handling and pattern-matching capabilities and is a favorite among CGI programmers.

plug-in. A Web browser add-in program that operates under the umbrella of the browser itself, thereby extending the program's overall capabilities.

point-of-sale (POS) equipment. A fancy term for a retail system that integrates a variety of features into one workstation or a group of networked workstations to process transactions.

postprocessing. Is the opposite of *preprocessing*, and supports operations that would be applied after a Web server has already responded to an incoming request.

preprocessing. Permits local programs to evaluate load associated with an URL and one or more servers before it attempts to access the Web documents. By doing this, it's possible to achieve a type of load balancing across multiple servers, or enact a method to redirect URL requests to other servers based on their contents.

Pretty Good Privacy (PGP). An encryption system developed by Phillip Zimmerman that has remained unbroken since its inception in 1991.

private card. An electronic commerce device similar to a credit card that allows monetary transactions to be made over commerce networks. The private card is used to approve or validate a transaction by scanning the card in a card reader.

private-key encryption. Also known as *symmetric cryptography*, uses the identical key to decrypt a message that was used to encrypt it in the first place.

processor-intensive. An application that consumes lots of CPU cycles (that is, runs for a long time) is said to be processor-intensive. Good examples include heavy graphics rendering like ray-tracing, animation, CAD, and other programs that combine lots of number-crunching with intensive display requirements.

proprietary. Technology that's owned or controlled by a specific company or organization, rather than a standards group, and that may or may not be widely used in the computer industry.

protocol. A set of rules and conventions by which two computers pass messages across the network. Networking software usually implements multiple levels of *protocols* layered one on top of another. Windows NT includes NBT, TCP/IP, DLC, and NWLink *protocols*. Windows NT Server also includes AppleTalk.

protocol suite. A collection of networking protocols that together define a complete set of tools and communications facilities for network access and use (for example, TCP/IP, OSI, or IPX/SPX).

public-key encryption. Also known as *asymmetric cryptography*, *public-key encryption* schemes rely on the use of two keys, one that's used to encode a message for transmission, and another that's used to decode that transmission at the receiving end.

public-key exchange. The action of exchanging public keys with individuals or groups so asynchronous encryption can take place between the two parties. There are some Internet organizations that are used as a directory service and store house for public-keys for many high-traffic vendors, companies, or individuals.

RC4-40. A 40-bit encryption key based on the RC4 algorithm developed by Ron Rivest of RSA Data Security Inc. This is the technology used in the export version of Netscape Navigator.

RC4-128. A 128-bit encryption key based on the RC4 algorithm developed by Ron Rivest of RSA Data Security Inc. This is the technology used in the domestic U.S. version of Netscape Navigator.

remote administration. The ability to control a computer from another computer via a dial-up connection.

RIP (Routing Information Protocol). The first major routing protocol used in the TCP/IP environment, now largely replaced by more modern routing protocols, such as OSPF (Open Shortest Path First).

router. An internetwork device or program that reads the addresses of incoming packets and forwards them to their destination, or to other routers that can bring them closer to that destination.

RSA (Rivest Shamir Adelman). An encryption algorithm named for its inventors at MIT, RSA uses a public/private key approach and is regarded as one of the secure methods for protecting data on the Internet. RSA is the best-known public-key encryption scheme in broad commercial use today.

sales slip. A form supplied by your processing network in which you, as the merchant, fill out the credit card and vendor information (or take an imprint of this information from the credit card and a plate which contains vendor information) for processing a credit transaction.

script. A program that contains the steps or actions to be performed on data received by a server from a client application.

search engine. A program that can search the contents of a database and other resources to provide information that relates to specific topics or keywords supplied by a user.

SEC (Securities and Exchange Commission). The U.S. regulatory body that governs stock, markets, and related financial exchanges.

secure Web server. An online Web server that takes security precautions to ensure data integrity and/or authorized access.

security. Of utmost importance in electronic commerce, *security* includes the steps taken to ensure that no sensitive information can be seen by would-be hackers on the Internet.

server. A computer and/or software that provides information services of any kind to clients, such as a Web *server*.

SET (Secure Electronic Transactions). A proposed open standard for conducting bank card transactions over the Internet.

.shtml (Secure HTML). A special implementation of the HypertText Transfer Protocol that's been enhanced to support encryption for the transfer of sensitive or commercial information via the World Wide Web.

S-HTTP (Secure HyperText Transfer Protocol). A security-enhanced version of the original HTTP application-layer Web protocol, released by EIT to members of CommerceNet in late 1994, which provides general transaction security services necessary to conduct electronic commerce, including transaction confidentiality, authentication, message integrity checks, and proof of origin.

SMB (Server Message Blocks). NetBEUI based application layer protocol, primarily used for access to LAN Manager and Windows NT file system files.

SMPS (Secure Merchant Payment System). Administers the details of CyberCash secure credit card processing; it authorizes transactions, handles voids and returns, and provides receipts. SMPS also lets merchants process orders from #800 telephone calls, e-mails, and faxes.

SMTP (Simple Mail Transfer Protocol). An electronic messaging protocol used on TCP/IP networks.

software payment systems. Systems that either supplant or enhance POS equipment. These solutions run on a regular computer platform, such as DOS, Windows, OS/2, UNIX, or Mac OS. There are even some that run on mainframe systems.

SSL (Secure Sockets Layer). A public-key encryption-based data security protocol, developed by Netscape, that provides a variety of security services including data encryption, server authentication, message integrity check, and optional client authentication for TCP/IP connection.

standard. A program, system, protocol, or other computer component that has been declared to be the common basis, foundation, method, or process by some standards-setting body, or it may simply have acquired that status through widespread or long-term use. When talking about *standards*, it's always important to find out if the designation is official or otherwise.

superuser. The name of a UNIX account with system wide privileges to all files and resources, often abbreviated "su".

symmetric cryptography. An encryption scheme in which data is encoded with the same key used to decoded the message.

T1. A digital transmission link with a capacity of 1.544 Mbps. Also written T-1.

tar (tape archival program). A UNIX utility used to compress and decompress files (files compressed with this program normally have the extension ".tar").

target audience. This is the group of people to whom you direct your Web site. For instance, if you are selling veterinary products, your *target audience* includes pet owners and veterinarians.

Tcl (Tool Command Language, pronounced tickle). A simple scripting language for extending and controlling applications. *Tcl* can be embedded into C applications because its interpreter is implemented as a C library of procedures. Each application can extend the basic *Tcl* functions by creating new *Tcl* commands that are specific to a particular programming task.

tcpd (TCP Daemon). The name of a UNIX program that handles the TCP/IP protocol stack.

TCP/IP (Transfer Control Protocol/Internet Protocol). The primary transport protocol used to communicate among systems on the Internet.

thread. In operating system jargon, a *thread* is a name for a lightweight process managed within the context of a complex program (for example, a Web server) where an executive process, called a Thread Manager, allocates execution threads as needed. When a user submits a request for an HTML document, for example, the Thread Manager would allocate a *thread* to handle that request.

track-two compatible. Magnetic strips on typical credit cards contain two tracks of electronic data. A magnetic strip reader that can read both strips is said to be track-two compatible.

TradeWave's Virtual Private Internet (TradeVPI). A technology that has been used for business-to-business electronic commerce, as an analog to EDI, except that it runs on the Internet, instead of using secured communications lines on private or public networks.

transaction processing network. The organization that you actually call—either data or voice—to verify the credit card information, and the ones who process the transaction in real-time or batch. They deposit the transacted money into your commercial bank account.

TSR (terminate and stay resident program). A TSR is a kind of program that stays installed within DOS memory, even when it's not in use, ready to be invoked at a single keystroke or system interrupt. *TSRs* are commonly used for utility programs or hardware drivers (such as NICs) that require instant access to the CPU.

turnkey. A complete system or solution delivered from a vendor that is ready to use.

UNIX. The powerful operating system developed by Brian Kernighan and Dennis Ritchie as a form of recreation at Bell Labs in the late 1960s, still running strong today.

URL (Uniform Resource Locator). The primary naming scheme used to identify Internet resources, *URLs* define the protocols to be used, the domain name of the server where a resource resides, the port address to be used for communication, and the directory path to access a named Web document or resource.

USENET. The TCP/IP-based collection of Internet newsgroups that today consists of over 15,000 named groups that regularly exchange collections of e-mail messages on a broad range of topics.

user authentication. An HTTP feature that allows you to protect document trees with password security. To access protected areas of your server, the user must have a username and password in your Web server's authentication database, and must login to retrieve the data.

verification certificate. A digital document, issued by a certificate authority, that validates the identity of its holder. Used in many commerce systems to authenticate the parties involved, and to provide non-repudiatability.

virtual hosts. An apparent independent host on the Internet, a virtual host is actually a unique domain name mapped onto another host (with its own unique domain name). This creates an aliasing mechanism that lets ISPs provide services for many Web sites without an equal number of separate servers.

virtual store. The Web-based, or electronic, equivalent of a commercial retail outlet.

VPI (Virtual Private Internet). The electronic commerce and firewall architecture devised by TradeWave to allow multiple intranets to be interlinked over the Internet.

VRML (Virtual Reality Modeling Language). A language for describing multi-participant interactive three-dimensional simulations—virtual worlds networked via the Internet and hyperlinked with the World Wide Web.

W3C (World Wide Web Consortium). The consortium that includes CERN, MIT, and other organizations that currently have custody over HTTP, HTML, and other Web-related software and standards.

Web browser. An Internet application that lets users access World Wide Web servers and view their contents.

webmaster. The individual responsible for managing a specific Web site.

Web merchant. A company that is running its own Web commerce server.

Web reporting software. A software package which can provide statistical data on your Web site, such as the number of documents accessed (hits), errors, server activity, and more.

Web site. A named collection of HTML documents and other materials accessible through the HTTP protocol.

world readable. In UNIX terminology, this means that anyone permitted to access the file system can read files with this permission designation.

World Wide Web (WWW or W3). The graphical, hypertext, TCP/IP-based service that provides access to document and information services around the world; the *World Wide Web* allows clients anywhere on the Internet to access information on any publicly-accessible Web server anywhere.

WSAPI (WebSite Application Programming Interface). Provides a fast, robust way to accommodate server side applications needs, and to handle Web-page-to-program-interfaces.

WYSIWYG (What You See Is What You Get). A term used to describe text editors or other layout tools (like HTML authoring tools) that attempt to show their users on-screen what final, finished documents will look like.

x-cert. X.509 is the name of a broad set of ISO security and authentication standards. Certification schemes that adhere to this specification are sometimes designated by this term.

Yahoo! (Yet Another Hierarchical Officious Oracle). A database written and maintained by David Filo and Jerry Yang, who style themselves "self-proclaimed Yahoos." This is an inauspicious introduction to one of the best search engines for the World Wide Web. When we go surfing, we often start from *Yahoo!*

INDEX

Internet Engineering Task Force
(IETF), 25
Internet Privacy Coalition site, 164
Internet Security SECRETS, 257
Internet Server Application
Programming Interface (ISAPI),
86
Internet service providers (ISPs),
210–211
accessibility via other TCP/IP
services, 211
file permissions, 211
firewalling, 210–211
and First Virtual, 228
need for UNIX servers, 72
user authentication, 211
Internet Shopping Network
security, 141
Web site, 9, 142
intranet manager, 206–209
accessibility via other TCP/IP
services, 208
file permissions, 208–209
firewalling, 207
user authentication, 208
ISAPI (Internet Server Application
Programming Interface), 86
ISPs. *See* Internet service providers
(ISPs)

J

Java, 86
JCB. *See* credit card payment systems
Jellinek, Brigitte, 261
JEPI, 30–31
Joint Electronic Payment Initiative,
30–31
junk e-mail, 281

K

keys. *See* encryption
Kiplinger Report, 7
KiwiClub server, 7

L

L.L. Bean site, 8
large site configuration
costs, 194–195, 199–200
hits per day, 72
requirements, 199–200
liability of consumers, 283
links, keeping current, 289
LivePayment, 154–157
benefits, 157
characteristics, 154–155
components, 155
future of, 157
LiveWire, 96, 155
merchant signup, 157
overview, 155–156
LiveWire, 96, 155
logging
log location, 217
Netscape Enterprise Server features,
95–96
security log, 287
low-volume sales
payment terminals, 61–62
telephone authorization, 60–61
See also small site configuration

M

MacAuthorize*Client, 64
MacAuthorize*Hub, 64
MacAuthorize, 63–65
Macintosh servers, 105–117
Mac advantages, 105, 106
recommended situations, 106–107

N

name of server, 217
National Center for Supercomputing
    Applications (NCSA), 188
National Institute of Standards and
    Technology (NIST), DES
    standard, 18
NCR's Web site, 63
NCSA (National Center for
    Supercomputing Applications),
    188
NetBEUI
    Samba, 255–256
    and security, 287
    Windows file sharing, 255
    Windows file sharing over TCP/IP,
        255–256
NetBill, 50–52
NetLink site, 152
Netscape bug-reporting form, 277
Netscape Enterprise Server, 94–101
    CGI support, 97
    compatibility, 103
    content development tools, 97, 102
    development tools, 97, 102
    drawbacks, 99–101
    management features, 94–96, 101
    O'Reilly's WebSite Professional
        compared to, 101–103
    price, 73, 99–100
    security, 97–99, 102
    UNIX versions supported, 73
    URL and evaluation period, 74
    See also Windows servers
Netscape LivePayment. See
        LivePayment
Netscape Secure Sockets Layer. See
        Secure Sockets Layer (SSL)

network file system (NFS) for TCP/IP,
    254
newsgroups, 278
Newshare, 43
    See also Clickshare
NFS (network file system) for TCP/IP,
    254
NIST, DES standard, 18
nonrepudiatability, 22, 283
Novell's Web site, 6
NT servers. See Windows servers

O

obtaining
    CyberCash CashRegister, 126
    CyberCash Wallet, 122, 147
    digital ID for WebSTAR/SSL,
        111–113
    Ecash coins, 128
    First Virtual API (FV-API), 227
    merchant number for credit card
        transactions, 245–250
    WebSTAR/SSL, 111
ODBC (Open Database Connectivity)
    tools, 85–86
Offline Group Only field (ICSETUP),
    175
Offline/Online Group Input File field
    (ICSETUP), 174
OM-Axcess, 80, 159
OM-SecureLink, 159
OM-Transact, 80, 158–159
OM-WebReporter, 80
online information centers
    elements of, 5–6
    as initial Internet presence, 5–6
    micropayments, 41–42
online payment systems. See third-party
        payment systems

Colophon

This book was produced electronically in Foster City, California. Microsoft Word Version 6.0 was used for word processing; design and layout were produced with QuarkXpress 3.32 on a Power Macintosh 8500/120. The type face families used are Adobe Garamond and Myriad Multiple Master.

Senior Vice President and Group Publisher   Brenda McLaughlin

Director of Publishing   Walt Bruce

Acquisitions Manager   John Osborn

Acquisitions Editor   Mike Roney

Marketing Manager   Melisa M. Duffy

Executive Managing Editor   Terry Somerson

Editorial Assistant   Sharon Eames

Production Director   Andrew Walker

Supervisor of Page Layout   Craig A. Harrison

Development Editor   Susannah Davidson

Copy Editors   Lothlórien Baerenwald, Katharine Dvorak

Technical Editor   David Elderbrock

Project Coordinator   Phyllis Beaty

Layout and Graphics   Laura Carpenter, Ritchie Durdin, Stephen Noetzel, Mark Schumann
Dale Smith

Quality Control Specialist   Mick Arellano

Proofreader   Christine Langin–Faris

Indexer   Steve Rath

Production Administration   Tony Augsburger, Todd Klemme, Jason Marcuson,
Christopher Pimentel, Leslie Popplewell,
Theresa Sánchez-Baker, Melissa Stauffer

Book Design   Margery Cantor, Kurt Krames, Mark Schumann

Cover Design   three 8 Creative Group

About the Authors

Ed Tittel is a columnist for *Windows NT* magazine and the author of numerous books about computing. He's the co-author of two best-selling *...For Dummies* books from IDG Books Worldwide, including *NetWare For Dummies* (co-authored with Deni Connor and Earl Follis, 1994) and *HTML For Dummies* (co-authored with Stephen N. James, 1995). Both books are in second editions. These days, Ed has turned his focus toward Internet-related programming topics, with recent titles on Java, VRML, Shockwave, and CGI programming to his credit. He's also active as a member of the NetWorld + Interop program committee.

Ed has been a regular contributor to the computer trade press since 1987. He has written more than 200 articles for a variety of publications, such as *Datamation*, *InfoWorld*, *IWAY*, *NetGuide*, and *ConneXions,* with a decided emphasis on networking and the Internet.

You can contact Ed at etittel@zilker.net, or visit his Web site at http://www.lanw.com.

Charlie Scott has been working with computers and networks for many years. His career path has put him in front of terminals at a variety of technology companies, including Texas Instruments, IBM, Wayne-Dresser, and Tomorrow's Technologies. Most of his experience lies with system and network analysis for the Windows, OS/2, and UNIX platforms. Charlie is currently the vice-president of Client Services at OuterNet Connection Strategies, Inc., where he oversees the development, administration, and promotion of Internet application services. In addition, he also provides consulting services for LAN and WAN administration, systems administration, and Internet connectivity. One of his current interests is technical writing, and he is a co-author (with Ed Tittel and others) of *Internet World's 60 Minute Guide to VRML*, *WWW Programming SECRETS*, and *More HTML For Dummies*, all for IDG Books Worldwide. Charlie can be reached at charlie@outer.net.

Paul Wolfe has done everything from driving an M1A1 tank in Operation Desert Storm to flipping computer chips for Motorola. For the last 10 years, he has served in various marketing and operations positions for technology companies, many of his own devising. He has worked on and with the Internet for 10 years, and on and with computers for 15. He has racked up several hundred hours attending various colleges around the world (Germany, Maryland, and Texas), though he never decided on a degree.

Paul currently serves as Vice President of Marketing and Communications for OuterNet Connection Strategies, Inc., where he provides Internet services to corporations worldwide. He edited a few Internet-related books for IDG Books Worldwide, and is a co-author of *Building Virtual Worlds with VRML* (Osborne/McGraw-Hill, 1996), with Ed Tittel and Charlie Scott. You can e-mail Paul at info@outer.net.

Mike Erwin is an entrepreneur and empresario of high-tech in Austin, TX. Frankly, he's obsessed with the Internet, with a particular fixation on CGI programming and Internet connectivity (the faster, the better). Mike also works part-time at Apple Computer, and is the president and CEO at OuterNet Connection Strategies, Inc., an Austin-based Internet service provider. He's a co-author of *The Internet World 60 Minute Guide to VRML*, and another member of the *Web Programming SECRETS* team.

Before his tenure at Apple Computer, Mike worked as a contract programmer for Microsoft, IBM, and the State of Texas. He contributed heavily to the CGI programs in both editions of IDG Books Worldwide's *HTML For Dummies*, and wrote science fiction and fantasy for TSR in the mid-1980s. Mike can be contacted at mikee@outer.net.

IDG BOOKS WORLDWIDE, INC.
END-USER LICENSE AGREEMENT

Read This. **You should carefully read these terms and conditions before opening the software packet(s) included with this book ("Book"). This is a license agreement ("Agreement") between you and IDG Books Worldwide, Inc. ("IDGB"). By opening the accompanying software packet(s), you acknowledge that you have read and accept the following terms and conditions. If you do not agree and do not want to be bound by such terms and conditions, promptly return the Book and the unopened software packet(s) to the place you obtained them for a full refund.**

1. **License Grant.** IDGB grants to you (either an individual or entity) a nonexclusive license to use one copy of the enclosed software program(s) (collectively, the "Software") solely for your own personal or business purposes on a single computer (whether a standard computer or a workstation component of a multiuser network). The Software is in use on a computer when it is loaded into temporary memory (i.e., RAM) or installed into permanent memory (e.g., hard disk, CD-ROM, or other storage device). IDGB reserves all rights not expressly granted herein.

2. **Ownership.** IDGB is the owner of all right, title, and interest, including copyright, in and to the compilation of the Software recorded on the disk(s)/CD-ROM. Copyright to the individual programs on the disk(s)/CD-ROM is owned by the author or other authorized copyright owner of each program. Ownership of the Software and all proprietary rights relating thereto remain with IDGB and its licensors.

3. **Restrictions on Use and Transfer.**
   (a) You may only (i) make one copy of the Software for backup or archival purposes, or (ii) transfer the Software to a single hard disk, provided that you keep the original for backup or archival purposes. You may not (i) rent or lease the Software, (ii) copy or reproduce the Software through a LAN or other network system or through any computer subscriber system or bulletin-board system, or (iii) modify, adapt, or create derivative works based on the Software.
   (b) You may not reverse engineer, decompile, or disassemble the Software. You may transfer the Software and user documentation on a permanent basis, provided that the transferee agrees to accept the terms and conditions of this Agreement and you retain no copies. If the Software is an update or has been updated, any transfer must include the most recent update and all prior versions.

4. **Restrictions on Use of Individual Programs.** You must follow the individual requirements and restrictions detailed for each individual program in Appendix D, "About the CD-ROM" of this Book. These limitations are contained in the individual license agreements recorded on the disk(s)/CD-ROM. These restrictions may include a requirement that after using the program for the period of time specified in its text, the user must pay a registration fee or discontinue use. By opening the Software

packet(s), you will be agreeing to abide by the licenses and restrictions for these individual programs. None of the material on this disk(s) or listed in this Book may ever be distributed, in original or modified form, for commercial purposes.

5. **Limited Warranty.**

   (a) IDGB warrants that the Software and disk(s)/CD-ROM are free from defects in materials and workmanship under normal use for a period of sixty (60) days from the date of purchase of this Book. If IDGB receives notification within the warranty period of defects in materials or workmanship, IDGB will replace the defective disk(s)/CD-ROM.

   (b) IDGB AND THE AUTHORS OF THE BOOK DISCLAIM ALL OTHER WARRANTIES, EXPRESS OR IMPLIED, INCLUDING WITHOUT LIMITATION IMPLIED WARRANTIES OF MERCHANTABILITY AND FITNESS FOR A PARTICULAR PURPOSE, WITH RESPECT TO THE SOFTWARE, THE PROGRAMS, THE SOURCE CODE CONTAINED THEREIN, AND/OR THE TECHNIQUES DESCRIBED IN THIS BOOK. IDGB DOES NOT WARRANT THAT THE FUNCTIONS CONTAINED IN THE SOFTWARE WILL MEET YOUR REQUIREMENTS OR THAT THE OPERATION OF THE SOFTWARE WILL BE ERROR FREE.

   (c) This limited warranty gives you specific legal rights, and you may have other rights which vary from jurisdiction to jurisdiction.

6. **Remedies.**

   (a) IDGB's entire liability and your exclusive remedy for defects in materials and workmanship shall be limited to replacement of the Software, which may be returned to IDGB with a copy of your receipt at the following address: Disk Fulfillment Department, Attn: *Building Web Commerce Sites*, IDG Books Worldwide, Inc., 7260 Shadeland Station, Ste. 100, Indianapolis, IN 46256, or call 1-800-762-2974. Please allow 3-4 weeks for delivery. This Limited Warranty is void if failure of the Software has resulted from accident, abuse, or misapplication. Any replacement Software will be warranted for the remainder of the original warranty period or thirty (30) days, whichever is longer.

   (b) In no event shall IDGB or the author be liable for any damages whatsoever (including without limitation damages for loss of business profits, business interruption, loss of business information, or any other pecuniary loss) arising from the use of or inability to use the Book or the Software, even if IDGB has been advised of the possibility of such damages.

   (c) Because some jurisdictions do not allow the exclusion or limitation of liability for consequential or incidental damages, the above limitation or exclusion may not apply to you.

7. U.S. Government Restricted Rights. Use, duplication, or disclosure of the Software by the U.S. Government is subject to restrictions stated in paragraph (c) (1) (ii) of the Rights in Technical Data and Computer Software clause of DFARS 252.227-7013, and in subparagraphs (a) through (d) of the Commercial Computer— Restricted Rights clause at FAR 52.227-19, and in similar clauses in the NASA FAR supplement, when applicable.

8. General. This Agreement constitutes the entire understanding of the parties and revokes and supersedes all prior agreements, oral or written, between them and may not be modified or amended except in a writing signed by both parties hereto which specifically refers to this Agreement. This Agreement shall take precedence over any other documents that may be in conflict herewith. If any one or more provisions contained in this Agreement are held by any court or tribunal to be invalid, illegal, or otherwise unenforceable, each and every other provision shall remain in full force and effect.

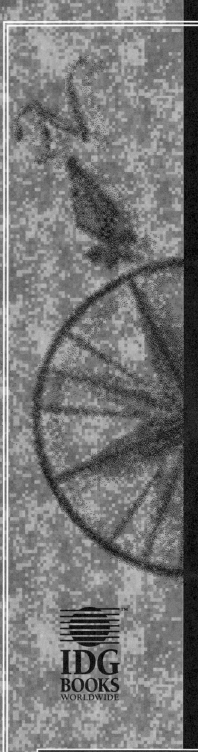

IDG BOOKS WORLDWIDE REGISTRATION CARD

RETURN THIS REGISTRATION CARD FOR FREE CATALOG

Title of this book: **Building Web Commerce Sites**

My overall rating of this book: ☐ Very good [1] ☐ Good [2] ☐ Satisfactory [3] ☐ Fair [4] ☐ Poor [5]

How I first heard about this book:

☐ Found in bookstore; name: [6]

☐ Advertisement: [8]

☐ Word of mouth; heard about book from friend, co-worker, etc.: [10]

☐ Book review: [7]

☐ Catalog: [9]

☐ Other: [11]

What I liked most about this book:

What I would change, add, delete, etc., in future editions of this book:

Other comments:

Number of computer books I purchase in a year: ☐ 1 [12] ☐ 2-5 [13] ☐ 6-10 [14] ☐ More than 10 [15]

I would characterize my computer skills as: ☐ Beginner [16] ☐ Intermediate [17] ☐ Advanced [18] ☐ Professional [19]

I use ☐ DOS [20] ☐ Windows [21] ☐ OS/2 [22] ☐ Unix [23] ☐ Macintosh [24] ☐ Other: [25]_____
(please specify)

I would be interested in new books on the following subjects:
(please check all that apply, and use the spaces provided to identify specific software)

☐ Word processing: [26]

☐ Data bases: [28]

☐ File Utilities: [30]

☐ Networking: [32]

☐ Other: [34]

☐ Spreadsheets: [27]

☐ Desktop publishing: [29]

☐ Money management: [31]

☐ Programming languages: [33]

I use a PC at (please check all that apply): ☐ home [35] ☐ work [36] ☐ school [37] ☐ other: [38] _____

The disks I prefer to use are ☐ 5.25 [39] ☐ 3.5 [40] ☐ other: [41]_____

I have a CD ROM: ☐ yes [42] ☐ no [43]

I plan to buy or upgrade computer hardware this year: ☐ yes [44] ☐ no [45]

I plan to buy or upgrade computer software this year: ☐ yes [46] ☐ no [47]

Name: _____ Business title: [48] _____ Type of Business: [49]

Address (☐ home [50] ☐ work [51]/Company name: _____)

Street/Suite# _____

City [52]/State [53]/Zipcode [54]: _____ Country [55]

☐ **I liked this book!** You may quote me by name in future
IDG Books Worldwide promotional materials.

My daytime phone number is _____

IDG BOOKS

THE WORLD OF
COMPUTER
KNOWLEDGE

❏ **YES!**
Please keep me informed about IDG's World of Computer Knowledge.
Send me the latest IDG Books catalog.

COMPUTER
BOOK SERIES
FROM IDG